Creative Negativity

Creative Negativity

FOUR

VICTORIAN

EXEMPLARS OF

THE FEMALE

QUEST

Carol Hanbery MacKay

Stanford University Press

Stanford, California

Stanford University Press
Stanford, California

© 2001 by the Board of Trustees of the
Leland Stanford Junior University

Printed in the United States of America
on acid-free, archival-quality paper.

Library of Congress Cataloging-in-Publication Data

MacKay, Carol Hanbery
Creative negativity : four Victorian exemplars of the
   female quest / Carol Hanbery MacKay.
      p.   cm.
   Includes bibliographical references and index.
   ISBN 0-8047-3829-7 (alk. paper)
      1. Feminism—History.   2. Women artists—Psychology.
3. Creation (Literary, artistic, etc.)   4. Women artists—
Biography.   5. Cameron, Julia Margaret Pattle, 1815–1879.
6. Ritchie, Anne Thackeray, 1837–1919.   7. Besant, Annie
Wood, 1847–1933.   8. Robins, Elizabeth, 1862–1952.   I. Title.
HQ1206 .M315   2001
305.42'09—dc21   2001020610

Original printing 2001

Last figure below indicates year of this printing:
10   09   08   07   06   05   04   03   02   01

Designed by Janet Wood
Typeset by James P. Brommer in 10/13 Galliard

To the memory of Shirley Wendt Hanbery
(1920–1998)

Contents

List of Illustrations

Preface

The reader of this book should expect a methodology that draws upon literary and gender studies as well as reaching out to other fields such as the fine arts, psychology, comparative religion, drama, and history. As an interdisciplinary scholar, I combine analysis of photographic images, of theatres as institutions, and "high" and "low" literary genres for an era in which that kind of eclecticism was common, and even valued. Previous Anglo-American scholarship has traced voices in this period for men or partially outcast women (notably the work of Nina Auerbach on the lauded but feared actress Ellen Terry), but not sufficiently for women with hard-won but apparently ordinary careers. In the midst of a sexist, racist, imperialist culture, I find covert revolutionaries. The kind of boundary-crossing that I am ascribing to Julia Margaret Cameron, Anne Thackeray Ritchie, Annie Wood Besant, and Elizabeth Robins might profitably be thought of as a "velvet revolution," by which I am acknowledging that they pushed boundaries with an uncanny awareness of the subtle implications of their transgressions. (Perhaps this is the real reason why Percy Shelley had to preface his wife's masterpiece, *Frankenstein*, with his own introduction, in the hope that it would be taken as mere horror story rather than as a parody of proto-Victorian maleness.) The subjects of my study are women who engage in active mimicry and play it as harmless or mainstream—all the while rewriting the social scripts assigned to them.

Traditional nineteenth-century studies have relied heavily on the tacit assumptions that artists either responded to their social and intellectual climate (given that the integrity of community structure seems so important) or revolted openly against it. The former assumption has been partially corrected by such recent work as that on the relationship between novelist Charles Dickens and his "shadow wife," the actress Ellen Ternan; he preserved the image of himself as family man (necessary to sell his works), while manipulating the social and literary markets (including archives and the historical record) to cover up this liaison for subsequent generations. The latter concept of the artist persists well into the twentieth century, where it recurs even in accounts of Virginia Woolf's emergence onto the literary scene. Note how she is cast as a rebel rather than as an innovative type of the late-Victorian eccentric (a true inheritor of her aunt, Anne Thackeray Ritchie), the role instead assigned to the likes of someone like Edith Sitwell, partly to consign her in turn to another century. By applying performance theory to the figures I have selected, I hope to make more obvious the ways in which social roles are reenacted or performed on a daily basis—with attendant opportunities to improvise, innovate, or downright subvert the expectations put upon them.

Additionally, I want to help reformulate genre theory with this undertaking, particularly with reference to the archetype of the quest and female autobiography. As women write biography, they (more than male biographers) tend to write a form of reflected or refracted autobiography, exploring the self (and selves) they and their societies have suppressed. As for writers of fiction, they have long acknowledged the subgenre of the *Bildungsroman* (and its artist subtype, the *Künstleroman*) as the novel of growth and development about a male protagonist. Extending the *Bildungsroman* concept to female protagonists has been a matter of critical controversy, however, not only because women have seldom been portrayed as active participants in the social and artistic arenas that showcased the maturation process, but because female novelists did not necessarily wish to adopt a male model of political and psychological development. At the same time, although a relational model goes a long way toward explaining how women's autobiographical enterprises—fictional and nonfictional—depict interdependent self-construction, this model also calls for recalibration, especially as we begin to uncover cleverly-concealed strategies deploying an ingenious array of creative tools.

The lives of the four Victorian women I have been studying and their creative reflections of their life experiences point up the ways in which women's self-expression can be reconceived as a manifestation of the female quest—a voicing of multiple lives and selves, both self and other, in myriad, even fantastical, domains of their own creating. All this suggests that these and other women who lived in an era that worked to infantilize, crush, and imprison them had stronger, more secure selves than heretofore acknowledged: it's primarily a matter for us to discover how they redefined the self as fluid and reinventive. In a sense, this was the task and the form of self-exploration that Elizabeth Barrett Browning set for herself in writing her epic narrative poem *Aurora Leigh* (1855), but the poem was received without much critical or popular acclaim largely because it fell through the cracks of rigid genre distinction. Someone like Elizabeth Robins met a similar challenge but overcame it with the success of her dual suffrage "polemics"—the play *Votes for Women!* and the novel *The Convert*—because she more wisely gauged her audience, doubly converting those who fell under the spell of both masterpieces of creative negativity.

As a model of cognitive self-definition, the theory of creative negativity that this study propounds may itself serve as a tool for scholars in other fields of research besides literary studies, fields such as anthropology, theatre arts, religious studies, and sociology. Beyond its applications to literature and the arts, it has implications for male and female psychology, intellectual history, cross-cultural studies, and feminism in general. By studying how the self is endlessly defined and redefined in various social contexts, I intend to provide a working model for how feminism has actually operated through history. The total achievement of Cameron, Ritchie, Besant, and Robins as seen in the light of my theory amounts to an astonishing series of connections and interactions both within and among their wide-ranging artistic and personal endeavors. Not only are their works far more remarkable than has been previously realized, but my theory forges them together in a powerful conceptual structure. Uncovering and extolling this structure will, I hope, augment and inform the larger structure of the feminism we know today.

This project has been long in the making, and as a way to acknowledge my debts and document the wellsprings of my own imagination, I think it is useful for me to trace the evolution of the book through my various critical forays into its subject matter, giving credit along the way to the many individuals, research libraries, and scholarly forums that have supported my endeavors. Accordingly, I here address my work on each of the women who constitute my subject matter in the order in which I first developed a critical interest in them and the concepts they inspired: Anne Thackeray Ritchie's *oeuvre* brought to the fore questions about the female quest and helped me to conceive the rhetorical practice I am calling *espièglerie*; the life and work of Elizabeth Robins first elicited the theory of creative negativity; Annie Besant's life story highlighted the intertwined issues of conversion and deconversion; and the photographic imagery of Julia Margaret Cameron motivated me to systematically apply the theory I had been perceiving until I recognized that it informed a coherent, shared strategy among all four women.

I suppose the real beginning of my interest in Anne Thackeray Ritchie dates back to my dissertation on the soliloquies in the novels of her father, William Makepeace Thackeray, for in writing about the father I increasingly discovered that the daughter's wit and intelligence evinced a perceptivity I wished to explore.

Jane Marcus provided the initial impetus for me to pursue my curiosity about Ritchie when she encouraged me to participate in the series of Virginia Woolf Centenary Lectures she organized at the University of Texas; for that lecture series in 1982 and the book it spawned, *Virginia Woolf and Bloomsbury* (1987), I examined "Aunt Anny's" influence on her niece Virginia. Subsequently, I tracked the development of Ritchie's essay on Jane Austen that eventually appeared in *A Book of Sibyls* (1885) by studying manuscript fragments held at UT's Harry Ransom Humanities Research Center (hereafter cited as HRHRC in notes and text) and the Special Collections at the University of California at Los Angeles, as well as the final state of the manuscript at Princeton University; these findings were published as "'Only Connect': The Multiple Roles of Anne Thackeray Ritchie" (1985). I am grateful to Director Tom Staley, Associate Director Sally Leach, Librarians Rich Oram and John Kirkpatrick, Manuscripts Librarian Cathy Henderson, Reading Room Director Rachel Howarth, and Library Assistant Pat Fox for their longstanding patience and assistance while I consulted the HRHRC's Rare Books and Manuscripts Collection for all four of my subjects, and I thank the Harry Ransom Humanities Research Center at the University of Texas at Austin for permission to quote from its unpublished holdings.

The concept of *espièglerie*, under the umbrella term "empathetic whimsy," has its origins in a paper I wrote for the 1986 Modern Language Association panel on "Hate and Humor in Women's Literature," presented with co-panelists Kay Rogers and Mary Ann Caws and organized by Regina Barreca, who later solicited additional essays to produce a triple-issue of *Women's Studies*, reprinted as *Last Laughs: Perspectives on Women and Comedy* (1988). Next, I began to develop the idea of the female quest in the context of Ritchie's "domestic" fairy tales for a paper presented on a panel devoted to Victorian women and publishing at the 1987 MLA; I am grateful to co-panelists Bradford K. Mudge and Catherine Golden, as well as to our respondent Patrick Brantlinger, for their constructive exchanges. During the years that followed, as I investigated Ritchie's introductions to her father's canon, I uncovered in them her reflected autobiography. This line of inquiry first led me to make presentations to the Victorian Studies Committee of the City University of New York and the UT Women's Studies Research Seminar (1985), then to the Narrative Colloquium at Harvard University and the Conference on Autobiography and Biography at Stanford University (1986), and finally to the Victorian Institute Conference on Gender at the University of North Carolina (1987), before I produced a chapter on the subject for *Revealing Lives: Autobiography, Biography, and Gender* (1990) as well as a two-volume edition of Ritchie's centenary biographical introductions to Thackeray's works (1988). By then my research had taken me to a number of additional rare book and manuscript collections, namely those at the University of London,

Columbia University, New York University (Fales Library), the Pierpont Morgan Library, the New York Public Library (Berg Collection), and the Huntington Library.

Subsequent years witnessed my honing the ideas that form the basis of my chapter on Ritchie. Focusing on a quotation from one of her letters written during the First World War, "There never was war until now" (1916), I analyzed her letter-writing technique for a paper delivered to the Dickens Project Biography Conference, "Letters and Lives," at the University of California at Santa Cruz (1989). Another quotation, "She lies not unremembered," taken from Ritchie's essay on Austen in *A Book of Sibyls*, helped to coalesce the concept of the female quest for a presentation to the 1996 Annual Eighteenth- and Nineteenth-Century British Women Writers Conference held at the University of South Carolina at Columbia. Chairing a panel for that conference the following year at the University of California at Davis prompted me to collaborate with fellow Ritchie scholars and panelists Manuela Mourão and Robin Sheets. All along, I have been supported and encouraged in my study of Ritchie by Bob and Vineta Colby, Bill Todd and Ann Bowden, John Sutherland, Michael Timko, Edgar Harden, Peter Shillingsburg, Uli Knoepflmacher, Sally Mitchell, and Abigail Burnham Bloom. To Belinda Norman-Butler, Ritchie's granddaughter, I owe an especial thanks for her scholarly acumen and her generous spirit in granting me permission to reprint quotations from Ritchie manuscript materials.

My interest in Elizabeth Robins stems from a search for an author who was equally successful at writing both fiction and drama, someone whose work I might compare with the more checkered careers of Thackeray and Dickens as novelists and would-be playwrights. My timing was also fortuitous, for the Special Collections at the Fales Library of the Elmer Bobst Library at NYU had only acquired the Robins Papers through the efforts of Literary Executor Leonard Woolf in 1974. By 1986, those papers were catalogued and open to the public, and I joined several other scholars who had begun to mine them. The growing critical interest in Robins was reflected by the five papers devoted to her work at the Women in Theatre Conference held at the Hofstra Cultural Center in 1994; my contribution, "Creative Negativity in the Life and Work of Elizabeth Robins," signaled my first public exploration of that key concept. This conference introduced me to a nucleus of Robins scholars with whom I have remained in close contact. Besides meeting and exchanging work in progress with Ann Fox, Susan Carlson, Jane Gabin, and Viv Gardner, I was fortunate to begin a long and happy correspondence with Joanne Gates, the first Robins biographer, to whom I am extremely grateful for her trailblazing research and willingness to share her expertise with me and other students of Robins.

Earlier installments of this chapter were presented in 1995 to the British Studies Seminar at the University of Texas and the Association for Theatre in Higher Education Conference in San Francisco. Revised and expanded, a substantial portion of my argument was subsequently published as "'Both Sides of the Curtain': Elizabeth Robins, Synaesthesia, and the Subjective Correlative" (299–316) in the volume 17, number 4, special issue of *TPQ: Text and Performance Quarterly* guest-edited by Lynn C. Miller and Jacqueline Taylor (1997); I am grateful to the National Communication Association for permission to reproduce portions of that article in my Robins chapter. In addition, I made a presentation entitled "Elizabeth Robins Performs Autobiography" for the 1997 Annual Fall Faculty Colloquium, "Women Challenging the Arts," sponsored by the UT Women's Studies Program under the direction of Lucia Gilbert, and two years later I delivered a paper, "Elizabeth Robins Outperforms Ibsen's New Woman," to the Baylor University Conference on Communities of Women.

I am thankful for the assistance of the late Frank Walker while I was conducting research on Robins at the Fales Library, and I appreciate the follow-up services of Reference Associate Maxime La Fantasie and Assistant Director Mike Kelly. Further thanks go to Melissa Miller, Humanities Research Associate for the Hoblitzelle Theatre Arts Collection at the HRHRC, and the various librarians who assisted me while I worked with the holdings at the Billy Rose Theatre Collection of the NYPL Lincoln Center for the Performing Arts and at the Theatre Museum, London. For their general interest and support of my Robins scholarship, I'd like to thank Colleen Hobbs and Leslie Hill. I am particularly grateful to Mabel Smith, Literary Executor of the Elizabeth Robins Estate, for granting permission to reproduce unpublished materials from the Elizabeth Robins Papers at the Fales Library/Special Collections, New York University, and I appreciate the role of the Society of Authors, London, for helping to obtain permission from the Estate of George Bernard Shaw to quote from his writings to and about both Robins and Besant. And lastly, I'd like to express my gratitude to Elizabeth Richmond Garza and Charlotte Canning for their critical insights in the final stages of revision.

My fascination with the multiple careers of Annie Besant grew out of encountering Robins's unfinished biography of her and my own interest in autobiography studies. Comparing and contrasting Besant's 1885 and 1893 autobiographies led me to submit a paper to the 1995 South Central Conference on Christianity and Literature on "Awakenings: Great and Small" held in New Orleans, and three years later I analyzed the creative tension between conversion and "deconversion" in Besant's life-writings for the Annual Eighteenth- and Nineteenth-Century British Women Writers Conference conducted at the University of North Carolina. These papers served as a catalyst for the presentation of a preliminary version of my Besant chapter to the UT British Studies Seminar later in 1998. I am grateful for the research opportunities at the British Library, London, particularly the Oriental and India Office Collections, and I have benefited greatly from the scholarly forum of the UT Center for Asian Studies as well. The Theosophical Society in America, centered in Wheaton, Illinois, has been extremely helpful in obtaining books and other materials related to Besant's Theosophical years, and I am especially thankful to its president, John Algeo, and his wife Adele, for their careful review of my writings on Besant. I further appreciate the responsive attention of D. K. Govindaraj, manager of the Theosophical Publishing House in Adyar, India, at the International Headquarters of the Theosophical Society, and I thank the Theosophical Society at both Wheaton and Adyar for permission to quote from Besant's *An Autobiography* (1893), which has been kept in continuous reprint by their joint publishing house. For their cheerful response to my many requests regarding hard-to-find materials on and by Besant, I'd like to convey my thanks to Nancy Payne and her staff in the Interlibrary Service Department at UT's Perry-Castañeda Library. And last but not least, I wish to express my gratitude to Gail Minault, Leah Madge Young Renold, and Dolora Chapelle-Wojciehowski for their willingness to read and debate my Besant findings.

The immediate impetus to my writing about Julia Margaret Cameron was an exhibit planned at the Harry Ransom Humanities Research Center for the fall of 1995. Curated by Andrea Inselmann and dedicated to Helmut Gernsheim (1913–1995), this exhibit was entitled "Gendered Territory: Photographs of Women by Julia Margaret Cameron." To coincide with the exhibit, a special issue of *The Library Chronicle of the University of Texas* was published in 1996 (26, no. 4), edited and introduced by Dave Oliphant. My contribution to that collection of essays was "'Soaring between home and heaven—': Julia Margaret Cameron's Visual Meditations on the Self" (63–87); I am grateful to the HRHRC for permission to reproduce some of that argument in my Cameron chapter and to quote from the manuscript holdings of the Gernsheim Collection. This issue and its reprinting published for the first time a catalogue of the HRHRC's Gernsheim Collection of some 250 Cameron images. At an earlier stage of preparing my Cameron chapter, I presented selected findings to UT's 1996 British Studies Seminar. I am thankful to Commander Roger Louis, Curator of Photography Roy Flukinger, and Assistant Curator Ann Paterra for their assistance and support in this endeavor, as well as to Humanities Research Associates Linda Briscoe and David Coleman for their subsequent support in tracking down Cameron photographs. The following year saw my presentation about Cameron's autobiographical fragment delivered to the Annual Eighteenth- and Nineteenth-Century British Women Writers Conference held at the University of California at Davis.

Ever since spring of 1997, when she was a Mellon Visiting Fellow at the HRHRC, Victoria C. Olsen has read my writing on Cameron and served as a

source of inspiration; her own critical biography of Cameron promises definitive status. The following spring, I received a UT Special Research Grant to
travel to the J. Paul Getty Center in Los Angeles to study the Cameron Family
Papers and Cameron's photographs housed there. The Cameron holdings in the
Getty Department of Photographs include 138 single images and 4 cabinet
cards; broken down, those numbers add up to more than 300 prints in total, 112
of which are part of the Overstone Album. I am thankful to Kate Ware, Department of Photographs, and Beth Ann Guynn, Reference Specialist for Special Collections in the Research Institute for the History of Art and the Humanities, for their help in arranging my study time at the Getty, and I thank the
Research Library of the Getty Research Institute for permission to print unpublished materials from the Cameron Family Papers (850858). I am especially
grateful to Julian Cox, Assistant Curator of Photographs at the Getty, for his
kind assistance when I was on site and in the writing of my Cameron chapter.

The complex, convoluted journey toward the discovery that my varied interests did indeed cohere into a single undertaking has required time and uninter-
rupted periods of focused energy; for the opportunity to launch, sustain, and
bring to fruition this book, I am grateful to the University of Texas at Austin for
funding a University Research Institute Assignment (1989), numerous travel
subsidies, and a Faculty Research Award (1998). I owe a special debt of gratitude
to Katherine Arens for the phrase "velvet revolution," which I have happily
adopted for use in this book; her warm endorsement of this project and her ability to synthesize its wide-ranging ideation have helped me enormously in bringing it to fruition. For their dialogue with me about the archetype of the quest, I
would like to acknowledge Betty Sue Flowers and Jerome Bump. For their stim-
ulating conversation and encouragement (whether they knew it or not, they kept
me on the right track), I'd like to thank the following friends and colleagues:
Linda Peterson, Adrienne Munich, Rachel Brownstein, Anne Humpherys, Gerhard Joseph, Jackie Jaffe, Elaine Showalter, Joe Donohue, Janice Carlisle, Jeff
Rosen, Ed Eigner, Bob Patton, Bob Gregg, Bill Worthen, Judith Fisher, Elisabeth Jay, Jackie Brattin, James Redmond, Angelique Richardson, Angie Mason,
Bill Livingston, Teresa Sullivan, Zipporah Wiseman, Deasley Deacon, Paul Wood-
ruff, Martha Newman, Shelley Fisher-Fishkin, Janet Swaffer, Michael Charles-
worth, Joni Jones, James Garrison, Linda Ferreira-Buckley, Rosa Eberly, Laura
Furman, Pete Smith, Susan Wing, and Mary Margaret Bowles.

Grateful for their camaraderie and shared vision, I extend profound thanks as
well to the following members of the UT English Department's Women and
Gender Studies Interest Group whom I have not otherwise mentioned: B. J.
Fernea, Leah Marcus, Theresa Kelley, Barbara Harlow, Susan Sage Heinzelman,
Elizabeth Butler Cullingford, Lisa Moore, Ann Cvetkovich, Mia Carter, Sabrina

Barton, Helena Woodard, Elizabeth McHenry, and Gerry Heng. To my former students, who have listened and responded to my ideas (and often attended my presentations), I convey a teacher's longstanding gratitude: Carol Rhoades, Tracy Seeley, Cheri Larsen Hoeckley, Patricia Myers, Peaches Henry, Catherine Yoes, Lynn Byrd, Mary Lenard, Alice Batt, Janet Hayes, Kim VanHoosier Carey, Amy Adams, Alyssa Harad, Crisi Benford, Elizabeth Dell, Kristen Hogan, Mary Grover, Susan "George" Schorn, Kathleen Vejvoda, Marilyn Lehman, Sarah Wakefield, Maeve Cooney, Kit Aldrich, and Sylvia Mollerstrom. And for their overall endorsement of the book's project, which has entailed writing in support of my grant proposals, I'd like to offer especial thanks to Alexander Welsh, Nina Auerbach, Rob Polhemus, and James Kincaid.

For her willingness to provide a complete reading of this text and give me an honest, constructive critique, I express my deep gratitude to Joss Marsh. I thank, too, Helen Tartar, Humanities Editor at Stanford University Press, for her advice and support so kindly given. As always, my greatest debt is to Kirk Hampton: most of the ideas generated in this book have their inception in lively dialogue with him, and his enthusiasm for this project from its onset has continually sparked my own. Finally, I'd like to dedicate this book to the memory of my mother, herself a twentieth-century exemplar of the female quest and a photographer who o'er-leapt her amateur standing. May she join my own four sibyls in the pantheon of my creation.

Carol Hanbery MacKay

The University of Texas at Austin

Creative Negativity

1. Creative Negativity and the Female Quest

In order to advance the subject of the female quest, I am introducing a vocabulary that I can call upon to address that quest in mythic, literary, and popular history. From the outset, I'd like to affirm that the concept of a female quest calls for a re-envisioning of women's lives and stories, that it calls forth its own language of self-defining in order to carve out for itself a space in which it can be retold and studied. Chiefly, I want to suggest that the female quest constitutes both a response and a strategy that can be read into lives lived and tales told—and that this activity emerges out of negation, creatively redefining women's roles and accomplishments. Tracking this activity points up key differences between female and male versions of the quest. Whereas the male quest tends to value process through its attempts to prolong activity in a linear drive, the female mode usually conceives of process as cyclic, as an ongoing effort at growth and self-understanding. The importance of the past differs for the two sexes, too. While the male typically looks to the past as an end in itself, the female tends to use a retrospective review as a means of gaining perspective, thereby acquiring the shaping language of self-naming and shared purpose in present time. And now we come to what may be the most distinguishing feature of all for gendered questing: the single-minded mode of the male quest contrasts sharply with the communal, collaborative quality of its female counterpart.

It should already be apparent that talking about the female quest necessarily seems to involve a comparison with the male variety. And, in order to establish my initial framework, I will need to employ a certain amount of essentialist language, often generalizing about composite male and female experience in Western culture, although the lives and work of the particular women I study should also ground this undertaking in the kind of specificity that will counterbalance some of these universalities. Needless to say, however, the idea of comparing the male to the female quest has not previously occurred to scholars with much force or regularity, and therein lies part of the problem for the male questor and his static, often facile formula. With the onset of feminism, particularly marked by Mary Wollstonecraft at the end of the eighteenth century in Britain, the roles of men and women have been undergoing their own processes of redefinition, much to the benefit of both sexes. Eschewing the unthinking imposition of roles and modes of arriving at them, feminists of both sexes have encouraged men and women alike to re-fashion themselves. This reflexivity of self-exploration through self-fashioning is a large part of what marks the activity of the female quest, although men have been and continue to be fully capable of this kind of self-transcendence.

The lineaments of the female quest can obviously be located and traced throughout human history, but like many other resonant myths it appears at its most vital—and open to productive analysis—during periods when it is both under attack and provoked by that opportunity to defend itself by evolving into a particularized response or configuration. Victorian England provides us with a prime occasion in this respect. This was a period of intense ontological ferment. Virtually any given self-definition seemed to be in peril. At the same time, however, the period was a highly reactionary one: the very boundaries and self-definitions which seemed constantly threatened were reaffirmed again and again, especially those related to gender roles. Thus, Victorian England was in one sense the height of the Western repressive tradition, and as is often the case with threatened or decaying belief systems, it tightened into a parody of itself.

Although much has been made of the sociological positions of women of the era, the psychological and rhetorical dimensions of those positions remain less clear. As a scholar of the Victorian period, I have for some time been investigating the mechanisms by which Victorian women interacted with their society's apparent compulsion to force them into such fixedly defined boxes. I kept asking myself, what bonded these women together, and how were those bonds forged and expressed? My study of various women artists from this period has filled me with a sense of uncanny cohesiveness among them, almost as if they were engaged in a powerful but elegantly concealed conspiracy. Convinced that a pattern of historical and philosophical significance might underlie these correlations, I began to apply the tools of rigorous rhetorical and semiotic analysis to the working lives of some of these women, most notably poet-photographer Julia Margaret Cameron (1815–1879), novelist-essayist Anne Thackeray Ritchie (1837–1919), activist-spiritual leader Annie Wood Besant (1847–1933), and actress-writer Elizabeth Robins (1862–1952). What has emerged from my work is the discovery of an intricate and heretofore undefined pattern of thinking or strategy for self-expression and self-identification—intuitive yet remarkably consistent, elaborate, and specific in its elements—employed by creative women in the Victorian-Modern marketplace.

I call this pattern *creative negativity*, a complex of rhetorical and performative techniques by which certain women of the period construct, deconstruct, and reconstruct themselves. This phrasing clearly owes something to the concept of "negative capability" advanced by John Keats, by which he referred to an ability to work with uncertainty, to negate the intellect so as not to reject anything categorically, but my terminology intentionally tries to exploit the powerful potential for creativity inherent in the maelstrom of negative emotions and circumstances.[1] Charting the careers of Cameron, Ritchie, Besant, and Robins, I believe I have uncovered a particularly female style of combined compatibility and subversion. Operating out of neither a male ego nor a posture of subservience, they bodied forth a mode of collaboration with form and other empathetic figures. In effect, the techniques employed by these and other women of the period constitute a complex rhetorical-psychological "machine" created within the dreamlike "fiction" of male Victorian society.

CREATIVE NEGATIVITY DEFINED

Occurring usually in a written text, but also analyzable within an individual's life story, creative negativity as I have been delineating it consists of a complex interaction among rhetorical, imagistic, and formal qualities, and it can be conveniently divided into six interacting elements, which I will elucidate in the pages that follow: (1) it grows out of *negativity*, either philosophical or emotional; (2) it evokes a *focal point*, often a place; (3) it combines *reality and illusion*; (4) it suggests a shift in *magnitude*, a sense of multifariousness or zooming out; (5) it includes an altered sense of *time*, by reaching backward, moving outside temporality, or attenuating time; and (6) it evokes *self-referentiality*, an aesthetic or formal invocation in a work of art, a sense of self-consciousness in social contexts.

Creative negativity primarily works to create serial selves: they comprise a sort of rhetorical and performative morphing from one fictional self to another, and the activity never stops, is never allowed to crystallize. The theory predicts, for example, an evocation of mass (solidification); liminality (boundary-crossing or dissolving); awe or wonder (but also surprise or shock); paradoxical communication; the release of powerful emotions (sometimes coalescence or healing); and microcosms eliding into macrocosms. Likewise, each of the six elements of creative negativity is ambivalent in its nature or treatment: each is used, often simultaneously, both to create and decreate the self. In this respect, creative negativity provides resourceful tools for enacting the female quest. After all, the female questor is profoundly ambivalent about creating a self, for her quest is never-ending. In its most mythic embodiment, the female quest involves a journey through layer within layer of dream, a breaking out of one illusion into another one, each one framed by the next and implicitly mocked by it. This double-edged quality explains how the six elements operate. As a formula, the operation is initiated by anchoring one's self in place; one next fires up the requisite negative emotions; and then one deliberately beats against the wall of rooted materiality. At this point, the creative negativist slips into illusion, regarding the self as a machine. Now one can negate time through repeating the pattern. Finally, one frames the whole activity with formalism or self-referentiality.

Instances of creative negativity tend to arise from negative emotions, but since this measure of *negativity* must necessarily be ambivalent if it is ultimately to serve an ongoing creative activity, certain negative emotions are invoked more frequently than others. For example, the emotion of anger risks asserting or crystallizing a self-definition, so its appearances are minimized or reformulated by the female creative negativist; suppressed or repressed, female anger proves to be highly resilient, often finding subversive outlets.[2] In contrast, the emotion of fear is intensely negating of the self; it, too, must be minimalized or ameliorated within the framework of creative negativity. In between, grief and despair are usually ambivalent emotions as they appear rhetorically, so they are ideal for the purpose. We can thus envision a spectrum of emotions, running from self-negating on the one extreme, through varying degrees of ambivalence, to self-asserting on the opposite extreme, and recognize that creative negativity will gravitate toward the mid-range. A powerfully emotional example of creative negativity, such as Annie Besant's first "deconversion," growing out of her feeling that God was letting her children suffer, balances anger at God with the fear of defying God, finally stressing the full complement of emotions in between. As a result, even this turbulent whirlwind across the emotive spectrum maintains the ambivalence essential to creative negativity's constant morphing among selves. Coupled with an increasing sense of spiritual vacuum, this negative emotional range propels Besant into a series of deconstructions that seem open-ended.

The notion of a *focal point* might seem to crystallize the self in an unmitigated fashion, but the very act of focusing intensely has a tendency to invite effacement. Photography provides an apt analogy, for excessive focusing in—in the form of enlargement of a tiny portion of the subject—breaks the illusion of solidity as the photograph disperses into a chaotic mass of emulsive grain. Likewise, we can begin to examine Julia Margaret Cameron's close-up portraits, which are deliberately soft in focus, as self-exploratory in resourceful new ways. Moreover, her frequent depiction of eyes as hooded or shadowed, hence losing the potent focus that eyes in photographic images naturally provide for the viewer, displays a propensity to decenter or destabilize accepted formulae about what constitutes the self, for subject and viewer alike. For Anne Thackeray Ritchie, the focal point is usually a place, a scene which serves as an occasion to recreate the environment of another author as a means of gaining insight into his or her creative source-points. In the process of weaving this scenic portrait, she draws upon her own wellsprings of imagination, thus providing her reader with yet more examples of her creative self-fashioning. In effect, these focal points permit Ritchie to try on the personae of her writer-subjects, empathetically recreating them while she displays for us her own limitless fecundity.

A ready willingness to play back and forth between *reality and illusion* marks the creative negativist as capable of perpetual self-creation. Cameron provides us with an intriguing visual record of this activity by posing real people—her friends and family, famous figures, even passers-by—as fictional characters. These instances recreate for all time a model of each self exploding the premise of the other. Thus, creative negativity can deploy reality and illusion against each other, such that they are mutually destructive forces in the employ of a larger creative structure. This operation is perhaps easiest to see at work in belief systems. For example, when Besant fights her way out of one belief system and into a new one, reality and unreality battle in earnest, each ultimately changing into the other. Meanwhile, for the actress Elizabeth Robins the interplay between reality and illusion takes on an especially unsettling aspect when her play-acting proves all-too-real for some members of her audience. One critic of *Alan's Wife* (1893), for instance, reported the depiction of a mangled corpse and the performance of infanticide on the stage, contrary to the objective facts: his "hallucinatory" response testifies not only to Robins's acting ability but to the intrinsic power of the text that she had co-authored.

With respect to a shift in *magnitude*, an intriguing example of two of my subjects converging occurs in Robins's unpublished typescript describing Besant's 1891 appearance at St. James's Hall, where Besant gave her farewell speech to the secularist platform. Evoking Besant as a kindred spirit, Robins establishes an initial feeling of multifariousness by describing the huge crowd as without a center. Then, moving through the negative emotion of disquiet to the focal point of Besant's actual appearance on stage, Robins utilizes the blending of reality and illusion to catapult herself into the shift in perspective that allows her to sort out the figure from the crowd—to freeze the frame, as it were, to set the tableau in her memory and that of her potential readers. In the process of creating this written account, Robins seems to tap into the same process that Besant herself enacts, thus suggesting the co-creative power of these two exemplars of creative negativity.

By now, the interrelatedness of many of these elements should become increasingly apparent. A sense of dilated *time* figures prominently in many of the scenarios I have been describing. This time dilation tends to take one of three forms—time attenuated, time frozen, and time reaching back into the past. Each of these forms has a powerful potential for crystallizing the self, which once again the practice of creative negativity cannot allow. As a result, we frequently recognize in instances of creative negativity a propensity to superimpose or double the self, as a means of undercutting the solidity of self-definition implied by any stretching of time. Note, for example, how Cameron counteracts her own efforts elsewhere in her canon to reach toward the solid essence of a frozen, timeless soul when she poses some of her famous "geniuses" as characters from Alfred Tennyson's *Idylls of the King* (1859; 1874–1877). Here we can witness the present breaking down the past, as ongoing life-identities are superimposed over mythic or historical ones. Another fascinating counter-activity occurs in Ritchie's doubling of a paradoxical self in her introductions to the works of her father, William Makepeace Thackeray, wherein the two selves of Ritchie and her father are simultaneously chronicled.

With *self-referentiality* we are finally dealing with an inherently ambivalent element, for the very act of referring to a self both underlines that self (crystallizing it, so to speak) and undermines it (by virtue of the implied creation of another self commenting on the first one). As a preeminent example, speaking or writing of oneself in the third person (a frequent case in creative negativity) at once asserts and denies the sense of an unchanging self. This is, in fact, the mode adopted by Cameron at the outset of her autobiographical fragment, "Annals of My Glass House" (1874; 1889). Repeatedly, the creative negativist draws attention to herself and the art forms she is exploring and exploding. Such, surely, is also the nature of Besant reading into or behind Christianity as she self-consciously leads herself and her reading public to the discovery of an "esoteric Christianity." And in both formal and social terms, Robins accomplishes the same thing for herself and Besant when she concludes her portrait of her fellow creative negativist (and women's suffrage advocate) by framing her description with the self-referentiality of the *raconteur* who favors the vividly remembered form of the evening's events over its specific content.

In sum, the machinery of creative negativity is anchored in space but fluid in time, fixed emotionally but unfixed cognitively, as it cycles between reality and illusion. Ideally, it is a machine that turns reality into illusion, illusion into reality, back and forth, again and again, as instanced in Besant's brand of Theosophy endlessly penetrating the shells of belief.[3] At its most intense, the techniques have the effect of making (male) figures perceive what is not there, preempting their fiction with a superfetated dream within the dream of Victorian gender divisions. Taken together, the elements of creative negativity comprise an ironic, circular creation-decreation myth. In its pure form, this myth tells the story of a birth from pain and entrapment, from chaos and multifariousness, into self-mocking transcendence, wherein the consciousness shucks off its old skin and steps outside the frame of its own defined existence. This activity dissects and lays bare the techniques which tell the tale of the female quest, anatomizing the tale for the four practitioners I am studying and providing us with insight into its general operation for other female questors. Essentially, the Victorian version of this myth undoes itself soon after it begins, involving a certain playfulness about its own primality, for in shifting beyond itself the creation looks back on the pathetic thing that was first created as a spur to new formulations.

FOUR VICTORIAN EXEMPLARS

All four of my subjects were prominent figures in their own time, immensely popular and well-received, yet today they remain largely out-of-print and under-studied in an age that has until recently relied on a hegemonically-determined male canon that has in turn dictated strict definitions of accomplishment and sharply delineated genre divisions. Cameron continues to be viewed as a scattered personality, a middle-aged amateur who stumbled onto an aesthetic technique, although recent exhibitions of her work have resulted in an increased awareness and appreciation of her as an artist. As for Ritchie, her achievements have been viewed in piecemeal fashion, as difficult to pigeonhole, and her works are available primarily in expensive scholarly editions. Robins has recently been rediscovered (between 1994 and 1995 she was the subject of two full-length biographies, the first to reach publication), but her work is still relatively unknown and underappreciated. Besant is, of course, an anomaly by almost any definition; her multiple careers have impelled many disciplines to claim her, but none has done justice to her overall accomplishment. She was both well- and ill-received during and after her lifetime. Highly controversial at all stages of her life experience, Besant inevitably remained in the public eye, but today she is chiefly remembered in India and in Theosophical circles, while social historians in the West seem to have lost sight of her impact and contributions. By examining a wide range of the creative expressions and performances of these women and finding heretofore undiscovered connections among them and their work, I hope to increase respect for and awareness of their achievements, both individually and as a group.

As an index of how these women have been shortchanged and marginalized by both history and the academy, it is instructive to look at how they have been represented in that bastion of British reference tools, the *Dictionary of National Biography*. Founded by George Smith, Thackeray's publisher, and first edited by Leslie Stephen, brother-in-law to Anne Thackeray Ritchie and father of Virginia

Woolf, this enterprise has been a dubious resource regarding my four exemplars. For instance, Stephen assigned the Cameron entry to his own wife, Julia, who in her turn provided a relatively short record based on "personal knowledge"; Julia situates her aunt within a large and loving "circle of friends," allotting only one paragraph to her photographic and literary accomplishments, which are presented in summary fashion. As for Ritchie, she does not even merit an entry under her own name; instead, she appears as an appendage or footnote to her husband Richmond, disparagingly reduced to the assessment that "it is in social life rather than in literature that her position was unique." Notably, Ritchie herself provided a much more sustained analysis of her friend and mentor Elizabeth Barrett Browning when she had an opportunity to contribute to the *DNB*. Besant merits the most extensive article of them all, but her early work in social reform takes a backseat to her political role in India, which is adjudged in equivocal terms: "Her facile but somewhat shallow eloquence also increased her following." Perhaps the *DNB* can be excused for overlooking Robins after her death in 1952 because she retained her American citizenship, but she was only belatedly picked up in the 1993 volume subtitled *Missing Persons*. Nonetheless, her somewhat brief account is the most balanced of all because it is written by one of her two recent (and only) biographers, Angela John.[4]

Uncovering and showcasing the lives and creative work of these four women allows me to proclaim them as exemplars who had to deal with and belie the then-prevailing images of women as "angels in the house." These women in many ways took the harder road; instead of becoming elite bluestockings, they carved a place for themselves within the cultural power structures of their day. Rather than taking the route of revolutionary nihilism, which would aim at dismissing those structures, they used strategies that I am calling creative negativity to negate the effects of stifling containment and to stage their own rebellions as a kind of loyal opposition. Within traditional feminist studies, especially those rooted in the Victorian period, scholarship has preferred either the victimology of the Victorian woman or its attendant pose of female survival-heroics. This practice has developed from Sandra Gilbert's and Susan Gubar's groundbreaking *Madwoman in the Attic* (1979) through Elaine Showalter's *The Female Malady* (1986), both landmark volumes for their time.[5] In contrast, my case studies demonstrate the mechanics of functional parts of Victorian culture rather than its dysfunctional mechanisms of stereotyping or the strictures of its class system. What I am describing in this study are real women with real achievements, considered as part of recognizable social and cultural space instead of being disentangled from the far fringes of psychological or social marginality.

Nonetheless, these four exemplars were empowered by some of the same kind of distancing that gave voice to women of the Empire, those women whose perspective on their homeland was magnified by their writing about it from abroad.[6] The cosmopolitan viewpoint that all four had in common allowed them an outsider status without relegating them to the ranks of the outcast. Cameron was born in India, educated in France, and finally returned to Ceylon (now Sri Lanka) to live out her last days on one of her husband's coffee plantations; she and her five sisters enjoyed a singular artistic community centered at Little Holland House on the outskirts of London before she removed her household to the Isle of Wight. Ritchie, too, lived abroad during her early years, receiving her early instruction in France from her paternal grandmother and then frequently traveling on the continent with her father. As for Besant, born of Irish heritage, she became a worldwide traveler as a result of heading up the worldwide Theosophy movement, and she spent almost half her life in India, where she found herself at odds with her homeland over the issue of Home Rule. American-born and -educated, Robins spent most of her adult life in England, yet she never gave up her American citizenship, making numerous transatlantic crossings, even during wartime, and journeying as far afield as the Alaskan gold country to recover her long-lost brother.

At the same time, all four women bore an equivocal relationship to the idea of Empire. Cameron's letters to her husband and sons when they were in Ceylon, as well as her correspondence with friends and family after she and her husband had retired to the Far East, show her openness to the experience of living outside English soil, but they also betray some of the Englishness ingrained in the colonial enterprise.[7] Ritchie came from a long line of Anglo-Indians (her father was born in India), and her husband, Sir Richmond Ritchie, dedicated his professional life to the India Office (it was this devotion that merited him his knighthood and thereby granted his wife the title of "Lady"). For her own part, Ritchie worked as co-author with Richardson Evans to produce one of the texts in the "Rulers of India" series, namely *Lord Amherst and the British Advance Eastwards to Burma* (1909). Besant's allegiance to the people of India can hardly be questioned, but like many British subjects she advocated a gradual journey toward independence, with the way station of membership in the Commonwealth holding out considerable appeal. As for the American citizen Robins, her so-called comic renderings of other national and racial groups in novels such as *Under the Southern Cross* (1907) remain uncomfortably dated, revealing her to be influenced by the imperialist prejudices of her day despite her democratic protestations.

Cameron, Ritchie, Besant—these are all married names, the surnames of their respective husbands. Robins, too, was briefly married (then widowed), and as an actress she was well within the common practice of retaining her maiden name as her stage one. Within the conventions of marriage and propriety, each carved out her niche and tried to work with the system, neither constrained by it nor openly rebelling against it. Moreover, although three of the four had children (we suspect that Robins may have had an abortion during her short-lived marriage) and they all extended their families by informal adoption (mothering younger men and women in Robins's case), their family lives proceeded along fairly smooth lines, not interfering with their creative endeavors. That such an observation can be made testifies in no small part to their fairly comfortable class positions, though both Besant and Robins did have to work to support themselves, and the dwindling Cameron family income was clearly boosted by sales of her photographs. But even within relative comfort these women knew how to turn circumstances to their advantage. For instance, I would argue that both Cameron and Ritchie used their eccentric personae as means to secure the space and time they needed to pursue their creative undertakings, effectively turning avocation into vocation.

In point of fact, each of these marriages could be called iconoclastic or unusual in certain key respects. Julia Cameron, née Pattle, surely benefited by marrying a man twenty years her senior, who in turn respected her right to explore her own interests and gave her the leeway to do so. Anne Thackeray's union was distinctive in the opposite direction; she married a man seventeen years her junior when she herself was thirty-seven and already an established author in her own right. Annie Wood's case runs against the grain in many ways, although she cannot be faulted for not trying to work from within the system. Finding herself married to a narrow-minded and abusive clergyman, she made the honest and reasonable decision to leave him, and she fought openly in the courts for custody of her daughter. Trapped by the laws of her time that denied her the right to sue for divorce once she had accepted the grounds for her separation (these included allowing her son to live with his father), she was forced into a marital limbo until her husband's death officially made her a widow. Nonetheless, she never remarried, and she retained the name of Besant throughout the remainder of her long life. As for Elizabeth Robins, after suffering from an unfortunate union with an unhappy actor who drowned himself four years into their marriage, she turned her widowhood into an opportunity to spurn attempts at coercion by would-be suitors. George Bernard Shaw called her "Saint Elizabeth" in consequence; in this respect, it is intriguing to contemplate the fact that Robins was reportedly the only woman whom Henry James wished to marry.[8] Ultimately, she established a long-term companionship with a younger woman, Octavia Wilberforce, whom she put through medical school and with whom she established a convalescent home for professional women that remained in operation for nearly eighty years.

Augmenting or in effect replacing their husbands, all four women at various times in their lives formed partnerships with other men, not allowing themselves to be constrained by either convention or the traditional limitations of marriage. Cameron, for example, adopted a series of mentors in such figures as astronomer Sir John Herschel, artist George Frederick Watts, and poet Alfred Tennyson; although she could be said to have idolized these famous men, her relationships with them clearly worked both ways, and her commercial status was shrewdly enhanced by association with them. Ritchie's chief male collaborator both predated and paralleled her life with her husband, for it was her working relationship with her father that provided her training ground as an author and then her editing of his works after his death that created an avenue for exploring her own evolution as a writer. As for Besant, she is infamous for the number of men she allied herself with—atheist and secularist Charles Bradlaugh, socialists George Bernard Shaw and Herbert Burrows, Marxist Edward Aveling, journalists John Robertson and William Stead, Theosophists William Judge and Charles Leadbeater, and World Teacher Jiddu Krishnamurti—but they all reflect working relationships that marked stages in her singular lifework's progress. Perhaps most savvy of them all, Elizabeth Robins chose collaborators from among her potential critics, enlisting the likes of Beerbohm Tree, William Archer, Harley Granville Barker, Shaw, and Henry James to help her revise her suffrage drama *Votes for Women!* so that she could anticipate and then quell likely male opposition to her line of argument.

Needless to say, however, I am not trying to suggest that the four women who inform the subject matter of this book were the only women of their era to develop the kind of subversive tactics I have been describing. Creative negativity constitutes a strategy that many women and members of other marginalized groups, male and female, could well derive and deploy. Among the Victorians alone, numerous other examples—canonical and non-canonical—come to mind. (In fact, Ritchie recommends many of these figures in her 1913 essay "A Discourse on Modern Sibyls.") To name just a few, the lives and work of all three Brontë sisters, Sara Coleridge, Anna Jameson, Elizabeth Gaskell, Charlotte Mary Tonna, Elizabeth Missing Sewell, George Eliot, Mary Elizabeth Braddon, Harriet Martineau, Elizabeth Barrett Browning, Mary Kingsley, Eliza Lynn Linton, Dinah Mulock Craik, Christina Rossetti, Charlotte Yonge, Margaret Oliphant, Adelaide Procter, Frances Power Cobbe, Rhoda Broughton, Mary Cholmondeley, Charlotte Mews, George Egerton, Sarah Grand, and Olive Shreiner certainly deserve examination or re-examination in terms of the techniques I have been delineating as creative negativity.[9] I am starting with Cameron, Ritchie, Besant, and Robins in large part because they stand out as case studies whose considerable talent and impact have been lost to subsequent generations. In addition, their accomplishments represent a range of fields with artistic interconnections that speak to one another in striking ways. This intertextuality among the works of these four women forms a fascinating narrative of how ingeniously and pervasively creative negativity can operate. Their combined tale is both extensive and persuasive—and hence exemplary for the purposes of this book.

As if to further confirm them in their remarkable paradigm, though by no means necessary to establishing its existence, the individual lives of the four women I have selected intersected in intriguing ways, suggesting that they were variously serving as models for one another or recommending alternative responses to equally negative situations. Julia Margaret Cameron, as the earliest of the four, predates the more overt feminism of her successors, but her proto-feminism engages her era by forcing it to confront multiple close-up photographic images of female subjects, even as her own autobiographical fragment disperses her sense of self across its few short pages. Cameron knew Anne Thackeray Ritchie through their complex network of shared family members and artistic mentors, and her photograph of Ritchie reproduced in this book is one of the most telling declarations of Ritchie's Victorian enmeshment (see Figure 10 in Chapter 3). In her turn, besides writing about Cameron, Ritchie acted as a distant link to Elizabeth Robins, via the same niece—namely Virginia Woolf—whom she had in common with Cameron, albeit through marriage and one rather than two generations removed. Ritchie's concern for her niece's health took the form of maintaining close ties with Virginia's husband, Leonard Woolf, who eventually became the executor of Robins's estate through his connection to Octavia Wilberforce, Robins's long-time companion, who was also consulting physician to Virginia. Moreover, Leonard and Virginia's Hogarth Press published Robins's *Ibsen and the Actress* (1928), and it was Virginia who suggested to Robins the title of her autobiography, *Both Sides of the Curtain* (1940). And finally, Robins openly joined Annie Besant in the fight for women's suffrage. The occasion of their sharing the stage of the Albert Hall in 1912 to promote "Votes for Women" contributed to Robins's fascination with the image and career that Besant fostered, culminating in her much revised yet finally unpublished biography of Besant.[10]

For my purposes, another serendipitous connection exists, centering on the art and writings of the Russian abstract painter, Wassily Kandinsky (1866–1944). The concept of synaesthesia, "the simultaneity and equivalence of sensations," contributed an essential element to his theory of creativity, much as I believe it did for Elizabeth Robins's boundary-crossing aesthetic. By comparing one art's fundamental elements with another's, Kandinsky believed he could foresee new "symphonic compositions" in his own impressionism and improvisations. In this respect, he acknowledged the powerful force of the "collision of different worlds . . . in their conflict with one another—through catastrophes, which, out of the chaotic roar of all instruments, create in the end a symphony known as the music of the spheres."[11] This orientation also opens up possibilities for expressing emotions in abstract forms through the strategic use of color and shape, much as Annie Besant and Charles Leadbeater had already articulated and illustrated in their jointly authored text, *Thought-Forms* (1905). This creative resource was clearly a spiritual one as well, as Kandinsky explained in *On the Spiritual in Art* (1912). Citing Besant's influence, Kandinsky proclaimed in 1935 that he viewed the artist very much as a microcosmic creator: "With each new instance of materialization, the divinity [or divine spirit in man] discovers yet another facet to its limitless potential."[12] By raising the intertwined issues of spirituality and creativity, Kandinsky suggests that there is something quite extraordinary about non-materiality and meta-materialization engendered by participating artists—including, I argue, those who employ the elements of creative negativity.

PLAN OF THE BOOK

Nevertheless, it is not my intention to mechanically proceed through a blow-by-blow elucidation of how each of the six elements of creative negativity operated for each of the four women I have selected. Instead, I want to allow them to tell their own stories, in their own words as much as possible, through the overall record of their lifework. Each of them engaged in multiple autobiographical enterprises; they were all prolific letter-writers; and their creative outpourings, individually and collectively, provide us with a panoply of redefinitions of what constitutes self-expression and self-performance. Thus, for each of these four women I will elaborate and explore the unique subtypes of creative negativity that her formal activities deploy and her personal vision develops. Moreover, I want to consider the elements I have described as comprising creative negativity as fluid, as useful for explicating complex lives and artistic accomplishments, not as ends in themselves. The plan of the book unfolds through the following four chapters and epilogue.

The chapter subsequent to this introductory one, "The Singular Double-Vision of Julia Margaret Cameron," documents this pioneer photographer as an intriguing precursor to the more fully realized creative negativists who follow her. Backing into feminism through multiple, incremental images of women, Cameron evidences a highly creative response to the gender-based dysfunctions she encounters in the Victorian marketplace. She bodies forth a distinctive set of images—both visual and verbal—which make available to her a kind of collaboration with form and with other empathetic artists, such as Poet Laureate Tennyson. Cameron's "creative economy" produces serial selves morphing from one fictional persona to another, and this activity never actually crystallizes. Her trademark photographic techniques include disturbingly soft-focused close-ups and group configurations of strangely dispersed individuals. This chapter explores how these and other images ultimately undercut our sense of coherent individuality, and how Cameron's methods—used simultaneously to construct and deconstruct the self—create an overall sense of ambiguity. This double-edged quality explains how Cameron can be so at home with negation and the challenges it poses to her gender. Like her sister proto-feminists, she learned that it takes an efficient creativity, a streamlined duality, to transcend gender considerations and celebrate them at the same time.

In Chapter 3, "Self-Erasure and Self-Creation in Anne Thackeray Ritchie," I trace the rhetorical development of creative negativity in an author who reveled in the full panoply of its variations. Ritchie's brand of creative negativity, which I have dubbed *espièglerie* (from the French word meaning prankishness), is a method of writing which strikes a deliberately and deceptively non-threatening pose, employing short units and overtly minor subject matter. In fact, she quietly evolved a new form of collection writing which succeeds in crossing superficial boundaries of magnitude, form, and subject matter. A case in point is her innovation of the "domesticated fairy tale." Through close textual analysis I show how Ritchie achieves many of the subversive goals of creative negativity through her mastery of *espièglerie*. Not surprisingly, her novels have been devalued as fragmentary, as failing to provide iron-clad plot structures. They do indeed read like a series of vignettes, easily amenable to Victorian serial publication, and, as small units, hardly threatening or revolutionary. In addition, this aesthetic pretends not to be serious writing—just fairy tales (and "domesticated" ones at that), or mere sketches. But a closer look reveals that these tales bristle with disturbing images. My analysis of these images (and Ritchie's other rhetorical stratagems) demonstrates how the forms of *espièglerie*, as with all instances of creative negativity, eventually transcend themselves, acting as image templates to express a cyclical erasure and re-creation of the self.

Chapter 4, "The Multiple Deconversions of Annie Wood Besant," elucidates how creative negativity can be used as a tool to shape life itself. In Besant, we can recognize a strong ratiocinative mind, relentlessly dissecting political, social, and religious belief systems in its quest for self-creation at the highest level. For Besant, this intellectual activity had the widest repercussions: she ultimately came to lead the worldwide spiritual movement of Theosophy. My study of Besant's life and writings suggests a pattern of painful deconversions, in which she first discovers the seeds of self-contradiction within her current belief system—the point where it fails in its unifying purpose—then turns to forbidden knowledge, and finally embraces a larger structure which offers a more convincing hope of dissolving the boundaries that separate human souls. As we see Besant break out of one Victorian box after another—utilizing creative negativity as a weapon in a quest for truth—we come to understand that it takes a strong sense of self to tinker with the self. Theosophy represented for her a system in which the process of deconversion is magnified into a metaphysic and a meditative technique, one that by its very definition endlessly tries to penetrate the shells of belief to realize an infinity beyond form. Thus, creative negativity leads Besant to the deeper mystical meanings lying behind, and eventually dissolving, all forms, making spiritual connections among all peoples and systems. Theosophy, in her hands, becomes a perfect creative negativity machine.

My penultimate chapter, "Elizabeth Robins Outperforms the New Woman," puts creative negativity on stage. Actress-manager, producer, playwright, novelist, suffragist extraordinaire, Robins outdoes the moral, social, and artistic boundary-crossing of even the mind-boggling New Women of her time by moving both inward and outward—inward to a realm of primal emotion and synaesthetic imagery, outward to a world of co-conspirators in the form of other performing women. Her subtype of creative negativity willingly enlists strong emotions, its aggressiveness sometimes actually distorting audience perceptions. If Keats's infamous "negative capability" invokes an ability to work with uncertainty—a general tolerance for ambiguity in order to transcend conceptual boundaries—Robins's more focused and precise use of negatives in her play *Alan's Wife* takes us across emotional boundaries, utilizing negation and opposition as tools to confront the unbearable, perhaps even to see the unseen. Robins played the lead character, Jean Creyke, who apparently views the mutilated body of her dead husband, smothers her deformed infant, and mutely accepts her death sentence. My study shows how Robins's brilliant acting and stagecraft make us see what are essentially non-actions—enabling the actress-playwright to convey the seemingly impossible. Something new is forged in the process of using a negative "action" to signal creative choice, something unexpected in its intensity, precisely because societal boundaries have been breached. What the play evoked is obviously central to Robins's aesthetic: it exudes a quality of life that ultimately refuses to stay in uncertainty, an engaged vitality that sets her in opposition to Keats's more sublime mode and shows her joining with her Ibsen heroines to say a loud "No!"

Lastly, in my epilogue, "The Female Quest Reconsidered," I explore some remaining aspects of the female quest highlighted by other authors and texts, which in turn reflect back on techniques advanced by my four Victorian exemplars. Besides reviewing pertinent aspects of Lewis Carroll's *Alice* books (1865 and 1872) and L. Frank Baum's *Wizard of Oz* (1900), I raise some final questions about the female quest in order to show how creative negativity can be utilized for parodic, ultimately constructive, purposes. If society alternately constructs and dismantles women, then the female practitioner of creative negativity may well decide to confound the enemy. In fact, an implied or formal parody is often at work in the writing of Ritchie and Robins, and men like Shaw, who call women humorless, miss the point precisely because they are often the target themselves. Even a rereading of a pre-Victorian novel like Mary Shelley's *Frankenstein* (1818; 1831) can demonstrate some of these principles in action. Within the confines of her male protagonist's grotesque attempt at creative negativity, the female novelist Mary Shelley explores female consciousness—cast as the monstrous creation—surrounded by a parodic plethora of formal framing devices.[13] In *Frankenstein* the elements of creative negativity are distorted at a primal level by the male would-be scientist's god-preempting creation of human life. Yet a constructive possibility is embodied in the creature himself: his central monologue represents an intuitive working out of all the basic elements of creative negativity. In keeping with the novel's inverted and parodic approach, Shelley places creative negativity in a vacuum, removing it from the social context that usually provokes it. Utterly isolated, the creature has to discover the very nature of family and society itself, for the full flowering of creative negativity's self-referentiality can come only when he re-creates himself as a social creature.

This epilogue concludes my book by showing how creative negativity is akin to an effort to create a bubble within a pressurized liquid. Its elements are designed to push against the societal pressures which attack it from all sides, yet the bubble is delicate, and the battle against the external forces must have a smooth and seamless quality. It must also be an unceasing—or at least recycling—effort. This activity, in sum, opens up and displays the complexities of the female quest. This quest's self-ironic nature tends to make it fragmentary, not given to coherent, epic form. As a form, the epic is itself a bit egotistical, suggesting a very large-scale, coherent self indeed, and such finality of self-creation runs counter to the ironic circle of creative negativity out of which the female quest spins itself. The consequence of the interaction of the elements of creative negativity is a crossing of societal or emotional boundaries, and as their combined activity creates a machine—a self-activated counter-dream within the generally accepted dream or fiction of the larger society—the effect is subtle or else skewed, risking horrific backlash. Avoiding a blunt confrontation with the fictional world-view it works within, this machinery subverts it, apparently on its own terms. So the form of the female quest is inherently problematical. As a result, we are more likely to encounter the quintessential female quest narrative in women's lives as fully examined. In this respect, it is appropriate that an actress figures prominently in my scenario, and that the biographies of the women I have chosen reveal many qualities of the actress and her multiplicity of personae. More precisely, these are women who repeatedly move outside their pre-existing roles to create new and more challenging ones.

2. The Singular Double Vision of Julia Margaret Cameron

At the age of forty-eight, Julia Margaret Cameron (1815–1879) took up the practice of photography, ostensibly to fill her idle hours once her children had flown the coop. She inaugurated her career in 1863 when she was living on the Isle of Wight, off the southern coast of England. Among her neighbors and friends was Poet Laureate Alfred Tennyson, one of a long parade of subjects who would sit to her increasingly practiced eye. Inspired by her daughter's gift of a camera, this pioneer woman photographer plunged into all aspects of the art, rapidly turning her deserted hen-house into a natural-light studio and the coal room into a darkroom. Chaos spread throughout Cameron's already frenzied extended household as her new passion began to engulf not only her life but that of anyone within her reach. It was not long before she started coercing people to become her sitters—relatives, friends, servants, and even strangers passing by who had somehow caught her attention. More and more driven by her newfound art form, Cameron became adept at orchestrating others into sharing her enthusiasm. Beginning with the 1864 annual exhibition of the Photographic Society of London, Cameron regularly submitted her work for public display. Rejected by many contemporary British academicians at first, she was faulted for her haphazard printing, her presumed lack of technical expertise in achieving a sharp focus, and her general disregard for the style of portraiture currently in vogue. But despite mixed reviews from critics in England, Cameron soon arranged for her works to be displayed and sold through a London print gallery. By then, she had received acclaim abroad, winning prizes at major exhibitions in Edinburgh, Berlin, and Paris. Controversial during her lifetime, Cameron and her work are still subjects of lively debate today.

Cameron's life was hardly empty when she began to assume her newly-discovered career, however. Daughter of an Anglo-Indian civil servant and a

FIGURE I.　Portrait of Julia Margaret Cameron (1815–1879) by her friend and mentor, G. F. Watts (1852). Platinum photograph of the oil painting taken by her son, Henry Herschel Hay Cameron (1846–1911) at the Cameron Studio in London (1890). 23.5 x 18.9 cm. Courtesy of The J. Paul Getty Museum, Los Angeles (86.XM.637.2).

mother of French descent, she was one of six accomplished sisters who eventually held salon-like court to artists, philosophers, and writers of genius. The young Julia Margaret Pattle was educated abroad, in both France and England. Then, returning to India via South Africa in 1835, she met and shortly thereafter married Charles Hay Cameron, a distinguished jurist and educator twenty years her senior. Back in Calcutta, the young wife quickly became chief hostess for English society, assisting Governor General Hardinge (whose wife had stayed in England) for some ten years, as well as raising a sum of £14,000 for victims of the Irish potato famine. Moving to England in 1848 with their five sons and one daughter, the Camerons lived in a variety of different locations that were part of Greater London, then and now, before settling down on the Isle of Wight. Back in London, at her sister Sara Prinsep's home, "Little Holland House," Cameron had been surrounded by many literary and otherwise artistic "lions," whose friendships she had also cultivated. By now Cameron's household, too, had swelled, with five adopted daughters joining the family as her own children grew up and left for school, and houseguests frequently dropped by and stayed for months at a time. Thus, occasions to photograph others were ready-made, providing an immediate array of subject matter as well as assistance in the difficult processing of the new technology. Moreover, Cameron was fortunate in having such mentors as Sir John Herschel, early innovator of the photographic art who also coined the words "negative" and "positive," and George Frederick Watts, a painter whose artistic aspirations she shared (see Figure 1 for his portrait of her).[1]

Knowing something of Cameron's life story and studying her photographic images can actually furnish us with lessons in how to read photographs as she saw them—as whole lives that deconstruct themselves only to reconstruct them as interacting with a network of many other lives, each with its own subjective center. In this respect, Cameron's photography may first impress viewers by what it omits: sharp focus, contemporary fashion styles, and other paraphernalia of conventional portraiture and time-bound identity. Take the example of the photograph entitled "The Mountain Nymph, Sweet Liberty" (Figure 2).[2] Gauzily out of focus, the background remains virtually nonexistent. The model's features are clear enough to present a striking image, but they are not rendered in the sort of overly-sharp contours that might atomize our attention, causing us to zoom in on details. Nor does the clothing consist of an easily definable style; instead, its ambiguity and lack of form suggest some sort of universal covering, which laps into the background in engaging but indeterminate folds.

Yet the artist behind the lens knew how to work with the tools that served her so well in pursuing her vision. Between the gestalt of soft focus and a diffuse source of light coming from above and off to one side, Cameron turns negation into a creation that emerges from her own inner wisdom. With an al-

FIGURE 2. Julia Margaret Cameron's "The Mountain Nymph, Sweet Liberty" (1866). Title taken from John Milton's poem "L'Allegro" (1632) and meant to symbolize the spirit of freedom; the model has been identified as Mrs. Keene (at Freshwater, Isle of Wight). 36.6 x 28.5 cm. Courtesy of the Helmut Gernsheim Collection, Harry Ransom Humanities Research Center, The University of Texas at Austin (964:0037:0112).

most gleaming paleness, the model's face thrusts itself forward out of the darkness, filling the space with her soft but penetrating gaze. The face is further framed by another Cameron signature—a mane of tousled, stormy hair. Then, by implementing the painter's use of *chiaroscuro*, releasing an interplay of lights and darks, Cameron both highlights and darkens the hair as it falls over a hint of the model's shoulders. The prominent neck—strong and solid—appears outlined against the darker tones receding into nothingness. All of these dampening forces around the face act as a visual magnet, and we as viewers are almost forced to zoom in to the eyes, to the point that we seem to discern something behind them. The centrality and intensity of the eyes, together with the figure's expression of emotional arrest, make it seem as if we are looking into a mind beset with overwhelming emotion, encouraging us to conjoin with that inner being in her ongoing moment of joy or suffering. By allowing focus and light to play back and forth across the model's face, Cameron invests it with a living quality, a kind of vitality, connecting the model with viewer, photographer, other photographs taken of the same model, other models posed in similar or contrasting ways—all of them forging a dialogue among a multitude of selves.

Over and over again, Cameron's photographic images entice and elude the onlooker. The figures she depicted are both present and not present; the eyes of these long-dead models stare out at us intensely yet blankly, their visages suggesting a trancelike or meditative state. And they induce in us a similar state, one that alternates between the focused and unfocused mental orientation that meditation engenders. Paradoxically, the meditator's unfocused stare belies his or her heightened awareness of both detail and a more holistic perspective. Behind these images and responsible for them is the primary meditator, Cameron herself. The body of her photography reveals three deliberate and consistent principles: the use of a soft focus in the service of portraiture, a personalized (even narrow) range of subject matter, and an almost obsessive, seemingly unphotographic iconography. These qualities derive from an imagistic meditation lying at the heart of her life and work. In an intuitive yet increasingly self-conscious manner,[3] Cameron repeatedly explored the relationship between the individual self and its apparent opposite—the transpersonal, divine, allegorical, or collective self. This exploration allowed her to confront and transcend gendered limitations, to become a proto-feminist for her time as well as our own.

Ambiguity is central to Cameron's visual meditation on this epistemological interrelationship. She did not insist upon either a oneness or a simple conflict between the individual self and a divine or transpersonal "meta-self." Looking ahead to the complexities later embraced by Annie Besant, Cameron sought to preserve both elements or qualities—so a mere melding or combining is also avoided. She strived to depict in her photographs the full range of interaction or intersection among qualities, without pinpointing any one as dominant. Hers is much more than the fairly clearcut storytelling art of Victorian narrative painting, particularly as exemplified by the Pre-Raphaelites,[4] and it is precisely when her meaning is most unambiguous that her art is least successful. Cameron's peculiar demand dictated—and limited—her aesthetic, her subject matter, and even her choice of models. Since specificity would seem to be generic to the art of photography, practitioners and critics of that art form might well tend to find Cameron's uniquely self-limited work inappropriate and even frustrating. Typical of her contemporary critics, Henry Peach Robinson accordingly opined, "Photography is preeminently the art of definition, and when an art departs from its *function*, it is lost."[5]

Cameron's soft focus served to maintain a degree of ambiguity across the panoply of her work. Furthermore, boundaries among photographs, models, and subject matter are blurred, as similar configurations—such as Madonnas—reappear incrementally; individual models assume many different roles, like actors who exist in our minds as both singular and multiple selves; and her famous contemporaries are posed as fictional characters, splitting or shattering their public selves, in effect breaking their singularity into facets.[6] Within this narrowness, however, Cameron deployed a vast visual armatorium which is anything but narrow. Its cumulative effect is a constant double vision, in which we see both the individual and the meta-individual. In order to elucidate this effect, I will be noting in particular her repeated use of veiled eyes; groupings in which individuals look in different directions; loose, unruly hair; working-class women serving as divine figures; people leaning on one another, as if melting together or acting as reflections; women and little girls in close arrangement, as if exploring the feminine or the relationship between adulthood and childhood; faces emerging from darkness; and conflations of time, such as the infant Jesus with a cross, or contemporary men and women assuming medieval guises. Moreover, Cameron's visual meditation on the ambiguous interaction between the self and the meta-self receives confirmation in the verbal analogues of her poems, reminiscences, and letters, which allow us to recognize the continuity and creativity of her interweaving life and art. I am borrowing the term "creative economy" from Ralph Waldo Emerson, who extols it in *English Traits* (1856) as "the fuel of magnificence," to highlight Cameron's efficient, almost streamlined, application of the components of creative negativity.

CREATIVE ECONOMY

Eyes constitute a key element in the iconography of meditation. In the scientific language of Cameron's acquaintance Charles Darwin, who sought to describe in detail "the expression of the emotions in man and animals," meditation is largely figured in terms of the eyes: "When a person is lost in thought with his mind absent, or, as it is sometimes said, 'when he is in a brown study,' he does not frown, but his eyes appear vacant. The lower eyelids are generally raised and wrinkled, in the same manner as when a short-sighted person tries to distinguish a distant object; and the upper orbicular muscles are at the same time slightly contracted."[7] Citing the more precise observations of several professorial colleagues, Darwin goes on to examine the peculiar aspect of this vacant expression: "The eyes are not then fixed on any object, and therefore not, as I had imagined, on some distant object. The lines of vision of the two eyes even often become slightly divergent" (227). Is this not a fairly accurate description of the eyes in many of Cameron's photographs? Those already familiar with her canon can probably recall numerous examples, such as Thomas Carlyle, staring eagerly into emptiness (1867); Sir John Herschel, intently seeing beyond the immediate present (1867); one of her Madonnas, serenely gazing at the child on her lap; or Cameron's niece Julia, contemplating her widowhood sadly yet steadily (see, for example, Figure 6; this photograph is discussed later in this chapter).[8] We may logically analyze the technique and ascribe the blank expressions to either an intense effort to hold the eyes open or to the recording of multiple blinkings, but the images that result still depict our sense of meditation and its concomitant state of mind.

Anyone knowledgeable about the long exposure times (anywhere between three and five minutes) and difficult postures that Cameron subjected her models to would probably scoff at the notion that they were meditating, but that is exactly my point about meditation: it promotes the ability to yoke together opposites, to be both focused and unfocused at once, to be in and out of time. Actually engaging in meditation may not have been a viable option to Cameron's sitters (although I suspect that some of them had recourse to it, especially after they became experienced models), but the analogy to meditation applies to the whole process of portraiture, which asks us to inscribe subject, image, viewer, and photographer in a relational scenario. As a result, even if we know about the discomfiture of the sitter—here I am thinking especially of Cameron locking one of her subjects in a closet to produce the emotion of "Despair"[9]—we can still be inspired by the image that is finally achieved, along the lines intended or envisioned by the photographer's guiding meditation. Once again, paradox or ambiguity comes to the fore, opening up a single reading of the image, permitting the viewer to suspend disbelief and hold opposites in abeyance.

As the reader might suspect, Cameron's use of soft focus has been the subject of considerable debate. Referred to disparagingly by many of her contemporary critics as her out-of-focus propensity, her soft focus signaled to her photographer-peers a lack of sufficient knowledge about her equipment as well as just plain poor technique. It is difficult today to challenge her on technical matters, however. As the developer and printer of her own photographs, produced from handling plates that were usually 12 x 15 inches and coated in a solution of silver-nitrate, Cameron created some 3,000 to 4,000 prints, with an overall image count of around 1,000, during her fifteen-year career. Although she herself was equivocal about whether soft focus (more a matter of depth of field, actually) was something accidental or intentional, she persisted in using lenses that were not appropriate for the design of either of her cameras. But questions of original intentionality aside, even Helmut Gernsheim, Cameron's groundbreaking promoter, writes of her use of focus in belittling terms, especially in contrast to the sharper images of Lewis Carroll (Charles Dodgson), whom he clearly favored over Cameron. Directly challenging Gernsheim's reading of the issues traditionally posed by focus and the Cameron–Carroll comparison, cultural historian Lindsay Smith argues that both photographers were working out of gender-inflected compulsions. While Carroll had in mind a particular modus that placed little girls in tightly controlled compositions, Cameron's proto-feminism directed her to explore new ways of bringing her female models to the fore. And by letting their modulated faces fill the photographic frame, she taught herself how to manipulate focus in order to study the full range of women's experience and aspirations.[10]

Regardless of how the question of focus is resolved (or even left unresolved), here I wish to emphasize the ways in which focus operates through attention to the eyes. From Cameron's own recounting in her autobiographical fragment, "Annals of My Glass House," we know that soft focus immediately served her desire "to arrest all beauty" that came before her: "when focussing and coming to something which to my eye, was very beautiful, I stopped there instead of screwing on the lens to the more definite focus which all other photographers insist upon" (298).[11] So even though Cameron's own text may show her sometimes agreeing with her son, fellow photographer Henry Herschel Hay Cameron, that "my first successes in my out-of-focus pictures were a fluke," she concurrently asks us to bear witness to an intentional aesthetic decision. This kind of ambiguous accounting is typical of Cameron's overall manner in life and art; it both obscures and highlights a technique that focuses on eyes. For Cameron, eyes acted as emblems to the ambiguity and paradox that informed her vision. Her one published poem, "On a Portrait," invokes eyes "full of fervent love," yet whose meaning remains hidden by lids "behind which sorrow's touch / Doth press and linger on." The poem's final yoking together of "immortal" and "face" conflates the very opposing qualities she sought to represent in her own portraiture. Just as tellingly, in a private poem Cameron sent to Clough's widow, the synaesthetic "sad and serious eye" that pays tribute to the music of Arthur Henry Clough's poetry devolves into a dual, fragmentary focus typical of Cameron's overall enterprise.[12]

Once we begin to attend to the eyes in Cameron's photographs, specific observations yield an intriguing array of thematic groupings which further confirm her double vision. We discover many faces in which eyes are almost decreated—blurred, hidden, multiply directed—paradoxically leading us to examine the notion of portraits without eyes, their apparent absence demanding that we explore them even more as "windows to the soul." Such deliberate blurring, or the valuing of such blurring by preserving it, brings out and serves the meta-personal, for too sharp a focus would conversely emphasize the individual. In almost every case, eyes seem important to the composition, even when they are not clearly visible. If they are hooded, the lids lowered sleepily as if the figure were in some sort of hypnotic trance, then the transpersonal is even more strongly implied, as evidenced by the mystical humanism of "The Dream" (1864). This figure turns her head in profile, her heavy lids only half open, while her covered head contains a mass of otherwise unruly hair that begins to blend into the heavy folds of her indefinable garment. This transpersonal state receives additional impetus from Cameron's inscription, "Methought I saw my late espoused saint," the first line of John Milton's sonnet entitled "On his Deceased Wife" (1658). Its final couplet reads, "But oh! as to embrace me she inclined, / I waked, she fled, and day brought back my night." In this respect, Mike Weaver has postulated, "[F]ar from accepting the ruthless dichotomy between divine and human love, [Cameron] acknowledged the interactive nature of God-given and sexual love" (*Whisper of the Muse* 45). Intriguingly, some prints of this same image are entitled "The Day-Dream."

Figures only rarely face the camera directly, only rarely are fully upright, and if several sitters are used, their line of vision is dispersed. One striking exception is the previously discussed image "The Mountain Nymph, Sweet Liberty"; her direct yet softened stare seems to see beyond any specific focal point to suggest the quintessential meditative state. As for images with multiple figures, the models often face in different directions, as they do, for example, in "Rosebud Garden of Girls" (1868). These four young women, sisters in real life, lean into one another as if creating a single form. Yet each is uniquely positioned and gazing in a different direction, as if to acknowledge her separate and subjective identity. Or, if the models face the same way, their eyes are usually looking toward different foci, as they are in "Summer Days" (1866). Roy Flukinger's more technical commentary on this image provides further confirmation of its narrative interest and tension: "Heads, hats, clothing, arms—all defy the rigid right angles which seek to frame the group in the traditional conformity of the commercial studio."[13] In either case, Cameron managed to emphasize a multiplicity that both verifies individual identity and disbands it. Perhaps this kind of configuration appealed to her from personal experience. Some five years before she took up the practice of photography, Cameron and two of her sons were photographed by her brother-in-law, Lord Somers (Figure 3). Grouped in a manner similar to that in the two images just discussed, these subjects appear not as a tight family unit but as individuals with their own thoughts and opinions. Nor is Cameron the typically maternal "Angel in the House," for she asserts her separate, singular identity by both gazing steadfastly at the camera and holding her pen poised to write.

As a whole, Cameron's subjects look pensive (one of her images is specifically titled "Il Pensorosa"). Her project was akin to using photographs to give us a series of silent soliloquies—providing us with access to a kind of imaginary internal discourse. If we speculate about these unvoiced soliloquies, they become our own imaginary meditations, while to the extent that they are also our projections, they assume a transcendent status, reaching across boundaries to join a participatory cosmic monologue.[14] Moreover, since Cameron often announced her subjects by labeling her prints with the name of a literary character or a line from a poem or song, we are invited into the minds of these figures as if they were living actors, shaped by our memory of the invoked work of art and amenable to our immediate scrutiny. Yet more often than not, an inchoate emotion, perhaps struggling to express the inexpressible, is implied by the rather limp and downcast demeanor of her models. So, Cameron in effect achieved both a focal point and a sense of multifariousness through the use of her figures' eyes—that is, the eyes at once center us and, through the varied treatments and directions of their gazes, provide a sense of transpersonal dispersion. Moreover, their hypnotic look evokes a curious quality of self-referentiality, one which turns back upon the photographer herself. Thus, the photographer's eye calls attention to itself, like a writer employing an eccentric or unusual style. Cameron thereby inserted herself uniquely into the longstanding history of those who seek to explore the interrelation between the human and the divine by focusing on the eyes. She added her visual meditation to the verbal symbols of Guillaume de Salluste ("These lovely lamps, these windows of the soul"), William Shakespeare ("The windows of my eyes"), and John Greenleaf Whittier ("The windows of my soul I throw / Wide open to the sun").[15]

Through photographic imagery, Cameron explored at a deep structural level the human–divine dichotomy that is central to High Church Anglicanism. Her interpretation of Anglo-Catholic Christianity led to the intriguing mixture—sacred and individually human—of her Madonnas. Strongly rooted in the secularity of the mother and woman, these Madonnas still interact with the divinity of the Mother of God and the Holy Virgin. Even more challenging is the risk

FIGURE 3.   Julia Margaret Cameron and her children Charles and Henry
(1859). Long attributed to Lewis Carroll (Charles Dodgson) but now believed to be
the work of her brother-in-law, Lord Somers (Charles Somers-Cocks, Viscount
Eastnor, 3rd Earl Somers). 20.3 x 16.2 cm. Courtesy of the Michael and Jane Wilson
Collection, London.

Cameron undertook by creating images of Mary Magdalene: How could she conjoin the fallen woman with the saint? This was a challenge doomed to failure within the plotlines of contemporary Victorian authors. Already breaching the moral code by casting the "fallen woman" as heroine, Elizabeth Gaskell, Thomas Hardy, and George Moore, for example, necessarily sacrificed her to society's dictates by novel's end in *Ruth*, *Tess of the d'Urbervilles*, and *Esther Waters*.[16] For Cameron's imagistic meditation, one answer to this self-imposed challenge lies in the power of eyes, their meditative gaze forcing us to acknowledge a suspension of opposing forces, perforce evoking a secular–sacred dichotomy. Another explanation lies in her repeated use of the same models, their incremental images bridging a spectrum from the human to the divine collectively, thereby increasing our propensity to read that same scope or range into single depictions. But perhaps Cameron's real coup in meeting this challenge lies in her extended visual meditation on women's hair.

For the Victorians, hair figured significantly in a mythology that tried to proscribe womanhood while worshipping it. A story about Ellen Terry, one of Cameron's models and briefly married to her artist-mentor George Frederick Watts, aptly conveys the practical force of this symbolism. Shortly after her marriage, the new wife apparently still wore her hair loose, in long cascades, but the matrons who had effectually acted as marriage-brokers were quick to correct and constrain the young bride in her new role by insisting that her hair now be bound and braided. Thus, an abundance of hair that had been free-flowing for the innocent child needed to be hidden and controlled for the child-bride, whose sexual knowledge would also presumably need to remain concealed and even denied. Interestingly enough, the women who were largely responsible for bringing about the marriage of the middle-aged artist to his seventeen-year-old bride were the Pattle sisters, Cameron among them, and from all accounts the unhappy union remained unconsummated, the ensuing legal separation eventually resolved by divorce. Moreover, Terry's subsequent life and career as an actress obviously opened her up to a sexuality which could be more openly acknowledged. In point of fact, Victorian attitudes presumed that the actress was the equivalent of the prostitute, whose loose hair would mark her both as sexual and as sexually compromised.

Intriguingly, Cameron's images of the young woman over a relatively short time span seem to navigate the full spectrum of Terry's potential range, and the photographer does so by utilizing hair as the predominant symbol in an overall scenario of her creation. At the one extreme, still during Terry's so-called honeymoon-stage on the Isle of Wight, Cameron presents us with a portrait of a sleeping Ellen. Self-contained and presumably self-controlled, the model has apparently pulled back her hair and concealed its length. Simply labeled "Ellen Terry"

(1864), this image depicts a demure innocent whose long hair is barely visible, her arm crossing her chest and clutching her necklace in a gesture of modesty. At the other extreme, Cameron anticipates the demise of Terry-as-wife and the vibrant embrace of her future self as an independent, freewheeling actress in an image entitled "The West Wind" (1864). In this allegorical portrait, Cameron has returned Ellen's hair to the original, liberated state of the Old Testament Eve. By releasing her subject's hair, by setting it free and wild in utter abandon, Cameron thus appears to recognize and reflect the free spirit in Terry that could not be long constrained by Victorian propriety. Indeed, it is almost as if Cameron prefigured the psychological insight into the subconscious that would eventually be heralded by Freudian and Jungian analysis alike. As the unconscious turmoil of Cameron's sleeping beauty gives way to the newfound power of the West Wind, the female creative energy shared by both artist and subject seems unleashed against a universal backdrop of endlessly flowing creation-out-of-negation.

Elisabeth Gitter points up how art and literature instance the Victorians' obsession with women's hair as complex and ambiguous: "Golden hair, through which wealth and female sexuality are inevitably linked, was the obvious and ideal vehicle for expressing their notorious—and ambivalent—fascination both with money and with female sexual power."[17] Further complicating the situation is another convenient dichotomy: "When the powerful woman of the Victorian imagination was an angel, her shining hair was her aureole or bower; when she was demonic, it became a glittering snare, web, or noose." The evocative power of women's hair is immense in its scope and potential for releasing opposing forces in this paradigm, and Cameron explores a panoply of graphic tones and narrative roles for hair in her photographs. Besides the ability to print her images darker or lighter or in a combination of different shadings, Cameron had a subtle spectrum of tones at her disposal, ranging through red, sepia, eggplant, and black, and her 1868 "Priced Catalogue" asked the purchaser to specify between gray or brown toning when placing an order. Not limited to the specifically "golden" symbolism of writers and painters, she dramatically highlighted hair, often using it as a framing device, and employed a dynamic asymmetry to convey a spiritual vibrancy that is even more potent in its quiet intensity.

Cameron's image of "The Angel at the Tomb" (Figure 4) is a remarkable case in point. Here Cameron posed her housemaid Mary Hillier in profile, the grandeur of her aquiline nose and upward-tilted head contrasting with a resplendent head of shining hair. This hair is unleashed in an especially wild and unruly manner, its tangled waves and swirls blending with the ill-defined drapery that extends upward, in wavelike fashion, and then drops to form the weighted baseline of the photograph. The light catches and highlights just a small portion of the model's forehead and tousled outcropping, providing an off-center focal

FIGURE 4. Julia Margaret Cameron's "The Angel at the Tomb" (1870), Freshwater, Isle of Wight. Portrayed by Mary Ann Hillier (1847–1936), one of Cameron's housemaids and her favorite model; Hillier was also the model for "The Angel at the Sepulchre" and regularly represented both Mary Magdalene and the Virgin Mary. 33.1 x 23.5 cm. Courtesy of the Helmut Gernsheim Collection, Harry Ransom Humanities Research Center, The University of Texas at Austin (964:0037:0025).

point above the profiled and hooded eye. No proper Victorian woman would have posed for her personal portrait with her hair so unrestrained, but Cameron could exercise her artistic freedom over her models because she was posing them as transpersonal subjects. Despite the reach toward the divine, the tension with the human individual remains solidly locked in place. We might note, too, that Hillier provided the model for "The Angel at the Sepulchre" (1869) as well. Using the same model as both angels doubly conflates the Magdalene with the biblical invocation to the divine, and the mirrored pairing allows an interplay between the overt devotion of the cloaked head and the subtle divinity of the uncovered one. For Mike Weaver, this kind of intersection replays itself as an "attempt to get the balance between the Madonna elements and those of the Magdalene exactly right in pictorial effect." He cites "The Dream," which Watts labeled "Quite Divine," as one of Cameron's finest efforts in this respect, but it is "The Kiss of Peace" (1869) which epitomizes for him Cameron's greatest success—her maid-model Mary Hillier's history of playing both Madonnas and Magdalenes once again contributing "an especially integrative factor."[18]

The impact of Cameron's close-ups enjoins us to compare and contrast her use of eyes and hair to specific interactive purposes. This juxtaposition allows us to read eyes as comparatively more personal and inward-focusing, while hair seems somehow more impersonal and reaching outward. Whereas eyes have a deliberate quality, hair promotes a sense of the accidental. Ultimately, hair—particularly female hair—takes on a life or personality of its own in the service of conveying a transpersonal tension. Hair in the panoply of Cameron's portraits is both weightless and heavy, highlighted and dark, free and bound, ordered and chaotic. It can alternately operate as a background or frame, or else be foregrounded. However it functions, Cameron's use of hair is visually remarkable, even when its meaning remains deliberately elusive. Moreover, hair conveys an inherent intensity while crossing boundaries. Even when it is contained in buns or braids, its abundance is emphasized, as it is in several portraits of painter and artist-model Marie Spartali (1867–1870). Posing her with head turned away, eyes hooded and hardly even visible, Cameron demonstrated how such images still convey a potential for wild disarray. Cameron employed yet another strategy to demonstrate how this tension inheres in hair. By utilizing a turban, as she did in her renderings of "Beatrice Cenci" (1866–1870), or by draping the heads of her Madonnas with cloths, sometimes extended down the length of their bodies, she reintroduced the weight and dimension of the covered hair she was apparently trying to obscure.

Upon closer examination, it would seem as if Cameron orchestrated her use of eyes and hair in tandem fashion. In the personal portraits of her women friends and family, hair arranged or done up neatly correlates frequently with a modest looking away, while in the allegorical or typological images, hair down and in slight disarray often corresponds to a more bold, straight-on look. At other times, however, the drawing-downward line of long hair is offset by the model's looking up and away, once more creating the ambiguity that serves so many of Cameron's visual meditations. In contrast, an instance of long streaming hair conjoined with a sidelong, glassy look is particularly intriguing, such as the one we find in her portrait of Eleanor Locker (1867). Locker's youth and innocence are underscored by the frank, full-flowing presentation of her hair, yet the sidelong gaze and frozen eyes suggest another tale. Biographical knowledge in fact informs us that this was the young woman who would soon become bride and widow to Alfred Tennyson's second son, Lionel.[19] Such retrospective awareness, extending beyond the photographer's conscious understanding, allows us to recognize again the foreshadowing vision in Cameron's imagistic meditations. Part of this vision, of course, consists of insight into women and their ambiguous roles in Victorian society. If loose hair can symbolize female sexuality, Cameron shows us how it can be muted, self-contained even in its abundance, curiously both assertive and non-confrontational, a matter of individual choice and transpersonal female identification. Implied, too, is the saving import of Christian iconography, which imbues long hair with the dual potential to dry Christ's feet and to conceal the body's nakedness, once again fueling the rich ambiguity that reasserts the divine–human dichotomy.

TRANSCENDENTAL FEMINISM

Cameron's *oeuvre* inverts the usual aesthetic of photography. Instead of capturing a compelling image already present in the outer world, she used her meditative vision to create or project a meaning, however ambiguously it might be interpreted. Furthermore, she exploded the traditional effect of typology, as it had been previously practiced in Western art largely to concretize or crystallize the (male) self.[20] By contrast, Cameron's repetitive photographic images of, say, her parlor maid posing as the Virgin Mary, or the same women and children configured in a variety of guises, tend to decreate one another, suggesting multiple selves. Her subjects, reconfigured again and again as a given biblical personage or as various fictional or allegorical characters, function more like actresses than the usual photographic models. In a household that included dressing up and staging *tableaux vivants*—striking poses from well-known mythical or theatrical scenes—it was not a far step to photographing any given subject or grouping in multiple roles and guises. Essentially, what we witness is a cumulative effect as of "morphing," wherein what was being photographed is the process of reformulating or redefining the self. And that self is primarily "woman"—in the individual and collective sense. The result, then, is not just a visual meditation on the un-gendered self but a photographic essay about women that details their ability to participate in a full range of roles. As models and the images they reflect, the per-formances of these women testify to their gender's ability to transcend its im-posed limitations.

So Cameron ended up using the photographic medium to record an overall imaginative performance that has practical implications for gender studies. In motion (despite the stillness of her images) throughout the body of Cameron's work are women emerging from darkness into light, moving from absence to dy-namic presence. Initially, famous men constituted the bulk of her semi-formal, personalized portraiture, but increasingly her less formal studies of women, whether for personal or typological purposes, began to consume her canon. Even her last major project, illustrating Tennyson's *Idylls of the King*, depicts women as more active, positive participants in the Arthurian legend than the written text delimits them.[21] In this respect, Cameron participated in the creating of serial selves, of herself and those who posed before her camera. This sense of individ-ual multiplicity speaks to both the changing self and its complexity, allowing her to identify a range of traits in the female characters she depicted from *Idylls*, themselves appearing serially from 1859 to 1885 (six years after her death). Not for her was it so simple as it was for the poet or his Age to blame womankind for the fall of Camelot; instead, Cameron provided her own reading of these women, whose faults and virtues commingle to create an in-depth interpretation of the Arthurian legends she illustrated.

Looked at individually, many of Cameron's illustrations for *Idylls* (taken over a two-year span from 1874 through 1875) strike us as clumsy and even artificial. Their resemblance to the *tableaux vivants* of the period inheres in their awk-ward, static posing of groups of figures, garbed in this case in fancy-dress styles that attempt to imitate those of medieval England. In large part the presumed failure of these illustrations within Cameron's *oeuvre* stems from her laying aside some of her key practices, most notably her severe close-ups and the ambiguity that had allowed her to maintain opposites in abeyance. In this respect, Nina Auerbach is right to see in such frozen scenes a heightened theatricality that re-flects the Victorian fear of change, for the *tableau vivant* required only putting on a costume and assuming a pose, not actively taking on another mindset by role-playing a character through a succession of scenes and actually speaking through another's voice.[22] But despite Cameron's apparent literality—her effort to capture the "truth" of the great poet's art—her preference for multiplicity in experimenting with a variety of postures for each character and reusing the same models in different scenes keeps her subjects alive. For the two volumes of *Idylls* that she eventually illustrated with twelve images apiece, Cameron made well over two hundred wet-collodion glass-plate negatives, thus providing subsequent generations of viewers with opportunities to see each character from many different angles and distances, these various vantage points always producing distinctive interpretations of character. And because Cameron also created more images of women than of men for this endeavor, she ended up reinventing Tennyson's heroines and villainesses alike.

Every time Cameron posed her models anew, she rewrote the specific passages of Tennyson's epic poem that she had sought merely to complement. Inevitably, then, her final choices for the published volumes underscore the potential for multiplicity within the individual self, for in most cases she illustrated a character's story with paired images. The two portraits of Enid are especially telling in this respect. In the first "Enid," the subject is about to accede to Geraint's baffling request that she clothe herself in her "worst and meanest dress / And ride with [him]" ("The Marriage of Geraint," ll.131–32). Standing in front of her cabinet, her head bowed, she recalls "when first he came on her / Drest in that dress, and how he loved her in it" (ll.141–42). Cameron's image conflates time as Enid's present-time meditation leads her back to a moment in her past. But Enid is not just the cowed innocent who dwells nostalgically on the past. The second illustration, "And Enid Sang," also involves a memory, this time Geraint's recollection of hearing her for the first time. Rather than showing him in contemplation, however, Cameron renders the object of his desire, namely Enid herself. This time the photographer is closer to her subject, whose hair is loosened and streaming freely behind her while she lightly holds her musical instrument diagonally across her chest. A stronger, more independent figure before her marriage, the early Enid is recorded in meditation as well, although this time Tennyson has not made us privy to her thoughts. Nonetheless, because Cameron has created her as self-contained, we may equally choose to see her as self-fulfilled. Such a reading would hardly be Geraint's, since he thinks he fulfills her destiny, but if, within the fictional world of the poem, the Enid of the first image should ever recall her premarital self-sufficiency, that memory might well undermine her later role as the devoted wife willing to endure a jealous husband's false suspicions of her infidelity.

Nonetheless, the paired portraits of Enid seem much closer to Cameron's previous body of work, so it is important to my argument to examine one of her multiply-figured pairings as well. Admittedly her two photographs of "Vivien and Merlin" hardly count as group shots, yet just pulling back enough to accommodate two figures already compromised Cameron's usual strategy. While Tennyson's text describes Vivien as avowedly evil, explicitly snake-like in her seduction of Merlin, Cameron's first image of the couple shows them on much more equal terms, Vivien's head only slightly lower than Merlin's as she gazes into his eyes. There is nothing wily about Vivien's posture, for she seems almost daughterly in her gesture of placing her hand on his chest, covered over as it is by the long white hair and beard of an elderly mentor figure. (Cameron's husband made an excellent Merlin.) The seduction complete, the second image reverses the head height of the couple, now standing and shown full-length. Merlin must already be under Vivien's spell, since he appears asleep, his arms hanging heavily against his robed body, which has already begun to recede into the background. Her power over him may coalesce into the frozen gesture of her pointed finger, but her change from sitting to standing seems active in comparison with his, since he barely holds himself upright in his suspended state. Yet we sense no evil here (perhaps partly because Vivien faces away from the onlooker), but rather authority and controlled power, attributes of a young woman taking charge of her own destiny. The pairing suggests stages in the life cycle, from dependency to independence in the case of Vivien, from venerable old age to the peaceful sleep that precedes death for Merlin. Thus what might have been mere theatricality turns into ingenuous performance, itself serving as critique of the patriarchal order endorsed by Tennyson. In the words of Carol Armstrong, we can now discover in the illustrations for *Idylls of the King* Cameron's "reading and seeing of the poem as a woman bringing out the gender instabilities that were already there in its surface."[23]

Although it is the beauty of Cameron's female subjects—in contrast to the character of the male ones—that has frequently been emphasized, these women are not exactly idealized. Instead, Cameron's aesthetic allowed her to explore issues and stages of femininity and femaleness. The aforementioned image "Summer Days" demonstrates this point rather nicely. Here we are confronted with four figures, two adult women and two androgynous children, of varying ages. Despite their frontal stances and the tightness of the circular composition, each of the sitters is granted an individual identity through a distinctive directional gaze. This very act of individualization encourages us to focus on the separate portraits, to speculate on their separate histories within the grouping. At the same time, the arrangement invites us to see the potential for interrelationship, either in terms of a specific familial scenario or a more general meditation on human growth and the nature of the feminine. For example, Nicole Cooley reads "Summer Days" along the following lines: "Rather than portraying woman's face as the object of the (male) gaze, Cameron invokes a secret, private world of women together, involved with one another." Similarly, Therese Mulligan finds in this grouping "self-absorbed females oblivious to their surroundings, the symbolic relationships between details, such as flowers, feminine beauty, and flowing hair, [signaling] intense, yet concealed emotions."[24]

This analysis helps us to understand and complicate Cameron's seemingly obsessive thematic return to the Madonna and child. Even her repeated use of the spectrum from secular to sacred can be viewed in this light, now seen as becoming circular or holistic. Individual secular portraits, set in opposition to the most sacred of the Madonnas, ultimately re-conjoin through the intervening examples and stages of womanhood that they thereby examine and explore. Here I must also stress that it is not a sentimental Victorian interpretation of femininity that is being equated with female experience in these images.[25] In fact, through her use of the little boy, Freddy Gould, and the Keowen sisters in various male-child roles (notably as Jesus and St. John the Baptist), Cameron further underscored her larger, androgynous vision of an ungendered humanity. Nonetheless, that vision lies in an undetermined future, operating in many respects as an ambiguous projection. Cameron remains perfectly capable of speaking out of her immediate, gender-specific present, as we find her doing when she writes to her friend and photographic model, epic poet and playwright Sir Henry Taylor, about the respective resources of the two sexes: she speaks of men as great "thro' genius," while women shine "thro' love. Love— that which women are born for" (1 July 1876, Bodleian Library; qtd. by Weaver, *Whisper of the Muse*, 30). Yet I would still argue that Cameron was not ultimately an essentialist but, in Weaver's terms, a "typological feminist"—an individual woman, grounded in the physical and spiritual experience of her time, whose love commingled with genius to project beyond her constrained present to a latent holism that constitutes her unique vision.[26]

Such transcendent feminism allowed Cameron to employ symbols and clichés which might otherwise suggest a static or stereotypical view of women for a new, more expansive purpose. A case in point is her use of flowers, particularly flowers utilized in conjunction with hair and eyes. With another artist or writer, such usage would merely evoke images of female fecundity, but Cameron opened up her exploratory process to make this connection emblematic of a state of mind as well. For example, her paired portraits of "Untitled (Ophelia)" and "The May Queen" (1875), both employing the same model, Emily Peacock, convey the potential range of female emotional experience from deeply disturbed to serenely calm by playing variations on the flower-hair-eye motif. In the former photograph, the subject is clutching her hair, which is bestrewn with flowers, while in the latter, she lightly suspends a wreath of flowers, her head framed in halo-like fashion by the circular brim of her hat. The parallelism between the two images is striking. Their heads held at precisely the same angle, the two figures look like duplicates of each other, the only slightly more pained expression in the eyes of Ophelia now seeming incipient in those of her "sister."[27] Turning this diptych into a triptych by adding a third image, namely that of "Little Margie" (ca. 1872), we may realize that the expansion can participate in the same ongoing visual meditation. Flowers and hair may both function as frames in the latter image, but such framing also protests too much the conventional image of femininity. Concurrently, the pouting mouth causes us to read into the open eyes more awareness and resistance—perhaps to a vision of the subject's future?—while the excessive use of flowers and hair here underscores the effort required to keep the girl-child in check in her journey to womanhood.

"ANNALS OF MY GLASS HOUSE"

Returning to Cameron's own life journey, I would like now to closely read her autobiographical fragment through some of the same terms and concepts I have been applying to her photographic art. "It may amuse you, Mother, to try to photograph during your solitude at Freshwater" (296). Cameron cites these words of her "cherished departed daughter," which had accompanied the gift of Cameron's first camera, in the autobiographical account she penned in 1874, some ten years after receiving that gift (see Figure 5). Entitled "Annals of My Glass House," the aborted autobiography is shaped by her activities as a photographer, her "glass house" in fact that former chicken coop she had reconstituted as her natural-light studio. But more busy with family and friends and her new art, Cameron never returned to the task of writing her "her-story." Not only did it remain unfinished (Gernsheim called it "a first uncorrected draft written on a sudden impulse" [180]), it is short for an autobiography—a mere 2,700 words. This autobiographical fragment did not reach even limited public access until catalogue publication for Cameron's 1889 posthumous exhibition, organized by her photographer son, and it was not until 1927 that her recounting became broadly available in an issue of *The Photographic Journal*.[28] Reading Cameron's self-record is like encountering a species of meta-photography, wherein the author-photographer details how she sees life as a photograph that consists of other photographs and the relationships they represent. In a sense, this fragmentary history worked so well for her that she hardly needed to complete it in the traditional manner.

Like the body of her photographic work, "Annals of My Glass House" itself consists of a series of dissolutions and recreations of the self. From the outset, Cameron speaks overtly in terms of birth: her camera is like a newborn baby— "from the first moment I handled my lens with a tender ardour, and it has become to me as a living thing, with a voice and memory and creative vigour" (297). Yet at the same time that we see selves being created, we also see them being uncreated. Holding up her first photograph, itself like another newborn, the novice photographer destroys it: "my first picture I effaced to my consternation by rubbing my hand over the filmy side of the glass" (298). Moreover, by creat-

FIGURE 5. Julia Margaret Cameron at the piano, Dimbola, Freshwater Bay, Isle of Wight (ca. 1863–1865). Photograph taken around the time she acquired her first camera; note the photograph's semi-candid, indoor-outdoor status (necessary, of course, to provide sufficient light). Most likely attribution to O. G. Rejlander (1813–1875), although possibly to Lord Somers. 15.5 × 11 cm. From "The Mia Album," courtesy of the Collection of Judith Hochberg and Michael Mattis, Los Alamos, New Mexico.

ing her own darkroom and studio out of her coal house and fowl house, Cameron has destroyed the original design of her home. Even "Annie—My first Success" (1864) seems a simultaneous act of creation and negation, as Cameron runs around the house searching for gifts to give to the model, who suddenly seems more the creator than the photographer herself—"as if [the child] entirely had made the picture." In this narrative, Cameron longs once again to see that model, now eighteen, so that she can engage in creative manipulation of a newly-formed imaginary self—in effect, desiring to recreate Annie with her master hand. Cameron then acknowledges that her first public exhibition in 1864, which marked her creation of a solid public persona, was displayed in a large, empty space. Coupled with an ironic, spiteful notice about her work that she cites from *The Photographic Journal*, the exhibit hall that Cameron describes almost seemed to conspire to negate or decreate her nascent public self.

The account asks us to witness a series of cyclic revisions of Cameron's new public self and the interactions with others that her art has brought to her. Her very language blends, merges, and multiplies the selves that constitute her models, moving between reality and fantasy and back again, mysteriously harmonizing once-separate lives. For instance, Taylor consented to a series of transformations, alternately thereby becoming Friar Laurence, Prospero, and Ahasuerus. Meanwhile, his 1865 Prospero-Miranda imaginary pairing led to a real-life marriage for Mary Ryan, the housemaid-model who played Miranda, for when Henry Cotton saw this image at the Colnaghi Gallery in London, he set off to the Isle of Wight to propose to Ryan. Shortly after Cameron had paired them in a photograph illustrating Robert Browning's narrative poem *Sordello* in 1867, they were married, and in 1902, when her husband was knighted, our Cinderella became Lady Cotton.[29] Before the fairytale ended, their real-life union produced children whom Cameron proudly claimed as "worthy of being photographed" (299). Once again, this time in verbal terms, a back-and-forth interweaving of reality and illusion carries a concomitant creating of new selves.

As "Annals" continues to spin out Cameron's story, it becomes clear that photographs of Mary Hillier retained for the autobiographer a continuous beauty that transcended their multiplicity: "in every manner of form has her face been reproduced, yet never has it been felt that the grace of the fashion of it has perished" (299). The unique and transpersonal are thus juxtaposed as Cameron goes on to explain Hillier's specific contribution to the photographer's communal experience: "The very unusual attributes of her character and complexion of her mind, if I may so call it, deserve mention . . . and are the wonder of those whose life is blended with ours as intimate friends of the house." As Cameron uses Hillier as a model for multiple roles, casting her alternately as Mary Magdalene and the Virgin Mary, the photographer embeds multiple—even potentially conflicting—narratives of class and lifestyle into the overall performance that constitutes Hillier's own life story. Class and race remain problematic issues in this respect, for Cameron obviously felt she could suborn her servants to her purposes, presumably more easily than the friends and visitors she otherwise wheedled and cajoled. And once again abroad, when she and her husband had returned in 1875 to Ceylon (now Sri Lanka) to live out the remainder of their days on one of the family coffee plantations, her portrayal of the native inhabitants lost some of her multiple perspective as she claimed a more anthropological role of record keeping. Nonetheless, singularity and plurality conjoined in the unique arrangements of the Cameron household, itself an environment that stressed the role of the individual even as it celebrated (especially female) community. As for Hillier herself, her story ended happily. After the Camerons left for Ceylon, she married someone who had worked as a gardener for Watts on his "Briary" estate at Freshwater Bay, and among her eight children, there was a daughter named Julia.[30]

With the correspondence she cites in "Annals," Cameron continued to shift and double relationships. At first she annotates an unidentified German correspondent, putting her not only outside him but outside his text. Then she finds herself laughing with him, in effect merging their two selves emotionally and confirming her empathy with others that we have already recognized in her photography.[31] This kind of playful empathy was a trait Cameron had in common with her good friend, Anne Thackeray Ritchie, and "Annie" was in fact the recipient of one of Cameron's first photograph albums, which secured their friendship via a special style of communication consisting of shared images of friends and family members.[32] But Cameron could also turn correspondence to a very different mode of shifting and redoubling. When the autobiographer refuses the offer of a woman who, as a "Carriage person," writes asking to be photographed "with her dress uncrumpled," Cameron negates in a telling manner the woman's projected selfhood as model: "I answered Miss Lydia Louisa Summerhouse Donkins that Mrs. Cameron, not being a professional photographer, regretted she was not able to 'take her likeness,' but that had Mrs. Cameron been able to do so she would have very much preferred having her dress crumpled" (300). Here we can observe the photographer's expressed preference that her hypothetical subject actually be "crumpled," revealing Cameron's brand of realism as a demand that the social selves of her models be decreated.[33]

The final section of Cameron's autobiographical fragment treats three substantial, great men whom she felt privileged to photograph—Carlyle, Herschel, and Tennyson. She speaks of these men as "Great Masters," and her discussions of them are by and large solid constructions of selves, yet she also offers up a small, final negation for each of them. For Thomas Carlyle, she asserts, "When

I have had such men before my camera my whole soul has endeavoured to do its duty towards them in recording faithfully the greatness of the inner as well as the features of the outward man" (300). Ultimately, however, that grand image elides for her into a simple prayer. With respect to Sir John Herschel, Cameron sees herself as responding to a high calling in photographing him: "The high task of giving his portrait to the nation was allotted to me." She elaborates on their long-term friendship, citing with great pride his early praise for her photographs as "perfection" (he singled out "The Mountain Nymph" as "absolutely alive and thrusting out her head from the paper to the air"). But actually photographing Herschel—the artistic consummation of their relationship—had to be postponed until 1867. Even though she is penning her autobiography some seven years after the fact, the act of posing Herschel before her lens is rhetorically put into temporal limbo, as Cameron describes herself waiting "patiently and longingly before the opportunity could offer."

Finally, the refractions in the conclusion to "Annals" multiply as Cameron's portrait of Tennyson's "immortal head" is transfigured by the poet's self-labeling into "The Dirty Monk" (301), which he in turn compares to a portrait of him taken by John Mayall, the leading commercial photographer of celebrities. All this playful diminution leads Cameron to suggest her own comical comparison of "The Dirty Monk" (1865), namely to one of Madame Tussaud's waxworks—that is, something insubstantial and easily melted down. Yet concurrently, in a more serious light, the waxwork simile also conjures up more disturbing images, such as an effigy, a death mask, or even an embalmed corpse. The Poet Laureate Alfred Lord Tennyson actually supplied Cameron with a rather convenient framing of her autobiographical narrative. Not only does the story of her portrait of him open her final paragraph, but it is to one of his poems, "The Gardener's Daughter," that she initially turns in order to apparently guard her own privacy:

> Be wise; not easily forgiven
> Are those, who setting wide the doors that bar
> The secret bridal chamber of the heart[,]
> Let in the day.[34]

But here again Cameron puts the "noble . . . teachings of one whose word has become a text to the nations" (296) to her own purposes. First, she uses this concession to empower the few personal references she does provide. Then, having introduced the language of high poetry into her narrative, she now feels free to pepper her account with poetic samples of her own devising.

Indeed, Cameron's artistic impulses were hardly limited to the visual realm. Early in her private career in India, she had translated and introduced Gottfried August Bürger's long narrative poem, *Leonora*, for an 1847 edition illustrated with steel engravings after Daniel Maclise.[35] Given her own choice of photo-graphic subject matter and her later desire to illustrate Tennyson's *Idylls of the King*, Cameron's earlier decision to translate *Leonora* can be viewed in retrospect as signaling the claims she all along wished to stake. Besides sharing other aspects of the tale of the woman who dies for love with Cameron's subsequent photographic image-making, *Leonora* depicts a woman driven to despair, on the brink of insanity:[36]

> They have passed on, the warrior host;
>   And wild is her despair;
> Upon the earth she madly rolls,
>   And tears her raven hair. (stanza ix)

Conjoining the bridal with the death "bed," Bürger's poem prefigures the verbal reversals of Emily Brontë's famous lovers, Catherine Earnshaw and Heathcliff, as Leonora announces to her mother, "To be with William, that's my heaven; / Without him, that's my hell" (stanza xxii). Cameron was justly proud of her translation as being true to both the letter and spirit of the German poem, which other translators had effectively rewritten to suit their personal purposes. As she pointedly remarks of William Taylor and Walter Scott in her preface, "These distinguished men have infused their own genius into their translations; and Bürger is forgotten." Furthermore, she goes on to argue,

> Masters of their own art, they could not be tied down to copy a portrait which
> another master had painted. They could not strike their lyre to sing without
> variation the song of a brother bard. A humbler disciple of the art can best
> do this; and the present translator, not aspiring to create, has studied only to
> catch the likeness of a beautiful picture, and to copy faithfully each feature and
> expression of the original.[37]

Like Nathaniel Hawthorne's Hilda in *The Marble Faun* (1860), Cameron here sets herself the task of the female copyist, modestly "not profess[ing] to have added anything to the original," yet still claiming the higher honor of "faithfully" capturing that primary image, her very language of self-deprecation heralding the insight that later directed the powerful aesthetic of her photographic eye.

Cameron's deference to male genius thus reflected a multitude of different meanings and operated to many—sometimes paradoxical—ends. She obviously admired, even hero-worshipped these men of genius, who were shining lights in diverse realms of the arts and sciences, their accomplishments made all the more possible because of the women at home who venerated and supported them. And Cameron did photograph more of these men than women in their own right, as themselves, that is, rather than as allegorical or fictional representations. Yet at the same time, by associating herself with great men, by crowning their achievements with her magnificent portraiture, as it were, she also elevated her own standing in the artistic community. It was not long before the charge of genius was being applied to her as well, an appellation that would in time be applied to the likes of Anne Thackeray Ritchie, Annie Besant, and Elizabeth Robins in the tradition I am recounting.[38] Cameron was in fact a key player in shaping the cult of the celebrity. "Perhaps more than anyone else," writes Raymond Blathwayt in an 1895 issue of *The Windsor Magazine*, Cameron "has preserved for us the features of the most celebrated and most interesting personages of the present century."[39] Of course, what this assertion conceals is Cameron's proactive role in selecting her subjects in the first place and then in bodying forth the qualities that she most respected. As a result, she did indeed assume a primary role in determining the high value placed on the painters, philosophers, scientists, statesmen, and literary figures of her own day, and she is largely responsible for the images that shape our view of them today. And for no one did she do this more than for her good friend Tennyson, whose home "Farringford" was an easy walking distance from Cameron's own home, "Dimbola Lodge," at Freshwater Bay on the Isle of Wight.[40]

A sense of dispersed selves, a propensity to self-negation, a tendency to revere great men and displace one's own accounting in favor of detailing their lives—these are all qualities of nineteenth-century women's autobiographies, and Cameron did not exactly provide a dissenting example.[41] In the first place, she did not even write her account until her sixtieth year, when she had been executing photographs for a full decade, and multiple commitments caused her to break off its writing after she had given only a brief sketch or overview. Moreover, she begins in the third person; she not only denies herself a personal voice in her first sentence, but she negates herself in favor of her work, her apparent subject, treating it as a published but checkered study in itself: *"Mrs. Cameron's Photography*, now ten years old, has passed the age of lisping and stammering and may speak for itself"* (296). Even the story of her work is ostensibly a "little history." Yet in equally typical fashion for women's self-voicing, Cameron subtly, perhaps even subversively, starts to build an incremental self-portrait that points up her creative energies. Her first sentence concludes by acknowledging the accomplishment of her body of work that has "travelled over Europe, America, and Australia, and met with a welcome which has given it confidence and power." Countering her own diminutive, she proceeds "to clothe my little history with light," admitting that her work is "indefatigable." And although she states that personal details should be avoided, by announcing that "it is with effort that I restrain the overflow of my heart," she concurrently asserts the strength of the very feelings that inform her powerful personality.

Part of what is at stake here is the question of authority—of who can best tell the subject's tale, of whether or not the autobiographer can establish her own truth claims.[42] Like many other autobiographers, Cameron has had her story contravened by critics, even those who consider themselves to be supporting her cause. Sometimes those critics, like Gernsheim, insisted on a literal reading that denies the creative, playful impulse that inspires storytelling in the first place. Thus, it would seem that Gernsheim felt compelled to correct what he considered outright "mistakes" or "slips of memory" in a series of footnotes appended to his reprinting of "Annals." Every one of these corrections is minor in nature and rather mean-spirited in tone, designed more to undermine Cameron as both amateur and member of the second sex. Sad to say, Cameron hardly fares much better in a more recent feminist assessment. Note the conclusion reached by April Watson, in her essay "A History from the Heart," who contradicts Cameron's dating of the inception of her photographic career accordingly: "We now know [otherwise], from the inscription in the Virginia Somers-Cocks Album that proves Cameron printed photographs prior to [January 1864]. While the *Annals* remains an important revelation of artistic sentiment, it falls short as an objective account."[43] Unfortunately, such a reading still devalues the subjectivity of autobiography, which acknowledges a fictional truth, or metaphor, as carrying as much or greater weight than objective fact. Even Joanne Lukitsh's critique of Watson, which rereads Cameron's stated date as marking her "identity as an artistic photographer," falls back on the same tired reasoning: "Although Cameron's essay has become an important text in twentieth-century art historical discourse, it was unfinished and unpublished in Cameron's lifetime and its status as an accurate narrative is arguably more qualified than Watson's discussion implies" (Lukitsh, "The Thackeray Album," 36).

Of course, Cameron's own double-consciousness, her dual message, contributed to such judgments. She was perfectly capable of writing in "Annals" two adjacent sentences that alternately questioned and asserted her own authority, contributing to the overall curve of the narrative as a movement from negation to creation. In this respect, I must cite again the juxtaposition of her son's observation that her soft focus technique was a "fluke" (298) and her clearly self-conscious admission that "when focussing and coming to something which, to my eye, was very beautiful, I stopped there instead of screwing on the lens to the more definite focus which all other photographers insist upon" (299). On a larger scale, we are thus encouraged to note the contrast between Cameron's early confession, "I began with no knowledge of the art" (298), and the fragment's final, exuberant words, "I felt as if I had wings to fly with" (301). Even the personal details that she only hints at demonstrate her transformative ability, as we observe her converting her domestic world into her workplace, metamorphosing the inhabitants of her glass house from hens and chickens into "poets, prophets, painters, and lovely maidens" (298). Art critic Lindsay Smith has done well to draw to our further attention the etymology of the Latin "focus" as meaning "hearth," for as Cameron "transform[s] everyday contexts into studio spaces," she can be seen to "question accepted hierarchies and begin to erode those fixed structures upon which they were based." For Smith, Cameron's "hearth"—the domestic or private space which by no means operates below the public sphere—functions "as a point of political re-definition," most notably for Cameron herself and then for the other women and children in her extended "household" ("Further Thoughts" 16–18).

Ultimately, then, Cameron's autobiographical fragment shows her at peace with her life and her art. She is comfortable with the criticism that finds her out of synch with the sharp-focused detail that others admire. Against the grain of many of her contemporary critics, Cameron confidently asserts, "I am content to compete"; she "valued" such criticism for its limitations—"at its worth," she wryly observes (298). She quickly learned to separate blanket dismissal from constructive engagement, to realize that it was fellow artists and exhibitions organized abroad that praised her and deserved her support in return. The question of soft focus remained a touchy one, in our day as well as in her own, but now we can recognize focus as a gendered issue with political implications for both changing the public marketplace and redefining the private sector. Integral to the self-conscious choice of focus is focal length. As Smith specifically points out, Cameron "removes the intervening distance between vantage-point and vanishing point," her close-ups filling the frame with faces "situated at the distance of a self-reflection in a looking-glass" ("Further Thoughts" 26–27). These mirror-image-like confrontations, akin to "seeing oneself seeing oneself," confirm Cameron in an art form that on this level is intensely autobiographical, the direct gaze of her subjects showing them as well as the photographer "at home" in the personae that they have elected to play out. The self-referentiality of the photographer's "eye" thus parallels that of the autobiographer's "I" as Cameron's mirroring and doubling weave an illustrated tale of transpersonal femaleness.

Moreover, if Cameron did not always get the public response she needed, she knew she could rely upon "personal sympathy" (298)—personal reactions which were favorable but which she often had to actively solicit. So she sent packets of letters and photographs to friends, mentors, and models, beseeching them to critique and rank their favorite images. Cameron's massive correspondence (she wrote on average some three hundred letters per month) reveals how these solicitations operate both personally and professionally. For instance, her letter of 23 January 1866 to Pre-Raphaelite William Michael Rossetti begins with a desire for "candid" feedback on her portrait of him—"I have never heard even whether you approve of yr picture!"—but quickly moves to a more commercial request—"now

if you would in any current paper notice that my Photographs are all for sale at
Colnaghi's you would I think help me on" (Gernsheim Collection, HRHRC; rpt.
Gernsheim 34–35). Apparently Rossetti acceded to her request, as is evidenced in
his reference to her current exhibit in one of his critiques of art criticism:

> Exceptional in the critical as in the photographic art are those productions
> which—like the surprising and magnificent pictorial photographs of Mrs.
> Cameron to be seen at Colnaghi's—well nigh recreate a subject; place it in
> novel, unanticipable [*sic*] lights; aggrandize the fine, suppress or ignore the
> petty; and transfigure both the subject-matter, and the reproducing process
> itself, into something almost higher than we know them to be. This is the
> greatest style of photography or of criticism; but it undoubtedly partakes of
> the encroaching or absorptive nature, such as modifies if it does not actually
> distort the object represented, and insists upon our thinking as much of the
> operator, and of *how* he has been operating, as of those objects themselves.[44]

In this respect, Cameron's photography once again returns us to the photographer herself, to the "eye" which is also so vehemently an "I."

Another good friend who was responsive to her request for public exposure
was Anne Thackeray Ritchie, who in January 1864 had recently experienced the
death of her beloved father and with her sister Minny found solace at one of
Cameron's Freshwater cottages, named "The Porch," just several doors down
from "Dimbola." Ritchie (still publishing anonymously or as "Miss Thackeray"
at the time) used the occasion to treat Cameron's 1865 commercial showing at
Colnaghi's as if it were a published artifact.[45] Her imaginative "review" of "A
Book of Photographs" opens up for purview the whole subject of the power of
photography before settling on the prime example at hand: "A book, or rather a
portfolio, although it may be here reviewed as a book, has been lately published,
in which as one turns over the pages one cannot but be struck by the indescrib-
able presence of this natural feeling and real sentiment of which we have been
speaking" (226). Ritchie goes on to advance a comparative study of Cameron's
style with that of the popular *carte de visite*—a miniature portrait resembling a
calling card—much to the detriment of the *carte*, with its heavy-handed use of
hackneyed props and stereotypical poses. Continuing her conceit of reviewing
this "unbound book," Ritchie then attempts a more positive comparison, this
time with her own verbal painting of a softly outlined scene, whose very "mystery seems in many cases to add to the wonderful charm" Cameron managed to
evoke (228). Finally, Ritchie reapplies a quotation from William Wordsworth
about the "Soul-soothing Art" of Sir George Beaumont to Cameron herself,
here boldly claiming for her friend the ability to give "To one brief moment
caught from fleeting time / The appropriate calm of blest eternity."

Cameron in her turn continued to evince an empathetic response to Ritchie, as well as to the full panoply of her correspondents over the years. Reading Cameron's letters is akin to experiencing stream of consciousness, for the flow of thought is both rapid and intimate. Weaver speaks of the "individualistic style" he encountered in the recently acquired archive of Cameron documents at the J. Paul Getty Research Institute for the History of Art and the Humanities: "best described as discursive," the style produced is "warm, compassionate, and eager to the point of breathlessness" (*Whisper of the Muse* 61). Even on her long journeys back and forth between England and Ceylon, Cameron maintained her communal ties with the extended community she had cultivated. "Off the Straits of Bab el Maandeb," in the Red Sea, she writes to Ritchie as both friend and co-professional: "I find your name, beloved Annie, like a household word in this ship, each one knowing about you and many a one carrying your book in their hand" (10 November 1875). Almost presciently, she goes on to discuss understanding "how hard that sorrow [of parting] hits"—"So did you, so have you often, for you have always shared my joys and pains and I have always vexed you with all my storms"—for Cameron could not have known about Ritchie's great loss that very month of her only sister, Minny. And after Cameron's death, Ritchie continued to write about this lifelong friend and confidante—her dear "Camme"—not only in her "Reminiscences" for Henry Herschel Hay Cameron's 1893 publication of his mother's photographs in *Alfred, Lord Tennyson, and His Friends* but also in her more personal, female accounting of friendship that conjoined her with both Emily Tennyson and Cameron in the 1916 article for *The Cornhill Magazine* entitled "From Friend to Friend: Mrs. Tennyson and Mrs. Cameron."[46]

Supported by the accolades of such friends as Ritchie and Rossetti, Cameron's own recollection of Herschel's impressive litany of praise for her *ouevre* in "Annals"—"wonderful," "too good," "astonishing," "beautiful," "fine," "admirable" (300)—adds up to a kind of self-induced source of encouragement for her burgeoning career. Furthermore, she was actually emboldened to quote it for posterity. Like the dynamic interaction of broken images created by a cracked mirror, her fragmentary autobiography reflects more from its scattered pieces than a highly polished and edited self-analysis of a solid public self possibly could. Cameron's out-of-focus technique was thus a fitting expression of an autobiographer who valued process over product, who viewed her life and her record of it as in progress. As a primarily female mode of storytelling, the unfocused memoir finally insists upon the autobiographer's creative engagement with all that she encounters. Avrom Fleishman mistakenly assumes that self-referentiality is absent from the subgenre of the memoir,[47] for if we read broadly in the sub-subgenre of the female memoir, we find precisely the opposite holds true. It is in this light that we can fully appreciate Cameron's boundary-crossing. Her networking, especially with some of the great male artists of her day, opened up possibilities for female subjectivities for all time.

TILL WE HAVE FACES

In his introduction to the 1926 Hogarth Press publication of *Victorian Photographs of Famous Men and Fair Women by Julia Margaret Cameron*, the Bloomsbury artist Roger Fry recalls that her career coincided with a period when "England was enjoying a spell of strong individualism" (23), yet from the foregoing discussion we can now more clearly recognize that the strong (male) egos captured by Cameron's photographs are also equivocated, rendered more "plastic" or diffuse—in short, complicated by an ambiguity that ensures both their individuality and connectedness. Fry finds nothing inappropriate, therefore, in comparing her work favorably to that of the great masters, as had her own contemporaries. Moreover, comparing one of Cameron's photographs of Carlyle to the portraits painted by her contemporaries and those executed by photographers of Fry's own day, Fry declares, "Neither Whistler nor Watts come near to this [image] in the breadth of the conception, in the logic of the plastic evocations, and neither approach the poignancy of this revelation of character. . . . The slight movements of the sitter gave a certain breadth and envelopment to the form and prevented those too instantaneous expressions which in modern photography so often have an air of caricature. Both expression and form were slightly generalized; they had not that too acute, too positive quality from which modern photography generally suffers" (26).[48]

Cameron's links to—and distinctions from—Bloomsbury have been variously noted. The key link in this scenario is Virginia Stephen Woolf, who published and co-introduced with Fry (himself the subject of one of Woolf's own biographical studies) the volume on Cameron's "famous men and fair women" cited above. Woolf's mother, Julia Jackson Duckworth Stephen, was Cameron's niece, namesake, and goddaughter, and as a young widow the frequent subject of Cameron's lens, her multiple images refracting the idea of beauty that Cameron so regularly sought (Figure 6). Thus, it was photographs of her mother that Woolf helped to make public when she brought Cameron, who had died three years before she was born, to the attention of a new generation. Intriguing for my purposes is another connection, for it was only after the death of Minny Thackeray Stephen (Figure 7) that Leslie Stephen could marry Julia, thereby fathering Virginia and forging an official link between Anne Thackeray Ritchie (see Figure 10, reproduced in the next chapter) and the Cameron clan.

FIGURE 6. Mrs. Herbert Duckworth—Julia Prinsep Jackson (1846–1895)—
Julia Margaret Cameron's niece, second wife to Leslie Stephen, and mother of Virginia
Stephen Woolf. A frequent subject for Cameron (who recorded this image in 1867,
the year of her niece's marriage to Herbert Duckworth), Julia wrote the *Dictionary of
National Biography* entry on her aunt. 31.7 x 25.8 cm. Courtesy of Helmut Gernsheim
Collection, Harry Ransom Humanities Research Center, The University of Texas at
Austin (964:0037:0101).

The contrasting styles that Cameron used to depict the two women who became Mrs. Leslie Stephen are worth noting at this point. While Minny is presented in three-quarter pose, her head turned away and her eyes cast downward, reflecting her mourning for her recently deceased father, Julia's face and neck here (and in general throughout Cameron's photographs of her) fill the entire frame. Minny Thackeray's image is captured in its singularity and labeled with her full name, even though the viewer could generalize her depiction as befitting other women subdued by grief. This modus appears more as an effort to record a specific period in Minny's life than as an abstract state, however. Given the details of Minny's mourning hat, jewelry, and clothing, which date and define her experience, Cameron's portrait confirms its status as a gift from friend to friend. In contrast, although Cameron labeled this and other images of Julia with either her maiden or first husband's name, the photographer's larger vision seems designed to explore the beauty and strength her subject exudes. This time we do not see the paraphernalia of mourning but are instead forced to concentrate on the head and profiled face of the model. Moreover, we cannot help but focus on the long neck which turns gracefully to one side, its taut tendons concurrently expressing an inner tenacity. Ultimately, the totality of Cameron's images of her niece Julia Prinsep Jackson Duckworth constitute a photographic essay on woman's resources of both strength and beauty.

Interestingly enough, Woolf found the means to tell her great-aunt Julia's story in *Freshwater: A Comedy*, her family theatrical (unpublished in her lifetime) that spoofs Cameron's eccentricities while it celebrates them. In parallel fashion, Woolf also paid mocking tribute to Ritchie, her other aunt (by marriage), by casting her as Mrs. Hilbery in *Night and Day*. A late-twentieth-century text by Lynne Truss picks up on this same spirit by casting Cameron as one of its protagonists. Entitled *Tennyson's Gift*, this novel productively works with Cameron's idiosyncrasies, much to her credit in contrast to the annoyingly repressed mannerisms of Lewis Carroll. Not to be excluded from this Bloomsbury scenario is Cameron's other grand-niece and Virginia's sister, namely the artist Vanessa Stephen Bell, who in fact played the part of Aunt Julia in a performance of *Freshwater* in 1935. Bell shared with her sister a double-edged respect for the Victorian family history, playing out her own versions of dressing up and constructing a sense of what constituted family through maintaining her own photograph album. In fact, the Bell family album bears testimony to the Bloomsbury inheritance of the practice of "dressing up to take pictures" that had been reported earlier by Ritchie and her daughter. Finally, bringing us to the mid–twentieth century, there is Clive Bell, Vanessa's art-critic husband, whom Gernsheim importuned for an introduction to his 1948 biographical study of Cameron.[49]

"Till we have faces": the faces that Cameron has brought into existence for us

FIGURE 7.   Harriet ("Minnie" or "Minny") Thackeray (1840–1875), sister to
Anne Thackeray Ritchie and first wife of Leslie Stephen. Albumen print taken by Julia
Margaret Cameron at Freshwater, the Isle of Wight, in 1865, about a year after the
death of William Makepeace Thackeray, father of Harriet and Anne. 25.6 x 21.6 cm.
Overstone Album, courtesy of The J. Paul Getty Museum, Los Angeles (86.XM.637.1).

all are a blend of the personal and the transpersonal.[50] Invoking in "Annals of My Glass House" the poetic language of Tennyson's "Locksley Hall" that inspired her—"The chord of self with trembling / Passed like music out of sight" (299)—she set her theme; she then sought in the body of her photographic *oeuvre* to record but not fix the passing image that is our individual experience. Reading those images as an extended meditation on the self allows us to explore with her all the intervening relationships—interactions, mergings, inseparability—between the self and the meta-self. This metaphysic already implies an out-of-focus aesthetic, lending itself to an imagistic fusion. Intuitively and deliberately, Cameron is breaking boundaries with her art, whereas her male critics resist such breakdowns, suppressing their recognition of the very personal-transpersonal meditation here discussed. No wonder Lewis Carroll expressed outrage at Cameron's photography, which was so much more honest and profound in scope than his own. His was a profane opposite—objects (not subjects), sexualized to a considerable degree and sentimentalized into other objects, namely Victorian-Imperialist ideals of the female child as other.[51] When George Bernard Shaw objected to Cameron's very different "photographs of children with no clothes on, or else the underclothes by way of propriety, with palpably paper wings, most inartistically grouped and artlessly labeled as angels, saints, or fairies," he really missed the point.[52] From our perspective, such photographs represent not some confounding loss of capability in the artist but rather the use of a willful aesthetic which successfully evokes an imagistic fusion between the individual and the meta-individual.

After Cameron and her husband had been in Ceylon for a year, she penned a two-page manuscript simply titled "Reminiscences."[53] (See Figure 8 for a photograph of Cameron taken just two years earlier.) Steeped in the language of creative negativity, the document speaks of Ceylon as a land of rebirth for anyone who is willing to experience its beauty and fecundity. Springing from negativity—ill health and old age—her account is replete with shifts in magnitude, with Ceylon constituting the focal point which transforms the effects of time. As reality and illusion turn on each other in the transmogrification of her impressions, they are either "confirmed or effaced." Her life itself was framed by the East; England marks a time of "severe bodily fatigue and much mental anguish." Cameron once again values the power of her language to make something real. We normally think of photography as creating microcosms of real things, but if her words here suggest her general outlook, then it is clear that she saw herself as creating something more real than her subject or temporal sitters. As she graduates her "jottings" to a higher level of existence, meta-materializing them into "the dignity of experiences," Cameron reflects, too, the generic language of the female quest. Both the photographer and the reborn questor are

FIGURE 8. Julia Margaret Cameron, Freshwater, the Isle of Wight (1874), wrapped in one of her many Indian shawls. Albumen print taken by her son, H. H. H. Cameron, during the year prior to her departure for Ceylon (Sri Lanka) and processed at his London studio. 25.6 x 21.6 cm. Courtesy of The J. Paul Getty Museum, Los Angeles (86.XM.737.1).

speaking when she acknowledges, "For dead indeed must be the soul who is not satisfied with Nature as here presented to the eye." Ever sensitive to new opportunities to blend the personal and transpersonal, Cameron calls herself not a preacher but a persuader, letting her language speak for itself—"My wonder . . . has been tamed but not my worship." In many respects, we can read "Reminiscences" as completing the unfinished "Annals of My Glass House."

The 1927 issue of *The Photographic Journal* that introduced Cameron's "Annals of My Glass House" to the general public prefaced it with the following retrospective assessment: "She was by nature a rebel. Her practice cut clean across the accepted traditions of the time, and it is small wonder that she received scanty appreciation from [other] photographers and had little following in her day" (296). Yet from her fellow artists she received the very praise that might have limited someone with a more confined vision. "Our English artists tell me that I can go no further in excellence, so I suppose I must suppress my ambition and stop—," she writes to Lord Overstone in 1867, breaking off only to expostulate on her art as "full of mystery and beauty" that compel her onward. She continued to flourish in a society very much of her own making. Writing in *The Dublin Review* in 1912, Wilfrid Ward later acknowledged, "The essential work of gathering together the interesting people who were to form the Tennyson society, the enthusiasm for the hero and for genius in general, was Mrs. Cameron's part, as it was Madame Recamier's." Although she seemed to refrain from linking female achievement with male greatness—resisting, for instance, Tennyson's tendency to speak of Jane Austen and Shakespeare in the same breath—others would accord her an even more telling distinction. Frederick Denison Maurice put it to her in no uncertain terms: "Had we such photographs of Shakespeare and Milton we should know more of their own selves. We should have better commentaries on 'Hamlet' and 'Comus' than any one now possesses, even as you will have secured for us a better commentary on 'Maud' and 'In Memoriam' than all our critics have given us or will give us."[54]

So in a fitting turnabout, Tennyson's brother, the Reverend Charles Tennyson Turner, expressed the gratitude he shared with both her contemporaries and future generations in a poem entitled "In Honour of Julia Margaret Cameron," which opens with the following quatrain:

> The sun obeys thy gestures, and allows
> Thy guiding hand, when'er thou has a mind
> To turn his passive light upon mankind,
> And set his seal and thine on chosen brows.[55]

This yoking together of a mere woman and the forces of nature almost presumes upon her godlike powers, an unlikely identification for a Church of England clergyman to make. Moreover, the sun himself is cast as passive against her strong-minded activity. But such was Cameron's ability to inspire in others a faith in her own extended reach. Her *oeuvre*, particularly her images of women, looks ahead a full century to the work of future women photographers. As curator Anne Noggle observes of the late twentieth century, "[W]omen are photographing women: deliberately and provocatively they are aiming their cameras at women as individuals, rather than as models or symbols. They are zeroing in on the essence. The results are head-on encounters with real people, projecting an identity of self. As a generalization, it is not so much a drastic change in subject matter as it is a more thoughtful and expressive look at the women being photographed."[56] Yet such subject matter, thoughtfulness, and expressivity were long present in the visual meditations of Julia Margaret Cameron, who recognized the individual in the meta-individual by employing her unique aesthetic to explore the essence that only begins to inform the female self.

3. Self-Erasure and Self-Creation in Anne Thackeray Ritchie

"It is true the string does not always unite the pearls; but the pearls are there, in tantalizing abundance—descriptions, sketches of character, wise and profound sayings, beyond the reach of any but a few modern writers, and well able to stand the ordeal of printing together in some book of selections" (281). So writes Virginia Woolf about Anne Thackeray Ritchie's works when she formulates her 1919 *Times Literary Supplement* obituary essay about her "Aunt Anny."[1] In this same piece, Woolf explores Ritchie's fading reputation by postulating a curious reader, who asks, "How is it possible . . . that a writer capable of such wit, such fantasy, marked by such a distinct and delightful personality, is not at least as famous as Mrs. Gaskell, or as popular as Anthony Trollope?" (279). Part of the answer for Woolf lies in the fickle public, which seeks diversion and entertainment in more sensational fare. In addition, argues the young modernist, none of Ritchie's novels has ever seemed sufficiently substantial to warrant the label of "masterpiece." I contend that the chief explanation for Ritchie's low profile in contemporary criticism is reflected in my opening quotation taken from Woolf's obituary notice. Ritchie's "little" writing is hardly something that the general public—then and now—is likely to read with an eye to its cumulative effect. Moreover, since subsequent generations have tended to situate Ritchie as a satellite to her famous father, novelist William Makepeace Thackeray, her works have not usually been read and studied unless they served as sources of information about him. Well-known, even popular in her own day, Ritchie and her writing have become increasingly less accessible to modern-day readers and scholars alike because most of her works are out of print. By acquainting more readers with the range and characteristics of Ritchie's *oeuvre*, I intend to raise awareness of her accomplishments. Interacting with her growing sense of a female literary tradition, Ritchie developed her own strategy to advance what I am calling the female quest.

Born Anne Isabella Thackeray in 1837, the young Anny soon found herself moving back and forth across the English Channel to be raised alternately by her father in London and her paternal grandmother in Paris. This unconventional lifestyle was forced upon the family by her mother's mental illness, stemming from a case of postpartum depression that required the lifelong supervision of a private institution. Both Ritchie and her younger sister "Minny" (Harriet) grew up in relatively cosmopolitan surroundings, with frequent exposure to Thackeray's literary endeavors and friends. These friends included Elizabeth Barrett Browning, Jane Carlyle, and Julia Margaret Cameron, who acted almost like surrogate mothers to the motherless girls. Thackeray singled out his elder daughter as a special confidante, treating her as his amanuensis (Figure 9) and hence primary reader of much of his work. Ritchie's first publications appeared in *The Cornhill Magazine*, which was founded in 1860 under Thackeray's editorship. After his death in 1863, Ritchie renewed her writing career while sharing a household with Minny. Soon after Minny married Leslie Stephen (later editor of *The Cornhill*), "Miss Thackeray" (as she would continue to be known to her reading public) married Richmond Ritchie, her second cousin and an undergraduate student seventeen years her junior. Having written short fiction, novels, and essays before her marriage, Ritchie then began to focus on memoir-writing, still using her personal voice as the unifying center to these apparently dispersed bits and pieces. At her death in 1919, her *oeuvre* consisted of twelve volumes in the John Murray Uniform Edition.

Ritchie's birth and death dates are telling: she was born the year Victoria ascended the throne, and she died the year after the Armistice for the Great War was declared. Framed by Queen Victoria and the moderns, she is herself a major linkage between the two generations, but it was for her father that Ritchie most wished to serve in this capacity. Hampered for years by Thackeray's proscription that she never write his biography, she became increasingly concerned about biographers who attempted to write his life story without correct information or whose portraits of him disagreed with her own. And so Ritchie hit upon an ingenious solution to her double-bind that fit elegantly with her own modus operandi: over a period of two years, she wrote biographical introductions to each of her father's works, which added up to Smith, Elder's thirteen-volume *Biographical Edition of the Works of W. M. Thackeray* (1898–1899). Obviously, the sum of her individual introductions to her father's works can be said to constitute her full-length biography of him. Ten years later, she embarked on a revised and enlarged set of eighteen introductions to coincide with the one-hundredth anniversary of Thackeray's birth, thus creating the twenty-six-volume *Centenary Biographical Edition* (1910–1911). Emboldened by her success, she even considered preparing a single volume that would allow the introductions

FIGURE 9.   Anne ("Annie" or "Anny") Isabella Thackeray (1837–1919), later Lady Ritchie, portrayed as "The Amanuensis," watercolor by William Makepeace Thackeray (ca. 1855). Reproduced in volume 26 of *The Centenary Biographical Edition to the Works of William Makepeace Thackeray*, edited and with an introduction by Ritchie (London: Smith, Elder and Company, 1910–1911). Courtesy of Belinda Norman-Butler, London.

to stand on their own, but unfortunately those negotiations fell through. Once conceived, the two multivolume versions of Thackeray's biography constituted for Ritchie what she repeatedly called her magnum opus, but today we might also read it as her own reflected autobiography.[2]

As Thackeray's writing partner, so to speak, Ritchie has the story of that partnership to tell when she writes his biography. As she narrates his work in progress, she discloses how closely she observed him and what techniques she learned from her primary mentor. Even events that occur before her birth spark recollections of people and places revisited with her father or after his death, and her almost eidetic memory produces portions of conversation or painterly descriptions otherwise lost to posterity. Most amazingly, Ritchie parallels or reflects Thackeray's style or focus for each volume of his works in its particular introduction. This subtle accomplishment is made possible in part because of her intimacy with the man and his work, but it takes a special sensitivity to capture and refine it. She is especially adept at using descriptions of gardens and other images of fecundity to express the complex interactions between her creativity and that of her father. Nonetheless, behind this kind of auto/biographical activity lies Ritchie's ambivalence about divulging any family secrets or revealing too much about the private self, much less for trying to condense a life into a single printed volume. If she never wrote her own autobiography as a separate text (or her father's biography in the same manner), she still created fragmented self-portraits throughout the body of her work—fiction and nonfiction alike. And these multiple portraits, refracted in a mode akin to Cameron's multiple images and serial selves, tell yet again the complex larger tale of women's interwoven relationships—the strategy and the story that constitute the female quest.

As I have been indicating, much of the challenge I face in working with Ritchie's texts is trying to familiarize my present-day audience with her work when most of it is not in print, but in her lifetime she was almost constantly in the public eye. Her first four novels—*The Story of Elizabeth* (1862–1863), *The Village on the Cliff* (1866–1867), *Old Kensington* (1872–1873), and *Miss Angel* (1875)—were serialized in *The Cornhill*, for which she continued to write through its jubilee year (1910). Her only novel to appear in first guise in volume format was *Mrs. Dymond* (1885). But more to my immediate interest is a listing of her various collections, which are based on individual pieces that appeared in a wide range of journals: *Five Old Friends and a Young Prince* (1868), *To Esther and Other Sketches* (1869), *Bluebeard's Keys and Other Stories* (1874), *Toilers and Spinsters and Other Essays* (1874), *Miss Williamson's Divagations* (1881), *A Book of Sibyls: Mrs Barbauld, Miss Edgeworth, Mrs Opie, Miss Austen* (1883), *Blackstick Papers* (1908), *From the Porch* (1913), and *From Friend to Friend*.[3] With respect to *Blackstick Papers*, Ritchie reveals in correspondence with Reginald Smith her own sense of her piecemeal approach: "Is it possible that these pretty pretty creatures are my untidy notes and scraps?"[4] Even her memoirs—*Records of Tennyson, Ruskin and Robert and Elizabeth Browning* (1892) and *Chapters from Some (Unwritten) Memoirs* (1894)—first appeared in series format in the periodical press, accentuating their atomized quality. Only Madame de Sévigné gets book-length treatment; Elizabeth Gaskell, Madame d'Aulnoy, Mary Russell Mitford, Maria Edgeworth—even her father—spark Ritchie's introductory, evocative spirit. Overall, women, women's concerns, and women's modus operandi inform this corpus.

Ritchie's approach to life and art reflects a willingness to actively engage with others, to use her empathetic spirit to explore complexities and differences even if that process threatens to overwhelm her with opposition. In fact, she repeatedly utilizes negative imagery for positive purposes, as if to say that investing in negativity causes it to implode, thereby revealing the creative potential within us all. And so self-erasure through playful self-effacement offers her its own impetus to self-creation as she rewrites fairytales, analyzes individual women writers, writes letters, and pays tribute to old friends. Sometimes the joke is on her subject, but always it is redirected back to herself for further reflection. This pattern helps me to explain why I connect Ritchie's particular brand of creative negativity with the French term for prankishness, *espièglerie*. Working from small units or pieces of "little" writing, Ritchie hardly seems dangerous or likely to undermine the status quo, but this technique can be deceptive. Its subversiveness lies in its ability to transcend boundaries by moving back and forth between separation and unity—slyly including the reader in her critique, or pretending to separate others from ourselves only to disclose an underlying connection. Against her father's life-journey through loneliness, loss, and despair, Ritchie exemplifies the female questor who learns from and overturns adversity. She rewrites Thackeray's cynical humor with her empathetic whimsy, not by denying his outlook but by reframing life from multiple perspectives. Woolf recognizes this practice in her aunt's manner of recording "the great and small figures of her own past": "Here the whimsical and capricious genius has its scope unfettered and exquisitely inspired. We should be inclined to put her at the head of all modern artists in this manner and to claim for her indeed, that she invented an art of her own" ("Lady Ritchie" 282).

This "art of her own" operated across a variety of different genres, allowing Ritchie to blend disparate elements and cross generic boundaries, particularly as they are defined in relation to gender. And like that of Julia Margaret Cameron, Ritchie's strategy may have been more intuitive than conscious, yet both of them learned to develop and refine their technique throughout their careers. In this chapter, I'd like to examine Ritchie's writing in a range of genres and over her lifetime. Although no single mode of writing will be treated to the exclusion of others, and I will not be insisting on a rigid timetable to account for Ritchie's level of expertise, the chapter will proceed as follows. I begin by situating Ritchie's work in relation to the Victorian publishing industry, which both discouraged and encouraged women writers. Looking first at her "little" writing, I review several of her short sketches before examining via *espièglerie* one of her fairytales for adults, namely, "Cinderella." Next I take up her *Book of Sibyls* as an example of a "major" text that has been constructed out of constituent parts, one that particularly illustrates the incremental model of the female quest. Having studied Ritchie through published fiction and nonfiction, I then turn to the private woman, reading through a selection of letters that help tell her life story and redisplay her technique. Finally, I conclude with a brief look at one of her early novels, *Old Kensington*, before encapsulating her strategy by examining her four tributes to Cameron. Woolf must have been thinking about both her great-aunt Julia and Aunt Anny when she remarked of Ritchie, "To embrace oddities and produce a charming, laughing harmony from incongruities was her genius in life and letters" ("Enchanted Organ" 74–75).

EMPATHETIC WHIMSY AND THE VICTORIAN PUBLISHING INDUSTRY

As Terry Eagleton and other Marxist critics have long argued, we can read any text for traces which reveal "how, by whom and for whom it was produced."[5] Examining nineteenth-century British texts for what they can tell us about their modes of production thus opens up for our consideration the multiple means of publication and variety of relationships among authors and publishers that the Victorian publishing industry and its reading public fostered. At the same time, however, we always have the choice of returning to the texts themselves to discover links between formal elements and a particular mode of production—a process which may or may not uncover conscious strategy but which will at least allow us to confront some of the literary consequences of publishing practices. And when we also highlight gender issues, we can reframe strategy as a survival construct that has psychological, sociological, and aesthetic implications, which in their turn encourage us to rethink previous formulations of canonicity as well.

The Victorian publishing industry, which collaborated for most of the century with the censorious control exercised by the circulating libraries, tended to enforce upon women authors a distinct magnitude, form, and subject matter— all of which downplayed substantive human conflict. These slight or limited domestic narratives, which could nonetheless be totted up or combined to constitute apparently large-scale works through serial or multiple-volume publication, discouraged sustained interactive energy. Of course, these observations hold true to a degree for male authors—Victorian publishers did not discriminate when their profit motive was at stake, and small-scale, outright copyright sale items always entailed less commitment and more potential long-term benefit—but men more than women in the Victorian age could treat writing as a full-time occupation, with its opportunity for acquiring skills in contract negotiation and artistic autonomy.[6] George Eliot (Mary Ann Evans) may often be cited as the exception to this last rule, but she proves a much more complex case upon closer examination. As N. N. Feltes points out, even her highly successful career demonstrates "the struggle between her vocation, her will to be a professional, and the dominant, patriarchal structures of professional authorship and publishing."[7] Her case also raises the issue of the literary agent, a role which George Henry Lewes in effect played for her. By century's end, literary agents and royalty contracts had begun to handle copyright and joint-profits abuse, but women were not immediately involved in the various societies for authors that led to these reforms.

In order to work within publishers' impositions and yet deal with serious human concerns, many women authors developed a rhetorical mode or strategy, which I have been characterizing as *espièglerie* (prankishness), and this form in turn constituted a basic building block for the female quest in the nineteenth century. At this point the writing of Ritchie comes to the fore to make my case across the spectrum of her *oeuvre*. Though often long enough to constitute full-scale prose fictions, her novels have been disparaged as either fragmentary or not tightly plotted. In fact, they frequently seem more like a series of vignettes, and, viewed as such, they were apparently quite acceptable when first encountered as separate units in serial installments. Thus, this publication mode and form, while tending to narrow the boundaries of human conflict, encouraged Ritchie and other women writers toward the exploration of *espièglerie*—the very strategy which could ultimately transcend those boundaries. And in the more developed language of creative negativity, that body of rhetorical and performative techniques allows Ritchie and her female cohorts to construct, deconstruct, and reconstruct themselves over and over again.

Women writers and their predominantly female readers apparently liked and fostered these little bits of publishing—which could be subtly powerful, even subversive. At the same time, however, piecemeal publication suited the time frames of both writer and reader, as well as reflecting their non-assertive sense of self-presentation. Ritchie's canon is a potpourri of small forms published through a great variety of publishers and modes of production—magazine articles, serialized novels, introductions to the works of others, short stories, domesticated fairytales, letters to the editor, and digressive essays. Specifically, her publishing history ranges from "Little Scholars," published in May of 1860 in her father's journal, *The Cornhill*, to *From Friend to Friend*, her 1919 posthumous collection of loosely connected essays.[8] In her own day, Ritchie was well-known because her public knew her over time through her various roles, initially as daughter of Thackeray, then as journalist, novelist, editor, introducer, and letter-writer in her own right.

What we can recognize at work in Ritchie's publication history is an example of the mixed messages and combination of advantages and disadvantages which are more likely to accrue to a woman writer than her male counterpart. In effect, her publishers treated her like a member of the family; after all, George Smith had known her since her youth when he visited her father to ask him to serve as the first editor of *The Cornhill*, and she maintained her ties with the firm of Smith, Elder and its next generation through the publication of her biographical introductions to her father's canon in his centennial year. Able to publish what she wanted with a relative degree of freedom, Ritchie was nonetheless limited by the firm's paternalism; like her protegée, Mary Cholmondeley, who was dubbed a "devoted amateur" by Percy Lubbock, Ritchie was often rushed into print, urged to reprint collections without revision, in general not shaped or groomed like the serious artists on the Smith, Elder roster.[9] In many respects, she remained Thackeray's daughter to her publishers. Yet, at the same time, not constrained by the kind of crippling self-criticism that her father often imposed upon himself, Ritchie managed to make her peace with Thackeray's memory by developing her unique mode of introducing him to her own generation.

What, then, is the aesthetic of this kind of writing? It almost pretends not to be real writing, but, for instance, "just" fairytales, themselves "domesticated," or "mere" sketches. In particular, the aesthetic of her domestic fairytale consists of disturbing images placed in minor, non-conflictive modern settings. *Espièglerie*— an often whimsical focal point—thus becomes part of a stratagem for expressing and getting around formal blocks, for making a virtue out of a weakness. In short, *espièglerie* operated as a means for overturning and transmuting the message that Victorian women received from their patriarchal world, namely that their frailty required that they be contained and controlled. As a rhetorical strategy, creative negativity lends itself to collection writing, which can transcend the apparent boundaries of magnitude, form, and subject matter. To review the points laid out in Chapter 1, creative negativity consists of certain recognizable elements: it grows out of a negative emotion; it evokes a focal point, usually a place; it combines reality and illusion; it suggests multifariousness; it includes a sense of time, often a reaching backward or outside of time; and it presents an aesthetic or formal invocation which may highlight or affect the form of the work. In the context of creative negativity, *espièglerie* acts like a template for symbols—in effect, a symbol-structure—which Ritchie and other women writers uncover and elaborate with characteristic qualities of intimate familiarity and generalized sensory detail.

In order to demonstrate how Ritchie develops the features that characterize creative negativity, especially as it is exemplified by *espièglerie*, I'd like to begin by introducing the reader to two of her sketches—one at the beginning, the other at the end of her writing career. In "Little Scholars" (1860), written at Thackeray's behest and "christened" by him, Ritchie describes her visit to several "ragged schools," namely, charitable institutions for the poor, in London. Thackeray submitted to George Smith this article "which moistened my paternal spectacles," and he later identified it with pride when an American reader singled out this anonymous piece for special praise. Writing to Smith in 1900, Ritchie acknowledged that her father had only just released her from an eight-year regimen of reading in order to write this piece, and in 1883 she wrote to Mary Cholmondeley's grandmother about how Thackeray had urged her not to overuse "little" in her first article.[10]

From the outset of "Little Scholars," Ritchie instinctively knows to place herself at the dramatic center of a particularized scene, for the author-narrator finds herself surrounded by a body of curtseying children. Immediately we recognize multifarious image-making, as well as an appeal to time and place, while the "irregular volley of curtseyings" also constitutes a formalized gesture, a prototypical formal invocation.[11] At the same time, however, the strategy summed up by the concept of creative negativity is not fully formed, probably not yet a conscious modality. The negative emotion remains weak, buried toward the end of the sketch—"there is often too great an inequality between those who teach and those who would earn, those who give and those whose harder part it is to receive" (115)—although it does harken back to her opening. And fourteen years later, when she collected "Little Scholars" with other essays under the title *Toilers and Spinsters*, Ritchie added an epigraph from Elizabeth Barrett Browning that manages to foreground the negative emotion while calling attention to formal qualities now more at her command: "Through the cruel social juggle, / Put a thought beneath the rags."

In contrast, one of her last essays, "From Friend to Friend" (1916), which also first appeared in *The Cornhill*, utilizes the full barrage of creative negativity from the outset: "When I read the address on some letters which have been lately shown me by the present Lord Tennyson, one of those wonderful mental cinemas we all carry in our minds flashed me back to the panelled rooms and the dark hall and the oak staircase and the benedictory Bishop."[12] Ritchie's cinematic metaphor moves us back in time, evoking a place and in turn unleashing multifarious imagery, which also serves as a formal invocation to the "child who was, I suppose, once myself" (21). The negative emotion—a child's loneliness—is implied by a succession of images, whose creativity equally suggests their inverse potential. In short, all the basic qualities of creative negativity are embodied in the flashback, which allows Ritchie to cross the boundary lines of fiction and nonfiction. Focusing on the correspondence of Julia Margaret Cameron and Emily Tennyson (the poet's wife), this essay imaginatively recreates women's friendship over time and place. By calling attention to itself as form, creative negativity increasingly formalizes its elements as powerful tools available to the woman writer who wants to transcend the confines of her delimited area.

Turning to Ritchie's short fiction, it is especially instructive to look at one of her retold fairytales through the elements of creative negativity and *espièglerie*. In this respect, I find it puzzling that a radical twentieth-century critic like Jack Zipes, who recognizes the subversive elements within traditional fairytales, reads Ritchie's "Cinderella" as an "example of female deprecation."[13] (See Figure 10 for a photograph of Ritchie close to the time her "Cinderella" was published.) I believe that Zipes errs in failing to perceive how style and mode, as much as characterization and plotline, combine to constitute a critique of society from its periphery. Grouping Ritchie with other female writers like Dinah Mulock Craik, Annie Keary, Harriet Parr, Jean Ingelow, Mrs. Molesworth, Christina Rossetti, Lucy Lane Clifford, Harriet Childe Pemberton, and Edith Nesbit, Zipes observes that they "conceived plots conventionally to reconcile themselves and their readers to the status quo of Victorian society" (*VFT* xxiii). Furthermore, he says, "their imaginative worlds could be called exercises in complicity with the various opponents of fairytales—for there is rarely a hint of social criticism and subversion in their works." But in the case of Ritchie in particular, subversion is a matter of extreme subtlety. Part of the problem may well be that Zipes is examining "Cinderella" out of the context of Ritchie's other fairytales and the rest of her *oeuvre*. She clearly develops a critical stance through the overall use of her character-narrator in the other tales collected along with "Cinderella" in *Five Old Friends and a Young Prince* (1868) and later in *Miss Williamson's Divagations* (1881), but given her current status as a writer largely out of print, Ritchie's subversion inevitably eludes all but the most persistent reader or scholar.

The Cinderella tale-type presents the reader or listener with a plotline and set of archetypal figures that cry out for feminist critique, from within and/or outside the text. Its various incarnations all contain a motherless girl-child who is a subservient worker, a wicked stepmother, cruel stepsisters who evidence sibling rivalry, a fairy godmother, and the saving prince.[14] Cinderella achieves her goal, namely marriage, through virtue, passivity, and obedience. Nonetheless, a re-imaging of the self is still central to that achievement, and, if this stage of de-

FIGURE 10. Anne Isabella Thackeray, taken by Julia Margaret Cameron about 1867, ten years before Anne's marriage to her second cousin, Richmond Ritchie. Reproduced in *Alfred, Lord Tennyson, and His Friends* (London: T. Fisher Unwin, 1893), which also contains Ritchie's "Reminiscences." 31.8 x 23.5 cm. Courtesy of the Gernsheim Collection, Harry Ransom Humanities Research Center, The University of Texas at Austin (964:0037:0109).

velopment remains unconscious or barely takes place, then the narrative mode may yet draw our attention to such inadequacy. In this respect, Ritchie's version of "Cinderella" utilizes serial instances of creative negativity presented through the vantage point of her spinster-narrator, Miss Williamson, who stands both inside and outside the domestic circle, commenting on its boundary line. That position, with all its advantages and disadvantages, is something that Ritchie frequently accentuated, most obviously with her article entitled "Toilers and Spinsters," which later designated an entire essay collection. Besides denoting an unmarried woman, usually one beyond the expected age of marriage, the appellation "spinster" also signifies someone who spins out tales and weaves spells,[15] while the name "Williamson" suggests an amalgam of Thackeray's given name and the son, that is, inheritor of his genius, whom he found and fostered in his daughter Anny.

By employing *espièglerie*, Ritchie saves her narrative from self-effacement because its very mode of whimsical exaggeration points to a (female) center that can always question the reality of the story it tells. For example, by opening "Cinderella" on the note that "[h]appiness is a fact: it does lie within some people's grasp" (32), Miss Williamson does not deny the existence of lives that may not be able to transcend unhappiness.[16] In this context, the narrator tells the tale of Ella Ashford, who lives happily with her widowed father until his second marriage to the conniving Mrs. Garnier and her two spoiled daughters. Shunted to the sidelines, deprived of her little treasures, Ella becomes lonely and despondent because she now feels unloved. Yet Lady Jane Peppercorne, her fairy godmother, easily cheers her up by dressing her in splendid finery and taking her to the ball at Guildhall. There she dances the night away with Charles Richardson, who has seen her before on several occasions but never known her name. Our hero is "a short, ugly little man, very gentleman-like," whom Ella finds "kind," "charming," and just plain "nice" (61). Despite the usual sibling rivalry and the machinations of the new Mrs. Ashford, Ella and her prince are united in marriage by tale's end. Along the way, a glass-studded slipper is nearly lost, and Richardson recovers an expensive yet paste buckle—which is hardly necessary for identifying Ella, since Richardson has the good sense to ask Lady Jane for her address.

At the center of Ritchie's retelling of "Cinderella" is an image of Ella dancing alone in a field. Her solitary dance establishes her form of freedom and provides the young Richardson, hiding in the tall grass, with the basis for what he later thinks is "love at first sight" (61). Yet this image also frames a critique of society's suppression of women: "Boys have a hundred other ways and means of giving bent to their activity and exercising their youthful limbs, and putting out their eager young strength; but girls have no such chances; they are condemned to walk through life for the most part, quietly, soberly, putting a curb on the life and vitality which is in them" (43–44). Against this reality, Miss Williamson can mix the reality and illusion of creative negativity, whose formal invocations to the fairytale mode remark on an inevitability that doesn't carry any guarantees. "What a fairy tale it was!" she exclaims when Ella appears in a "lovely little chariot, galloping down the Brompton Road, with all the little boys cheering and hurrahing" (59), the outcome still an uncertainty. Then, by announcing the ending before it actually occurs—"We all know what is coming, though little Ella had no idea of it" (69)—Miss Williamson allies herself with the reader in recognition of how the fairytale plot is exactly expected in everyday life. Finally, Miss Williamson provides a rather commonplace send-off for her hero and heroine— "Dear little couple; good luck go with them, happiness, content and plenty" (78)—her parting words sounding more like what the average wedding guest might say about any newlyweds leaving on their honeymoon.

A comparison with other Victorian retellings, such as the one by George Cruikshank, "Cinderella and the Glass Slipper," or Louisa May Alcott's "A Modern Cinderella; or, The Little Old Shoe," underscores how much more they serve Victorian values than Ritchie does with her imaginative boundary-crossing.[17] Cruikshank, for example, treats his "Cinderella" primarily as another occasion to preach his message of abstinence from alcohol. As for Alcott, her tale ends with the princely John asking the heroine Nan to be "my 'angel in the house,'" promising her that "you shall never know a weariness or grief I have the power to shield you from" (69). Her exuberant reply—"Oh, John, I never can be sad or tired any more!"—strikes us as highly ironic, given the likelihood that this household angel will undoubtedly tire again under the weight of being a dutiful wife and homemaker, her "weariness" in this case something the new husband will probably still expect of her. A more apt comparison with Ritchie's version of "Cinderella" can be made by looking at Anne Sexton's innovative rendition of the tale.[18] Her poetic variant has its own prologue, which provides us with multifarious examples pointing to "that story" as a type (53–54). Unabashedly, Sexton announces the purpose of the ball: "It was a marriage market" (54). In effect, the story continually validates itself by mixing fantasy with elements of realism. Thus, Sexton's parodic ending, with its implied unhappiness—"never," among other things, "telling the same story twice" (57)—can be read as a linear extension of Ritchie's technique. And given Ritchie's own whimsical treatment of Cinderella's tale, I suspect she would have fully appreciated Sexton's added layer of black humor.

Although Ritchie's "Cinderella" does not present itself as an example of the feminist utopian tale, such retellings do—according to Zipes—"allow for women's voices and needs to be heard" (*VFT* vii). In contrast, the classic tale, coming down to us through the Brothers Grimm and Charles Perrault, seems less gender-specific. In Bruno Bettelheim's terms, "Cinderella" is primarily "about the agonies and hopes which form the essential content of sibling rivalry; and about the degraded heroine winning out over her siblings who abused her" (*Uses of Enchantment* 236). When Erikson introduces his interpretation, the tale becomes even more universal, for he reads the story as essentially about identity formation in the life cycle of humankind. Unfortunately, an otherwise thoroughgoing critic like Marina Warner shows no awareness of Ritchie's role vis-à-vis the history of fairytales in her landmark study *From the Beast to the Blonde: On Fairy Tales and Their Tellers* (1994). Nina Auerbach and U. C. Knoepflmacher, on the other hand, observe in *Forbidden Journeys: Fairy Tales and Fantasies by Victorian Women Writers* (1992) that Ritchie's retellings of "Cinderella" and other tales demonstrate how "childishness is kept at bay by the invitation to re-inspect from an ironic adult perspective the archetypal relevance of tales removed from the confines of the nursery" (13). Furthermore, they argue, Miss Williamson's status as spinster is significant: "Her aged youthfulness makes her perfectly suited as a purveyor of the old but ever-fresh tales she merely needs to replant" (14). In *Ventures into Childhood: Victorians, Fairy Tales, and Femininity* (1998), Knoepflmacher goes on to discuss how such tales replanted from an adult perspective are clearly gendered by Ritchie and other women writers in the period, allowing them not only to express their adult female voices but to highlight the maturation process for their girl-children as well.[19]

Continuing with Zipes's reading of Victorian versions of "Cinderella" and other fairytales, we do well to note that he considers such contributions "part of the general reutilization of the traditional fairy-tale motifs and topoi," and their "formal aesthetic changes"—especially as I see them evidenced by creative negativity—are "connected to an insistence that the substance of life be transformed" (*VFT* xxvi). If romance can indeed be deflated, then the quest for the female self in such tales has already been domesticated and its goal rendered more feasible.[20] For one of many examples of how the female quest can deflate romance elements we have only to look to a work like Charlotte Lennox's *The Female Quixote; or, The Adventures of Arabella* (1752). In this comedic romance that mocks romance, Lennox manages to explode the tenuous relation between illusion and reality, all the while maintaining empathy toward her charming heroine. It is not hard to see that Lennox's text has successors in such Jane Austen novels as *Emma* (1816) and *Northanger Abbey* (1818). Thus, we recognize that the familiar homelike or family sphere—supportive of the Victorian woman's sense of community as well as limiting her options—was capable of witnessing a rebirth. On their own terms, within a liberated confinement, women could begin to postulate mental and physical independence from an externally defined order. This language seems, appropriately enough, to echo that of Jane Eyre—herself another Cinderella figure—when she cries out, "Grant me at least a new servitude!"[21]

At this stage, we can begin to recognize elements of the female quest in this body of Ritchie's "little" writing. Such writing considers the question of what constitutes the full self through its various transformations, particularly through a woman's way of seeing herself. In this manner, "little" writing represents how Victorian women writers can be said to have anticipated modern psychology. After all, we create for our own purposes a coherent whole when, after the fact, we put together the pieces of this kind of writing, even as we know the whole can always be broken down into the fragments from which it has been constructed. This kind of success story is reflected in Ritchie's frequently piecemeal approach, for the Victorian publishing industry inadvertently enabled such accomplishments to take place. Women like Ritchie have often been forced to employ a disguised understanding and expression of self: their ways of knowing themselves have been unconscious—only brought to the surface through multiple increments, emerging from subservience in a forceful voice even years after their regulated lives lived out their course.

"SHE LIES NOT UNREMEMBERED"

Anne Thackeray Ritchie's 1883 evocation of the lives of four eighteenth-century British women of letters, *A Book of Sibyls*, exemplifies the techniques of this uniquely interactive form of writing that I am calling the female quest. To reiterate, the female quest does not usually occur as a chronological story but emerges rather through a complex, multiple vision—interweaving past and present, reality and illusion, in a manner which tends to dissolve both traditional literary form and its modes of characterizing a singular self. It is inherently a subterranean mode, one suited to both the external limitations imposed upon women and the internal shared sensibilities which may ally women across time. Hence, it was doubly appropriate for Ritchie to write her appreciation of fellow women writers in this fashion. *A Book of Sibyls* invokes the lives and accomplishments of four literary foremothers—Anna Letitia Barbauld (1743–1825), Maria Edgeworth (1767–1849), Amelia Opie (1769–1853), and Jane Austen (1775–1817). Ritchie dealt with them individually in four articles published over a twelve-year period before she perceived that the true form of her tribute added up to a single volume.[22] Studying this extended writing process more fully reveals the developmental strategy of *A Book of Sibyls*. In effect, Ritchie's text showcases itself from different angles, different periods of time, as Ritchie cooks it, allows it to blend and mellow, so as to uncover even more connections.

Let me sketch a hypothetical definition of the female quest by once again contrasting it to the elements of the prototypical male quest, which entails movement toward a spatially separated, discrete goal across a vast span of time. Male quests, whether the classic tales of Gilgamesh or Beowulf or dramatizations of athletic competition, can be characterized as dualistic: they portray a single, singular individual, who seeks a distant, isolated goal; linear in time and space, they imply an activity of keeping things separate, especially self from others, emotion from reason, reality from fantasy, past from present; their goal is ultimately perfection, implicitly understood as total separation. In sum, the male quest proceeds by the logical structure of a conscious mind engaging with a clearly perceived "other," as does the Prince in the classic version of "Cinderella."

In contrast to the male quest and in the language of creative negativity, the female quest involves neither distance nor separation in time. More specifically, the female quest embodies the effort to unify (in some sphere) apparently discrete formal units. It occurs more through form than through story; it is not ultimately a chronological experience. If the female quest dons the trappings of a story, it perforce assumes the guise of a quest for sanity—perhaps more precisely, the effort to awake from a nightmare, or more generally to wake up. In addition, the female quest usually possesses a double vision, with two perspectives interacting, as we have seen in the examples of Cameron's transpersonal and serial images. This quest may occur on two levels at once, and it is not usually one individual's quest alone. It thus possesses in its forms the female quality of collaboration and actual intersecting of selves—a community. The female quest is also a struggle to transcend time. It may be instigated by a hint of time—an intuition, detail, or clue which transports one to a different time or communicates from it. Often, too, this quest experiences a pressure of time. Suddenly, the nature of reality seems to have become distorted. Although illusion is central to the female quest, it is never really illusion in the negative sense, but rather the imaginative material for the creation and re-creation of reality itself. The world of the female quest is not so much one of opposites fighting each other as of relative contraries creatively interacting and interweaving. And while the clashing opposites of the male quest create resounding tales, the merging, interactive qualities of the female quest dissolve stories and forms and even characters.

If the traditional male questor marches resolutely through time, tracking down his dragon or grail, what does the female questor—inasmuch as she has a coherent self—seek within her problematic, mixed universe? What, exactly, is the direction of the female quest? Clearly it bears little resemblance to the linear directness and assuredness of the hegemonic male version, which follows a horizontal line. In contrast, the female quest is more akin to a rising up, an enveloping movement—creating a supra-image. This is a quest which crosses boundaries in order to encompass them.

A key passage from *A Book of Sibyls* can demonstrate this activity very effectively. I quote this passage at length to showcase Ritchie's brilliant subtlety as a practitioner of the subliminal methodology I am elucidating. Much more than a mere digression from her study of Austen, it shows Ritchie not split from her subject but absorbing and absorbed by it:

> What a difficult thing it would be to sit down and try to enumerate the different influences by which our lives have been affected—influences of other lives, of art, of nature, of place and circumstance,—of beautiful sights passing before our eyes, or painful ones: seasons following in their course—hills rising on our horizons—scenes of ruin and desolation—crowded thoroughfares— sounds in our ears, jarring or harmonious—the voices of friends, calling, warning, encouraging—of preachers preaching—of people in the street below, complaining, and asking our pity! What long processions of human beings are passing before us! What trains of thought go sweeping through our brains! Man seems a strange and ill-kept record of many and bewildering experiences. Looking at oneself—not as oneself, but as an abstract human being—one is lost in wonder at the vast complexities which have been brought to bear upon it; lost in wonder, and in disappointment perhaps, at the discordant result of so great a harmony. Only we know that the whole diapason is beyond our grasp: one man cannot hear the note of the grasshoppers, another is deaf when the cannon sounds. Waiting among these many echoes and mysteries of every kind, and light and darkness, and life and death, we seize a note or two of the great symphony, and try to sing; and because these notes happen to jar, we think all is discordant hopelessness. Then come pressing onward in the crowd of life, voices with some of the notes that are wanting to our own part—voices tuned to the same key as our own, or to an accordant one; making harmony for us as they pass us by. Perhaps this is in life the happiest of all experience, and to few of us there exists any more complete ideal. (211–13)

The question of influence for women writers has long been a vexed one, largely because it has not always been sufficiently acknowledged. Ritchie was in fact privy to a keen insight on this subject, when she heard George Eliot say in conversation with her and Leslie Stephen that "[w]e ought to respect our influence": "We know by our own experience how very much others affect our lives, and we must remember that we in turn must have the same effect upon others."[23] Now, in her volume of *A Book of Sibyls*, Ritchie seeks to make her own contribution to the history of a female chain of transmission not only by demonstrating it with her four subjects but by overtly addressing the subject of influence as well. She begins the above passage with a series of packed exclamations, impressionistically and synaesthetically rendered so as to give us a sense of the teeming quality of a fully-lived life. Implicitly using herself as a model for others, she generalizes from her own subjective experiences in an empathetic tone that still seems individualized by her style. Then she moves to abstractions about humanity—"[m]an seems a strange and ill-kept record of many and bewildering experiences"—calling upon us to be self-reflexive in the abstract. Invoking the ungendered third person of "one," Ritchie asks that one reflect upon the human potential for creating opposites, for ignoring our gift of being "lost in wonder" because we must also encounter "disappointment perhaps, at the discordant result of so great a harmony." At this point, author and reader seem rendered almost helpless—overwhelmed and unable to comprehend the scattered pieces which should be able to unite us all.

Yet out of decreation and dispersal are born creation and unification. As individuals, we may not grasp the whole, but, amidst the mysteries of life and death, we all share the same longing and frustration to see the total picture. Against the immediate assumption of "discordant hopelessness," Ritchie introduces her conception of "the great symphony" of life. At this point, if we are open to her viewpoint, we can start to find in others harmonics of ourselves that help us achieve our own completion, the result "making harmony for us as [the voices of life] pass us by." Ritchie does not try to sugarcoat the lived life—she knows it includes pain, loss, and destruction—but she gives us a wake-up call when she reminds us that happiness is available in experiences that offer connection with others. Her "seize the day" message carries with it the impetus to continue the activity of re-creating our lives, thereby acknowledging what is for her the most "complete ideal" that we could possibly find. Ritchie carries us through images of unity and separation in order to show how opposites can creatively interact to produce a temporary sense of collaboration and community that can be perpetually re-created. Interweaving personal and generic voices, she demonstrates how the female quest can operate from dual perspectives, distorting reality only to explore its illusions and distinguish among them the ideals that can be realized. Moreover, Ritchie's encompassing sense of time allows her to transcend it, to let time present and time past inform each other, even as she projects her own vision of an interactive future.

If I had to assign a "supraimage" to the passage I have just been examining, I would say it is Ritchie's metaphor of "the great symphony." After going inward to particular-yet-general experiences, "jarring or harmonious," she rises to a level of abstraction that must deflate itself because mankind can only focus on discord. But next comes Ritchie's overarching image of the symphony. She has been listening to its harmonies even if many of her readers could not hear them unless she were to draw their attention to them, as she in fact does by reaching out to the entire human community. In contrast to Ritchie's modus operandi, her father was more inclined to notice splits and divisions—and then to dwell on them. In *Pendennis* (1848–1850), for example, Thackeray's omniscient narrator directly addresses the male reader by saying, "Ah, sir—a distinct universe walks about under your hat and under mine," his reference to "infinite isolations" emphasizing the author's perennial theme of human loneliness. Subsequently, in *The Newcomes* (1853–1855), character-narrator Pen observes, "So every light in every booth yonder has a scheme of its own: every star above shines by itself; and each individual heart of ours goes on brightening with its own hopes, burning with its own desires, and quivering with its own pain."[24] Given this contrast, perhaps we could describe the activity of the female questor as akin to going inward to center in order to discover a self or selves. Yet to employ the verb "discover" falsely implies uncovering a spatially separated other—isolated, in the same sense that anything in space is isolated from anything else. Instead, what Ritchie is repeatedly doing with *A Book of Sibyls* is finding connections and making linkages, so that an individual (female) quest ends up being a shared enterprise with other women readers and writers.

In this context, Ritchie's choice of title is worth remarking. On the eve of her book's publication (1 September 1883), she writes to her publisher, George M. Smith, "Since I saw you, as I was crossing Lynton moor in a storm, with the children tucked up on my knees, and the wind whirling, I thought of Macbeth's Three Witches, and then it suddenly occurred to me [what] my new book ought to be called. . . . It would also give a sort of point to my volume, for the Sibyls were certainly authoresses. . . . To return to my Sibylline metaphor, I am rather in the condition of the Sibyl myself, coming with my small shreds of literature and large demands" (*Letters* 204–5). (See Figure 11 for a photograph of Ritchie from around this time period.) Note the "inspirational" quality to her choice, coupled with a willingness to invoke both divine and demonic female power. "Authoress" and "prophetess" conjoin here, too, as Ritchie permits herself to join the ranks of her subjects in a lineage which could well continue into an indefinite future and which could easily accommodate someone like Annie Besant. And in the immediate past, Ritchie could look for inspiration to sibylline images of the long-gone past created by Cameron, namely "A Dantesque Vision" and "Lady Elcho as a Cumean Sibyl," both taken in 1865 and on view at Colnaghi's later that year when Ritchie wrote her review of the exhibit.

Of course, a text must be linear in some sense, so the female questor has to create a rhythm of coalescence by which the subjective impression of timelessness and unification can be achieved. Structurally, the essay form allows some of this free play, especially as Ritchie redefines it from the progression-by-logic model of the typical male essay.[25] If the female quest proceeds in a manner akin to the rising of a thought from the subconscious to the conscious, no wonder she has to break form and not tell a story in the traditional way. Finding and making connections, Ritchie transforms potential otherness into oneness, opening

FIGURE 11.   Anne Thackeray Ritchie around the time of the publication of
A Book of Sibyls (1883), herself looking very sibylline; photograph by Elliott and Fry,
London. Courtesy of the Fales Library, Elmer Bobst Library, New York University.

everything up into a widening sphere—which she in turn embraces. All her techniques operate to prevent a conscious delineation of the other or to dissolve the cognitive and emotional dualisms she has already perceived. For Barbauld, Edgeworth, and Opie she displays echoes of her own practice, while in Austen she encounters a blueprint for her very activity. Quoting "a little extract" from one of Austen's letters to a niece, Ritchie highlights a shared propensity for apparent digression—in actuality, for exploration on a broader, more intuitive level. "I allow much more latitude than [your Aunt Cassandra] does," Austen admits to her niece, "and think nature and spirit cover many sins of a wandering story" (203). Here we see Ritchie's subject, Austen, engaged in a parallel process of encompassing and grouping, rather than separating and delineating; moreover, so-called sins are covered by "nature and spirit," which themselves seem to dissolve boundaries rather than providing a single cover or masking distinctions.

But how, you may ask, can I present this simple, unpretentious collection about so-called minor authors as an embodiment of a quest? The disarming form is in fact the essence of the female quest. It is more a form than a story, since it seeks to do other things with time and opposition than does the typical male quest. In a sense, it must overcome storytelling and chronology—and this feat is well accomplished through form. Its main goal may in fact be to counter the separations—dualisms, conflicts, death itself—that seem so central to existence. It is, ultimately, an art to achieve unity through separation, to make the reader feel that opposition is not the last word.

As an exemplary demonstration of the female quest at work, *A Book of Sibyls* introduces us to a corporate female self, engaged in a multi-formal quest to make connections, to find her progenitors, and to discover her own uniqueness within their framework. Ritchie went about this process of embodying the quest in a typically—and even necessarily—piecemeal fashion. Writing individual articles or reviews, she came to understand the unifying spirit of apparently discrete documents, giving them new form and substance. Her other works employ a similar modus operandi. As I have indicated, her biographical introductions to her father's works ultimately constitute her implied autobiography—an autobiography that clearly devolves upon a complex of literary and familial interrelationships merging past and present. Moreover, Ritchie can be fruitfully compared with her father on several pertinent counts. With respect to *A Book of Sibyls*, the obvious point of comparison is with Thackeray's *English Humourists of the Eighteenth Century* (1853). Taking up Swift, Congreve, Addison, Steele, Prior, Gay, Pope, Hogarth, Smollett, Fielding, Sterne, and Goldsmith by turn, the father conveys a much more competitive edge than does the daughter. Ultimately, Thackeray dwells more on the lives of his subjects, not their literature, which receives more balanced attention from Ritchie. Ritchie's many other quasi-collections highlight the rich array of imagistic and rhetorical techniques at her disposal as she guides us through the multi-leveled, storyless story comprising this most covert of literary forms.

The female quest is reified in *A Book of Sibyls* as a combined verbal and structural technique, which close readings can reveal. In this text, Ritchie takes us through a dazzling series of crystals of time, or windows, through which intuitions, details, or clues transport us to realms where different times coexist, where dream and reality cooperate, and where the ostensible form of the essay and individual personality are dissolved. Cumulatively, they maintain a multiple perspective connecting Ritchie, her subjects, and her readership. Again and again, these time-crystals (or foci) evoke hints of time, in which one time touches another, or time infolds upon itself. A newspaper in a library is thereby described as "stray sheets of to-day that have fluttered up the hill, bringing news of this bustling now into a past serenity" (4). A hint of time can itself be a work of art, such as a portrait or some written record (letters are ideal for Ritchie's purposes).[26] Time-windows are often embedded, as when the historical narrative of Barbauld's childhood is interrupted—or is it augmented?—by a "pretty little story," the modifier "little" enhancing the feeling that this is a tiny crystal, itself now found or "interleaved" in a book that tells her story on multiple levels, from manifold angles (8).

I'd like now to guide the reader through a quietly breathtaking passage at the start of Ritchie's essay on Barbauld which sweeps us through several layers of time and reality (3–6). Ritchie describes in present tense the Hampstead Library—an ideal storehouse of time-windows—and figuratively presents the conjunction of past and present in the image of newspapers as "stray sheets of to-day that have fluttered up the hill, bringing news of this bustling now into a past serenity." Notice that the people in the past are reading present-day accounts, a reversal of the usual relationship between the past and present. Ritchie launches this section of her text with a shifting series of narrative tenses. We enter the library first through present-tense mode (as in a newspaper story), then briefly hear of Barbauld's life via third-person narrative past (as in a story), next encounter a first-person past-tense narrative (as in a memoir), and then fall into a "waking dream," evoked by the past conditional ("one could picture to oneself"). The permutations continue as the fantasy shifts into a near-conditional state ("I could almost see the lady") and is then solidified in past-tense narrative. At this point the gradations are so subtle that the fantasy eventually shades into reality. Ritchie as narrative voice announces, "I pictured [a dapper figure]," then drops that imaginative frame around the scene ("The lady came forward"), at which point expressing herself like the character-narrator in one of her own novels, "Was she going to speak?" After this multifold onslaught of fantasy, the bubble of illusion is finally burst, yet even here we are not sure of the "reality" which awakens her:

"My young companion laughed and opened an umbrella, or a cock crew, or some door banged, and the fleeting visions of fancy disappeared." Such a reading vividly demonstrates how Ritchie manages to conflate time—the literal and conditional—creating a subjective mental universe in which all things connect.

Along with the windows or crystals of time that cause us to enter into the past and the imaginary, we also encounter exits, frequently abrupt yet themselves subtle recrystallizations or awakenings. An apt example occurs when Ritchie's description of the fictional world that Austen created in *Pride and Prejudice* zooms out to recall Austen's "bright eyes," and we are pulled back "some seventy years ago to an old mahogany desk in a quiet country parlour" (199). Because the female questor is often lonely, working in solitude, the female quest (in dramatic terms) involves its own time travel to compensate for its isolation. This time travel occurs within the context of a specific place, often taking the form or appearance of a dream—or in Ritchie's case, a daydream. Following the embroidered passage describing the Hampstead Library, the permutations of time and reality (past-present-conditional, real-unreal) continue, building through an allusion to ghost stories and leading to another hint of time in the form of letters from a "*confidante* of Mrs. Barbauld's early days, the faithful friend of her latter sorrows" (6). Ritchie may begin an account by launching into a narrative, but she likes to interweave these subtle disruptions of time and reality, frequently by employing the introductory clause, "One can imagine," or even its conditional, "One could imagine." Abruptly throwing herself and the reader into a dreamlike state, she forces us to ask if her tale is accurate, helping us in turn to recognize that it can coexist as both reality and imagination. This ability to juggle the real and the imaginary is something that Ritchie has in common with the character of Mrs. Hilbery in Woolf's *Night and Day* (1919)—"Aunt Anny on a really liberal scale."[27] Mrs. Hilbery is engaged in an endless process of writing the biography of her poet-father: "She drafted passages to suit either [of several competing explanations], and then liked each so well that she could not decide upon the rejection of either" (*Night and Day* 41). This interplay between opposites, a willingness to hold both in abeyance, constitutes Ritchie's double perspective. The lives that Ritchie relates and the activity of presenting them indeed demonstrate the female quest's characteristic double vision.

Ritchie's portraits of Opie, Barbauld, Edgeworth, and Austen reveal her subjects as female questors in their own right and highlight their own crystallizing techniques, giving form to the themes of connectiveness, communication across time, and the cooperative interaction of reality and illusion. Moreover, they conjoin with Ritchie to develop an aesthetic of orderly fecundity, in which control itself seems to elicit powerful reactions—and this can all be seen as a fundamental means of connecting and networking among women, especially across the chasm of time. Although the lineage is not always fully conscious, Ritchie's many writings about women would suggest that she became increasingly aware of its operations. For example, individual essays like "Heroines and Their Grandmothers" (1865) and her full-length study of *Madame de Sévigné* (1881) bring other women writers to the fore. The collection entitled *Blackstick Papers* (1908) alone contains essays devoted to Felicia Hemans, Elizabeth Gaskell, and George Sand, while "A Discourse on Modern Sibyls," her 1913 Presidential Address to the English Association, features George Eliot, Gaskell, Charlotte Brontë, and Margaret Oliphant, while introducing Charlotte Yonge, Mary Elizabeth Braddon, Emily Lawless, Mrs. Humphrey Ward, Rhoda Broughton, Margaret Woods, and Mary Cholmondeley to a contemporary readership.[28] This same concern about filling in the missing pieces of the history of women writers is exactly what Woolf later manifested in her lecture-text *A Room of One's Own* (1929).

Time-windows interact richly in *A Book of Sibyls*, reaching an apotheosis in Ritchie's verbal duets with her subjects, who are performing parallel techniques. For example, the opening section of the Austen essay begins with a window into *Pride and Prejudice*—an extended quotation of dialogue among Bingley, Elizabeth, Darcy, and Mrs. Bennet (197)—followed by Ritchie's rhetorical underscoring of windows as a merging technique. After likening the characters in the novel to "living people out of our own acquaintance transported bodily into a bygone age" (198), she proceeds to use fancies to meld reality and imagination: "Could we but study our own bores as Miss Austen must have studied hers!" Note here the double embedding of conditionals—the "could" we imagine, within which Austen "must have" performed. Ritchie then closes the scene with a drawing back into reality, acknowledging that the whole tapestry of imagination that she evokes "never lived except in the imagination of one lady with bright eyes" (199). Finally, in an especial coup, Ritchie wittily embodies the minor magnitude of Austen's genius by employing characteristic tools of the female quest to reach the incontrovertible conclusion, "Her picnics are models for all future and past picnics" (201). Such scenes—rendered by Austen, evoked and contained by Ritchie—themselves serve as windows, conjoining past and present, real and imagined.

Austen would seem to command Ritchie's particular attention, even though this essay in *A Book of Sibyls* is the shortest by far (it is half the length of those on Barbauld and Opie, which are half again the length of the one on Edgeworth). Austen could already be said to assume preferential status since the volume's preface consists entirely of an anecdote about "five out of six people sitting round a table, nearly a hundred years after her death, who all recognise at once a chance allusion to an obscure character in one of her books" (v). But Ritchie herself was not always compared favorably with Austen. Leslie Stephen, Ritchie's brother-in-law, elsewhere calling her a "genius," once opined accordingly, "[Anny] showed more perception and humour, more delicate and tender and beautiful emotion, than would have made the fortune of a dozen novelists, had she had her faculties more in hand. Had she, for example, had as I often thought, any share of Miss Austen's gift for clearness, proportion and neatness, her books would have been much better and incomparably more successful."[29] Perhaps as a corrective, Woolf cites her father's quibbling words in her own obituary notice of her aunt and follows up with the assessment cited at the head of this chapter. Note, too, that Woolf's epithet of "genius" for Ritchie is the inheritance of three generations of appreciators—Thackeray, Stephen, and now Woolf herself.

As the opening sections about each one of her subjects in *A Book of Sibyls* attest, Ritchie likes to evoke large and complex webs of interrelations among people, real and fictional. This generalization is particularly true of the Edgeworth essay, for which family lineage provides yet another large cast of characters, including the additional implication of connections across space and time. Ritchie is thereby encouraged to look back on her own childhood, where she finds "a delightful host of little playmates" from among Edgeworth's "inheritance" of fictional creativity: "All Mr. Edgeworth's varied teaching and experience, all his daughter's genius of observation, came to interest and delight our play-time; and that of a thousand other little children in different parts of the world" (53–54). Another line of connection to Edgeworth may also not have been fully conscious to Ritchie, but she certainly set us up to uncover it. Besides reading Edgeworth as a child, Ritchie informs us on the first page of *A Book of Sibyls* that she had actually learned to read by reading Barbauld's books. Subsequent scholarship has revealed that Edgeworth, too, first learned to read by reading Barbauld. Although this latter fact is not something that Ritchie necessarily knew, she intuited it, I might argue, by selecting her subjects and setting up the lineage of her sibyls in the first place. Ritchie's six Edgeworth introductions—to *Castle Rackrent* and *The Absentee* (1895), *Ormond, Popular Tales, Helen* (1896), *Belinda*, and *The Parents' Assistant* (1897)—could certainly be read as another literary-biographical essay on Edgeworth. In this case, it's the reader who would have to put together the cumulative picture, since Ritchie never chose to edit the essays together as a continuous text. But such piecemeal writing adds up for Ritchie in terms of giving her the self-confidence to continue challenging herself with additional projects—most obviously the major project of reintroducing her father's canon to her own contemporary audience.

In effect, dissemination of experience is a structural element in the female quest, for loss of emphasis on the individual self opens up the real possibility of an intense communal experience. In fact, the female quest resonates with the invocation to communal experience—a relationship one cannot limit temporally or spatially. Inasmuch as we have come to see the female quest in terms of story, it is the casting of a spell, a spreading enchantment—often featuring the rising of something from one level of existence to a higher one (closer, more vivid, more powerful), and frequently using humor to smooth over the movement (here I can't resist citing again how Austen's picnics become "models for all future and past picnics"). This kind of invocation incites to magnification, an increase in intensity, a widening sphere of dreamlike power. So if opposites are reconciled in the female quest, this technique entails, not so much a simple bringing together or mere melding, as an encompassment. And this process has the advantage of avoiding direct confrontation—which, after all, might break the spell. This magical, enchanted quality of Ritchie's writing recalls her authorship of two collections of modern, "domestic" fairytales—namely *Five Old Friends and a Young Prince* and *Bluebeard's Keys and Other Stories*—which somehow manage to balance reality and fantasy as well.

The female quest brings forth a feeling generally induced by subliminal techniques. It acts to coalesce time (past and present, present and future) and space (conditional and indicative, physical and mental), ultimately existing as a timeless expanse in which all boundaries have been transcended. (In this case, I have deliberately chosen "coalesce" over "deconstruct," because the former implies a blending or merging rather than fractioning; another verb utilizing the prefix "trans" might also be appropriate.) This sense of timeless unification is the goal of the female quest—something ever-present and within, as opposed to a singular, distant object to be attained by arduous progression through time and space. In *A Book of Sibyls* we can recognize that Ritchie has chosen empathetic authors with whom she can in turn be empathetic. (In fact, I would argue, she would probably find grounds for empathy with any woman writer.) In the very selection of each subject, we witness the structuring of the study, as she casts her spell, finding connections as well with herself and her own works. Here I might note the parallel between Ritchie's citation of Opie's "pretty reminiscence of her childhood from a beginning of the memoir which was never written" (155) and her own later collection of semi-autobiographical essays, *Chapters from Some (Unwritten) Memoirs* (1894). It's remarkable how this almost magical endeavor grows out of technical activities. Art, literature, music are all invoked, "absorb[ed] . . . into the mind of the writer," Ritchie reports, in the context of explaining how in reading Opie she realizes "some kind of metempsychosis takes place" (151). Moreover, Ritchie creates a sense of endlessness by employing a series of such microstories. Through subtle gradations of style, we soon find we're in yet another story, or looking at the first one from a different temporal perspective, or starting to flow into still one more story. Without telling any single story, Ritchie creates the sense of a vast cosmic tale.

In general, Ritchie reserves biographical facts and dates for the second movement of each essay in *A Book of Sibyls*, when genealogy and a sense of family history are clearly established. At the same time, however, she also employs lengthy quotations from the authors themselves or their memoirists in order to give the tone and style of the times. And imaginary extrapolations continue to occur, as Ritchie repeatedly paints vivid scenes of "what might have been"—a theme so germane to her father's works, yet for the daughter and her subjects not entailing such a note of regret for the unlived or unfulfilled life. By using degrees of conditionality, wherein everything becomes more and more hypothetical, Ritchie develops the theme of incompleteness or fragmentation in these lives and works, suggesting a whole which is always imminent but never fully created. Yet in the end, some form of encapsulation becomes crucial to the female quest. Each concluding section draws heavily on the present tense and tries to recreate the given author's last days and characteristic emblem—Ritchie's mode of summing up or encapsulation. Even if this type of quest-story never ends, it has its epiphanies— its own time crystals. In this respect, I think we can observe that Virginia Woolf may well have been introduced to the tradition of subjective biographical-literary criticism by her aunt Anny. Furthermore, Woolf's review-essays on the Edgeworths, Austen, the Brontës, George Eliot, Mary Russell Mitford, Mary Wollstonecraft, and Elizabeth Barrett Browning—published in *The Common Reader* (1928) and *The Second Common Reader* (1932)—show her sharing many of the same subjects with her aunt.

Examined holistically, the female quest is chiefly governed by the two principles of separateness and unity. As Ritchie embarks on the concluding section of each of the mini-biographies in *A Book of Sibyls*, separateness is acknowledged by an evocation of the perennial process of creation, while unity is expressed by a mood of calmness—separate universes becoming one in their mutual stillness. Ritchie plays up the absence of fear in all of these passings. For each of the writers, she illustrates a lack of resistance to her own death—a one-pointed simplicity of mind, without messiness or unraveling. The image of Opie's approaching death, as she lies among the prismatic colors she loved, makes a case in point. Ritchie begins by quoting Opie—"My prisms to-day are quite in their glory. . . . [T]he atmosphere must be very clear, for the radiance is brighter than ever I saw it before"—and then enters the dying woman's thoughts, as she "wonders whether the mansions in heaven will be draped in such brightness; and so to the last, the gentle, bright, *rainbow* lady remained surrounded by kind and smiling faces, by pictures, by flowers, and with the light of her favourite prismatic colors shining round about the couch on which she lay" (196). This peace can come about through the completion of a long and rich life, but it can also occur after a painful illness, as is the case with Austen, whose simple desire for death at the very end conveys her emotional exhaustion. Ritchie tries to make this last, most "unsatisfactory" of deaths seem like a purgation; it is to Austen that she makes her final tribute, and these last words of her essay conclude the entire collection: "she lies not unremembered" (229).

"ONLY CONNECT"

In *Madame de Sévigné* (1881), her book-length study of the famous seventeenth-century letter-writer, Ritchie describes a certain process of alternating self-creation and destruction:

> There is something almost of a great composer's art in the endless variations and modulations of this lady's fancy. She laments, she rejoices, she alters her note, her key; she modulates from tears to laughter, from laughter to wit. She looks round for sympathy, tells the stories of the people all about her, repeats their words, describes their hopes, their preoccupations. Then she remembers her own once more, and repeats again and again, in new words from fresh aspects, the fancies and feelings which fill her heart.[30]

Here we witness a rhetoric of fecundity informing Ritchie's description, characterized by a continuous teeming of multiple qualities, fertile duplication, a creative movement among spheres of discourse, and above all the assertion of a magical and cyclic nature to existence. In her private correspondence, Ritchie herself engages in the sort of activity she so exuberantly evokes in the above passage: she rhetorically creates and destroys various images of herself and others in a process of alternate construction and deconstruction, enabling her to establish and explore the multiple relationships that women especially try to foster. Having looked at several of Ritchie's short sketches and one of her fairytales, as well as a collection of her essays, in terms of her rhetorical strategy, I'd now like to turn to the personal recording of selves that a selection of her correspondence provides.

For example, in a letter written to her cousin Emmy Irvine in 1859, the twenty-two-year-old Anne Isabella Thackeray begins in a large and imposing manner, employing an inflationary rhetoric of the self: "[My sister] Minny says that if the Angel Gabriel came to fetch me I should say, 'Just a minute till I have finished this note . . .'" (*Letters* 119). Having thus presented herself as a distinctly formidable figure, capable of making even an Archangel wait, young Miss Thackeray turns the tables on this image of herself, and ends the sentence accordingly: ". . . and in the meantime with all this scribbling I have kept you waiting ever so many days." Thus, the letter's first sentence and paragraph conclude in a deflationary gesture that is at once trivializing and uniquely personal.

As a budding author, this letter-writer often uses the very rhetorical and imagistic tools by which one might inflate an image of self only to deflate it. In the domain of her letters, she alternately builds up and tears down herself, other people, situations, the world itself. She presents a series of such examples virtually by the paragraph: a military relation's bravery is in effect reduced to "whatnot"; the presumably great artist "Sir Edwin Landseer" becomes little more than his gift of "a little dog picture"; a dinner guest, one Dr. Sandwith, is "covered with Victoria Crosses"—that is, almost obliterated by the very symbols of his valor. Even "the grandest dinner I ever went to" ends up not "near as alarming as I expected," for Anny and her father are wrongly announced—albeit by "an imposing voice at the door"—as "Mr. and Mrs. Tackey" (120)! Often accomplishing her act of inversion by a single word, Miss Thackeray employs the conditional and subjunctive modes, as well as simple negations, frequently setting one figure off against another for a final deconstructing contrast.

Midway through her life, in 1877, at the age of forty, Anne Thackeray celebrated her engagement to Richmond Ritchie. A letter from this period, addressed to well-wisher Andrew Hichens, already exhibits a much more flexible range of rhetorical and linguistic tools by which she can accomplish her inflationary-deflationary cycle. Anny begins with an exuberant paragraph, creating the image of a happy self whose happiness can inform that of others: "It is very nice to get a friend's good will and wish and may yours bring us in as good fortune as ours brought to you. How happy your marriage did make my sister and me!" (192). But the next paragraph creates a negation or deflation by calling up a conditional voice: "If it were not Richmond, I should be afraid to take such a life's gift. . . ." Then, the bride-to-be (she outlived her mate by seven years) creates a brilliant image of her future husband—"he knows his own mind so clearly"—and offsets this "blessing of affection" with her own "darkness." In this case, we uncover the letter-writer employing one strong projection of a self to undo another. Finally, that image of the "happy" pair is both undercut and reaffirmed by the interplay of qualifications and double negatives: "and now at last I feel as if it were ungrateful indeed if we did not take the happiness which has come like a sort of miracle."[31]

The older Anne Thackeray Ritchie can often achieve her inflationary and deflationary effects simultaneously. At the turn of the century, now over sixty, she writes from Brighton to her workaday husband at the India Office (10 January [1899]). Beginning on a note she calls "most agreeable," she ever-so-gently modifies the tone a bit in the subsequent two paragraphs by announcing and narrating "two rather amusing things" (267). Besides operating through expansion and contraction, Ritchie likes to work through anecdote. She uses the language of others in quotation to deflate: Beethoven never knew when to "leave off"; the "life is scarcely bearable" is softly mocked by the "making life worth having"; the

"O" in Romeo "should come from your bowels" (268). Qualifications can slip in unobtrusively—"I love some of his books," she quietly observes about William Black. Or they can be developed through elaborate anecdote—as is the case of her story about Kipling. Stranded in midstream in America, Kipling anticipates that his own name will appear on the lips of a curious stranger who has been informed that the visitor is the "only one man in England who can write." Ritchie then relates how Kipling's self-ascription is soundly undercut by the man's response by way of the monosyllabic *"Black."* By contrast, inflation shows up her own exuberant embrace of life—"O how nice it is to be going to do just as I like all this evening!"—her image-making revealing the artist she is at heart: "The sky was like a divine Parrot's breast just now with a deep deep flapping sort of sea."[32]

Ultimately, Ritchie employs the battery of techniques she has spent a lifetime developing in order to express another vision of life—the inexpressible horror and heroism of life during the Great War. Writing to American poet and editor Robert Underwood Johnson (27 January [1916]; HRHRC), she negates her selves—the personae of her entire previous existence—in the service of an unfolding vision of the world:

> How many years have passed since we met, when life was not as it is now. But we feel the same as we did then, only we know alas more than we then could imagine possible to believe. I write of this terror, but a vision of noble goodness & courage comes before me also. Your beautiful lines speak of it—"The weak is stronger than the strong" in truth;—now at the end of a full life, this awful realization rises before me and one can but accept the fact that life *is* a more terrible & noble thing, than one knew before.

This letter shows Ritchie, in her seventy-seventh year, still growing and changing. The process of self-creation and self-destruction remains active in her—not slowed down and congealed, as it often is with older people. Moreover, Ritchie does turn this letter to a substantially positive purpose as she goes on to request aid for a group of nuns outside Rheims who have been caring for wounded soldiers. Subsequent correspondence with Johnson and his wife illustrate how Ritchie continues to relate the saga of the nuns' contributions to the war effort. In even more tangible terms, Ritchie and her longtime friend Kate Dickens Perugini later that same year (22 November 1916) organized a sale of their fathers' rare books and manuscripts to assist the Belgravia War Supply Depot.

Ritchie lives emphatically in the present, while characteristically using affirmations and negations to express it: "In all my life there never was war until now," she writes to Marie Belloc Lowndes after reading the letters and journals of her own nephew, who had just been killed near Ypres (4 December [1914]; HRHRC). Against her relatively positive past, softened by the passage of time,

Ritchie juxtaposes the violent reality of a war brought suddenly home by the death of a young member of her family. Two years further into the war, she writes again to Lowndes: the people of the past "seem to me almost *asleep* compared to the men & women lying awake at night & anxious now" (8 or 9 [? 1916]). Invoking a dual perspective on the past and the present, Ritchie's comparison mixes and merges negation with affirmation. The past—the now-dead generation that preceded her own—has always held a special place for her. Now, however, Ritchie's affection cannot conceal her distance from her predecessors, whose innocence, she implies, was perhaps the kind of naivete that contributed to the war in the first place. Lying in bed awake and anxious may not constitute a desirable state, yet it does reflect an awareness that suggests responsibility, possibly even heroism. Ritchie's choice of correspondent for expressing these reflections is telling, for she knows that her recipient understands and shares her outlook. Ritchie's friendship with Lowndes, sister to Hilaire Belloc, spans several generations, going back to their childhood when Mme. Belloc held forth to Ritchie about Elizabeth Barrett Browning, and Lowndes could evoke her shared past with Ritchie simply by mentioning Thackeray's name. With this history between them, the two correspondents together face the barbarism of a new century's warfare.

From the other side of Ritchie's correspondence, Henry James provides a useful point of comparison, for he, too, expresses himself in terms of self-negation and self-creation. Writing of the death of one of their friends, Hamilton Aidé, James declares, "But I shall miss him, oddly (*we* shall miss him) beyond the use, as it were, that we had for him; he *was* such a pleasant part of our past going on into one's present and vouching still for the reality of vanished things" (21 December 1906). However, in typical Jamesian fashion, he turns the focus of his correspondence back to himself, for this same letter reveals him accepting Ritchie's sympathy for *his* loss of Leslie Stephen, surely a death that has hit close to home for her. James's letters to Ritchie and his other correspondents reflect an exuberance that he shares with Ritchie, but reading over a collection of his letters suggests that he is inclined toward self-indulgence with his enthusiasm, for working himself up rhetorically almost seems like a substitute for real-life engagement. Still, it is apparent that he and Ritchie express a genuine rapport and share a similar response to the changing world order: "How beautiful and brave of you to have been so moved to write to me—though not more moved than I have been by the generous act itself. You are the kindest of old friends and the vividest of old correspondents, and the much-to-be trusted fellow-partaker of all the pangs and prides of this terrible time" (30 May 1915). Their friendship dates back over thirty years, and James was yet one more appreciator to acknowledge Ritchie's genius, albeit anonymously. In his essay "On the Art of Fiction" (1884), James refers to a friend, "a woman of genius," whose invocation of a childhood memory infused one of the key scenes of her first novel (namely *The Story of Elizabeth*) with "experience." In turn, this recollection prompts James to make his often-cited pronouncement to beginning writers, "Try to be one of the people on whom nothing is lost!"[33]

Reading through a large body of Ritchie's letters, published and unpublished, we experience a very complex set of linguistic interactions. It is almost as if we are witnessing a series of flash-images of selves, which may in part be created by her responses to another such series, from the other side of her correspondence. As we wonder or speculate about the other half of a letter exchange, we recognize the essential quality of *relationship* that letter-writing points up. Ritchie assumed myriad roles in her lifetime, many of them contemporaneous, some of them contradictory. The common element in this role-playing and her letter-writing in general is a woman's desire to mediate larger considerations, to cross boundaries of time and space, while at the same time to make the smaller connections—in letters of invitation and acceptance, news and gossip, condolence and congratulations—in short, to weave together the minutiae that constitute the basic social fabric. In this respect, I find it only too appropriate to invoke again the subheading of this section and the epigraph to E. M. Forster's *Howard's End* (1921): "Only connect." Women have always responded to the multiple demands placed upon them with a multiplicity of selves, and like Ritchie many of them have discovered that they can vastly increase their connections with people by defining themselves—alternately creating and re-creating themselves—in relation to others.

The destruction, or at least the incompleteness, of the self is of course inherent in any discussion of the self as manifest in letters. After all, we virtually never have a totally full set of anyone's letters—there are always ones missing, if only the drafts that were destroyed before final copies were sent. The natural, or accidental, gaps and presences are thus significant to acknowledge when we try to talk about a life as constituted by a subject's letters. Moreover, there is also the crucial question of conscious (and not-so-conscious) editing, by the self and others. In Ritchie's case, it is instructive to trace the publication of her letters as edited by her daughter, Hester Thackeray Ritchie Fuller. Fuller's initial purpose in 1924 (she was as yet unmarried) was to select a body of letters that would convey the fullness of her mother's personality—but primarily in relation to well-known literati. Twenty-seven years later Fuller tried to reconstitute the more intimate side of her mother's life, this time by weaving together some of the more personal correspondence in memoirlike form. Yet in both instances, the figure of the father (and grandfather) looms large as a defining or limiting presence—the two volumes were published under the titles *Thackeray and His Daughter* and *Thackeray's Daughter*.

An anonymous reviewer for the *Times* comments on the latter publication by saying, "Anny Thackeray's gay, haphazard personality, which would have been buried for ever under the incongruous weight of a formal biography, emerges clear and sparkling from these seemingly casual pages."[34] Ignoring for the moment the reviewer's slight acknowledgment of the shaping role of layers of selectivity, we can nonetheless recognize his subscription to the belief that biography is often thought to be best served by autobiography—by apparently allowing the subject to speak for himself or herself. This is indeed very much the case with Winifred Gérin's full-length biography of Ritchie (1981), which has paradoxically been faulted for being too uncritical, for in fact relying too heavily on quotations from Ritchie's own writing.[35] But more to my own purpose, here and elsewhere, has been the task of isolating various discrete bodies of Ritchie's correspondence to tell different stories and understand her complex interrelationships. Examining her epistolary self-presentation and negation in her dealings with her publishers is especially interesting. These letters reveal both her assertion of her own creative work in novels, short stories, essays, and memoirs, and her creative engagement with her father's *oeuvre* in a variety of different articles and her biographical introductions to Thackeray's canon.

It is through these manifold groupings that I came to see how this daughter of genius adhered to a Victorian father's proscription against writing his biography while drawing on a woman's special genius to create both his piecemeal biography and her reflected autobiography. Perhaps private letters in general could inherently be said to set up a rapid series of rhetorical images of oneself and others and then destroy them. This instinctive purpose of letters would appear to contradict the traditional purpose of biography, which is ostensibly to construct a single, if complex, and coherent definition of self. But if letters can thus be fundamentally deconstructive, especially of the self, then we can also observe how Ritchie's biographical introductions, for which she uses her own and her father's letters, serve as a subversive—because at first view hidden—form of self-creation. We might therefore come to hope that future critical biographers would engage in a special format for editing letters—not just the one which inevitably constructs the form of the traditional biography, but one which also highlights the process of self-erasure.

"WE THINK BACK THROUGH OUR MOTHERS
IF WE ARE WOMEN"

Looking back through Ritchie's canon to her third full-length fiction, *Old Kensington*, set in the time and place of her own childhood, we can now more fully recognize her early exploration and even experimentation with negation and erasure. In this novel, she employs the image of a microcosm in order to create minor yet disturbing domestic tragedies, which feature an ironic inversion of growth and fulfillment. Taking a 180-degree turn from the muted mode of her domestic fairytales, Ritchie informs this troubled world with events that fail to occur, thereby creating a haunting psychological universe of isolation and disconnection:

> People think that what is destroyed is over, forgetting that what has been is never over, and that it is in vain you burn and scatter the cinders of many a past hope and failure, and of a debt to pay, a promise broken. Debts, promises, failures are there still. There were the poems George had tried to write, the account-books he had not filled up, the lists of books he had not read, a dozen mementoes of good intentions broken. (*Old Kensington* 21.180)[36]

Ritchie's is a disturbing vision—constituting almost an anti-universe—of an untouchable yet inescapable world of failed communication, a seemingly impossible quest. At the end of this passage, however, there remains a "not yet" quality—a negation that nonetheless contains something. Ritchie evokes this undefined element as if it were a memory trace—a tracking of aspiration, even if it is not fulfilled.

In tandem with the thought processes of her protagonist Dolly Vanborough, Ritchie utilizes free indirect discourse to express how unfulfillment and sadness can create the emotional effect of an almost ghostly universe: "She had taken up some work, but as she set the stitches, it seemed to her,—it was but a fancy—that with each stitch George was going farther and farther away . . ." (33.294). Dolly's "work"—her stitching—is overtly connected with the haunting microcosm of isolation with which Ritchie's characters have come to some kind of accord. At the conclusion of the novel, Dolly finds a packet of letters, which embodies this microcosm (56.530). The packet is burned in the fireplace, and Frank kisses her hand as the story ends—but the gesture amounts to a weak, rather subjunctive image of connection. The narrator then undercuts any possibility of even initiating a quest by calling forth the fire in the following image: "Here, within, the fire leaps brightly in its iron cage" (56.531). The boundaries between painfully separated universes are here affirmed rather than dissolved as the novel concludes with a final, ironic meta-materialization in which "the sunlight . . . extinguished the flame." If the sun constitutes the meta-universe, then the flame is now the microcosm, destroyed by—rather than united with—the higher reality.

Against the sense of loss and failed communication interrogated in *Old Kensington*, Ritchie celebrates connection—particularly through a female lineage—valuing it all the more because she never denies the negations that permeate our life experience. In typically fragmentary fashion, Ritchie writes about her friend and mentor Julia Margaret Cameron on four separate occasions, treating her story as the epitome of a personal female quest-story. At the same time, Cameron inspires her kindred spirit Ritchie to great heights, as herself another exemplar of the archetypal female questor. Starting in 1865 with "A Book of Photographs," as we have seen, Ritchie anonymously reviews an exhibition of Cameron's photographs as if it were a published volume. By depicting photographic portraits as, in effect, microcosms of personality, the unnamed author explains how they can tell more about a character or a person "in one minute than whole pages of elaborate description" ("A Book of Photographs" 224). Yet she also acknowledges the feeling of mystery that Cameron evokes through her signature soft focus (227–28). Essentially, Ritchie here engages in her own form of verbal painting, especially when she describes the scene she sees through a window while she is actually writing the review:

> As we are writing, at this moment, we look through a window into a garden, and across a sloping country, where the bare trees have not yet put on their leaves, and stand out in soft and delicate lines against a gentle spring mist, through which the birds are singing. A thatched cottage roof, the hedges, the distant clump of trees, are all painted with the soft mysterious grey. (228)

Author and subject thereby coalesce in the dramatic timeless present as Ritchie remarks on the similarity of recording this scene with Cameron's own art, the process itself a technique of concurrent self-erasure and self-creation.

With the passage of three more years, Ritchie embarked on her serialized novella, *From an Island* (1868–1869). Set on the Isle of Wight, home to Cameron and refuge to Ritchie, this diffuse tale presents no single protagonist, content to tell its story through fragments, letters, and multiple viewpoints. Yet in the relationship of the narrator to Mrs. St. Julian, clearly modeled after Cameron, we can recognize some of the intensity of the life Ritchie shared with her friend and mentor. And the diffusion is itself telling about Cameron. In many respects, she is so much larger than life that she must be refracted among three characters—Mrs. St. Julian, her artist husband, and the photographer Hexam. For the Smith, Elder reprinting of *From an Island* (1877), Ritchie in fact provided a dedication to Cameron, who in her turn had previously dedicated her illustrated edition of Tennyson's *Idylls of the King* (1874) to Ritchie. In addition, comparisons abound between *From an Island* and Woolf's *To the Lighthouse* (1927), which was undoubtedly influenced by Ritchie's work. Ritchie's St. Julian is an amalgam, with traces of both Tennyson and Browning, while Hexam bears a slight resemblance to Charles Dodgson. Once again we enter a universe packed with vivid microcosms, replete with images, phrases, characters, and mini-stories invoking the techniques of creative negativity. Even a footnote can become a microcosmic arena for Ritchie to proffer in the third person her own gratitude to the Cameron clan who had extended their hospitality to her and her sister when they were in mourning for their recently deceased father: "[A]nd to these kind and tender friends and relations, if she were to attempt to set down here all that she owes to them, to their warm, cordial hearts, and bright sweet natures, it would make a story apart from the one she has in her mind to write to-day" (*From an Island* 4.166).[37]

To understand creative negativity and the female quest, we can do no better than to read Anne Thackeray Ritchie, the more so when she is evoking a sister-practitioner of the same body of techniques. What we especially encounter in a work such as *From an Island* is a mirror-effect, with one image bouncing off another, both reflecting the self and refracting the other-self, in a seemingly endless succession of epiphanies or near-epiphanies. For example, love (or friendship) is invoked in two different ways in one mini-essay within the novella, beginning with a query about its apparent negation:

> What is a difference? A word that means nothing,—a look a little to the right or to the left of an appealing glance. I think that people who quarrel are often as fond of one another as people who embrace. They speak a different language, that is all. Affection and agreement are things quite apart. To agree with the people you love is a blessing unspeakable. But people who differ may also be travelling along the same road on opposite sides. And there are two sides to every road that both lead the same way. (8.180)

Time is never a simple linear matter for Ritchie either, and memory is a tricky affair, sometimes best handled by evoking or narrating a relived past in the dramatic present. Accordingly, the narrator of *From an Island* tries to explain a critical turning point in the following terms: "I do not know how it was,—certainly at the time I could not have described what was happening before my eyes; but afterwards, thinking things over, I seemed to see a phantasmagoria of the events of the day passing before my eyes" (10.189–90). In characteristic and charming fashion, the novella concludes self-reflexively, providing a final postscript to the direct quotation already supplied by a letter: "What strange reports get about! One should be very careful never to believe anybody" (13.201).

More than a decade after Cameron's death in 1879, Ritchie was called upon by her photographer-son Henry Herschel Hay Cameron to provide "Reminiscences" to accompany a limited edition of their photographs.[38] Entitled *Alfred, Lord Tennyson, and His Friends* (1893), this volume contained twenty-five portraits of many of the friends shared by Cameron and Ritchie, including a portrait of Ritchie herself. Taken circa 1869, when the unmarried Ritchie was thirty-two, this image depicts her in a cumbersome midcentury gown that seems more appropriate for a younger woman; looking very Victorian, Ritchie seems to belong in the company of her father's peers, who had of course continued their friendship with the daughter for a third of a century beyond Thackeray's death. (This portrait appears earlier as Figure 10; see Figure 12 for a photograph of Ritchie contemporaneous with this publication.) Ritchie's own verbal contribution brings out some of her best writing as she uses the techniques of creative negativity to create an image of a parallel creator of the female quest. Evoking both place—Freshwater Bay on the Isle of Wight—and its inhabitants, Ritchie sets Cameron at the focal point as "the lady of the green hospitable bower" ("Reminiscences" 10). And Cameron's photographic activity constitutes a mini-materialization in Ritchie's eyes as she extols Cameron's intuitive wisdom for having "clothed great spirits in the flesh for the admiration of succeeding generations": "The sun paints the shadow of life, and the human instinct and intelligence bestowed upon this shadow create in it that essence of life and light which is so priceless in a picture" (11). Here Ritchie pays homage to someone who "made every day of the week a Saint's day, every commonplace event into something special, just as she transformed a village maiden into a Madonna or a country bumpkin into a Paladin" (12). Ritchie drives her point home with both images and abstraction. Cameron and her sisters "realised the artistic fitness of things," for example, and thus they "were able to live out their own theories and to illustrate them" (13). In effect, their family constitutes yet another microcosm, in which they "were unconscious artists, divining beauty and living with it."

If we in turn treat these "Reminiscences" as biographical fiction, they become a distinct evocation of the female quest. Seeing herself in the microcosm, Ritchie announces, "Indeed we all seemed to be performing parts in some fanciful pageant, making believe, and yet thoroughly in earnest as children at their play, and most entirely enjoying our holiday" (14). Constantly entering into her own wonderlands, the author evokes "one holiday moon" (15), and the whole scene comes flooding back to her, to be replayed before her discerning yet enchanted eye. The unseen director behind the former scene thus conjoins with the participant and recorder of both of them to co-create their essence in picture and word. Ultimately, this recollection reads like an essay on the female quest—both performing and defining it.

Ritchie's final tribute to Cameron occurred in 1916, in the midst of the Great War, when she wrote for her old friend *The Cornhill* an essay simply entitled "From Friend to Friend." Ostensibly about the friendship between Emily Tennyson and Cameron, it is also about the sorority among all three of them. In fact, it almost seems as if Ritchie is attuned to some discrete realm in which all female questors are joined, and she continually enters this universe and evokes it for her readership. Having access to the correspondence between the two women,

FIGURE 12. Anne Thackeray Ritchie (ca. 1891); photograph by Lord Battersea at Overstrand. Courtesy of Belinda Norman-Butler, London.

Ritchie pulls out images and events that act like epiphanies in the lifetimes that cross over into one another. Although these moments share many of the qualities of those celebrated by James Joyce, they bear a distinctive female stamp. Joyce's epiphanies are more like moments frozen in time, while Ritchie's windows of time are both crystallized and dynamic, drawing us into microcosms only to project us outward into the universes that frame them. Her worlds-within-worlds framework causes her to see in Cameron's verbal descriptions of a living woman, namely Emily Tennyson, "the sketch of the heroine" ("From Friend to Friend" 27). The heroine is both an individual female questor and an archetypal one— whom both Cameron and Ritchie wish to exalt, with whom both of them seek to identify. Emily Tennyson once wrote to Edward Lear about Cameron in words that certainly can be applied to Ritchie as well: "It is really wonderful how she puts her spirit into people" (qtd. by Ford, *The Cameron Collection*, 127). Ritchie's final summation of Cameron is unselfconsciously self-reflective: "Torch-bearers sometimes consume themselves and burn some of their own life and spirit in the torches they carry" (35).

Leading up to her description of Ritchie's death in 1919, biographer Winifred Gérin observes that Ritchie was finally granted "her one remaining desire: to see the war end, and the assuaging of the world's sufferings" (Gérin 275). Ritchie herself experienced "only a gentle and gradual decline," expiring "in a quite exceptional tranquility of mind" in the arms of her daughter at "The Porch," her cottage on the Isle of Wight that Cameron had once made her refuge from sorrow at the loss of her father. It is almost as if Ritchie had been preparing herself for her own end by celebrating in *A Book of Sibyls* and in her writings about Cameron mentors whom she could follow beyond material existence. In Gérin, too, we encounter another "sister," doing for Ritchie what she does for her own "sibyls." Perhaps one of the most significant accomplishments of the female quest lies in its insight into death—that it does not have to be a rupture. By its very definition, the mechanisms of the female quest work against the multiple separations of time. As for the seemingly ineluctable separations of life, Ritchie's treatment of the "ultimate separation" demonstrates that even death can constitute a rounding out, a sense of completion that concurrently exists as connection and continuity. And once again, it is form which achieves this effect. Upon first reading *A Book of Sibyls*, Robert Louis Stevenson penned the following two quatrains, in direct-address to Ritchie:

> The faces and the forms of yore
> Again recall, again recast;
> Let your fine fingers raise once more,
> The curtains of the quiet past.

And then, beside the English fires
That sing and sparkled long ago,
The sires of our departed sires
The mothers of our mothers show.[39]

Stevenson was only one of many of the next generation—including George Meredith, Thomas Hardy, George Moore, Henry James, and T. S. Eliot—to salute her.

All along, whenever Anne Thackeray Ritchie wrote about other women, she sought to find and forge connections—to understand "[t]he mothers of our mothers." Some of those women whom she counted among her friends in adulthood—Barrett Browning, Jane Carlyle, and Cameron—had in fact acted like mothers to the young Anne Thackeray when her own mother had to be placed under private care.[40] When Isabella died in 1894, Ritchie became a mother to her own mother, just as she would soon come to foster a mother-mentor relationship with her troubled niece-by-marriage Virginia Woolf. But Woolf also served her aunt in her turn by variously reviewing her work and life in her own initially anonymous publications. Reviewing Ritchie's *Blackstick Papers* in 1908, Woolf is clearly in sympathetic accord with her subject, capturing the spirit of the writing with her own amazing acumen: "If we try to discover what her method is we must imagine that she looks out of a window, takes somehow the impression of a gay, amusing world, turns over the leaves of her book and seizes a sentence here and there, remembers something that happened forty years ago, and rounds it all into an essay which has the buoyancy and the shifting colours of a bubble in the sun."[41] Surely Woolf is here displaying some of the same impressionistic style she shares with her aunt, a style that verges on her own stream-of-consciousness. Nor does her aunt's use of *espièglerie* elude her: "Lady Ritchie will surprise us again and again by her flitting mockery" (228). At the end of the review, Woolf concedes the power of examination to example itself, concluding with a direct quotation which gives "what analysis fails to give" (229). In that same spirit, I now choose to conclude my chapter with another quotation from Ritchie, this time from the fittingly titled 1873 essay, "In Friendship":

> It will all be a dream to-morrow, as we stumble into the noise, and light, and work of life again. Monday comes commonplace, garish, and one can scarce believe in the mystical Sunday night. And yet this tranquil Sunday night is more true than the flashiest gas-lamp in Piccadilly. Natural things seem inspired at times, and beyond themselves, and to carry us upwards and beyond our gas-lamps; so do people seem revealed to us at times, and in the night, when all is peace.[42]

4. The Multiple Deconversions of Annie Wood Besant

Annie Wood Besant (1847–1933) began her tumultuous engagement with problems of personal belief almost from the start. As a young woman, she was a problematic figure in Victorian England, openly questioning and then breaking from the Anglican Church to become an atheist, a Freethinker, a Neo-Malthusian, and then a Fabian Socialist—all the while exasperating the general public with her writings and legal and political battles. Her inner peace came only when she embraced the worldwide social and mystical movement known as Theosophy in 1889. Its etymology signifying "wisdom or knowledge concerning things divine," Theosophy drew artist-figures like William Butler Yeats, Wassily Kandinsky, and L. Frank Baum to its ranks, and it generated offshoots led by Rudolf Steiner, Alice A. Bailey, and "World Teacher" Jiddu Krishnamurti. After the death of its founder, Madame Blavatsky, in 1891, Besant headed the Theosophical Society in her typically controversial style for over forty years, writing prolifically on the subject and actively participating in the stormy politics of India (she influenced as much as she provoked Mohandras K. Gandhi and Jawaharlal Nehru) as the ancient tradition struggled to free itself from British colonialism.

Despite the death of her father when she was six years old, Annie Wood grew up under favorable circumstances. Not only was she encircled by a mother's love, but she received a zealous education conducted by Ellen Marryat (sister of novelist Frederick Marryat), an Evangelical who nevertheless taught Annie to seek direct proof and think for herself. Married at the age of twenty to Frank Besant, the former Annie Wood soon discovered how inappropriate it was for her to have allied herself with this future Reverend of the Church of England. Their six years together were marked by his physical and verbal abuse, leading Annie to file for a legal separation. A custody battle ensued in 1879 for their daughter Mabel (son Digby was already living with his father), but even though Besant eloquently argued her own case in open court, her religious views (she was by then an atheist) denied her the legal rights of motherhood. Still products of the nineteenth century, however, neither husband nor wife sued for divorce, and Annie retained the technical status of wife until her husband's death in 1917. Besant had recently figured prominently in another legal battle, namely the infamous Bradlaugh–Besant trial of 1877–1878 over the right to publish and disseminate birth control literature, specifically Charles Knowlton's *Fruits of Philosophy: The Private Companion of Young People* (1832).[1] Besant had met Charles Bradlaugh, president of the National Secular Society, in 1874, and together they worked assiduously for the Freethought cause for a full decade. Moved by the need for more active social reform, Besant left Freethought behind in 1885 when she became a Socialist and joined the Fabian Society. The year 1888 saw Besant's success in helping the Match Girls of Bryant and May win their strike, as well as her election to the London School Board.

The major change in Besant's life occurred in 1889. After reviewing Blavatsky's *Secret Doctrine*, Besant met with the author and converted to Theosophy. Within two years, Besant became leader of the Theosophical Society in Europe and India, making India her permanent home after visiting it for the first time in 1893. While seeking to uncover the ties between Theosophy and the ancient Hindu religion, Besant transferred to India her zeal for political and educational reform. Her early support for Home Rule, albeit within the British Commonwealth,[2] led to her internment in 1917, but that act turned against the authorities, for she was elected the first woman president of India's National Congress the following year. As her leadership brought more Indian nationals to the fore, she devoted more time and energy to Theosophy and education. With Bhagwan Das, Besant had founded the Central Hindu College in 1899, and in 1911 they conjoined it with a girls' school to form the nucleus of Benares Hindu University. She became Dr. Annie Besant when she was awarded an Honorary Doctorate by BHU, where she remained on the board of directors until 1932 and occasionally lectured. Her legacy in India continues to be demonstrated in positive terms today—women who were educated at BHU still speak of Besant with great gratitude, and students pay tribute to her at the pavilion on the grounds of the Central Boys' School by daily performing the devotional service of *puja*.[3]

But it was Theosophy that brought Besant to India, and it was Theosophy that inspired Besant for the second half of her life. Theosophy was founded in New York City in 1875 by the Russian linguist and clairvoyant Helena Petrovna Blavatsky (1831–1891). With Henry Steel Olcott, HPB, as she was affectionately called, began to spread the word about the truth that underlies all religions, one that acknowledges the higher faculties of humanity and encourages their development. As the theosophical movement spread around the world, Blavatsky expounded her views in a series of texts, most notably *Isis Unveiled* (1877), *The Secret Doctrine* (1888), and *The Key to Theosophy* (1889). When Besant assumed the leadership of the Theosophical Society in Europe and India in 1891, she found a hard-working co-enthusiast in Charles Leadbeater, who joined her in conducting scientific research which presaged many of the findings of the New Physics during the 1930s.[4] Relocated to India, Besant then became the official worldwide head of the organization with her election in 1907. Besides fueling her political and educational reforms with the inspiration she drew from pursuing the higher goals of Theosophy, Besant took on the endorsement of a new Messiah, or World Teacher. Helping to educate Jiddu Krishnamurti and prepare him for his future role constituted a major investment of her time and energy, making his 1929 dissolution of the Order of the Star, founded to promote that cause, all the harder to accept. Looking at Theosophy's impact today, we can see that it has been substantially responsible for introducing to the West the "ancient wisdom" of China, India, Egypt, and Greece, as well as for reintroducing the esoteric knowledge of early Christianity. Although it retains a fringe status in the eyes of many, Theosophy permeates New Age elements in the populace at large, subtly continuing to inform the thought and lifestyles of people who remain unaware of its specific tenets.[5]

Besant penned two autobiographies, one of them pre-Theosophy in 1885, the other post-Theosophy in 1893. During the remaining forty years of her life, she never again directly addressed her own life story in her writings, but her many lectures, pamphlets, and books published by the Theosophical Publishing Society form a non-personal testimony to her soul's progress to find further peace and insight. For my purposes in examining and analyzing her conversion pattern, this process both conforms to and breaks from our expectations governing women's lives and life-writing. On the one hand, hers is a highly dispersed story, one which confirms a woman's tendency to operate from a less ego-centered agenda and which usually emerges from the variety of documents that testify to her multiple roles and the many demands placed upon her. On the other hand, Besant quickly came to live a highly public life, and in this arena she can hardly be described as either self-effacing or merely fulfilling the duties usually assigned to her gender. However, conjoining women's autobiography criticism with that of conversion narrative reaches an apparently strategic impasse in the writings of Mary Mason and Felicity Nussbaum because they argue that conversion can only represent a denial of women's sense of selfhood. In this respect, the work of Virginia Brereton and Peter Dorsey only constrains itself by its enforced tie to patriarchal authority, even as it grants women's subversive potential within such confinement.[6] What Besant accomplished most importantly was an explosion not only of belief systems but of the conversion process itself. Her life pattern opens up the ongoing questioning of authority in order to embrace a larger whole that transcends all human attempts at boundary-making.

Confronted by some of the apparent paradoxes in Besant's life story, we would be well-advised to note that a theory of "deconversion" helps to deal with her complex journey chiefly because it constantly confronts the overall curve and pattern of her life search. Because they understand this spiritual quest better than most Westerners, Indian biographers have served an important role in redressing our often-imbalanced perspective on Besant's life, even if some of them have engaged in open hagiography. Too many of her Western biographers have failed to achieve that key quality of balance, and as an unfortunate result, they tend to deride her apparent lack of commitment. For example, Arthur C. Nethercot's two-volume biography (1960 and 1963), in deciding to break down Besant's life into nine stages, necessarily becomes satiric in its analogy to a cat's nine lives. Nonetheless, his divisions do provide us with some useful categories: volume 1—the Christian wife, the atheist mother, the martyr of science, the Socialist labor agitator, and the *chela* (disciple) of the Mahatmas; volume 2—the Indian educator/propagandist/mystic, president of the Indian National Congress, the deserted leader, life in death. Anne Taylor's 1992 biography, adjudged by many as definitive, is a disappointment largely because of its lack of empathy for its subject.[7] A much more balanced accounting occurs in Geoffrey West's earlier text, *The Life of Annie Besant* (1929). West proffers an interlude chapter on conversion, opening with the words, "With regard to Mrs. Besant's conversion to Theosophy nothing needs more to be stressed than that it was, absolutely, a logical conclusion to all that had gone before. It might almost have been prophesied, had anyone possessed intimate knowledge and subtle perception" (143).[8]

As applied by John D. Barbour in *Versions of Deconversion: Autobiography and the Loss of Faith* (1994), the term "deconversion" helps him to focus on rejection of religious faith and the ways in which autobiographers have interpreted that loss. In his four-step breakdown, deconversion moves through the following stages: intellectual doubt, moral criticism, emotional suffering, and disaffiliation from community.[9] This line of analysis is certainly applicable to Besant, but what I find missing from Barbour's program is an acknowledgment that this pattern might well be repeated, as it is in the case of Annie Besant, leading to increasingly larger and more encompassing belief systems. In this light, it is perhaps not so surprising that Besant does not even figure into Barbour's otherwise thoroughgoing schema, remarkable especially for the ways in which it explores loss of faith "as a metaphor for interpreting other kinds of personal transformation than conversion to Christian faith" (34). Barbour is useful, too, for expanding the definition of *apostasy*, originally denoting "public renunciation of faith . . . reserved for those who abandoned Christianity for another exclusive and institutionalized religion" (139). As a narrative of crisis, deconversion, and conversion, Besant's quest recalls that of renowned Victorian sage Thomas Carlyle, whose hero in *Sartor Resartus* (1836) moves from "The Everlasting No" through his "Centre of Indifference" to "The Everlasting Yea." Yet our heroine—and very few women, for that matter—has never been granted the appellation of sage by previous critics, despite the fact that the body of her lifework and eloquence attest to a spirit and oratorical intelligence that have moved millions.[10]

Besant's life story, as articulated through her multiple deconversions, forms the core subject of this chapter. Thus far, I have been providing an overview of her life through the language and perspective of biography, and I have introduced the concept of deconversion because it serves to explain how her life decisions cohere as part of an overall pattern. To demonstrate how this pattern of deconversion governed Besant's life, I now want to turn to the language of autobiography. First, by reading her *Autobiographical Sketches* and *An Autobiography* in conjunction—treating them as a consolidated resource—I illustrate how each can supplement the other to uncover and explicate the motif of deconversion in her self-accounting. Secondly, I reread the two autobiographical texts in the manner of a compare-contrast essay to show how Besant variously employs the elements of creative negativity in each of them, as well as to argue that the earlier text prefigures the second version's open tale of deconversion to Theosophy. Finding consistent elements in both of them further demonstrates how Besant's pre-Theosophy years set her up for the deconversions that she continued to experience within Theosophy itself. Finally, I address some of the vehement criticism of Besant's life pattern as it has commonly been read, namely as inconsistent and superficial. In this respect, George Bernard Shaw's various attempts to encapsulate Besant provide a representative case of how much she has been misunderstood. By remaining at the forefront of so many controversial causes, Besant has aroused the animosity of a considerable number of detractors who apparently never read her autobiographical writings closely enough (if at all) to recognize her insight into her own evolution. In fact, Besant's literary-critical reading of her own rhetoric in her autobiographies constitutes a deconstruction that parallels her pattern of deconversion. Besant's self-writing thus confirms the potency of self-producing a complete life-as-model, in her case dismissing or at least compromising the project of humanist-secularist biography, which can merely approach her life history.

A PATTERN OF DECONVERSION

Besant tried twice to tell her complex story, once in 1884–1885 and then again in 1893, at two key moments in her life journey. The first of these two records, entitled *Autobiographical Sketches*, initially appeared in monthly installments in the magazine she edited, *Our Corner*. Published when she was only thirty-seven, this first self-accounting was written largely in response to inquiries about her notorious life experiences (thus far) and was intended "to satisfy friendly questioners, and to serve, in some measure, as defense against unfair attack."[11] Immediately thereafter available in book form through the Freethought Publishing Company, *Autobiographical Sketches* featured her detailed—and dramatic—narrative of the Bradlaugh–Besant trial of 1877–1878. But Besant grants her *Sketches'* primary appeal to the account she reserves for endpoint—the tale of her struggle for custody of her daughter and her eventual separation from both her children, powerfully marked by an unembittered willingness to give them up for the sake of their emotional well-being.

Eight years later the second account was dignified by the more self-assured label, *An Autobiography*, prefaced with the hope that her example might serve as solace and beacon to other like-minded seekers: "the tale of one soul that went out alone into the darkness and on the other side found light, that struggled through the Storm and on the other side found Peace, may bring some ray of light and of peace into the darkness and the storm of other lives."[12] *An Autobiography* signaled a major revision of the previous *Sketches*. It can be distinguished from the prior account chiefly through Besant's attention to shaping devices, notably chapter divisions and titles at close range, and the retrospective awareness of her gradual growth toward Theosophy at long range. Most significantly, she opens this volume with the mystical invocation, "Out of the Everywhere into the Here," and concludes with the grand finale, "Through Storm to Peace," its last words reading, "PEACE TO ALL BEINGS" (A364). Somewhat fittingly, *An Autobiography* begins by reproducing her astrology chart. Although she immediately qualifies the value of such rigid attempts at self-interpretation (A11–13), her audacious beginning this time primarily signals to the reader a contrast with the (relatively) more traditional commencement of *Sketches*.

As the following passage from *An Autobiography* makes clear, Besant had the will to convert from a very young age:

> From the age of eight my education accented the religious side of my character. Under Miss Marryat's training my religious feeling received a strongly Evangelical bent, but it was a subject of some distress to me that I could never look back to an hour of "conversion"; when others gave their experiences, and spoke of the sudden change they had felt, I used to be sadly conscious that no such change had occurred in me, and I felt that my dreamy longings were very poor things compared to the vigorous "sense of sin" spoken of by the preachers, and used dolefully to wonder if I were "saved." (A43)[13]

At this very vulnerable stage and age, Annie and other young women are only too ready to be "saved" by Jesus Christ, in her words "my ideal Prince" (A45). Looking back, she sees quite clearly how Christ elides into the "Ideal Man" (S36). In this respect, she recognizes how "the loving side finds its joy in religious expansion, in which the idealised figure of Jesus becomes the object of passion, and the life of the nun becomes the ideal life, as being dedicated to that one devotion. . . . But analysing it now, after it has long been a thing of the past, I cannot but regard it as a mere natural outlet for the dawning feelings of womanhood, certain to be the more intense and earnest as the nature is deep and loving" (S36). Unfortunately for all concerned, adulation of Christ in her own case was displaced onto his earthly representative, namely a member of the clergy, and Annie assumed that her highest aspirations could be achieved only as a clergyman's wife.

What Besant soon found was that she had to convert in reverse fashion—through a series of deconversions, backing her way out of restrictive dogmas into more inclusive belief systems. Her odyssey of personal awakenings reveals a pattern of painful deconversions: first, she uncovers the elements of self-contradiction within her current belief system, that is, where it fails its unifying goal; then, she explores forbidden knowledge; and finally, she embraces a more encompassing structure—one which promises a more optimistic program of dissolving those boundaries that separate human souls.

Like many a troubled adult, Besant could look back to a youthful period of emotional harmony. Real or imagined, this Edenic period is sensed as something which must be regained. For Besant, that period of life was inherently fragile, built upon an exaggerated religious foundation. Her times of innocence involved a hypnotic pleasure at the "sonorous cadences" of the Bible and Milton as she sat "swinging on some branch of a tree, lying back often on some swaying bough and gazing into the unfathomable blue of the sky, till I lost myself in an ecstasy of sound and colour, half chanting the melodious sentences and peopling all of the blue with misty forms" (A43–44). Lost in the ecstatic moment, when everything is passive or robotic, as in a dream, Besant is here experiencing the polar opposite of engagement with pain we will be seeing later in her deconversions. In a sense, she often seems more involved in what she loses than what she moves toward, but in what follows, we also witness her penchant for martyrdom—the will to suffer, wishing she lived when she would have to suffer for a new religion. Besant goes on to detail how a prolonged stay in Paris awakened in her a primal sensuous aesthetic: "I discovered the sensuous enjoyment that lay in introducing colour and fragrance and pomp into religious services, so that the gratification of the aesthetic emotions became dignified with the garb of piety" (A51–52). Soon she was brooding on the martyrs, reading the early Church fathers ("my chief companions"), even fasting—essentially responding to the mystical appeal of Catholicism in her desire to "sacrifice to something greater than myself" (A52–57).

Her first fall from grace—a fateful near-deconversion at the age of eighteen— emerged from an innocent application of the intellect to her harmonious world of faith. Attempting to map out the events of Easter week as recounted in the four Gospels, the young biblical scholar confronted a horrifying discordance in the apparent contradictions among the four versions: "I became uneasy as I proceeded with my task, for discrepancies leaped at me from my four columns; the uneasiness grew as the contradictions increased, until I saw with a shock of horror that my 'harmony' was a discord, and a doubt of the veracity of the story sprang up like a serpent hissing in my face" (A61). From the outset, Besant's keen mind threatened to tear apart whatever comforting structure she accepted, or created, for herself. Despite a will to believe, her inherent skepticism always entertained negation, which she then transformed—through the tools of creative negativity—into an ever-expanding creative process.

Besant's first real deconversion took an even more profoundly painful and personal form and was based uncompromisingly on her sense of a lost world of emotional harmony. Both of her children became seriously ill, and the perennial theological question of suffering took an agonizingly concrete form for the young mother:

> There had grown up in my mind a feeling of angry resentment against the God who had been for weeks, as I thought, torturing my helpless baby. . . . More than once I cried aloud: "O God, take the child, but do not torment her." All my personal belief in God, all my intense faith in his constant direction of affairs, all my habit of continual prayer and of realisation of his presence, were against me now. To me he was not an abstract idea, but a living reality, and all my mother-heart rose up in rebellion against this person in whom I believed, and [in] whose individual finger I saw my baby's agony. (S50)

The sequence of events following this trauma reveals the essential pattern of Besant's lifetime experience of deconversion. Even after the immediate emotional crisis has ended, her mind begins ruthlessly probing the contradictions of her beliefs, seeking deeper and more mystical meanings behind unsatisfactory forms— all in an effort to recover an earlier sense of divine harmony. Once more we witness her militant, analytic mind at work, putting the forms of her belief to the test. Now she begins reading both heretical and orthodox works, and she starts actively consulting clergymen (notably not her clergyman husband), resolving that, "whatever might be the result, I would take each dogma of the Christian religion, and carefully and thoroughly examine it, so that I should never again say 'I believe' where I had not proved" (S55). Her alienation from her husband was undoubtedly further provoked by Walter Besant's meddling in his brother Frank's affairs: "But unfortunately a copy [of my anonymous pamphlet "The Deity of Jesus of Nazareth"] sent to a relative of Mr. Besant's brought about a storm. That gentlemen did not disagree with it—indeed he admitted that all educated persons must hold the views put forward—but what would Society say?" (S71). Significantly, Annie is absent from Walter Besant's *Autobiography*, where he otherwise confirms his commitment to social work (247–49 and 256–60) and to a genuinely moral interpretation of the role of religion (273–76). Ironically, her brother-in-law's interference may very well have helped to launch Annie Besant on her separate path.

Besant continued to seek answers in doubt. She embraced the inner discomfort expressed by the poet John Keats's negative capability, "when man is capable of being in uncertainties, Mysteries, doubts," riding a whirlwind of doubt to the core of existence.[14] We see this propensity confirmed by her effort to align herself with her own mother, whose dying wish was that her daughter join her in taking communion even when Besant no longer subscribed to the divinity of Christ. (See Figure 13 for a photograph of Besant with her mother taken seven years earlier.) Mrs. Wood considered taking the Sacrament necessary to salvation, yet she refused to do so "'if darling Annie is to be shut out'" (S80); on her part, Besant insisted that she would have to tell the officiating clergyman of her heresy. In despair, Besant sought someone who would perform the Sacrament under such conflicted circumstances—when she finally recalled Dean Stanley, "known to be of the broadest school within the Church of England." Stanley informed Besant that "conduct was far more important than theory," that he regarded "all as 'Christians' who recognised and tried to follow the moral law" (S81). Once again her willingness to work through discord to harmony was rewarded: "Well was I repaid for the struggle it had cost me to ask so great a kindness from a stranger, when I saw the comfort that gentle noble heart had given to my mother."[15]

Nonetheless, the result of Besant's continual questioning was deconversion to atheism. Applying her intellect to a partitioned belief system in a manner akin to what she had undertaken in her earlier Easter analysis in 1866, Besant was in effect pursuing emotional continuity. Atheism thus held out for her a hope of renewed harmony. We can recognize this pattern at work when she describes her first encounter with the public rhetoric of Charles Bradlaugh (1833–1891), the atheist and freethinker who became her mentor for many years:

> Eloquence, fire, sarcasm, pathos, passion, all in turn were bent against Christian superstition, till the great audience, carried away by the torrent of the orator's

FIGURE 13. Emily Wood (1816–1874) and her daughter Annie (1847–1933) photographed the year of Annie's marriage to the Reverend Frank Besant (1867). With permission of the Theosophical Society, Wheaton, Illinois, and Adyar, India.

force, hung silent, breathing soft, as he went on, till the silence that followed a magnificent peroration broke the spell, and a hurricane of cheers relieved the tension. (A136)

Her language echoes that of a religious (not to mention sexual) experience—both she and the speaker embrace a spirit of totality and harmony. Besant even goes on to express the nature of her friendship with Bradlaugh as recovering an "ancient tie":

From that first meeting in the Hall of Science dated a friendship that lasted unbroken till Death severed the earthly bond, and that to me stretches through Death's gateway and links us together still. As friends, not as strangers, we met—swift recognition, as it were, leaping from eye to eye; and I know now that the instinctive friendliness was in truth an outgrowth of strong friendship in other lives, and that on that August day we took up again an ancient tie, we did not begin a new one. (A137)

Of course, Besant now sees that "tie" as part of a divine plan. Her newly adopted belief in reincarnation affirms a connection that transcends earthly divisions and partings—a precept that would hardly be acknowledged within Bradlaugh's atheist ranks.

Besant's next major step—that of embracing Socialism—amounted to a deconversion from her mentor. Feeling like a traitor, she nonetheless found herself responding to a sense that something was missing in the social order and in Freethought's failure to provide a systematic program to indict suffering. By 1885, Besant had become increasingly active in promoting political as well as legal causes. Three years later, along with fellow Social Democrat Herbert Burrows, she helped establish the Matchmakers' Union after both had successfully led a strike of girls working in match factories. Her Irish legacy (she boasts in both her autobiographical accounts of being three-fourths Irish) aligned her with Irish Home Rule long before her commitment to Indian independence and made her agitation on British soil doubly fearsome to her opponents. All her life, Besant had demanded that both her emotions and her intellect submit to rigorous testing: "Socialism in its splendid ideal appealed to my heart, while the economic soundness of its basis convinced my head" (A304). In the private and public debate that followed, Bradlaugh's magnetism remained the form Besant had to overcome in order to deal with the content at issue. "Could I take public action which might bring me into collision with the dearest of my friends, which might strain the strong and tender tie so long existing between us?" she implored (A305–6). Still problematic for Besant was the disharmony of Socialism's sharply antagonistic approach to its opponents, Bradlaugh chief among them. Finally, however, Besant cried out, "A conflict which was stripped of all covering, a conflict between a personal tie and a call of duty could not last long, and with a heavy heart I made up my mind to profess Socialism openly and work for it with all my energy" (A306). Now she could find intellectual allies galore, most notably her old friend (soon to be sparring partner) George Bernard Shaw, but she would still be lacking that key component of spirituality that always underlay her questing.

Besant's lifetime of spiritual development consisted of three general stages—first a series of Christian deconversions, next a group of secular ones, and finally those embodied within Theosophy itself. The first two stages characterized her tumultuous early life in Victorian England, while Theosophy crystallized for her a system in which deconversion is heightened into a metaphysic and meditative technique—one that continually tries to penetrate its own layers of belief to reach the infinity that transcends all form. Of course, all conversion experiences involve the dissolution of old patterns and boundaries, the negative aspect of spiritual growth for which I have employed the term "deconversion." But Besant's personal style of awakening so strongly features this negative aspect that the concept of deconversion serves to highlight the backing away which may be a component of all forms of renewal in general and to explain the appeal of Theosophy for her and other seekers in particular. Barbour's parallel discussion reads as follows: "In one sense, every conversion is a deconversion, and every deconversion is a conversion. The 'turning from' and 'turning to' are alternative perspectives on the same process of personal metamorphosis, stressing either the rejected past of the old self or the present convictions of the reborn self" (*Versions of Deconversion* 3).

Theosophy provided Besant with the deeper mystical meanings lying behind—and ultimately dissolving—all forms, making spiritual connections among all peoples and systems. Mme. Blavatsky actually preempted Besant's deconvertive proclivities in bringing her to Theosophy. When Besant expressed a desire to become a Theosophist, Blavatsky asked her to read a recent, scathing attack on Blavatsky's character. Considering the strongest possible arguments against her chosen belief system was something Besant would do anyway, so even the process of conversion into this most capacious of belief systems took the form of probing the negative, of first backing away from the claims of its leaders. Against the attack, Besant recalled the clear blue eyes of Blavatsky. Returning to request that she be accepted as a pupil, Besant looked straight into Blavatsky's eyes: "Her stern, set face softened, the unwonted gleam of tears sprang to her eyes; then with a dignity more than regal, she placed her hand upon my head" (A344). The motif of eyes, eye contact, and eyesight figures prominently in both of Besant's autobiographical renderings. This last reference recalls an epiphany—her moment of immediate intimacy with Bradlaugh—and later she would fear the look in his eyes when he learned of her conversion to Theosophy. Eyes operate as a focal point for Besant, epitomizing the deepest of human contact, sometimes agonizing, which constitutes the real goal of her lifelong quest, when "eyes [are] made luminous with the radiance of Eternal Peace" (A364). Besant here gives voice to the motif of eyes that I began exploring in a previous chapter with regard to the visual meditations of Julia Margaret Cameron's photographic images.

So Blavatsky's technique worked. Besant encountered in Theosophy a belief system in which no knowledge is really forbidden, a system that could even allow her to view Christianity as an esoteric science. Now we witness a continued pattern of deconversions within the sphere of Theosophy, for this open system ensured for Besant a greater success at bringing people closer together and fulfilling her larger social vision. Thus Besant came finally to an inner peace. Through anxieties heavy and long she came to know bliss—engagement without pain. And significantly, Besant's Theosophical writings, her expositions of its beliefs and her analyses of the elements of Christianity and other religions, tended to take precisely the tripartite form of her own inner development. For example, her lectures on the three Christs, the sacraments, and the three realms of existence seem oriented to reenacting her own deconversion process, moving from form to allegory to spirituality, employing the painful struggle of her early life as a pedagogical tool. This is precisely the case, too, with her arguments in such books as *Esoteric Christianity* (1901) and *Theosophical Christianity* (1922). Both of them show her continuing to seek the truth behind all religions—using one or many to connect them all, going back through the Lesser Mysteries to discover an early essence, uncovering in the Greater Mysteries a singular interpersonal connection.[16]

In her political activities as a Theosophist, Besant's work in India may be seen as an exfoliation of the dynamic inner process which guided her life. In Victorian England, she had found herself further and further beyond the pale of acceptable belief. Moving from a materialistic, traditionally Christian status into the forbidden realms of atheism, Freethought, and Socialism—much less the occultism of Theosophy—was too much for her native West. The British had nothing to deconvert to. But in India her social and religious activism could take the form of the deconversion which had so powerfully dominated Besant's life. The years 1917–1918 alone saw her interned by the British government for three months, released to an enthusiastic following, and then elected president of India's National Congress. Theosophy was essentially outward-turning; it allowed her to pull others out of negation, to return India to spiritual traditions crushed by British colonial rule.

In a lecture delivered at the 77th International Convention of the Theosophical Society at Adyar in 1952, Sri Prakasa summed up Besant's impact on India:

> If today we are a free people politically, and have also shed many of the shackles that bound our bodies and minds and souls socially and spiritually; if men and women in our land are working in close cooperation in many fields of national endeavour; if there is a consciousness of human dignity among the humblest, and the evil aspects of caste are being thrown aside; if we are proud of our religion, our culture and our heritage—much credit for this consummation must go to Mrs. Besant.[17]

Prakasa's remarks are contained in a volume of lectures "delivered in memory of the great servant of India and of humanity, Dr. Annie Besant." These twenty-four lectures, presented between 1952 and 1988, appear under the following four wide-ranging headings: The Role of India; Man—His Problems and Role; Philosophical Presentations; and The Modern Crisis. The very spiritual traditions Besant revitalized had inspired her own belief system, and out of gratitude she returned them to their origins. In effect, in India Annie Besant had only to take the people back to their roots, bearing out the reverse, form-dissolving process of deconversion, functioning as a sort of anti-missionary. It was far easier to try to deconvert India to what it once was—an old harmony—than to convert England to something it despised and did not understand.

HER-SELVES, HER-STORY

Given the complexities of Besant's life quest and the intricacies of the deconversion process, to read in close conjunction her two full-length autobiographical excursions—*Autobiographical Sketches* (1885) and *An Autobiography* (1893)—entails much more than a simple comparative exercise. These two texts, published a mere eight years apart, do tell somewhat different stories and apparently depict different selves, yet they also cover much of the same ground and reveal some remarkable continuities. Incredible, too, is the fact that after engaging in these two acts of self-writing within such a short time span, Besant never again attempted such an openly self-reflective activity for her public, even though (or perhaps because) she would live such a highly exposed life for the next forty years. There are, however, several shorter autobiographical undertakings from around the same time period of the two full-length accounts, all of them in response to specific circumstances. "How I Became a Theosophist" constituted her immediate follow-up in the *Star* to her 1889 review for the *Pall Mall Gazette* (25 April 1889) of Blavatsky's *The Secret Doctrine*. Recast and expanded as one of her lecture-pamphlets, it was reborn as *Why I Became a Theosophist*, published by the Freethought Publishing Company later that same year. As an intermediary text to the two full-length volumes, she then produced *1875 to 1891: A Fragment of Autobiography* under the auspices of the Theosophical Society. This twelve-page pamphlet prints the text of her last remarks delivered to the Hall of Science (30 August 1891), a lecture primarily intended to announce that she would not speak there again. The hall was about to pass into the hands of the National Secular Society, which had imposed on Besant the restriction that she not say anything "that goes against the principles and objects of the society" (12), a condition she declared she would never agree to meet. Finally, Besant's preface to the second impression of *An Autobiography*, republished by the Theosophical Society in 1894, as well as the one to the third impression (second edition) from Adyar in 1908, filled in some additional gaps in her spiritual and activist journey.

Keeping all this information in mind and knowing about Besant's subsequent life events, the reader may want to respond to an unspoken challenge to project a speculative third autobiography or even a series of volumes. After all, the indefinite article "an" (implying one of several) in the title of *An Autobiog-*

raphy almost sets this challenge in motion. But the two published full-length texts already give us more than sufficient basis for understanding Besant's personal evolutionary style. It is not just a matter of recognizing how she changes or reconceives the same experiences upon recasting them a second time, however. We need to examine as well the points of continuity and shared allegiances, for the seeds of Besant's overarching curve of self-creation are present even in the first volume. In this respect, the language of creative negativity helps to unpack the layers of similarity and difference to uncover hidden layers of meaning in the lifelong quest of this amazingly complex and compelling personality.

First of all, Besant does not simply treat her initial text as a template upon which she will make slight embellishments and merely plug in appropriate additions second-time round. She truly takes up the task of writing her life story anew, drawing on the first one for general guidelines and borrowing from the original only when its wording fits her current sense of self-conception. What we are privileged to witness by examining these two texts together is no less than an in-progress rewriting of the self, one that self-consciously recognizes the patterns reflected in the first rendering and that now can more clearly trace the growth toward her present spiritual state as worldwide leader of the Theosophy movement. In one sense, Besant did not need to undertake the writing of any subsequent autobiographies, for she undoubtedly felt she had arrived at her goal—albeit one of perpetual spiritual evolution—and in another sense, she must have felt that her second autobiography should have made her life pattern quite clear to her sensitized readership. At the same time, she also provided us with a test case in that first example of self-writing, for even without the opportunity to compare it with the second version, the alert reader can find clues in her original work to the restless, questioning style that would fuel future deconversions.

So the original text must be taken uniquely—viewed in its own right—before it can be profitably compared with the second, apparently more definitive version. In this respect, the status of the first version as a published work already marks it as more than a draft, yet its manner of publication and very title nonetheless signal Besant's present-time awareness of her ongoing evolution. (See Figure 14, frontispiece to the book publication of *Autobiographical Sketches*; this photograph is described and discussed later in the chapter.) She began by publishing this text serially in her own journal, *Our Corner*, over a period of a year and a half in 1884–1885, writing to self-imposed monthly deadlines. Meanwhile, she continued to edit the journal and make other contributions to it, and at the same time she was becoming increasingly involved in the Fabian Society. Her involvement with *Our Corner*, which ran from 1883 through 1888, tells its own implied autobiography. As the years wore on, before any explicit contact with Theosophy, Besant can be seen as retreating from her Freethought and Socialist

FIGURE 14. Annie Besant in her lecturing dress (1885). Photograph by
H. S. Mendelssohn, London, for the frontispiece to *Autobiographical Sketches*; this
text was reprinted from her journal *Our Corner* (1884–1885) and published by the
Freethought Publishing Company.

roles, suggesting again the pattern of her search for something—not just something new, but something with meaning. Besant would continue to co-edit a variety of journals, whose titles tell their own tale—*The Link* (the journal of the Law and Liberty League, with W. T. Stead), *Lucifer* (the Theosophical monthly, meaning "The Light," with G. R. S. Mead), and later in India the new *Commonweal* (named after the Socialist League journal which had recorded many of her activities in the late 1880s) and the refurbished *New India*—both with the able assistance of B. P. Wadia.

Moreover, Besant titled her *Our Corner* installments *Autobiographical Sketches*, thereby acknowledging a certain piecemeal quality, although by now it should be clear to readers of my text that such a quality is fairly typical of women writers and can in fact operate as a tool toward more full-fledged self-assessment than society (or even oneself) can readily allow. But for Besant, fragmentary self-writing is hardly delimiting. She is not just being self-effacing in her prefatory paragraph which announces her intention "to satisfy friendly questioners, and to serve, in some measure, as defence against unfair attack" (S3). By this time, Besant was only too well aware of the profound impact her personal experiences—however briefly here outlined in these mere "sketches"—had already had on British politics and the issue of free speech.

Finally, despite the fact that Besant began publishing *Sketches* in 1884 before she had written it in its entirety, she knew from the outset that she would end it not simply by bringing it up to date with her present embrace of Socialist activities but rather with the heart-rending loss of her daughter through an egregiously unfair custody battle waged in the British court system. Focusing on this endpoint, she can plant earlier references to that final shaping event, and we can recognize the themes of motherhood, marriage, law, self-sacrifice, and principle interwoven throughout the text as interconnecting organizing links. In contrast, Besant writes *An Autobiography* after she has converted to Theosophy, and since her self-definition as a Theosophist has become paramount, her newly-discovered inner peace serves as a focal point for the second text. Throughout the body of *An Autobiography*, Besant's quiet strength of purpose is apparent, something that she was still clearly striving toward in *Sketches*.

In many respects, the preface to the second edition of *An Autobiography* (1894) sets the stage for what will ensue. This time Besant concedes that the autobiographer's life story "reflects many others," that it "may give the experience of many rather than of one," and she concludes these prefatory remarks with the following periodic sentence:

> Since all of us, men and women of this restless and eager generation—
> surrounded by forces we dimly see but cannot as yet understand, discontented
> with old ideas and half afraid of new, greedy for the material results of the

knowledge brought us by Science but looking askance at her agnosticism as regards the soul, fearful of superstition but still more fearful of atheism, turning from the husks of outgrown creeds but filled with desperate hunger for spiritual ideals—since all of us have the same anxieties, the same griefs, the same yearning hopes, the same passionate desire for knowledge, it may well be that the story of one may help all, and that the tale of one soul that went out alone into the darkness and on the other side found light, that struggled through the Storm and on the other side found Peace, may bring some ray of light and of peace into the darkness and the storm of other lives. (A5–6)

Dealing with the loss of her daughter from the distance of another eight years, Besant is no less poignant in telling this part of her-story, but she can now place it in perspective, knowing full well that both of her children have returned to her on their own as thinking adults who embrace her same philosophy. Later in the chronology of *An Autobiography*, she reports with joyful satisfaction that "both are treading in my steps as regards their views of the nature and destiny of man" (A225), that is, both have reunited with her within Theosophy. In fact, Digby later provided an informed and sympathetic account of his mother's legal and marital struggles in his family history *The Besant Pedigree* (1930).[18]

Another shift in focal point or center occurs between the two texts as well, although a significant overlapping remains. In *Sketches*, it is Charles Bradlaugh who serves as Besant's mentor and moral guide, while in *An Autobiography* that focus has shifted to H. P. Blavatsky, tellingly still a powerful presence even after her physical death. Bradlaugh's influence on Besant's life is self-apparent from their first meeting:

And let me say here that among the many things for which I have to thank Mr. Bradlaugh, there is none for which I owe him more gratitude than for the fashion in which he has constantly urged the duty of all who stand forward as teachers to study deeply every subject they touch, and the impetus he has given to my own love of knowledge by the constant spur of criticism and of challenge, criticism of every weak statement, challenge of every hastily-expressed view. (S90–91)[19]

Yet even though that guiding force will eventually be replaced, Besant does not lower him from his pedestal in her recasting of her life. In fact, this time round she devotes two full chapters to Bradlaugh—one detailing their early work together, another recounting his struggle to take his seat in Parliament despite his professed atheism (he eventually became the Member for India). But now Besant can look back on that first meeting and see it from a larger sphere: "Long afterwards I asked him how he knew me, whom he had never seen, that he came straight to me in such a fashion. He laughed and said he did not know, but, glancing over the faces, he felt sure that I was Annie Besant. . . . And so in lives to come we shall meet again, and help each other as we helped each other in this" (A136–37). Moreover, she even brings him into the maternal fold that Blavatsky currently oversees. When Besant breaks down after the loss of her daughter, Bradlaugh nurses her back to health, "behaving more like a tender mother than a man friend" (A218), she reports.

The role of the mother, mothering, and the whole subject of motherhood repeatedly surface in both autobiographical texts, reinforcing how the love Besant bore toward her own mother—"that absolute idolatry of her, which has not yet faded from my heart" (S15)—was for her an insatiable energy always in search of an appropriate channel. As a young bride, Besant embraced the arduous work of caring for her husband's parishioners. When the Sibsey villagers (Lincolnshire) suffered from a typhoid epidemic, she replaced exhausted mothers in order to monitor their children's sleep: "I take sheer delight in nursing anyone, provided only that there is peril in the sickness, so that there is the strange and solemn feeling of the struggle between the human skill one wields and the supreme enemy, Death" (S71). With her mother's death and her parting words, "You are all alone" (S84; A127), Besant was consigned to a solitude only partially satisfied by her long-distance mothering of her own children, and she continued to seek and find surrogate mothers and children to mother throughout her lifetime. Yet before long she also found peace in a love that surpasses human understanding and a new homeland where hundreds of thousands gratefully called her "Mother."

Both texts depict Besant struggling with negative emotions, but in the earlier of the two she recalls crises as part of an ongoing response mode, while in the latter she recognizes that every occurrence fits into a larger plan. The despair and anguish that she experiences with the illness of her daughter and her subsequent questioning of her long-held faith are rendered with equal force in both *Sketches* and *An Autobiography*, but a sense of emptiness reverberates in the former, despite the energy with which she undertakes her subsequent deconversions. Each text establishes the young woman's essential religiosity: they both quote Mrs. Wood on her deathbed saying to her daughter, "You were always too religious" (S87; A24). But the propensity toward religion often remains repressed or buried in *Sketches*, such that when Besant experiences her "dark night of the soul," she emerges only by rationalizing to herself, "Truth is greater than peace or position" (S64).[20] "Position" may never satisfy the Besant of *An Autobiography*, but "peace" that can be paired with "truth" becomes her final goal and appropriately enough constitutes the last word of that text:

> Quiet confidence has taken the place of doubt; a strong security the place of
> anxious dread. In life, through death, to life, I am but the servant of the great

Brotherhood, and those on whose heads but for a moment the touch of the Master has rested in blessing can never again look upon the world save through eyes made luminous with the radiance of the Eternal Peace. (A364)

To this she appends the slogan, "PEACE TO ALL BEINGS." In contrast, *Sketches* ends on the word and note of continued "strife." With reference to her daughter Mabel, Besant concludes her first self-accounting:

I had hoped to save her from the pain of rejecting a superstitious faith, but that is now impossible, and she must fight her way out of darkness into light as her mother did before her. But in order that she may do so, education now is of vital importance, and that I am striving to obtain for her. I live in the hope that in her womanhood she may return to the home she was torn from in her childhood, and that, in faithful work and noble endeavor, she may wear in future years in the Freethought ranks a name not wholly unloved or unhonored therein, for the sake of the woman who has borne it in the van through eleven years of strife. (S169)[21]

Because Besant writes *Sketches* from the viewpoint of a fundamentally spiritual being who has not yet found peace, she inevitably expresses nostalgia for the youthful harmony she has lost. Concomitantly, she is unwilling to look too deeply into the despair that she finds welling up inside her, lest it prove overwhelming. Reluctant to abandon the past, often despairing of the present, she cannot claim a future without seeing it riddled with strife. But the assured voice of *An Autobiography* can confront her earlier sense of futility precisely because she can leave the past behind her and welcome a glorious, never-ending future. As a result, the author of the second autobiography can do what the first could not: she can admit to and describe her close brush with suicide. Readers of *An Autobiography* thus learn about Besant's suppressed previous temptation to take her own life in a highly dramatic recounting: "No door of escape? The thought came like a flash: 'There is one!' And before me there swung open, with lure of peace and of safety, the gateway into silence and security, the gateway of the tomb" (A93). Once again, the note of peace is sounded, along with the concept of a gateway that marks a passing into another realm, but this time it is rendered as negation, in sharp contrast to the joyous affirmation that will later displace it.

At the same time, however, both texts reiterate a key attribute that shows Besant engaged in shifting degrees of magnitude. This quality inheres in her growing awareness of her power to move others with her own oratory. It begins when she is still studying with Miss Marryat. Asked to pray aloud at "the often-recurring prayer meetings," she reports initial dread: "But the plunge once made, and the trembling voice steadied, enthusiasm and facility for cadenced speech always swallowed up the nervous 'fear of breaking down'" (S20;

cf. A44 for similar phrasing). Later, as a young bride, Besant locks herself in her husband's church and delivers her first lecture to the empty pews:

> I shall never forget the feeling of power and of delight which came upon me as my voice rolled down the aisles, and the passion in me broke into balanced sentences, and never paused for rhythmical expression, while I felt that all I wanted was to see the church full of upturned faces, instead of the emptiness of the silent pews. And as though in a dream the solitude became peopled, and I saw the listening faces and the eager eyes, and as the sentences came unbidden from my lips, and my own tones echoed back to me from the pillars of the ancient church, I knew of a verity that the gift of speech was mine, and that if ever—and it seemed then so impossible—if ever the chance came to me of public work, that at least this power of melodious utterance should win hearing for any message I had to bring. (S72)

What better predictor of the writer of the second autobiography, namely, the head of the Theosophical movement and the future spokesperson for Indian Independence? But subtle differences between the two texts reveal that the author of *An Autobiography* is more prepared to emphasize the word "power," twice more highlighting it and acknowledging it as something "that was to mould much of my future life" (A116). Pertinent to Besant's second accounting is her timely recollection of her ability to move others: "And now the time had come when I was to use that gift of speech which I had discovered in Sibsey Church that I possessed, and to use it to move hearts and brains all over the English land" (A181).

Nonetheless, Besant's self-awareness of her oratorical abilities and her desire to move others to action with her own words is clearly present in *Sketches*, which begins to outline her complex relationship with "the crowd." Crowds are almost symbolic in both these self-reflective texts, for they signify the capability of the many to become one. Initially, however, Besant is more inclined to mix reportage and drama in recounting crowd scenes, as she does with the "angry crowd" and Fenian trial in Manchester (S42), while her later re-rendering partakes much more freely of the dramatic, providing the kind of reenactment that the savvy rhetorician might be likely to use in the courtroom or on the platform (A75–77). Oratory once set in motion allows the orator to zoom out, as it were, to rise above the mundane and material world and discover larger meanings—in short, to cross apparently uncrossable boundaries. These are the wings Besant is trying on in *Sketches*, the ones that she has mastered in *An Autobiography*. Yet in both texts she still finds it important to explain to her reading public, and to remind herself, that the ability to give speeches always involves overcoming weakness and conquering fear. Recalling her first public lecture, "The Political Status of Women" (1874), she compares her feelings unfavorably with the worst anticipation of a visit to the dentist: "All this miserable feeling, however, disappeared the moment I rose to my feet and looked at the faces before me. No tremor of nervousness touched me from the first word to the last. And a similar experience has been mine ever since" (S93). The only real difference between this recollection and that of *An Autobiography* again pertains to the word and concept of "power." This time she re-remembers that "as I heard my own voice ring out over the attentive listeners I was conscious of power and of pleasure, not of fear. . . . Once on my feet, I feel perfectly at my ease, ruler of the crowd, master of myself" (A182).

A curious example of self-revelation occurs in both texts regarding Besant's passionate investment in the power of speakers to move crowds to action. After relating an incident of stone-throwing while she was on tour as a Freethought speaker, depicting a protest against spending £142,000 to send the Prince of Wales to India, and recounting how she found herself as a woman "physically unfit to push her way through the dense mass of people" in Hyde Park, the writer of *Sketches* next provides a detailed description of the Radicals' method of organizing large orderly meetings in such outdoor settings (S102–4). She follows this prelude with a discussion of her preparation for delivering and publishing a course of six lectures on the French Revolution. After extensive research into the subject, she acknowledges that it "became to me as a drama in which I had myself taken part, and the actors therein became personal friends and foes" (S108). The only significant difference in this accounting in *An Autobiography* involves a slightly greater degree of pulling back through generalization: "That stormy period had for me an intense fascination," she confesses (A202). In both cases Besant seems almost innocently unaware of how close she comes to admitting to an obsession on this topic. Yet I suspect that there is more here to challenge such a ready assumption (itself innocent) on the reader's part. In context, what emerges more decisively is a recognition of the careful, studious grounding that underlies Besant's commitment to each cause she endorses. Given this diligent, even impartial baseline, she is finally prepared to launch herself wholeheartedly into her chosen enterprise, granting it a deservedly zealous — even dramatic—devotion.

Oratory and drama go hand in hand for Besant, as they do for many public speakers, but she is not afraid to claim the tools of an early-day performance artist in both living her life and telling her life story. While this observation has some validity for her first undertaking, it comes much more into its own by the time she writes the second. Note the evocatory, even incantatory mode of the recalled resolve to give herself "wholly to propagandist work, as a Freethinker and a Social Reformer, and to use my tongue as well as my pen in the struggle":

> But the desire to spread liberty and truer thought among men, to war against bigotry and superstition, to make the world freer and better than I found it—all

this impelled me with a force that would not be denied. I seemed to hear the voice of Truth ringing over the battlefield: "Who will go? Who will speak for me?" And I sprang forward with passionate enthusiasm, with resolute cry: "Here am I, send me!" Nor have I ever regretted for one hour that resolution, come to in solitude, carried out amid the surging life of men, to devote to that sacred cause every power of brain and tongue that I possessed. (A188)

Despite the peace that eventually replaced the strife of the first volume, however, the language of the battlefield pervades this passage, recalling as well the tone of the old-time male questor. The two modes merge when Besant rewrites, in even more chivalric imagery, her decision to go public as the writer who has been signing her *National Reformer* articles under the name "Ajax": "Thus I threw off my pseudonym, and rode into the field of battle with uplifted visor" (A190). Perhaps because she is so confident in her inner peace, Besant can now afford to playfully invoke this male-identified discourse, knowing full well that it represents a conquered past. In this spirit, penultimate chapters can still be entitled "At War All Round" (A245), "Mr. Bradlaugh's Struggle" (A253), and "Still Fighting" (A277), especially given the fact that the final one will read "Through Storm to Peace" (A329).

Overall, Besant's viewpoint on time supports her manner of expression as both an autobiographer and an orator. She realizes in both instances of her life-writing that reviewing a life entails reliving it; for her, looking backward really means bringing the past forward into the dramatic present, where she can draw it out and explore its nuances. Both texts tellingly provide the reader with a mini-essay (some would say digression, but that misses the point) on the subject of memory:

What a pity it is that a baby cannot notice, cannot observe, cannot remember, and so throw light on the fashion of the dawning of the external world on the human consciousness. If only we could remember how things looked when they were first imaged on the retinae; what we felt when first we became conscious of the outer world; what the feeling was as faces of father and mother grew out of the surrounding chaos and became familiar things, greeted with a smile, lost with a cry; if only memory would not become a mist when in later years we strive to throw our glances backward into the darkness of our infancy, what lessons we might learn to help our stumbling psychology, how many questions might be solved whose answers we are groping for in vain. (S7; A19–20, which adds "in the West" to the last sentence)

Clearly the writer is someone for whom present-time speculation builds from vivid memories, ones which not only serve her as fodder for telling her life story but provide insights which match our own present-time understanding of psychology and the human mind. In this respect, Besant's penetration also supplies her with a personal metaphor that acknowledges the solace that such memories can carry into the long-term future: "I have a long picture-gallery to retire into when I want to think of something fair, in recalling the moon as it silvered the Rhine at the foot of Drachenfels, or the soft mist-veiled island where dwelt the lady who is consecrated for ever [*sic*] by Roland's love" (S22; A49).

As the writer of the second autobiographical text reviews and recasts her life anew, she increasingly moves outside of time, attenuating it, becoming less bound by its rules. Although hints of this perspective are vaguely present in the yearnings of the first volume, the woman who pens *An Autobiography* can unequivocally declare, "[L]ooking back, I cannot but see how orderly was the progression of thought, how steady the growth, after that first terrible earthquake [of doubt], and the first wild swirl of agony" (A99–100). Now secure in her belief system of Theosophy, she can rise above the particular past, the clinging present, and a merely mortal future to a larger view of mankind: "He is a spiritual intelligence, eternal and uncreate, treading a vast cycle of human experience, born and reborn on earth millennium after millennium, evolving slowly into the ideal man" (A241). This point of view allows Besant to think both concretely and abstractly at the same time, to see her own specific life and the evolution of the species as one: "So does each man create for himself in verity the form wherein he functions, and what he is in his present is the inevitable outcome of his own creative energies in his past." As a result of this frame of mind, she can take responsibility for her life as an individual while entrusting it to a "peace which passeth understanding."[22] When she speaks in this spirit, it is hard for a present-day reader to accuse her of sexism for her propensity to refer to human beings as "men" or "mankind." Not only is this practice the expected mode of reference for her time, but Besant espouses a belief system that so genuinely sees beyond the time-bound concepts of sexual difference or gender politics that it makes that ideal world seem close at hand.[23]

Thus it is that Besant turns creative negativity into a rhetorical technique that permits her to engage in the boundary-crossing that was so startling to her contemporaries—both those whom she leaves behind and those whom she comes to join. (See Figure 15 for a photograph of Besant eight years after she became a Theosophist.) As each belief system she embraces becomes her reality, her passionate drive to pursue truth in turn sows the seeds for seeing through the false guises that that reality assumes, and her honesty compels her to eventually call that reality an illusion. This pattern is clearly established in *Sketches*, such that the sensitized reader should be prepared for its continuation in *An Autobiography*, where its apparently ever-growing paradigm reaches a paradoxical goal in the perpetually re-creating or evolving formula that constitutes Theosophy. Theos-

FIGURE 15. Annie Besant in her Indian robes (1897). She had made India her permanent home shortly after first visiting it in 1893, the year that she published *An Autobiography*. With permission of the Theosophical Society, Wheaton, Illinois, and Adyar, India.

ophy's endorsement of a progressive program for humanity inevitably reflects its own theory of human evolution. Yet Besant still recognizes that there may be one more mystery that may need to be solved for a resistant readership: How could such a staunch Atheist ever become a Theosophist?

In characteristic fashion, Besant overtly anticipates and addresses this question, stopping the chronological flow of *An Autobiography* by declaring, "And at this stage of my life-story, it is necessary to put very clearly the position I took up and held so many years as Atheist, because otherwise the further evolution into Theosophist will be wholly incomprehensible" (A139). Next she boldly announces to her readers her intention to quote from her own Atheistic pamphlets: "No charge can then be made that I have softened my old opinions for the sake of reconciling them with those now held" (A140). What follows is an entire chapter, "Atheism as I Knew and Taught It," replete with self-quotations that demonstrate how the "incomprehensible" should have been "comprehensible" all along—not just to readers of *Sketches*, but to close listeners and readers of her many lectures and subsequent pamphlets of a full decade earlier. For instance, she observes how her 1874 pamphlet "On the Nature and Existence of God" ultimately argues "that a profound unity of substance underlies the infinite diversities of natural phenomena, the discernment of the One beneath the Many" (A141). In effect, Besant asks readers of *An Autobiography* to reread her early self, to see now what they could not see then. Ideally, she wants her readers to move step-by-step with the author, deconverting in her company to her inevitable reality.

In this respect, it is instructive to note Besant's "List of Books Quoted" at the end of *An Autobiography*—J. S. Mill's *Autobiography*; *The Christian Creed*; *The Freethinkers' Text-book*; *The Gospel of Atheism*; *Gospels of Christianity and Freethought*; *Life, Death, and Immortality*; *The Link*; *The National Reformer*; *Our Corner*; *The Theosophist*; *True Basis of Morality*; *Why I do Not Believe in God*; and *World without God*—most of which supply instances of self-quotation. Although she draws upon a much wider reading base, particularly in terms of literary references, Besant here chooses to emphasize her own previous writings and those publications which supported her views at given times. In *The Origins of Theosophy: Annie Besant—The Atheist Years* (1990), J. Gordon Melton provides an edition that openly supports this orderly progression in precisely the same manner, namely by reprinting many of the pamphlets cited above. Melton writes, "Thus, as with so many occultists, Besant's atheist years become an important bridge on which she walked from belief in unbelief straight to the acceptance of a new faith" (iv). So perhaps Besant's path wasn't quite so unusual after all. In fact, many Secularists showed an interest in comparative religion, and they were especially intrigued by Eastern philosophies.

Reviewing her lifework and retelling it provoke from Besant increasingly heightened degrees of self-referentiality. Initially, the author of *Sketches* happily acknowledges her Irish heritage and describes in detail a range of family members who variously influenced her, but by the time she writes *An Autobiography* her political involvement with Ireland leads her to streamline the anecdotal Irish relationships and reclaim her Irishness more in her own right.[24] Similarly, on a religious or mystical note, the earlier text contains a lengthy description of Mrs. Wood's visionary experiences regarding her husband's funeral and her infant son's impending death, as well as announcing that the hair of the wife and mother turned white the day after Dr. Wood's death. However, the second text introduces that description with an explicit connection that the current author recognizes with herself, both as an individual and as a self-claimant to a much-maligned ethnic identity: "For as a child I was mystical and imaginative, religious to the very finger-tips, and with a certain faculty for seeing visions and dreaming dreams. This faculty is not uncommon with the Keltic races, and makes them seem 'superstitious' to more solidly-built peoples" (A24–25).[25] These are not admissions that the author of *Sketches* was prepared to make, largely because her social and religious growth was still much more in-process, her understanding of her own motivations still less conscious and less self-aware.

Self-consciousness elides smoothly into retrospective projection or outright self-analysis as the autobiographer speaks about herself in the third person. This practice is lightly employed in *Sketches*, most notably through the recasting of secondhand accounts about her early childhood, as when Besant jokes about how the infant "Miss Pleasantina determined to show that she was capable of unexpected independence, and made a vigourous struggle to assume that upright position which is the proud prerogative of man" (S6).[26] More seriously, and with growing awareness of her share of responsibility in her failed marriage, Besant provides for *An Autobiography* the following incisive self-portrait of the repressed twenty-year-old bride:

> And, in truth, I ought never to have married, for under the soft, loving, pliable girl there lay hidden, as much unknown to herself as to her surroundings, a woman of strong dominant will, strength that panted for expression and rebelled against restraint, fiery and passionate emotions that were seething under compression—a most undesirable partner to sit in a lady's armchair on the domestic rug before the fire. (A82)

She rounds out the passage by openly admitting that "self-analysis shows the contradictories in my nature that led me into so mistaken a course."

Now operating from an even more ironic perspective on her marriage—"strange that at the same time I should meet the man I was to marry, and the doubts which were to break the marriage tie" (A59)—Besant is prepared to devote an entire chapter to the subject in *An Autobiography*. "Looking back over twenty-five years," she writes about an almost other self, "I feel a profound pity for the girl standing at that critical point of life, so utterly, hopelessly ignorant of all that marriage meant, so filled with impossible dreams, so unfitted for the *role* of wife" (A65). At this point, she can address more explicitly the whole topic of failed marriages:

> Many an unhappy marriage dates from its very beginning, from the terrible shock to a young girl's sensitive modesty and pride, her helpless bewilderment and fear. Men, with their public school and college education, or the knowledge that comes by living in the outside world, may find it hard to realise the possibility of such infantile ignorance in many girls. None the less, such ignorance is a fact in the case of some girls at least, and no mother should let her daughter, blindfold, slip her neck under the marriage yoke. (A71)

So, too, can Besant see "religious wretchedness" in light of a problematic marriage. Her own example clearly provides the model from which she self-reflexively generalizes: "And, truly, women or men who get themselves concerned about the universe at large, would do well not to plunge hastily into marriage, for they do not run smoothly in the double-harness of that honourable estate" (A97–98). In *Sketches* Besant only obliquely hints at the dissolution of her marriage over several pages (S73–74), while in *An Autobiography* she openly declares, "In 1873 my marriage tie was broken" (A117). Much later in the latter text she was well-prepared to evaluate her distinctive role as "the most religious of the Atheists" (she had in fact written a Secularist funeral service). In filling that role, she recognized the "very natural outcome of a sunny nature, for years held down by unhappiness and the harshness of an outgrown creed. It was the rebound of such a nature suddenly set free, rejoicing in its liberty and self-conscious strength, and it carried with it a great power of rousing the sympathetic enthusiasm of men and women, deeply conscious of their own restrictions and their own longings" (A157–58). Such ingenuous self-analysis quickly blends into apt insight into those whom she would lead—although it is not hard to imagine that one of her detractors might label Besant's self-analysis as self-justification.

As Besant's self-referentiality reconfigures into aesthetic invocation or formal choice, her metaphors cohere into three patterns—one focusing on "light," another on imagery of water flow, the last on the tension between strife and peace. I have already discussed how strife figures into the language of the quest in both texts—how it dominates the first version, and how peace resolves all things by the end of the second endeavor. The trope of "light" operates in a similar vein. Generally recalling the biblical injunction "Let there be light!", both texts introduce the concept of light emerging from darkness through the specific agency of

Besant's pen name "Ajax," inspired by the Crystal Palace statue of "Ajax crying for light." "The cry through the darkness for light, even if light brought destruction, was one that awoke the keenest sympathy of response from my heart," Besant acknowledges in both texts, concluding her peroration by invoking mankind's shared "pleading, impassioned cry: 'Give light!'" (S91; A180–81).[27] Predictably, however, the second version appends another layer, one which readily admits to resolution: "The light may come with a blinding flash, but it is light none the less, and we can see" (A181). Out of darkness and negation emerge light and creativity for the author who has already transformed strife into everlasting peace.

Developing a more definitive measure of this ultimate sense of achievement, Besant employs the figurative language of water flow to convey her sense of equanimity. Not yet available to her when she pens *Sketches*, this language is reserved for *An Autobiography*. Here we find her summing up her adolescence accordingly: "[M]y life flowed smoothly, one current visible to all and dancing in the sunlight, the other running underground, but full and deep and strong" (A54). Later, she cheerfully observes, "The hidden life grew stronger, constantly fed by these streams of study; weekly communion became the centre round which my devotional life revolved, with its ecstatic meditation, its growing intensity of conscious contact with the Divine" (A57). Then, more ominously, she reports, "I drifted into an engagement with a man I did not pretend to love" (A70). In consequence, she concludes, "I sailed out of the safe harbour of my happy and peaceful girlhood on to the wide sea of life, and the waves broke roughly as soon as the bar was crossed" (A80–81). Throughout the remainder of her life story, Besant continued to compare rough with still waters as a reflection of the inward peace she has achieved no matter how turbulent the outer life. She begins the final paragraph of *An Autobiography* with these words of wisdom: "And thus I came through storm to peace, not to the peace of an untroubled sea of outer life, which no strong soul can crave, but to an inner peace that outer troubles may not avail to ruffle—a peace which belongs to the eternal not to the transitory, to the depths not to the shallows of life" (A363–64).

Self-referentiality may breed self-analysis and self-consciousness, but for Besant and other female creative negativists that propensity does not deny its opposite—self-effacement. As she deems it appropriate, Besant can also pull back the egoistic self in favor of the larger community or the greater good. She does so in *Sketches* primarily to protect her daughter from the wrenching partings she would have suffered by her mother's retaining visiting rights: "By effacing myself then, I saved her from a constant and painful struggle unfitted for childhood's passionate feelings, and left her only a memory that she loves, undefaced by painful remembrance of her mother insulted in her presence" (S168–69). In contrast, that private sacrifice is reconfigured in *An Autobiography* as a more public one,

one that now helps to explain part of Besant's motivation as a Socialist while looking ahead to the worldwide scale of rescuing mankind: "Resolutely I turned my back on [my children] that I might spare them trouble, and determined that, robbed of my own, I would be a mother to all helpless children I could aid, and cure the pain at my own heart by soothing the pain of others" (A220). This "mother of them all" could again have been predicted, in Besant's own terms, from her backward- and forward-looking perspective throughout *An Autobiography*: "Looking back to-day over my life, I see that its keynote—through all the blunders, and the blind mistakes, and clumsy follies—has been this longing for sacrifice to something felt as greater than the self" (A57). Continuing in the same vein, she reiterates in the third person, that it was "the wailings of the great orphan Humanity" that "drove her finally into the Theosophy that rationalises sacrifice, while opening up the possibilities of service beside which all other hopes grow pale" (A58).

That movement concurrently away from self while asserting the right of the self to act in the service of a larger sense of self is symbolized by use of various self-portraits and other photographs in the two versions of Besant's life story. Initially, in its serial guise, *Sketches* appeared without any visual accompaniment, but when it was published in book form in 1885 by the Freethought Press, an individually mounted mezzotint photograph of Besant taken by H. S. Mendelssohn appeared opposite the title page (see Figure 14). Wearing what became popularly known as her "lecturing costume," Besant stands serenely in three-quarter pose, gazing meditatively in the viewer's direction, her head haloed by a raised collar rimmed with pearls, her eyes seeming to see beyond the immediate present. That photograph is reproduced as a photogravure frontispiece for the first edition (second impression) of *An Autobiography* published by the Theosophical Society in 1894 (it is in the body of the text in the first impression published by T. Fisher Unwin in 1893), but this time the viewpoint pulls back to show more of the costume and both of her hands, one of which is resting on a desk or podium, while a potted bamboo plant stands to the right and behind her. The effect is more active, as it were, giving Besant a more solid three-dimensional form and practical substance, convincingly demonstrating the balanced merging of her spiritual and earthly identities. So once again *Sketches* recognizes and prefigures the evolution that *An Autobiography* confirms, while the latter text conveys that complex self that both is and is not of this world.

In addition, *An Autobiography* goes on to reproduce multiple images of Besant, alone and in the company of others, as well as her horoscope and portraits of Thomas Scott, Charles Bradlaugh, Henry Labouchere, and members of the Matchmakers' Union. These various illustrations depict Besant at different ages and in different contexts, especially in political and socialist terms, and thus they comment more fully on her sense of community and relationship than does the single image of *Sketches*. Yet there are also some curious omissions from this group of images. Conspicuous by their absence are depictions of any family members or of anything related to Theosophy except a photograph of Blavatsky in the 1893 first edition and one of her statue at Adyar in the second edition (1908). We can only assume that in her lifetime—there were two editions and five impressions through 1920—Besant guarded a measure of her privacy and her most intimate (although admittedly highly public) self-identification. In effect, she could control her daughter's story and her own coming home to Madame Blavatsky by rendering them primarily in the rhetoric that had become her personal voice and not exposing any of the participants to the intrusive visual gaze of the public at large. In fact, even the other individual and group shots that she provides are posed formally, already intended primarily for public consumption.

It was only some six years after her death, when the third edition was published in India, that Besant's more private images were employed. There are two impressions of this third edition, both made at Adyar, India, in 1939 and 1983; the significant personal images include one of Annie at sixteen and another of her with her mother (see Figure 13). Gone are most of the group configurations, replaced by a wider range of ages and more informal poses of Besant. Appropriately enough, Bradlaugh and Blavatsky (her infamous eyes staring hypnotically into the camera) constitute the only two other individual portraits. First and last, Besant now appears alone, yet prominently displaying Blavatsky's ring. Additional images are available through the Theosophical Society (London, Adyar, and Wheaton, Illinois), most notably one of Besant standing in the rain in Trafalgar Square, the shock of her uncovered white hair causing her to stand out from the other protesters who are hidden from view by a sea of umbrellas. This visual image recalls the one verbally evoked by Elizabeth Robins in her suffrage novel—serendipitously entitled *The Convert* (1907)—which I will be addressing in the next chapter in the context of Robins's unfinished biography of Besant as well as their shared contribution to the suffrage platform.

After *An Autobiography* develops in detail the trial for custody of her daughter (the section with which *Sketches* concludes), the second text proceeds through nearly a hundred more pages before coming to its final chapter, "Through Storm to Peace." While ostensibly serving to bring the reader up to date on Besant's political and social causes, these intermediate chapters look ahead not only to the Theosophist who will conclude this volume but the activist who will work for Home Rule in India in the four decades to follow. (See Figure 16 for a photograph of Besant when she had achieved international stature.) Reformulating her Socialist position in more general ethical terms, Besant thus declares her ded-

FIGURE 16. Annie Besant as elder statesman; photograph taken at Wimbledon in 1924 during her annual summer trip to London, when she was publicly honored for her fifty years of public service. With permission of the Theosophical Society, Wheaton, Illinois, and Adyar, India.

ication to helping all those who suffer from man's inhumanity to man in eloquent, dramatic apostrophe:

> O blind and mighty people, how my heart went out to you; trampled on,
> abused, derided, asking so little and needing so much; so pathetically grateful
> for the pettiest services; so loving and so loyal to those who offered you but
> their poor services and helpless love. Deeper and deeper into my innermost
> nature ate the growing desire to succour, to suffer for, to save. I had long given
> up my social reputation, I now gave up with ever-increasing surrender ease,
> comfort, time; the passion of pity grew stronger and stronger, fed by each new
> sacrifice, and each sacrifice led me nearer and nearer to the threshold of that
> gateway beyond which stretched a path of renunciation I had never dreamed
> of, which those might tread who were ready wholly to strip off self for Man's
> sake, who for Love's sake would surrender Love's return from those they
> served, and would go out into the darkness for themselves that they might,
> with their own souls as fuel, feed the Light of the World. (A317–18)[28]

The rhetoric of self-sacrifice and boundary-crossing here unite with the persistent strand of light imagery to prepare for her final proactive repose. Then, with
the advent of her final chapter, Besant appropriates the language of traditional
quest imagery, transfiguring it by conjoining it with morality and the so-called
new religion of Theosophy to fully confirm "the Ancient Wisdom":

> Still the quest of the Holy Grail exercises its deathless fascination, but the seekers
> no longer raise eyes to heaven, nor search over land and sea, for they know that it
> waits them in the suffering at their doors, that the consecration of the holiest is
> on the agonising masses of the poor and the despairing, the cup is crimson with
> the blood of the "People, the grey-grown speechless Christ." . . . If there be a
> faith that can remove the mountains of ignorance and evil, it is surely that faith in
> the ultimate triumph of Right in the final enthronement of Justice, which alone
> makes life worth the living, and which gems the blackest cloud of depression
> with the rainbow-coloured arch of an immortal hope. (A331)

This closing social and aesthetic invocation confirms Besant in her inherently
paradoxical mode as self-assertive and selfless worldwide leader for human rights
based on a program of shared goals and common understanding.

CONFOUNDING OR AMAZING?

Reading through the literature about Annie Besant, it is not difficult to come to
the conclusion that she has not been well served by most of her Western biographers, who I can only assume have not been reading her autobiographical

texts very carefully. One hope for unbiased accounting occurs in articles like Mark Bevir's "Annie Besant's Quest for Truth: Christianity, Secularism and New Age Thought" in *The Journal of Ecclesiastical History* (1999), which studies her life stages "in the context of the Victorian crisis of faith and the social concerns it helped raise" (62). In time, though, I suspect that she will be best understood by spiritual feminism.[29] For to read Besant's texts closely is to run the risk of being radicalized, maybe even converted to a succession of her belief systems, culminating with her grand vision for the future of the human race. The line of resistance to her siren song seems to have taken the form of personal attack and disparagement, chiefly through the charge or innuendo that she was easily swayed by others and always "needed a man in her life." These assaults uncannily resemble the jeering she had experienced on the platform and the derision of the mainstream press, so it is perhaps not so surprising that Besant knew to anticipate them in her self-writings. She answers these criticisms in advance for those who are willing to listen—who can discern her sincerity, consistency, and integrity. The self-questioning that consumes her prior to joining the Theosophical Society sums up her position succinctly, for it shows her unclouded recognition of the losses entailed by her choice:

> For I saw, distinct and clear—with painful distinctness, indeed—what that joining would mean. . . . Was I to plunge into a new vortex of strife, and make myself a mark for ridicule—worse than hatred—and fight for an unpopular truth? . . . Must I leave the army that had battled for me so bravely, the friends who through all brutality of social ostracism had held me dear and true? And [Charles Bradlaugh], the strongest and truest friend of all, whose confidence I had shaken by my Socialism—must he suffer the pang of seeing his co-worker, his co-fighter, of whom he had been so proud, to whom he had been so generous, go over to the opposing hosts, and leave the ranks of Materialism? (A342–43)[30]

Equally important, this passage does not mark Besant as the antagonist who loves a good fight and always needs another cause—with its male leadership—to champion. It instead exposes a tired, compassionate "soldier," one who takes the next necessary step in her evolution even if it means hurting those she loves because she cannot deny a greater truth.

All along Besant has been noting and underscoring, with increasing self-insight and audience awareness, the underlying logic of her social and spiritual evolution, yet she still realizes that she needs to address directly the criticisms that continue to be leveled at her, criticisms that will haunt her life story as rendered by biographers in the many decades to come. It is in this knowing spirit that she openly asserts, "I have been told that I plunged headlong into Theosophy and let my enthusiasm carry me away. I think the charge is true, in so far as the decision was swiftly taken; but it had been long led up to, and realised the dreams of childhood on the higher planes of intellectual womanhood" (A345). What more can she say on this point? To say more would be to incur the critique of her detractors that she is being repetitious and even defensive, yet history has borne out her prescience in recognizing the necessity of risking overstatement to the resistant reader. To the reader or listener willing to trace her steps, Besant was more than generous in her explanations and explications, as witnessed in her two autobiographical accountings, two lectures which she delivered and then subsequently reprinted entitled "Why I Became a Theosophist," and the entire body of her writings on Theosophy that followed over the remaining four decades of her fully-lived lifetime.[31]

In this context, it is fascinating to introduce the tension between Besant and George Bernard Shaw, a tension that transcended Besant's death and continued to resurface in Shaw's repeated jibes at her seriousness of purpose and her ultimate success. Nine years his senior, Besant was in fact responsible for the young Shaw finding a periodical audience and financial security. She arranged for serialization in *Our Corner* of two of his unpublished novels, namely *The Irrational Knot* (about the marriage tie) and *Love among the Artists*, as well as signing him on as a regular contributor to the column entitled "Art Corner."[32] Their friendship deepened, although he remained jealous of the influence of the "other men" in her life—co-workers and collaborators like freethinker and radical Bradlaugh, editorial assistant John Mackinnon Robertson (later a Member of Parliament of considerable stature), fellow scientist Edward Aveling, editor and co-seeker William Thomas Stead, and reformer-turned-Theosophist Herbert Burrows. But collaboration was not really a concept that Shaw could fathom. He was too much of an individualist and an egotist to work in equal partnership with anyone, least of all a strong woman, in actuality a Superwoman who could outperform his Superman. Even in a movement that espoused cooperation, namely the Fabianism to which Shaw nominated Besant in membership, he remained competitive, and when Besant moved beyond the more moderate Fabians to embrace what Socialism fully entailed, he expressed exasperation and a sense of betrayal.

After Besant's deconversion to Theosophy, Shaw found an outlet for his contradictory feelings about her in his portrayal of the character Raina Petkoff in his play *Arms and the Man* (1894). Besant's idealism gets transformed into a mixture of Romanticism and realistic self-knowledge in this heroine, whose "noble attitude" and "thrilling voice" provoke both mockery and admiration from the practical but equally Romantic Swiss mercenary, Captain Bluntschli.[33] This role very much captures Shaw's own position. Torn between seeing Besant as a genuine reformer and a quixotic dreamer, he fights to resist her charisma even as he is compelled to appreciate it. We can gain some insight into his understanding of this melodrama of male-female relations (and perhaps his personal feelings about Besant) by reading his correspondence with the actress Lillah McCarthy, who played the part of Raina in the play's 1907 revival. Ranting about McCarthy's failure on opening night to carry "dramatic indignation to the point of totally forgetting your clothes"—because she still does not "sweep with a sufficiently majestic unconsciousness of them"—Shaw launches into an even more vitriolic attack a month later, when he declaims that "Raina has gone to bits" because she is no longer on her "high horse." "What Raina wants," he goes on to explain, "is the extremity of style—style—Comédie Française, Queen of Spain style. Do you hear, worthless wretch that you are?—STYLE."[34] Hands-on about the productions of his plays, Shaw nonetheless seems even more carried away here than usual, as if he indeed has a living model he is trying to approximate, someone with whom he has a longstanding love-hate relationship.

Four decades later—fourteen years after Besant's death, only four before his own, and the centenary year of her birth—the perennially pugnacious Shaw felt constrained to challenge an article in *The Freethinker* and to assert his own active role in her deconversion to Theosophy.[35] Entitled "Annie Besant and the 'Secret Doctrine'" (1947), Shaw's response tries to rewrite the history of Besant's reviewing of Blavatsky's *Secret Doctrine* at the request of Stead. Ignoring (or perhaps unaware of) the accounts published by all three participants, he insists on attacking Stead as "a complete Philistine" and casting himself in the rescuing role that Besant had earlier played for him. Yet Shaw's assessment was privately countered and Stead's sensitivity confirmed in a letter Stead wrote to Blavatsky (8 December 1888), in which he also acknowledged that "you have a genius quite transcendent, and an extraordinary aptitude for both literature and propagandism, which the rest of your fellow-creatures may well envy." Meanwhile, Besant went on to report in *An Autobiography* that she reviewed the Blavatsky text for *The Pall Mall Gazette* (25 April 1889) explicitly at Stead's behest, requesting from him as well "an introduction to the writer" so that she might send a note "asking to be allowed to call" (A308–10).[36]

According to his rewritten scenario, Shaw declares that it was he who turned the review assignment over to Besant out of concern for her "serious want of money" and the fact that it was "a huge tome which I contemplated with dismay." Given Shaw's gratitude to William Archer for doing the same for him by planting him on the reviewer roster of *The Pall Mall Gazette*, it is not hard to see in this account a retrospective desire to repay a long-held debt to Besant for boosting his career in journalism. And it was hardly the first time that Shaw had misremembered his earlier history in such a public way. In 1938 he was responsible for the Limited Editions Club's publication of Charles Dickens's *Great Ex-*

pectations with its original manuscript ending as the final chapter, but he accomplished this feat despite his attempt to trace that ending through his false memory of having read it in novel form as a child. It would seem that he had somehow conflated his disappointment with the revised conclusion recommended to Dickens by Bulwer Lytton with a passage in John Forster's 1870 biography that reproduced Dickens's original intention.[37]

Continuing with his revisionist history about Besant's conversion to Theosophy, Shaw goes on to report that he had been "utterly confounded" by reading Besant's 1889 article in the *Star* entitled "How I Became a Theosophist." "I had done a trick I never intended," he confesses, though not without some pride in his apparent influence despite his face-to-face accusation that "she was quite mad." He was, however, disturbed by her jocular response, all the more so because he found it uncharacteristic: "She said she supposed that since she had, as a Theosophist, become a vegetarian, her mind may have been affected." (Shaw was himself notoriously vegetarian.) Then, after declaring that this occasion marked "the end of our collaboration" and that their "separation was entirely of her doing," Shaw launches into the oft-quoted tirade that has fueled the negative rhetoric of many of Besant's detractors:

> Like all great public speakers she was a born actress. She was successively a
> Puseyite Evangelical, an Atheist Bible-smasher, a Darwinian Secularist, a Fabian
> Socialist, a Strike Leader, and finally a Theosophist, exactly as Mrs. Siddons was
> a Lady Macbeth, Lady Randolph, Beatrice, Rosalind, and Volumnia. She "saw
> herself" as a priestess above all: That was how Theosophy held her to the end.
> There was a different leading man every time: Bradlaugh, Robertson, Aveling,
> Shaw, and Herbert Burrows. That did not matter.
>
> Whoever does not understand this as I, a playwright, do, will never under-
> stand the career of Annie Besant. ("Annie Besant and the 'Secret Doctrine'"
> 450)

In spite of himself, Shaw here pays tribute to Besant's great powers of oratory, but his "actress" label misses the point that she had been repeatedly making about the nature of her deconversion process. Not giving credence to her self-accountings (again, possibly because he has never read them), he provides his own rationale in the language of the theatre, his false analogy suggesting that she took on a jumbled assortment of roles, not the successive ones that she so carefully researched and agonized over.

As for Shaw's intimations regarding her "leading men," Besant seems to have had a precise rebuttal in mind over half a century prior to his attempt to impugn her character:

I may add that such shafts are specially pointless against myself. A woman who thought her way out of Christianity and Whiggism into Freethought and Radicalism absolutely alone; who gave up every old friend, male and female, rather than resign the beliefs she had struggled to in solitude; who, again in embracing active Socialism, has run counter of the views of her nearest "male friends"; such a woman may very likely go wrong, but I think she may venture, without conceit, to at least claim independence of judgment. (A316)

The integrity and independence that Shaw denies for Besant are manifest in her lifetime struggles and her self-writing. That so many of her contemporaries as well as most biographers should fail to see these qualities speaks more to their own efforts to resist the strength of her argument and the potency of her rhetoric than anything else.

On a more constructive note, it is worth our while to observe how Besant's spiritual journey resembles one of popular culture's most widely loved female quests, namely L. Frank Baum's *The Wonderful Wizard of Oz* (1900). Apart from the actual connections between Baum and Theosophy, Dorothy's multiple challenges in the land of Oz, the interplay between reality and illusion, and her spirited desire to return home all find parallels in the experiences and self-recording of Besant's complex life story. Moreover, at least one literary critic reads Baum's tale as a Theosophical allegory. Specifically citing Besant's and Blavatsky's metaphorical description of the quest to find Truth, John Algeo makes the connection fairly explicit: "There is a Road, steep and thorny, beset with perils of every kind, but yet a Road, and it leads to the very heart of the universe."[38] Algeo goes on to summarize, "Dorothy's quest is for salvation, liberation, enlightenment, freedom from birth and death" (295), adding, "If there is a 'moral' to *The Wonderful Wizard of Oz*, this is it: we must rely on ourselves, for we alone have the power to save ourselves" (297). Besant's real strength lay in precisely that ability to combine self-reliance with a relentless pursuit of the truth synonymous with ultimate liberation.

Controversial in life and death, Besant continues to vex would-be biographers with her rich complexities. The best accounts—because fairest and closest to the experience of their subject—reproduce at length her own words. At the same time, they also support the position that no accounting can be definitive, that we as would-be readers of such a complex life story need to track it down from multiple sources, putting together a narrative of our own making even as we recognize that it will need to be reformulated again and again.[39] In trying to tell the story of the multiple deconversions of Annie Wood Besant, I have followed a much more winding trail of resources than was the case for the other creative negativists I have been studying. More has been written about her, of course, because she had such a broadly based public career, but by the same to-ken there have been more veils thrown over her activities and the assessments of them. Serving so many different agendas, Annie Wood Besant has appeared in multiple guises, which have in turn obscured her all-too-singular multiplicity. Without engaging in hagiography ourselves, I think we can join with my col-league Desley Deacon, who speaks with quiet amazement of lives so lived: "You just gaze in wonder."[40]

5.   Elizabeth Robins Outperforms the New Woman

An awed witness to Annie Besant's last appearance at the Hall of Science in 1891, Elizabeth Robins (1862–1952) recognized in her a sister performance artist. In fact, Robins's career embodies all the components of performative autobiography: she was an actress who performed and who directed other women, an episodic biographer and autobiographer, a writer of plays and novels drawing on personal emotional experience, and a spokeswoman for the women's movement. Yet the combination of autobiography and performance is deliberately, even inherently, problematic. A traditional autobiography is in a sense the opposite of a performance. Historically a male construct, the autobiography has tended to involve an epic effort at self-crystallization, a period distinctly separated in time, existing outside the autobiographer's present experience. In contrast, performance—and women's lives—could be described as ephemeral, aleatory (improvised), working more through surfaces and effects than from concepts and solidity. Thus, for Robins (as for most women) autobiography has needed to take a new form, with characteristics akin to those of performance, evolving its own distinctive traits. Piecemeal, rife with multiple selves, female autobiography is comfortable with internal contradictions. It accepts above all the employment of surrogate autobiographies—the use of others' lives, others' performances—to reflectively evoke one's own multiplicity.

American born and educated, Robins played over three hundred roles in two old-fashioned stock companies, touring in romantic melodrama with the father of Eugene O'Neill and acting Shakespeare with Edwin Booth, before she settled down on her own in London in 1888. Born in Louisville, Kentucky, Robins spent her early years on Staten Island before entering Putnam Female Seminary in Zanesville, Ohio, in 1872. Despite family protests, she became an actress, first with James O'Neill's traveling company in 1881 and then with the Boston Museum Theatre, where she met and then married fellow actor George Parks in 1885 (see Figure 17 for a photograph of Robins from this time period). Upon learning about their marriage, Robins's manager did not renew her contract, forcing her to return to the touring circuit. Meanwhile, her mother's mental health had deteriorated to the point that she had to be institutionalized, and, within two years of Robins's long-distance marriage, her depressive husband committed suicide by throwing himself over a bridge on the Charles River. Grief-stricken at Parks's death and overworked by nationwide theatrical touring (this time with Booth and Lawrence Barrett), Robins sought a change by traveling to Norway and London with her good friend Sara Bull in 1888. Welcomed by such powerful luminaries as actor-manager Herbert Beerbohm Tree and playwright-novelist Oscar Wilde, Robins decided to make London her home.

There she excelled in her Ibsen roles but increasingly became critical of the elements of patriarchy still present in his plays. Robins started out in 1889 with the part of Martha Bernick in *The Pillars of Society*, which she followed up with the role of Mrs. Linden in *A Doll's House* two years later (Marie Fraser played Nora). Ibsen productions were already being met with considerable resistance by the public, including most of the theatre reviewers. But Robins accomplished a real breakthrough for both herself and the playwright with her stellar première performance on the London stage of the lead character in *Hedda Gabler*, its 1891 production under the joint management of Robins and her sometime collaborator, Marion Lea. By now Robins was even involved in translating Ibsen, not only to create the best possible acting text but also to insure that the female voices were rendered with more nuance. The year 1893 saw another success for her in *The Master Builder*, for which she enacted the role of Hilda Wangel, who ushers in the modern spirit. A significant shift occurred during the course of that year as Robins went on to co-write with Florence Bell their own New Woman play, *Alan's Wife*, for which Robins played the highly controversial title role. The play's immediate closure testifies to the public's (and critics') aversion to forbidden topics like infanticide and euthanasia.[1] Robins proceeded to play leading roles in the premières of Ibsen's next two plays, *Little Eyolf* (1896) and *John Gabriel Borkman* (1897), but by 1899 she was stating her express disillusionment with his last play, *When We Dead Awaken*, consenting to participate only in its copyright reading, pointedly not participating in its eventual English performance (1903).

Since her arrival in Britain, Robins had been a fixture on the London stage. Besides her Ibsen roles throughout the nineties, she played a wide variety of parts from melodrama to Shakespeare, often under her own co-management, but, discouraged by Ibsen's final offering at the end of her Ibsen decade, when she was also preparing to write novels under her own name, Robins acted in only two

FIGURE 17.   Elizabeth Robins (1862–1952) in costume for the New York production of James Albery's play *Forgiven* (ca. 1882). Later a cigarette card and, at Bernard Shaw's goading, the frontispiece to one of her autobiographical accountings, *Both Sides of the Curtain* (1940).

more professional productions. Both in 1902, these final performances were in Stephen Phillips' *Paolo and Francesca* and the adaptation of Mrs. Henry Wood's novel *Eleanor*. Robins continued to juggle her multiple roles in a range of genres and venues: increasingly behind the curtain as a playwright; regularly writing novels as well as contributing to the women's movement; and always trying to bring to fruition numerous auto/biographical accounts, including her unpublished biography of Annie Besant. From the outset of her dramatic engagements, Robins found herself dealing with a number of men who ruled the London stage from various angles and positions of power. Besides falling in and out of rapport with actor-managers like Beerbohm Tree and Charles Wyndham, she discovered herself in an antagonistic relationship with novelist-playwright George Bernard Shaw, an equivocal friendship with would-be playwright Henry James, and a close alliance with theatre critic and Ibsen translator William Archer.

The new century witnessed Robins carrying out her ideals in the social and political realms, primarily by writing and staging *Votes for Women!* (1907), which she concurrently adapted as the novel *The Convert*. Her involvement with the women's suffrage movement began slowly and carefully, for she shared with her heroine Vida Levering an initial aversion to speaking in public for a cause that aroused such belligerent opposition. But Robins, too, experienced her own conversion to this kind of ideological performance, as recorded in her publication of *Way Stations* (1913), for which she gathered together most of her suffrage speeches as well as a variety of her articles published in both England and America. Meanwhile, Robins had been active as a novelist. Before the turn of the century, she had published four works of fiction under the pseudonym "C. E. Raimond," namely *George Mandeville's Husband* (1894), *The New Moon* (1895), *Below the Salt and Other Stories* (1896; American title *The Fatal Gift of Beauty and Other Stories*), and *The Open Question: A Tale of Two Temperaments* (1898). Then, after journeying to Alaska and rescuing her younger brother Raymond in 1900, she began publishing articles and novels under her own name, starting with the Alaskan novels *The Magnetic North* (1904) and *Come and find Me* (1908). She proceeded to produce another eight volumes of fiction at a steady pace: *A Dark Lantern* (1905), *The Florentine Frame* (1909), *My Little Sister* (1913; British title *Where Are You Going To . . . ?*), *Camilla* (1918), *The Messenger* (1919), *The Mills of the Gods and Other Stories* (1920), *Time Is Whispering* (1923), and *The Secret That Was Kept* (1926). By the 1920s, Robins began to focus on collecting her own writings about the "Woman Question" in her anonymous edition, *Ancilla's Share: An Indictment of Sex Antagonism* (1924). And, as always, she continued to probe her own experiences in a series of autobiographical forays, ending with *Raymond and I*, published posthumously by Leonard Woolf in 1956.

In her personal relationships, Robins valued her independence but relished the wide variety of alliances she was able to maintain. Perhaps feeling guilt about her husband's suicide (there are reasons to believe that she may have had an abortion), she kept his memory alive in her private records. Some of the men in London whose advances she regularly rejected implied that this early experience with Parks made her reluctant to consider marriage again, or even to engage in a heterosexual affair. Archer may have been the exception to these assumptions. A theatre critic of considerable merit, he had laid the groundwork for the acceptance of Ibsen's *oeuvre* in Britain and America, as well as advising and supporting Robins in her theatrical endeavors. If he hadn't already had a wife, it seems quite plausible that Robins might have married him. Moreover, although no evidence survives to confirm their conjecture, several Robins scholars speculate that she and Archer did consummate what was at the very least an emotionally intimate affair. Despite these speculations, it is clear that Robins did not enjoy the pursuit of a bevy of would-be male lovers, usually preferring the company of other women, especially if they could collaborate to achieve artistic or social goals. In particular, she formed a close friendship with a woman some twenty-five years her junior, Octavia Wilberforce, whose medical education she financed. Together they converted Robins's home, Backsettown Farm (Sussex), into a woman's shelter that remained in operation for over sixty years. Again the sexual nature of the relationship remains uncertain, largely because Robins worked so hard to preserve her privacy, although the emotional bonds were obviously extremely intense, eventually to the point of obsession on Wilberforce's part.[2]

Upon reevaluating Robins's theatrical performances, I am convinced that she sought to induce in members of her many audiences a dissolution of inner boundaries. At its most intense, this process might result in the experience of synaesthesia or of perceptual delusion. More broadly, her autobiographical performances could provoke in audiences something akin to a conversion experience. Robins's acting crossed the boundary line between what occurs and what is seen. Some members of her audiences had "false memories"—virtually hallucinatory experiences—of what actually took place on the stage. For her own part, Robins always found points of identification in her roles. As the lead character she played in her drama *Alan's Wife*, for example, Robins reconnected with her own impetus to oppose the status quo—to seek both intensity and extreme situations. The kind of life-changing events that preoccupied Robins involved the dissolution of subjective boundaries, at times even the merging of opposites, and her aesthetic was developed to induce just such a dissolution. If T. S. Eliot's "objective correlative" implies the conveyance of a relatively static inner experience through an objectively perceived image or symbol, Robins's more dynamic technique acted as a "subjective correlative"—a process of infecting audience members with an uncomfortable inner change.

Feminist performance critic Sue-Ellen Case has elected to describe what she calls a "feminine morphology," or structure, accordingly: "It can be elliptical rather than illustrative, fragmentary rather than whole, ambiguous rather than clear, and interrupted rather than complete. . . . [I]t abandons the hierarchical organising-principles of traditional form that served to elide women from discourse."[3] In particular, these distinctions allow us to view Robins performing Ibsen's New Women anew, seeing in these performances a form of surrogate autobiography that provides her and her audiences—male and female—with multiple opportunities to explore new subjectivities. After examining Robins's extended commentary about her Ibsen years, prompted by the occasion of the 1928 centennial celebration of his birth, I proceed in this chapter to explore how her autobiographical and biographical impulses often interact, even conflate, as she develops various projects designed to come to terms with both "the atom that was I" and her sense of the larger female community that connects all women in a collective identity.[4] In this respect, Robins's unpublished biography of Annie Besant provides a prime case in point, especially as the biographer sees in her subject a shared propensity to perform one's life, encouraging Robins to disclose her own ability to co-conspire with a sister creative negativist by interrogating how extreme emotions can cross apparently impassable boundary lines. Next I take up three of Robins's most powerful boundary-crossing texts, namely *Alan's Wife*, *Votes for Women!*, and *The Convert*, in order to demonstrate her amazing ability to transcend limitations that have so long confined women to passive roles. These examples compel me to analyze her aesthetic technique as combining the use of synaesthesia and an inverted form of Eliot's objective correlative that I am calling subjective correlative. Finally, I look to Robin's empathy with other performative women and her astute collaborative enterprises as the key components in her drive to construct a worldwide feminist community.

IBSEN AND THE NEW WOMAN

The concept of the "New Woman" emerged near the turn of the last century, in the 1880s and 1890s, and it was invoked again at the end of the twentieth century. "New," "odd," "wild," "superfluous," these women didn't posit marriage, children, and home as their chief goal, and hence they were considered sexually suspect. Perceived as committing transgressions against gender and class distinctions, they transformed themselves from "relative creatures" to independent women.[5] Resultant fear-mongering postulated the second fall of man, and cries of nihilism could be heard emanating from the status quo. Elaine Showalter is just one of several culture critics who has noted the parallels between the change of century then and the subsequent change of millennium a hundred years later.[6] What is perhaps the most significant recursion here lies with women who choose to be creatively independent. Into this expanded comparative arena I elect to insert Elizabeth Robins. Robins outperformed the moral, social, and artistic boundary-crossing of the New Woman that was already considered outrageous by her contemporaries by moving both inward to a neurological, basic, or core fusion and outward to co-conspirators in other performing women like Annie Besant and Marie Bashkirtseff. This scenario puts into perspective Henrik Ibsen's innovations and limitations in portraying the New Woman in the first place: he could approach but not finally fulfill the actress in Robins. In point of fact, his genius merely inspired her own.[7]

Elizabeth Robins went beyond even what the New Woman was said to do in part by being not only the première Ibsen actress of her time but by outgrowing the playwright who helped define her contribution to the stage. Robins could be said to go beyond the New Woman by not just doing things singly or one-dimensionally. As with her own New Woman play, *Alan's Wife*, she combined and built upon her multiple roles. Inspired by what women usually do anyway, Robins reenergized the female relational experience by her own creative leaps and bounds. In effect, Robins evinces an extra quality—something outside or above her immediate environment, providing a larger perspective—which encourages her to transcend and cross boundaries, leading her to exceed even the outstanding accomplishments of her New Woman peers. And this extra dimension in her lifework informs her autobiographical performance of creative negativity.

Robins's *Ibsen and the Actress*, published by Virginia and Leonard Woolf in 1928, shows her recognizing in Ibsen "a bundle of unused possibilities" (18). In effect, we could say, she saw more in Ibsen than he saw himself. Certainly Robins saw more to espouse in Ibsen than did most of her male contemporaries.[8] For example, Herbert Beerbohm Tree rewrote *A Doll's House* (1889) so that Krogstad could star as its villain (making Dr. Stockman a comic entertainer to boot), while critic Clement Scott attacked the lead role of Nora (played by Janet Achurch) as an exemplar of the "New Creed"—"a mass of aggregate conceit and self sufficiency who leaves her home and deserts her friendless children because she has *herself* to look after" (*Theatre*, July 1889). Intuitively, then with increasing self-consciousness, Robins responded to the multifarious prospects set in motion by Ibsen, scanning her personal and professional environments for the elements which served her as openings—the means to forge connections, to discover soul mates. Noting that "Ibsen still seems to me to side with the actress" (19), Robins seized upon his work for the "acting opportunity" it provided in general and accepted the specific challenge of *Hedda Gabler* (1891) for "the need to put meaning in [a woman's] life" (21). Even more particularly, Robins was intrigued by the awareness she shared with Hedda about what the ability to commit suicide might mean for a woman: "The power to end it rather than accept certain slaveries," in other words, the power to escape from a slavery that seemed so unreal to most men that they judged it to be mere "melodrama" (30). Intriguingly, Robins was compelled by growth out of negativity, by someone "so *alive* as Hedda" contemplating suicide (31).

"How should men understand Hedda on the stage," Robins astutely asked, "when they didn't understand her in the persons of their wives, their daughters, their women friends?" (18). Yet somehow Robins made them accept her even if they could not understand her. Rising above the prejudices of male actor-managers, who expressed "indifference" and "loathing" for *Hedda* and derided it as merely "a woman's play" (15), Robins and Marion Lea acquired the acting rights to the drama and decided to co-produce it in 1891, further collaborating with translators Sir William Gosse and William Archer to make it a "more speakable version for stage use" (16). Winning over some of her most resistant critics with a vehicle she had made very much her own set Robins up for her next Ibsen triumph as Hilda Wangel in *The Master Builder* (1893). One might even say she enlisted the playwright himself in her creative endeavor, for as she later acknowledged, "More than anybody who ever wrote for the stage, Ibsen could, and usually did, collaborate with his actors" (52). Without mentioning Robins specifically, Ibsen had once reversed the terms, for she cites him as finding in the generic actor a "fellow-creator" (53).

At the time, Robins said that Ibsen had "nothing to do with the New Woman" (32) — although with hindsight we could argue that this was all part of the larger picture that feminism posits when it seeks equality and freedom for both women and men. Instead, at this point, Robins reported that the Ibsen experience had "everything to do . . . with the art of acting" (33). Actresses had been starved throughout the nineteenth century for good roles; all the best roles were reserved for men, usually the actor-managers. But finally, women had the sense of "playing with the full orchestra," as her friend Marion Lea said, her expression once again evoking multiplicity (34). Robins even saw her perplexing friend, George Bernard Shaw, as capable of heightening and prolonging the value of an Ibsen actress through his own plays. Each time a new Ibsen play came out, there was a competition among actresses as to who would get the leading role: "The actress"—namely Robins herself, speaking here for all performing women—"recognized [an Ibsen character] as life—the kind of life that is most real in the theatre, that breathes freest on the stage" (39). And, we might add, the surrogate self embodied in the Ibsen character—the illusion that becomes reality for the actress—inspired Robins and the women of her era off-stage equally well.

BIOGRAPHY OR AUTOBIOGRAPHY?

In Joanne E. Gates's 1994 biography of Robins, the biographer utilizes such key expressions as "multiple identity," "double duty," "competing obligations," and "duality of her own voice" to describe her subject.[9] These terms highlight the mechanics of the female quest as it exists within a woman's lifetime—and the difficulties inherent in narrating "her-story." As further support for this contention, I can point to Robins's 1875 childhood story, "The Herstory of a Button."[10] Surely it is unusual for a girl-child, especially at this time period, to compose an autobiographical feminist parody of female education. Although Robins spent the last twenty-four years of her life working on multiple autobiographical and biographical projects, she brought to the public only three scattered volumes of memoirs, leaving the majority of her self-accounts unfinished or unpublished. Aptly, Angela John has chosen to title each of the part-divisions of her full-length biography of Robins with the appropriate name by which Robins was best known at its given time: Bessie, Lisa, C. E. Raimond (her pseudonym), Elizabeth, E. R., and Anonymous. Robins even evaded a sense of singular self in the playful composition of her will: "I have a constitutional unwillingness to letting people know what seems to be the real 'me.' . . . I must content myself with trying to warn my relations and my friends that they will not find me or any explanation of me in any one's description or in any letter or diary of my own. I have partly deliberately and partly unconsciously 'cooked' my accounts" (16 March 1895; Fales: Series 1C, box 13, folder 2). Her reticence to settle on a delimited identity, a reluctance that is one of the by-products of creative negativity, resulted in a repeated re-creation of the self, the tendency to continually transcend inner as well as outer boundaries.

In keeping with this self-recreative propensity, Robins was working out different kinds of autobiographical statements or position papers, as it were. This piecemeal approach contrasts with the totalizing attempts of contemporary male autobiographers, such as Walter Besant and H. G. Wells, for whom narrating "his"-story was a much more straightforward affair; for them, the separation between nonfiction and fiction was a more ready assumption. Robins's published autobiographical accountings represent a range of genres in themselves: a lecture for the Royal Society of Arts, under the auspices of the British Drama League, produced *Ibsen and the Actress* in 1928; correspondence with Henry James led to an edition of their epistolary history in *Theatre and Friendship* in 1932; and a desire to record more fully her early years in London, to tell more than just the story of an Ibsen actress, finally resulted in *Both Sides of the Curtain* in 1940. Yet, at the same time, many other autobiographical writings—including an epic-length, three-volume autobiographical novel—never reached the public. Robins's correspondence with Virginia Woolf in fact details the challenges to her self-writing from frequent interruption.[11] For all the while, Robins continued to act, stage-manage, and write plays, novels, and other polemics related to the women's movement.

The sheer amount of Robins's incomplete or unpublished autobiographical renderings bears testimony to her undaunted efforts to tackle all the pieces of her life story. For example, even though she successfully published recollections about touring with the Barrett–Booth company (*Universal Review*, 1890), her two follow-up pieces—"An American Actress at Amergau [Oberammergau]" (1890) and "An American Actress at Balmoral Castle; or, A Close up View of Queen Victoria and the English Stage" (1895)—met with no interest from the periodical press. Within fifteen years, she was at it again, this time with an autobiographical trilogy entitled "Theodora; or, The Pilgrimage" (1910–1911), which she subdivided into "A Study in Egoism," "Theodora at Home," and "Theo on Stage." Robins intended this "composite portrait" to take her self-writing through her choice of profession, to show how the tension between career and passion played out on the American scene.[12] Picking up the controversies surrounding her Hedda Gabler role, Robins originally planned "Wither and How," which exists in several typewritten drafts (Fales 7A.78.1), as the final chapter of *Both Sides of the Curtain*, but because of its length, the chapter developed into what Robins later hoped would be published as a sequel volume. This particular unpublished typescript actually provided biographer Gates with the raw material to create an extended scene of dialogue between Robins and Marion Lea at the home of Edmund Gosse for Gates's study of Robins, itself a text that experiments with multiple genres to tell a life story. As a title, "Wither and How" is also eerily reminiscent of *Man: Whence, How and Where*, co-authored by Annie Besant and C. W. Leadbeater in 1913, the year after Robins and Besant shared the stage together at the Albert Hall. Robins continued to mine her autobiographical materials throughout her lifetime, sometimes even putting a fictional guise on her personal experiences to provide telling examples for her feminist political agenda.

If the creative negativist perceives and intuitively treats herself—any self—as ever-changing, then perhaps Robins found constructing biography just as problematical in terms of form and content as creating autobiography. Conversely, experimentation with one form could produce insights into the other. Biography, of course, has affinities and overlaps with both autobiography and fiction, as Rachel Brownstein, author of *Tragic Muse: Rachel of the Comédie Française* (1993), emphasized in her keynote address to the Hofstra 1994 Women in Theatre Conference.[13] Robins directly challenged herself on these questions, variously writing notes and observations to herself on "The Art of Biography" and

"Fiction versus Biography" (Fales 7C.87–88). On the subject of biography, she records the following consideration that inevitably slides over into autobiography: "Of the cloud of witnesses to this individual life some of the best have been women. Those that I personally prefer have come from women who had not before made writing their business" ("The Art of Biography"). Then, on another occasion, Robins comments to herself, "To turn from Biography to fiction is like being let out of school." As she continues in this vein, she assumes a second-person address to an unspecified but personalized reader, providing a window into the creative process she empathetically shares with that unknown reader and potential fellow writer:

> If you are accustomed to the pleasing exercise of story telling[,] you know well those gentle slaves of one's invention. They are so ready to do their best, to feed the creator's illusion of the power to shape and sway all things to the writer's will. You are tempted to think of the novel as a tractable beast of burden[,] a poor ambling ass in comparison to this untamed Arab, that refuses to obey the bridle of the rider's wishes and carries him where he will. ("Fiction versus Biography")

An intriguing case study of Robins's approach to both biography and autobiography exists in her extensive notes, manuscripts, and typescript drafts about Annie Besant, whose multiple deconversions, as I have argued, mark her as another re-creator of the self. Clearly, Robins was writing an extended memoir of Besant, with whom she found considerable empathy and rapport. (Other Robins "little portraits" unfinished, unpublished, or printed for private circulation include those of Alice Duër Miller, Bret Harte, Dorothy Grey, Oscar Wilde, W. T. Stead, Gertrude Bell, and Elizabeth Thompson.) Throughout the typescript drafts of her Besant biography, Robins maintains a first-person perspective that shows her self-reflective examination of this other life she sets before herself. In particular, she recognizes in Besant someone who was "ready to do what few men in public life have dared. She was never afraid to say she had been mistaken. She could turn round on her old self, look at it with cleared vision, leave it like a cast off cloak by the wayside and press on—without the cloak."[14] That ability to leave the past behind and create herself newly, to deconvert as decidedly as to convert, is what Robins admires in Besant and in herself, and what she fails to find in so many of the men she encounters. Willing in the course of her account to variously identify with Besant, Robins comes to value Besant's achievement, thereby realizing that insight demands a willingness to see through another's eyes, to risk the conversion process itself: "It might be a Something which, for understanding, required a new and different set of perceptions."

In describing one of Besant's key appearances, her final hearing sponsored by the Secularists at St. James's Hall in 1891 (soon after Besant had become a Theosophist), Robins evokes her as a kindred spirit.[15] Assuming the role of both the dramatist and the theatre-reviewer, Robins begins by placing herself in the scene and describing its parameters. "I was there early," she reports, "watched the place fill, saw people jostling for standing-room." She establishes an initial feeling of multifariousness by describing the huge crowd that is without a center, while at the same time emphasizing the potential confrontation with negativity in the crowd's growing impatience:

> But the crowd inside was less disposed to wait after the advertized time. Those in no mood to be patient began to argue, and drum with their feet. As I heard that old warning of sinister significance to player-folk, I listened with new concern to the talk that ran about. A feeling of dread came over me as though I had been the woman back there behind the scenes who had been given her cue, and did not pick it up. Every second she delayed she was losing ground with the audience.

But eventually a focal point emerges with Besant's actual appearance: "A statuesque figure swathed in white silk was moving slowly down toward the footlights." Robins then blends reality and illusion, seeing Besant as an "apparition," before she effects a shift in perspective or magnitude by zooming back, separating out Besant's voice and calling her a "white shining presence." Finally participating in a sudden self-referentiality or framing, the memorialist eschews content in favor of the vividly recalled form of the evening's events: "But, as I find so often in reviewing the past, I seem to keep with curious vividness the picture, the voice, above all the feeling of a scene but few of the words and for the most part only those deeply charged with passion." Ultimately she concludes:

> As I say, I have to go to others for the words [of the speech], but I remember, as though it happened last night that while she was speaking, the audience hardly noticed that she was moving backward. Or, if some noticed, they must have waited in all confidence for the moment when with some tremendous word, she would come down stage. And then—a thing that took your breath. On the fall of a sentence, the white vision melted through the arrangement of screens at the back—. She was gone.
>
> The second's stupefaction exploded in a scene unforgettable though I find no record of it in print. It is hard to believe people would care so fanatically to-day. They made me wonder what they would do to her! It was impossible to go home till I was sure she had really escaped from the Hall and not been caught in the mob outside. I remember only moving about among a protesting crowd and nothing more.

Besant's disappearing trick feeds into Robins's own sense of the dramatic moment, a moment so astonishing that it apparently confounded the ordinary rules
of reporting, its official unreportability lending it some of the status of myth.
When elements of creative negativity fuse in this manner, the result is akin to a
mini-creation myth. Taken together, such inchoate myths constitute the form-
less cycle of the prototypical female quest-story I too have been relating.

Robins and Besant later shared the platform at a public meeting in the Albert Hall on 15 June 1912. The would-be biographer of Besant builds toward her
account by declaring, "It has not been easy—it is impossible even with the ten-
league boots of synopsis—to keep pace with the main events of her Pilgrimage." Then she begins the description itself. Facing an audience of some twelve
thousand people for or against the measure "Votes for Women," Robins reports that she and Besant were the only two among all the practiced speakers
who were heard "in every corner of the great Acoustic-defying Auditorium."
Recollecting Besant's powerful oratory presence, Robins writes, "I remember
thinking: what an ease in command! *What a voice!*" This vivid auditory impression recalls Besant's own awareness of the power of her voice when she first unleashed it to the empty pews at Sisby church some forty-five years earlier, a
memory she had of course shared with Robins and other readers of *An Autobiography*. Curiously, Robins had a similar epiphany. Trying her luck in New York
City, the struggling young actress was discouraged by criticism of her "old-
fashioned" acting style. Alone in her room, she began reciting some of Ophelia's lines from *Hamlet*. Suddenly her voice actually set a brass curtain rod vi-
brating, its "faint singing overtone" renewing her faith in her calling. Or at least
that's how Robins reports the experience, which stems from a real-life counterpart, when she fictionalizes it in the last volume of her projected trilogy, "Theo
on Stage" (Fales 7A.66.20).

With the advantage of hindsight, Robins could eventually affirm that in Besant's response to the events of the Bloody Sunday riots (1887) she was "the spiritual mother of those twenty years later militant Suffragettes." Sadly, most of the
suffrage workers of Besant's own time viewed her as too radical, as someone
"beyond the pale" because of her earlier atheism and support for birth control,
and hence they had refused her tainted allegiance. Besant's earlier membership
in the National Secular Society was actually significant, however, for it was the
first political organization to openly endorse women's suffrage. Robins was certainly less outspoken and controversial than Besant, yet her own 1912 speech at
the Albert Hall endorsing suffrage conveys all the fervor of an informed zealot.[16]
As an actress and playwright supporting women's right to vote, Robins knew
only too well how to write and perform her role. Jane Marcus further reminds
us of the performance history of the suffrage cause when she rewrites George

Dangerfield's reading of its history in her introduction to *Suffrage and the Pankhursts* (1987): "The women's suffrage movement was a 'drama,' the women were 'actors' and 'actresses' in a 'scene' of the 'real' drama of the decline of the Liberal Party" (3). Recognizing the suffrage movement as drama made available to Robins and her fellow suffragists the tools and strategies of the theatre, eventually granting them the stage from which to declaim and then later refine their message of female liberation.

In Robins's fragmentary biography of Besant, we see one female practitioner of performance art applying shared linguistic and dramatic tools toward the evocation of another. What is particularly striking here is the almost total emphasis on form: Besant's voice, her presence, her white, apparitional appearance, the environment in which she appears. The circular, self-erasing quality of creative negativity tends to dictate this treatment, even more than the obvious fact of Robins taking a professional actress's approach to another public figure. Performers like Robins and Besant create selves, then step outside of them almost immediately; they are never granted much solidity or duration, so in describing themselves or their counterparts, why pin down the ephemeral self?

In this respect, it is interesting to note that during the period shortly after Besant's death in 1933, Robins met with little encouragement in her efforts to write and publish a biography of Besant. Chief among the Besant detractors, once again playing the devil's advocate in both Robins's and Besant's lives, was George Bernard Shaw. Robins wrote to Shaw several times during the mid-thirties, describing her biographical project and asking him questions about the Besant he had known.[17] Of Besant she herself writes in personal, almost evangelical language: "She blocked my way, made me stop, throw everything to the winds, and write a book about her—a small book, but a great undertaking and a great expenditure of time." But Shaw tries to warn Robins off. His first attempt at intervention occurs within five days of her query: "I hadnt the least idea that you and Mrs. B. had ever met. She was what Ibsen calls an episode in my life, and I in hers. It came to nothing. Nothing *from the inside* ever did come to anything with her: she was a public person first and last." Later, after detailing his own role in the disbursement of funds to support the striking match-girls and acknowledging his relative cowardice in response to Bloody Sunday, the inimitable G.B.S. tries to undermine Besant's overall significance: "She was great in impulse and action; but she contributed nothing to the doctrines she preached here. I know too little of her Indian career to say whether she achieved anything original theosophically. She was not an original thinker, just as Napoleon was not an original soldier." Not to be put off by this dismissal, however, Robins responds, "The warning comes too late, dear G.B.S." She goes on to observe in her own quiet way that his long letter obviously shows him protesting too much. The former colleague whom he so vehemently asserts "left no trace on [my] mind" was also the woman whose "voice in its best order" was "irresistibly authoritative."

Robins and Besant seemed equally to provoke Shaw to verbal attack. He worked closely with both of them, clearly admiring them for their talents as writers and performers. But perhaps that admiration was a large part of the problem: they may have come too close to the mark as competitors. And so he lashed out, as a humorist best can, by writing them off as humorless. Given Besant's seriousness of purpose, she was an easy target, but as I think Shaw's own reports quoted in the last chapter demonstrate, she was certainly capable of a teasing rejoinder. As for Robins, she was much more sorely tried. A young woman alone in London, recently widowed and trying to find work as an actress, she was extremely vulnerable to male advances, and Shaw's insensitivity to her situation led him to abuse his many privileges as a male, a theatre-reviewer, and a dramatist. He has been having the last laugh for some time now, thanks to his many biographers and the editors of his self-serving, clever letters. One wonders, too, how Robins would have fared at the hands of Leon Edel, who was in correspondence with Wilberforce between 1959 and 1963 about writing a biography of Robins; throughout his accounts of Henry James's theatre years, which he labels "treacherous," Edel casts Robins in the role of self-centered seductress.

An exception to the observation about Shaw's latter-day adherents is Sally Peters, who casts the infamous story about Robins threatening Shaw with a revolver in a new light. As rendered by Shaw, the incident marked the conclusion of an interview with Robins which Shaw only later promised not to publish, given her vehement objections. His letter to her the following day (5 February 1893; Fales 2B.23.171) mocks up a dummy article with a series of tantalizing headings that he labels "SENSATIONAL": LUSTROUS EYES; IBSEN'S MASTERPIECE; IF YOU DO, I WILL SHOOT YOU; and THE REVOLVER IS THERE. Teasing Robins with this tabloid fodder, Shaw then proceeds to lecture her on the art of giving a good interview, concluding with the offhand comment, "I could never have convinced you of the impolicy of your frightful and quite undeserved mistrust of me except by mystifying you as I have done." This one-sided account of the incident has been frequently reproduced at Robins's expense, misrepresenting her sexual skittishness and hinting at Shaw's aspiring prowess. Rather than simply assuming that Robins was overreacting to Shaw's advances, however, as have most of his male biographers, Peters helps us to recognize the self-deprecating humor and melodrama in Robins attempting to dissuade the ardent Shaw from making public her unauthorized comments: "Like Hedda, the Ibsen heroine at ease with revolvers, Elizabeth gestured sensationally toward her own weapon" (*Bernard Shaw: The Ascent of the Superman* 231).

Shaw's supposed "sacrifice" in denying himself the "professional success" of printing the interview becomes more disturbing when Robins's private response to the encounter comes to the surface. Buried among her papers at the New York University Library lies an empty envelope from Octavia Wilberforce, who had sent Robins a report of Shaw retelling the story yet again. Robins apparently seized the moment to record her version of the incident, her hurried remarks on the envelope testifying to the rage that had never subsided. According to Robins, Shaw tried to turn what she considered a private conversation into an opportunity to break the story about "my own excited reaction to Hilda" and the confidential plans to stage Ibsen's *Master Builder* (Figure 18). In response to his selfish and unethical intention, she recalls declaring, "You deserve to be shot," and then, almost as an afterthought, she observes, "The rusty old Texas pistol was on the mantel piece."[18] Records like this private note to herself and Robins's side of her correspondence with Shaw, missing of course from collections of his own letters, now begin to supply a resource for examining his attempts at intimidation and his failure to recognize the sense of humor that Robins and Besant shared. Not only do Robins's letters to Shaw show her feisty fortitude and unacknowledged parodic wit, but her unpublished study of Besant's subversive choice to downplay her drollery provides Robins her own last word:

> There have been Laughing Philosophers: have there been laughing Saints and Martyrs? Annie Besant's composition was mixed with the stuff of both,—and both at war with her practical genius.
>
> Pace Mr. Shaw, if Annie Besant had had a sense of humour she would not have been able to work with men as effectually as she did. The mass of men do not take kindly to humour in women. It may for the moment amuse them, but it makes them uneasy, puts them off the main track, and Annie Besant was all for the main track. (Fales 7A.4)

For women to have the true last word, they must often hide it and their ability to produce it. While Robins's insights into Besant's strategies helped to confirm them both as fellow tacticians, they also demonstrate how both of them managed to keep to "the main track" of changing the world one step at a time.

SYNAESTHESIA AND THE SUBJECTIVE CORRELATIVE

Putting herself to such tests, Robins discovered a solution to the challenge she saw of understanding and narrating the self by going inward to a kind of synaesthesia, wherein all boundaries melt, all perceptions merge. In her autobiographical accounting of her early years as an actress in London, *Both Sides of the Curtain* (1940), she expressed the genesis of her enterprise in the following manner:

FIGURE 18. Elizabeth Robins as Helda Wangel in Henrik Ibsen's *The Master Builder* (1893). The choice of costume is Robins's, in contradistinction to Henry James's request that she wear something "agreeable," that is, something more becoming by his standards of femininity. Courtesy of Mabel Smith, Literary Executor, Elizabeth Robins Estate; The Elizabeth Robins Papers, Fales Library/Special Collections, New York University.

It did not yet trouble me that my particular limitations, as well as the age I lived in, would not allow me to be myself. I hadn't any self as yet. I didn't even want any self that I could see in the offing. What I wanted was to be everybody. I *was* everybody.

And that loosed the lightning. It showed my dazzled eyes a divine right to ambition. No limit. (328)

This language of the self echoes that of Case accounting for the sense of "her"-self displayed by Rahel Varnhagen (1771–1833), who performed in the Berlin sa-lon-theatre at the turn of the eighteenth century: "Rahel didn't imagine herself as a whole self, complete, discrete and independent. She had a sense that her self could only exist in mutuality—through the perception and interactions of others. Rahel's self was constructed in social interchanges, just as her dialogue was" (*Feminism and Theatre* 49). Neither Varnhagen nor Robins accepted circumscribed or narrow definitions of the self, and hence they frequently crossed boundaries between the self and others, freely reconstructing themselves in ways that allowed them to reconfigure outward social structures as well.

Far from being unaware of boundaries or denying separateness—after all, this is the actress who portrayed a mother apparently murdering her child, the woman who fought for suffrage, the friend who admitted to a necessary separation from Henry James—Robins made the most of them and highlighted them as challenges, finding within boundaries and separateness the means to overcome division. This synaesthetic mentality feels the torment of isolation, but at its height it knows it can produce union from apparent opposites. Robins likes to evoke isolation—Jean Creyke (Alan's wife) confined by utter silence, Victorian and Edwardian women constricted by outmoded traditions, crowds stripped away to separate atoms—and to create out of such separation a oneness. Sometimes that inner struggle or turmoil of one thing to overcome its sense of separation suggests parody, as we can recognize in some of the suffrage crowd scenes in both her 1907 play *Votes for Women!* and its novelization, *The Convert*, but as the audience or reader is enjoined to participate in the crowd's performance, we get a measure of how drama, fiction, or autobiography can work to knock down and eliminate a panoply of boundaries.

In *Alan's Wife*, staged after her Ibsenian successes as Hedda and Hilda, we witness Robins applying the precepts of creative negativity to take an audience across emotional boundaries, in effect using negation and opposition to confront intolerable circumstances, perhaps even to make the audience see the unseen. By emphasizing the act of negating the ego, she urges her audience to perceive and embrace everything, in short, in the Keatsian mode to negate the intellect so as to not reject things categorically, to lay aside dogma and preconceptions. In the words of William Archer, her chief defender, the play depicts its female protagonist in "one of those agonizing dilemmas where it seems equally impossible, equally inhuman, to act or to refrain."[19] Archer found himself caught up in writing an extensive introduction in support of the play for J. T. Grein's Independent Theatre's anonymous edition of *Alan's Wife* (ix–lii), which he supplemented with two appendices, one reproducing the critical response in an exchange of letters in *The Speaker*, the other consisting of a letter to the editor of *The Westminster Gazette* (9 May 1893) by Thomas Hardy regarding his protagonist's baptism of her dead infant in his 1889 novel *Tess of the D'Urbervilles*. In the meantime, the already sacrilegious baptism had in fact become the crux of Hardy's stage version of the novel. On both stage and page, this controversial scene predated the immediate impetus to *Alan's Wife*, the Swedish source "Befriad" (1891), by Elin Ameen, whose title translates as "The Release" or "The Liberation." However, Ameen and co-adapters Robins and Bell took an even more radical step with the key scene said to bear such a resemblance to Hardy's: their female protagonist moves resolutely toward an act of infanticide in the name of euthanasia.

The story of *Alan's Wife* is brief but compelling. The first scene begins with Jean Creyke eagerly awaiting the arrival of her husband Alan, who should be returning for his noonday meal from his job at the local works; it concludes with her lifting the cover of a litter carrying his dead body, crushed in an industrial accident. Scene 2 discloses the interior of Jean's cottage, where her mother, a neighbor, and the minister try to rouse her back to life and the care of her infant son. Left alone with the child, who has been born weak and deformed, Jean debates with herself whether he should live in pain or be released from his suffering. After performing a makeshift baptism, she moves "stealthily towards [the] cradle with a long wailing cry, the eider quilt hugged to her breast as the curtain falls" (37). The last scene takes place in prison, where Jean is urged to confess to temporary insanity. Remaining silent during almost the entire scene, she speaks at the end only to declare her acceptance of the consequences of her choice, "I had to do what I did, and they have to take my life for it" (47–48). Playing the protagonist, Robins sees her husband's mutilated body, smothers her own child, and receives her death sentence in silence. Yet all of these actions are really reactions or implied actions, requiring the actress to convey (according to her own stage directions) the seemingly unimaginable. Letters published in *The Speaker* provide telling testimony to her phenomenal success: in this open forum, theatre critic A. B. Walkley repeatedly insists, "We are shown the stretcher, the mangled corpse, the [deformed] child" (6 May 1893), while the play's champion, Archer, retaliates, "Mr. Walkley's [subjective] impression does not correspond with the objective reality" (13 May 1893). At its most intense, creative negativity's juxtaposition of reality and illusion can, for some, turn one into the other, perhaps even causing them to merge.

At this point, I would like again to invoke T. S. Eliot's conception of an "objective correlative" in order to demonstrate how Robins's personal and artistic endeavor acts as a "subjective correlative." In his famous essay "Hamlet and His Problems," Eliot pronounces, "The only way of expressing emotion in the form of art is by finding an 'objective correlative'; in other words, a set of objects, a situation, a chain of events which shall be the formula of that *particular* emotion; such that when the external facts, which must terminate in sensory experience, are given, the emotion is immediately evoked."[20] Eliot's proposition establishes an external object or image as a vehicle through which the author re-creates an original set of feelings or emotions, and then postulates that the reader can tap into this line of inspiration to experience the same or similar feelings, thereby according the author the power of evoking a conditioned emotional response. In contrast, Robins's subjective correlative does not posit an intermediary object but aims directly at the audience member or reader by creating an absence that must be filled. In other words, she treats the audience or reader as a co-creator (recall what she later said about the playwright and the actor in *Ibsen and the Actress*), forcing in the case of *Alan's Wife* a degree of uncomfortable inner change.

The subjective correlative in this instance operates chiefly through silence — through Jean's unspoken reaction to the uncovered stretcher, her measured movements as she slowly approaches the baby's crib, her looks and gestures during the entire last act. Robins runs an immense risk with this technique (witness the extraordinary result of the critic Walkley, whose subjective experience is so fueled by his fears that his interpretation rewrites the actress's experience on stage), but she is clearly willing to accept the ultimate lack of control the artist has when she unleashes the unconscious. Moreover, she has tapped into a reservoir here that has the potential to be seriously affected and perhaps changed by the demands she has placed upon it. Also significant is what both sides of the curtain entail — Robins as anonymous co-scriptor behind the scenes creating a character whom she then enacts on the stage (in front of the curtain, so to speak), all in an effort to pull each audience member out of the safe confines of his or her theatre seat, onto the stage, and into the mind/heart of the dramatic character living out a present-time fictional existence that has far-reaching potential to change future real-life experiences. When Robins decides to abolish the curtain — to cross that final theatrical boundary of the fourth wall — she does so to phenomenal effect.

Robins gives us here a world that is horrifyingly stable, and in turn its inevitability creates a discordant tension that presses for resolution. Her character struggles against the attenuation of time, trying to accept the unacceptable, experiencing life as excruciatingly conflicted. But to ask Jean to pull back is to ask the impossible; she must look deeply at negation — the reality of her deformed child in the long-term future—and make her decision accordingly: "I seem to see you in some far-off time, your face distorted like your body, but with bitterness and loathing, saying, 'Mother, how *could* you be so cruel as to let me live and suffer?'" (36). In an unusual move, Robins shows Jean using her mind to negate "the darling little face all the same" (30) as she has Jean utilize a unique mental computation to cross over a difficult emotional boundary. But if the attenuation of time is fundamental to Jean's agony, making her every minute insupportable, barely endurable, then future projection allows her to extrapolate the impact of that attenuation for her child and bring about her resolution quickly. The communication achieved via this imaginary interchange bridges the isolation that has become so pervasive in this modern tragedy and modern life in general.

Delineating deliberate opposites, setting them side-by-side, pushing extremes to further extremes—this methodology produces a cauldron of energy on the stage and in the audience. We recognize that something new is forged when negation or absence is employed to signal a creative choice, something unexpected in its intensity precisely because societal boundaries have been breached. By exploding a fixed belief system, such as that about infanticide or euthanasia, Robins takes her audiences about as far as any artist can. She had already done so as an actress in *Hedda Gabler* with respect to suicide, and she would do so again as a playwright and novelist in *Votes for Women!* and *The Convert* regarding abortion. And audience response confirmed the power of her ability to provoke reaction: *Alan's Wife* was closed after only two performances! Archer reports that there was no middle ground; the play was "either mercilessly condemned or highly praised" (vi). A play that is not graphically lurid but that causes audience members to conjure up images they are unwilling to see is both highly effective and ineffective: it works only as long as it remains in the public eye. Yet what *Alan's Wife* evoked is obviously central to Robins's aesthetic. By refusing to remain in uncertainty, Robins as playwright and actress rejects the sublimity of the Keatsian model, opting instead for the more forthright denials she voiced through her Ibsen heroines.

The concepts of synaesthesia and the subjective correlative constitute more than just technique for Robins, for they infuse her writing and performance across the board, their boundary-crossing creating a new and distinct form of self-expression.[21] The negative response to *Alan's Wife* continues to provide a telling example. Here we have a case of the critic Walkley seeing what's not there—"the mangled corpse and the hideously deformed baby"—but in many respects his response is absolutely appropriate to this unique art form, for silence can sometimes tell more than words, as we witness unbearable isolation leading to connection, unity, love, sisterhood. Silence is a key element in women's writing in general and in Robins's case in particular, as Elin Diamond demonstrates in her various analyses of the actress enacting the hysterically unspeakable. Later, in 1907, Robins pointedly expounded on the subject of silence in her Women's Social and Political Union (WSPU) pamphlet, *Woman's Secret*, in which she discusses woman's "success in keeping her mental processes to herself" (16) and her acceptance of "the yoke of silence and of service" (18). Noting what it means when woman dares to speak out (20), Robins concludes, "[I]f our parts had been reversed, if woman had been the dominant partner, men would have exercised precisely those arts of dissimulation and of long silence, alternated with brief outbursts of bitterness, that always characterise the unfree" (26).[22]

Through one form of expression we experience another—a deeper, more internal boundary-crossing. Perhaps this process points toward women's more fluid communication between the two hemispheres of the brain, a modus operandi less spontaneously available to men. The hallucinatory experience of the reviewer is profoundly disturbing because it seems to confirm that the actress-playwright has successfully made something happen in the viewer's mind. This kind of communication and change may in fact have been Ibsen's goal in *A Doll's House* as well. Note how Nora Helmer hopes against hope for the miracle that never happens, namely a husband and wife relating to each other outside and beyond social dictates, but it is only she who acts in accord with this ideal by signing her father's name for her husband's sake, something most men at the time didn't (or couldn't) understand. Robins's performances as Hedda Gabler (Figure 19) went on to seem terrifyingly real, so much so that critics imagined multiple bodies onstage and even conflated the actress with the character, expressing consternation at the prospect of ever meeting "Elizabeth Gabler."[23] Even forty years later, when writing about Robins's production of *Hedda Gabler*, Charles Archer vividly recalls, "The effect produced bordered on hallucination in some cases" (176), turning to the (unsigned) remarks of the *Daily Telegraph* for his evidence: "It was like a visit to the Morgue. . . . There they all lay on their copper couches, fronting us, and waiting to be owned. . . . There they all were, false men, wicked women, deceitful friends, sensualists, egotists, piled up in a heap behind the screen of glass which we were thankful for" (21 April 1891). Of course, it was only Hedda's body on the stage, barely in view as the final curtain descended.

Robins was understandably cautious as she anticipated public reception of her dual suffrage enterprise in 1907. How could she remain true to both her aesthetic and her ideology and yet not run the risk of having her play closed or her novel panned? Already the choice of two genres reveals her strategic maneuvering, hedging her bets, so to speak, but that Robins was so successful with two such distinctive projects attests to her skill and fortitude. Clearly she had learned from her experience with *Alan's Wife* without having to compromise either her

FIGURE 19. Elizabeth Robins as Hedda Gabler for the New York City production in 1898 (she originated the role in London in 1891, co-producing the play with fellow American actress Marion Lea); photograph by Aimé Dupont, New York. Courtesy of Mabel Smith, Literary Executor, Elizabeth Robins Estate; The Elizabeth Robins Papers, Fales Library/Special Collections, New York University.

goals or her beliefs. This time she embedded her key conversion scene between more familiar material. In fact, Marcus has summed up *Votes for Women!* as "two acts of Shavian comic moral melodrama flanking the Trafalgar Square scene" (viii). As for the middle act, Jan McDonald has already examined the script used by one of the actors in the crowd, Campbell Cargill, who played "one of the trio of 'decently dressed' men" (145) in order to "shed some light on how this 'most brilliant piece of stage-management we have ever had in an English playhouse' (*Sunday Times*, 14 April 1907) was effected" (139).[24]

In *Votes for Women!* Robins calls upon a variation on the subjective correlative. In this case, the audience member is not impelled to fill a silence but rather to discover a point of identification with another audience member (or members) presented or projected on the stage itself. This process works through layering: for her suffrage rally in Trafalgar Square, Robins creates central characters, who are in effect on an inner stage; her crowd then becomes a middle ground through which the theatrical audience views the action; and thus the audience is once again pulled up onto the stage, seeking a vantage point with which to identify in order to interpret the inner drama. This kind of subjective involvement differs from that elicited by *Alan's Wife*, however. In the earlier play, Robins sought to effect non-volitional change, whereas in *Votes for Women!*, overtly subtitled "A Tract" for the stage production, she seeks to bring about a volitional shift. Non-volitional change operates more at the unconscious level, where it can bring to the surface deep-seated fears and emotions, forcing audience members to grapple with them, while volitional change is more likely to move into the political arena, where change or conversion is measured by active choice in supporting legislation or working more directly for reform. As a measure of how one reviewer of *Votes for Women!* could identify with being an audience member in the Trafalgar Square scene, and thereby feeling moved to action, we have on record the following assertion from *The Evening News* (10 April 1907): "For my part, I felt like climbing over the footlights and inviting the dirty, drink-sodden ruffians who interrupted [Miss Wynne-Matthison, playing Vida Levering] to come outside one by one and have their heads punched into rice-puddings!" The (obviously) male critic goes on to explain, "Yes; it makes you feel all the time, this wonderful scene. It is by far the best-written and best stage-managed thing of the kind that has ever been done in London or (I should think) anywhere else. . . . The air of reality is never absent."

Nonetheless, volitional conversion still requires nurturing. Let us observe how the gradual movement calling for degrees of viewer participation parallels the plot movement onstage. Vida Levering, a reflection of Robins herself, goes from being an interested observer of the Woman's Movement, to an active speaker on a public platform, to an effective behind-the-scenes manipulator of a potentially powerful political advocate. Meanwhile, the misogynist Geoffrey Stoner, her former lover, eventually makes the volitional—conscious, albeit hardly altruistic—decision to support the Woman's Cause. From the outset, Robins challenged herself to bring about a specific miracle: how could she transform her melodramatic villain into an adherent for women's rights by play's end? Because transposition is central to suffrage itself, Robins wisely focuses on the ability of men to reposition themselves, both seriously and comically, vis-à-vis women. We may laugh at Richard Farnsborough's banter with Lady John Wynnstay that results in his willing acceptance of her declaration, "[T]he penalty is you shall stay and keep the others amused between church and luncheon, and so keep me free" (42), but we are also forced to recognize the social implications when an inversion of domesticity is deployed by the working-class Pilcher, who openly takes the stand to acknowledge the inability of many of his fellows to give women a home in the first place (66). Negating or complicating traditional male roles clearly sets up the last act for whatever change Stoner can undergo in response to the elliptical demands Vida makes of him: "Give me back what you took from me; my old faith. . . . Or give me back mere kindness—or even tolerance. . . . Give me back the power to think fairly of my brothers—not as mockers—thieves" (82).

In parallel fashion, we witness the women in the play lining the men up in various positions, only to repeatedly reveal that the structure of society is beholden to the subordinated female. Unless men can discover an ability to redefine themselves in the social context, they betray themselves as diminutive and negative; in effect, they demonstrate how they are less causal, dominant, or significant than the women. Nowhere is this conclusion more obvious than when Vida reports on the little girl, dying in the Tramp Ward, whose chief concern is to protect the pride of her ineffectual father. No wonder, then, that Vida can eventually distance herself from her sense of shame and personal loss with respect to Stoner's betrayal and her secret abortion: "For me he's simply one of the far back links in a chain of evidence," she finally declares (80). Watching both sexes realigning men, we come to realize that Robins's reconciliation can occur only if men will take advantage of their flexibility and reposition themselves with women, thereby making it possible for women to define themselves less negatively.

When the curtain comes down on *Votes for Women!*, destructive negativity in the form of ignorance has been banished in favor of a creative negativity that puts "political dynamite" in the hands of a suffragette (87). We have heard Greatorex's absurd dismissal of "a few discontented old maids and hungry widows" (47) corrected by Vida into compassion for a more accurately estimated 96,000; we have witnessed hecklers overturned by a specific recital of historical tactics; and we have even learned that Vida's story of desertion is more complicated than she had originally represented it to be. Robins thus argues that if information can replace ignorance, and facts can overcome hostility, it is still equally important that individuals come to terms with their own pasts by reconciling their self-stereotyping. Accepting her own denials ultimately allows Vida—through Stoner—to reverse ignorance on a larger social scale. This effort to reduce reform to a dramatic reconciliation, an emotional relationship of opposites, may suggest something like wishful thinking, but Robins invests it in a structure that is both coherent and sound. To call Robins a "propagandist of genius," as Jane Marcus does, is not just to acknowledge her ability to focus on her audience but to credit her skill in creating this play's resolution. In this case, Robins manages to negate and transform her own brand of self-invoked melodrama.

Robins's diaries record a tension between writing and performing, the two activities competing with each other, sometimes finding an uneasy coexistence. But even when she could not find the time to perform or to engage in overt autobiographical accounting, her fiction found a way to fuse the two. In this respect, we can track the evolution of her record keeping of suffrage debates in Trafalgar Square. Not only did these records inform the central scene in *Votes for Women!*, but they also grew into an opportunity for Robins to explore her own relationship to impromptu public forums in *The Convert*. Thus, we can start reading Vida Levering in both texts as a stand-in for the erstwhile autobiographer.[25] The question of open self-assessment remained unsettled for the individual woman who constituted Elizabeth Robins, who continued to straddle the Victorian and Edwardian value systems. She had published her fiction under the pseudonym "C. E. Raimond" until the turn of the century (her stage name through 1892 was "Claire Raimond," also derived from the name of her favorite younger brother Raymond), and over a quarter of a century after the anonymous publication of *Alan's Wife*, she yet again chose anonymity for *Ancilla's Share* (1924). At issue here are the perennial questions regarding respect and reputation for women: How can the female novelist, playwright, or social critic guarantee that her work will be taken seriously once her gender is known?

Although most critics have assumed that *The Convert* is simply a novelization of *Votes for Women!*, a careful reading of the two texts in juxtaposition proves otherwise.[26] More precisely, in terms of my thesis, Robins's technique of creative negativity becomes multidimensional as she turns it to novelistic account. In the hands of a lesser artist, the novel's necessarily greater length might merely contribute to its verisimilitude, but Robins puts fictional realism to a more severe test by treating it as an occasion to explore levels of negativity.

As a result of all its contending forces, *The Convert* finds Robins constituting herself in a complex blend of protagonist and narrative voice. The novelist depicts Vida smiling at a charge of Chartism, for example, but then she finds a way to express a penetration or plunging from external events to unconscious mergings by evoking "some dim sense"—"two-thirds fear"—that arrests and stirs to "unsuspected deeps" (85). Vida's "strange new sense of possible significance in this scene" here embodies the experience of synaesthesia. Or take what starts as "a significant Babel" when Vida joins a group (54). A merger occurs, everything conjoins in unity, yet at center "unfinished questions" remain. Robins even turns the occasion of relating a mini-biography into a synaesthetic opportunity. Observe how the following narrative begins as a parody of male neurological operations, invokes singularity, and then flips over into a shared experience in which two become one, making the isolated expression transcendent without violating it:

> A little wearily, without the smallest spark of enthusiasm at the prospect of imparting her biography, Miss Claxton told slowly, even dully, and wholly without passion, the story of a hard life met single-handed from even the tender childhood days—one of those recitals that change the relation between the one who tells and the one who listens—makes the last a sharer in the life to the extent that the two can never be strangers any more. Though they may not meet, nor write, nor have any tangible communication, there is an understanding between them. (156)

Thus, technique goes well beyond a matter of mere aesthetics for Robins, for it answers the key question of how to save the world, namely through unity, the miracle Ibsen was only talking about.[27] Both *Votes for Women!* and *The Convert* bring to the fore questions of violence and sexuality in ways that were clearly disturbing to theatergoers and readers of the time, yet Robins learned to work with these threats with varying degrees of subtlety and success. In sum, she developed her concept of creative negativity into a feminist philosophy that allowed her to redirect her specifically female rage into an effective aesthetic.

This aesthetic technique also helps to explain the pivotal importance of crowd scenes in *Votes for Women!* and *The Convert*, wherein we witness one person's neurons sparked by another, the power of anticipation or the expectation to incite unity recalling Besant's commanding emergences onstage. Robins's shaping of these crowd scenes dramatizes the struggle of the individual to remain isolated versus the desire to be joined. One might even say that these scenes disclose an atomization of the dialectic between mind and heart. Ultimately, Robins depicts the separation created by an angry mob transformed not only by the right speaker or event but also by something already present within the crowd itself. The paradox of isolation becoming unity occurs in one instance when it starts to rain, and only one member of a crowd observes it; then one by one "umbrellas blossom" (113). Thematically, Robins is addressing the question of what constitutes leadership—a major challenge to the women's movement—and she answers it by demonstrating how to join those who are in love with isolation. This is what happens when one woman starts to speak and the audience "went for her" (193). First positing another negative example of unity, something that portends complete disaster, Robins then has a character observe, "If she weathers this, she'll be a speaker someday," prefacing her remarks by noting that the would-be speaker is "not half so bad as lots of men when they first try." Here we see how Robins dissects crowds, laying bare their hostility and isolation, then shows them quieting down, in this case through a heckling male being isolated, chased away, his own weapons of isolation finally used against him (194).

Robins's synaesthetic technique essentially operates in *The Convert* to expose gender politics. Initially, we see it at work between the sexes—"The women grew more insistently vivacious in proportion as the men's minds seemed to wander from matters they had discussed contentedly enough before" (10)—but it also functions within them. Note how in the following passage Robins develops the interplay between isolation and unity, studying its evolution: "Between these two daughters of one father existed that sort of haunting family resemblance often seen between two closely related persons, despite one being attractive and the other in some way repellent. . . . [T]he slight disparity in age fails to account for a difference wide as the poles" (37). What has not yet been merged remains as "the sum of their unlikeness," recalled again by "that more disquieting reminder of the ugly and over-elaborate thing life is to many an estimable soul." Yet even the isolate finally merges, despite her profound disharmony: "Janet Fox-Moore had the art of rubbing this dark fact in till, so to speak, the black came off," while her sister seems destined, all along, to exist "in perfect because unconscious harmony with [her] environment" (38).

Without a doubt, *The Convert* benefits from its use of embedded parallelism as well as its protracted development of the plotline established by *Votes for Women!*, all the more so because it coopts the play's direct dialogue at end-point, allowing the last five chapters to stand in dramatic contrast to the novel's overall multi-dimensionality. Boundary-crossing and conflation sound the keynote here; the result is rich and subtle, a narrative that blends linguistic flexibility and satirical interaction to create an authorial voice that is simultaneously disruptive and harmonious. Early in the text, for example, Lord Borrodaile (a character who exists only in the novel) is astonished that "our Ernestine" can overwhelm class differences (176). Physically, he cannot cross the distance the "mob" sets between them, but at the same time he is "stirred . . . even thrilled," his own differences overcome by both argument and demonstration. Robins's chief retooling of her final chapter involves the addition of free indirect speech, that narrative conflation that blends the voices of character and narrator. Interestingly enough, she has utilized this technique sparingly in the body of her text, reserving it primarily for Vida. Its particular power derives from her now applying it to both Vida and Stoner, whose privacy she has previously safeguarded. Going behind the thoughts of her protagonists in tandem at once conjoins and divides them, however, for they misread each other (302). Nonetheless, by moving forward to acknowledge her misreadings of herself, Vida is finally able to shape a major social change at its crucial turning point. Having developed the grounds for personal and political reconciliation through the mutual potential for boundary-crossing, Robins opts for a subdued but assured resolution, a balance of emotional opposites.

In many respects, *The Convert* becomes an extension of the *Bildungsroman* (perhaps more precisely for our purposes, the *Künstleroman*), a novel of development that unlayers the process and significance of conversion. On this subject, Vida in fact takes the bait when Lord Borrodaile patronizingly but affectionately asks, "And did you find there was 'something new under the sun' after all?" She is quick to reply, "Well, perhaps not so new, though it seemed new to me. But something differently looked at. Why do we pretend that all conversion is to some religious dogma—why not to a view of life?" (143). Change in this novel is not just presented through multiple examples, coupled with a sudden leap in consciousness. Rather, it advances through parallelisms—psychological, formal, and social—creating a multivalent aggregate that accurately reflects the complexity that engenders transformation. At the center of this growth process is Vida, both protagonist and self-reflective artist-author, who moves from being "ruffled" into a retreat, able to speak only under her breath (65), to someone who can mount a public platform and hold forth at length before an unruly crowd (262–70). Such a transformation makes sense, moreover, because Vida is not alone in her tendency to hide, to put up boundaries, so to speak. Setting and character conjoin to underscore that propensity, whether we witness it in the seclusion of an old-order estate (209) or in Stoner's desire to be incognito at the suffrage rally (244). These are instances of clinging to the private sphere. Their self-negation, revealed through the desire not to change or to remain unseen, serves to spur Vida's growth, which in turn informs the gradual conversion of social and personal forces that constitute her surround. Out of deadness and neutrality emerges the new order.

PERFORMING COLLECTIVE AUTOBIOGRAPHY

Speaking of all the warring religious sects performing in the 1890 Passion Play at Oberammergau, Robins recognized in *Both Sides of the Curtain* that they "seemed to have found at last a common ground of agreement—and found it on the Stage!" (305). This autobiographical text is the one in which she also reports, "That is what the despised Theatre could do for you," namely provide that sense of having no self, of being everybody, of experiencing no limit (328). Such insight inspired Robins to reflect on not only her own history but that of other women: "I had been collecting, unconsciously, a store of information about the experience and the prospects of other women on the stage" (231), she acknowledges.[28] Playing back and forth between others' stories and "the atom that was I" (330), Robins shows herself to be a unified-field thinker. She continually evokes in her writing and performance options a realm where everyone is connected, where opposites meet, and where the relatively powerless individual becomes a powerful, superpersonal force. How could one write a singular autobiography with such an un-Victorian viewpoint? The answer is complex—only by utilizing a special brand of rhetoric that involves a plunging into unconscious realms, toward the unified field of combined selves and synaesthesia, and by acting out and forging links among different forms, so that autobiography ultimately becomes performance, and vice versa.

After reading the *Journal of Marie Bashkirtseff* (1890), the memoir of the short-lived Russian artist (1860–1884), Robins observes, "There are pages about her Journal in my journal" (261). But then she goes on to contrast their styles, describing her own notes to herself as indecipherable, hiding an essence available only to herself (262).[29] In this respect, Bashkirtseff constitutes an ambivalent spur to self-assessment, as Robins rhetorically evokes an unconscious world of conjoined opposites which she herself reaches toward. Robins's evocation underscores both the separateness of forms and the ultimate unity that lies beneath them: "I both despise and love her," she declares, "but I weep for the bottomless yearning, the infinite striving and toil, the glad hope, the half-expressed terror, the torrent of palpitating eager life that ends in this helplessness and silence" (261). Once again we can note Robins's conjunction of opposite emotions (hate and love), the sense of great effort and energy ("striving and toil"), the probing within or beyond language (only "half-expressed"), and the paradoxical silence lying within that "palpitating eager life." Robins in no sense suggests that Bashkirtseff's journal denies separateness; on the contrary, it somehow shows unity and conflict existing at the same time. And this is the very world-view that Robins's own life and work body forth.

Had she brought to fruition a sequel to *Both Sides of the Curtain*, Robins might well have publicly explored more of the quest that we must otherwise piece together out of a combination of her published and unpublished accounts, both of which she variously presented under the guise of fiction and nonfiction, autobiography and biography. "Wither and How," the typescript of the unfinished sequel, opens with the following declaration, "To write this book was to set out on a voyage of discovery," and Robins goes on to express that intention in the explicit language of the creative-negativist-as-questor:

It is no very useful quest, for all that I go to find is my lost self—or, to be as honest as possible—I go to find such fragments as I shall be willing to declare. Though, like other travellers, I shall have snapshots to show of people I met by the way, the Theatre is my main theme. Yet the record will show less how I "did" plays—and other things—than how I did not do them. (Fales 7A.78.1)

Just as she spoke of "cooking" her accounts when she was writing her will, Robins here acknowledges the same ambivalence about encountering herself and setting down that self in writing. On the one hand, she clearly wants to embark on this journey of self-discovery, while on the other she denies its validity from the outset. Juxtaposed with establishing her goal are statements that either disparage or belittle it, yet at the same time she retains creative control over her subject, announcing that a future readership would discover only those "fragments" that she chooses to share. The apparent negativity of presenting how she did not act in "plays—and other things" carries with it a concomitant affirmation, for it continues to underline the willful element of choice that was so strong in Robins.

If the sequel to *Both Sides of the Curtain* remains unfinished and unpublished, the life matter that occurred next in the Robins chronology emerges in multiple public accountings, and these chronicles involve the usual layering and obfus ·a-tion we have come to expect of the Robins narrative. The official record consists of Robins traveling to Alaska in 1900 in search of her beloved younger brother Raymond. To assist her undertaking, she was offered an advance by her editor friend, W. T. Stead, who planned to publish her correspondence in his London journal. In addition, Robins maintained a detailed diary of her experiences, which was not published until 1999. Although Stead printed only one of her letter-articles in the *Review of Reviews*, Robins turned her saga into a fascinating array of other narrative accounts. One set of her annals retained the voice of the journalist, namely the reports that were published in the *Seattle Post Intelligencer*, the *Pall Mall Magazine*, *Harper's Magazine*, and the *Fortnightly Review*. The fiction writer variously came to the fore with short stories and eventually a total of three novels—*The Magnetic North* (1904), *A Dark Lantern* (1905), and *Come and Find Me* (1908). The first and third of these works of fiction have been widely praised as examples of both the male and female quest story. Upon its publication, *The Magnetic North* was touted as "an extraordinary book for a woman to write" by the *Daily Telegraph*, while *Come and find Me* has more recently been described as a revisioning of "the Alaskan adventure as one of female faith, perseverance and women's bonding." Meanwhile, *A Dark Lantern* constituted a darker, more personal examination of Robins's own rest-cure experience, itself a response to the lingering effects of her Alaskan travels. Lastly, we can recognize the work of the playwright and the biographer in "Bowarra," an imaginative reworking of Eskimo tales as children's theatre, and *Raymond and I*, a memoir of her relationship with the brother who provoked this much-mined stage in her life journey.[30]

The years that followed this extended episode in Robins's lifelong quest witnessed her increased politicalization, primarily as it was directed by the movement for women's suffrage and its attendant feminist concerns. Her 1913 novel, *My Little Sister* (published in Britain as *Where Are You Going To . . . ?*), exemplifies the very union of propaganda and art that her detractors had not recognized in the 1907 dual suffrage vehicles that constituted Vida Levering's tale of deconversion. While the anti-prostitution campaign of the Women's Social and Political Union took its lead from Christabel Pankhurst's well-documented *The Great Scourge and How to End It* (1913), Robins elected once again the subtle strategy I have characterized as creative negativity. As is so often the case in such an accounting, the chief difficulty emerges in trying to move from one reality system to another. The unnamed narrator of *My Little Sister* tries in vain to explain to the outside world the experience of the white slavery ring that has claimed her sister Bettina, but no one seems to really understand or fully believe her. She is assumed to be mad, and in fact she falls into a form of hysteria, moving in and out of consciousness, and requiring the assistance of a male surrogate who can move more efficiently in the patriarchal world in search of the lost Bettina. Her sister is not recovered, but by novel's end it is clear that the narrator will dedicate her life to reforming society, and that her story will move others to similar action.

By choosing this personalized, subjective mode of narration, Robins develops a powerful (female) empathy that quite simply could not have been so effectively evoked through a traditional, linear (male) argument for social reform.[31] From the outset, the narrator draws the reader into her agonizing attempt to recall her wrenching past feelings: "I did not know then how hard this was to do"—to show the face of memory—"or that the faithfullest [*sic*] intention must fall short; that genius itself cannot pass on to others all the poignancy of past Hope, or—mercifully—more than a pale reflection of past Despair" (116). At the same time, however, the narrator's own growth toward self-actualization provides a more positive spur to reader identification: "I had that feeling of the creature who has been straining long at bonds, and finds the sudden loosing a test of equilibrium" (190). In her life journey, this protagonist goes on to pursue a medical education and jettison her own marriage plot before she settles on her life purpose: "That was the day I came to know the steadying influence of a call to face great issues. They bring their own greatness with them. They wrap it round our littleness" (196). Moreover, she will develop this insight through her close observation of gender roles: "[G]irls seem to 'care' more than men do. . . . Men had so much to do. Life was so full for them" (250). The novel's last chapter, "The End Which

Was the Beginning," concludes with this final, ongoing invocation to heal societal ills:

> Was there, then, some life-principle in such pain?
> A voice said, "You shall find in mortal ill, the seed of Immortal Good."
> I knelt by the window and thanked my sister.
> Others shall thank her, too. (344)

In the letters written to her by the novelist Henry James that Robins preserves and comments upon in *Theatre and Friendship* (1932), James rhetorically presents himself as a creature of emptiness and division, who is appealing to Robins as the one who will mend or cure him.[32] James portrays himself as the divided melancholic, Robins the unifying soul to whom he can surrender for reconstruction. In 1892, the year following her performance as Hedda, he experiences her absence as "the loss of intenser light I was hoping for" (85). The following summer he writes, "I am in London again after a vast absence, and nothing that it contains presents itself to me more imperatively than the opportunity of seeing you again" (137). And later that fall he commences another letter, "I shall look out for you feverishly to-morrow . . ." (139). James constantly speaks of dichotomies and boundaries which he cannot overcome but Robins can: "I want on my side to be shown *your* horizons," he insists (140). A decade later, in 1903, her correspondence still evokes both pleasure and pain in him, for it signals both the joy of seeing her again and a reminder of her "*missing*" presence: "Most happy and beautiful and touching to me the inspiration that dictated your letter, and striking that chord of the unforgotten past that ever, for me, vibrates with a force of which the pleasure is half the pain—I mean the pain of intensity itself" (185).

Theatre and Friendship functions as yet another unique approach to the autobiography of Elizabeth Robins. After all, these letters by James were chosen and edited by her, shaped and arranged by her commentary. In addition, the volume serves another more personal, subversive purpose, for it allowed her to include the correspondence of her dear friend, Florence Bell, who had died just two years previously. James's words confirm the picture of Robins that I have been sketching, but at the same time, they—like all of her writing at our disposal—have been sifted by her discerning eye. Robins had played the female lead Claire de Cintré in James's stage adaptation of his novel, *The American*, for its London run in 1891 (he had been impressed by her portrayal of Mrs. Linden in *A Doll's House*). Subsequently, he hoped to cast her in the lead role of Mrs. Vibert in *Tenants*, written in 1890 but never produced, despite the encouraging words of producer John Hare, who called it "a masterpiece of dramatic construction" in the foreword to its published version.[33] James had even written the scenario for

"The Promise," which became the novel *The Other House* (1896), with Robins in mind, and his short story, "Nona Vincent" (1891), plays out a version of the thinly disguised triangle of Bell, Robins, and himself. In the wishful thinking of the tale, Robins is the actress Violet Grey, whose "transformation" saves both play and playwright from public failure. Now the history of the theatrical relationship between Robins and James moves toward an inevitable climax of separation, the end of a collaboration that was not meant to be:

> While Mr. James retained, with any force or continuity, the idea of his own practical connection with the theatre, he and I had his hopes as well as mine, for a common bond. As long as he could believe, and I could hope, that I might venture again to play one of his graceful and gracious ladies, or make myself responsible for the production of one of his plays, he would naturally feel there was still a possibility of making something, to the general gain, of me as "colleague." The time never came. (216)

Yet the closure is both quiet and gentle, prefiguring a continued, if different, friendship: "The stage door closed for both Mr. James and me, with no slam from either of us. It closed quietly, gently, without bitterness, without even the decency of sharp regret" (216–17). Moreover, Robins retains an implied union in the last paragraph of this climactic chapter, engaging in her characteristic rhetorical technique of producing unity from (apparent) separateness by "valuing, perhaps, most of all, those kindnesses of [James] that marked the years after our common Theatre-love grew cold" (217).

Where women's rights were concerned, Robins was innovative and courageous, but she also showed the good sense to work with collaborators—male and female, opponent and proponent. In her hands, collective autobiography is also a collaborative performance. Astutely aware that the creative process does not just operate in isolation, she turned collaboration, with its negative connotations, into creative networking. The actress who could collaborate with the unseen playwright recognized the power of engaging other empathetic artists and art forms to forge her own aesthetic. Neither limited by the competitiveness of the male ego, nor inclined toward a posture of subservience, Robins could accept an equal partnership, as she did with Marion Lea in their shared enterprise of translating, producing, and performing *Hedda Gabler*. Crafting her own dramatic vehicle, in which she would also star, marked another major step in her artistic development, but Robins also guaranteed herself an empathetic sounding board by co-scripting *Alan's Wife* with her close friend and supporter, Florence Bell. Correspondence with Robins attests to the pleasure Bell derived from their collaboration: "Il n'y a une plus haute collaboration que celle de la plume" (There's no higher collaboration than that of the pen).[34]

Episodic or sustained, collaborative undertakings served Robins well. For example, as a test case dramatizing the suffrage movement, *Votes for Women!* ran a pronounced risk. Accordingly, Robins enlisted a wider network of collaborators than usual, sharing her script in various stages of completion with "fellow" suffragists like Emmeline Pankhurst, producer Harley Granville-Barker, and would-be playwright Henry James. Letters exchanged with Emmeline show Robins renaming her heroine so as not to confuse her with Christabel Pankhurst, as well as discussing platform tactics, while Granville-Barker's letters reveal the give-and-take involved in the actual staging (he was responsible for renaming the play from Robins's original choice, "The Friend of Woman"). All told, Robins enjoyed a productive collaboration with a range of notable males besides James and Granville-Barker, including Ibsen, Archer, Shaw, Tree, Oscar Wilde, James Barrie, William Heinemann, and John Masefield. But it was collaboration with Florence Bell that was most meaningful to Robins, for their work together inspired the creativity of women's collective spirit. Case pinpoints that sense of connection for feminist scholars in the introduction to one of her collections: "A different kind of pleasure in the texts resides in the community of feminist scholarship created in the citations. . . . This interaction signals not only the community of scholars in the field, but also their direct interest in one another's work. Thus, a kind of dialogue is signalled in the citations that marks a sense of nourishment and dialectic."[35]

In the mode of creative negativity, Robins could be both compatible and subversive. The record of her correspondence with James about *Votes for Women!*, taking place in the decade after their apparent separation, demonstrates Robins turning potential opposition to extremely useful account. In her hands, James, no longer actively involved in the theatre nor a proponent of women's rights, becomes the excited ghost collaborator on a project that endorses militant suffrage. Eventually acknowledging himself "a captive warrior," he insists, "Don't be afraid I don't understand (or shouldn't, on seeing it) every (or any) development or trait the closer working out of your scheme imposes on you as you go" (*Theatre and Friendship* 259). Welcoming James into the collaborative process meant that Robins could benefit from his reactions, sometimes realizing that she needed to shore up her structure, at other times being alerted to just what it would take to forestall and persuade her male critics.[36] When she finally shared her completed script with him, he was clearly won over to her cause on more levels than he realized: "How perfectly delightful and adorable and how absolutely and as it *should* be!" (261).

Shaw was yet another of those male critics, someone who could be both supporter and provocateur. Robins actually took more advice from him than she did from James—after all, who was the better dramatist?—but she also rejected many of his later suggestions as grossly misreading her intentions. By the time that she was developing *Votes for Women!* she demonstrated a remarkable ability to turn Shaw's irritating tendency to tease or insult to good purpose, alternately letting his negativity provoke her to greater creativity and treating him as a very effective devil's advocate. Before long, Robins was ready to play his game from the safety of the anonymous critic. Her witty attack on Shaw's play *Great Catherine* (1913) for its "amoristic content" and its failure to acknowledge the achievements of female leadership shows her calling his bluff: "In the face of Mr. Shaw's failure before a fine opportunity, we are not consoled by the fact that in cheapening Catherine he cheapens his own talent." Continuing in this vein, she concludes, "Whether for purposes of jest or earnest, it is clear that intelligent representation of women cannot be left to men who, however modern they think themselves, have as regards women the medieval mind."[37] The so-called humorless actress whom Shaw called "Saint Elizabeth" was now ready to call him to account on his own terms. She was even ready to use his name for its market value when she published some of their correspondence as prologue to *Both Sides of the Curtain*. Furthermore, after he teasingly proposed that she use a youthful photograph of herself playing the heroine in James Albery's *Forgiven* as the book's frontispiece (already reproduced as Figure 17), she pragmatically and gleefully seized upon his recommendation, dismissing his provocation as "some gibe which I have unfortunately forgotten." Nonetheless, the strain of dealing with such an obnoxious personality still shows in her private notes to herself: "The Shaw letters not only by his later consent but by virtue—if virtue is the right word—of his repudiation of discretion made useable to illustrate his violent detestation of many of my views and decisions" ("The Art of Biography," Fales 7C.87–88).

What Robins had learned from collaborating with others she applied to the task of adapting herself for both the stage and page. More than just an example of self-adaptation, the dual project of *Votes for Women!* and *The Convert* signaled an ability to let no single or one-dimensional genre take artistic precedence. She consulted her own reader-responses just as she actively solicited the suggestions of others, writing herself notes "to remember," and in the case of *The Convert*, urging herself to remain "in consonance with my own desire to be at the matter exhaustively, *if* at all, in book form."[38] Talking to herself on paper, Robins extended the creative dialogue into a private arena, where she gained increasing fortitude to act according to her own convictions. Then, once again, she was able to return to the public sphere, not just in subject matter and in her willingness to put herself on the line, but in terms of the material measure of her artistic and commercial success. *Votes for Women!* ran to sold-out crowds, extending beyond its original contract and daily increasing its receipts, and Robins split a percentage of her profits between the longstanding Suffrage Society and the more recently established Women's Social and Political Union. In a letter to the *Daily Mirror* (23 April 1907), she announced her intention, describing the WSPU as "that younger society which has done so much to bring the question of women's enfranchisement to the position of political and public significance that it now occupies." As for *The Convert*, one of several covert autobiographies, it was a bestseller, and proceeds from the combined sales of both suffrage vehicles purchased the Sussex property which served as a rest home for professional women through 1988. (See Figure 20 for a photograph of Robins from the post-suffrage years.) Reversing the movement from private to public spheres that had characterized the life story of Besant, Robins in private retirement nonetheless continued her quiet, unstinting support of other women in need of her resourceful measures.

Historically, Robins's position as a feminist and as a woman of the theatre induced her to cross formal and structural boundaries and virtually create new forms of expression, for herself and other women but ultimately for anyone who endorses her outlook. The furthest extrapolation of Robins's technique—and possibly of performing autobiography in general—goes beyond the re-formation of the self to its dissolution. Her career in this respect could be described as a deliberate and continuous process of confounding others' perceptions of her as an individual, or even of the concept of singular, distinctive autobiography. Moreover, her championing of Ibsen helped significantly to introduce a new type of theatre and assist the recrudescence of British drama that was already underway with the likes of Ibsen and Shaw. Robins persevered and succeeded despite (and perhaps because of) the resistance she and her colleagues encountered—equivocal translations, access to the plays themselves, male actor-managers, an unwilling public. She overcame major limitations in a theatrical tradition that had long excluded real roles for women. Her sense of community always assumed a grand design. With Oscar Wilde, she had worked for the dream of a National Theatre, and when she had to pull back, she successfully turned her energies to breaking new ground with the 1897 founding of the New Century Theatre in London. Her collaborative-communal model in all things still stands today as the ideal that feminist networking only begins to approach.

The kind of velvet revolution Robins helped to foment cut to the heart of what was wrong with nineteenth-century English culture—the sexism, or misogyny, that she called "sex antagonism" that did such a disservice to both men and women. In this respect, we might do well to rewrite a claim made by Hélène Cixous in "The Laugh of the Medusa": "Woman un-thinks the unifying, regulating history that homogenizes and channels forces, herding contradictions into a single battlefield." For Robins that "un-thinking" eventually created a positively charged field of unification, an arena where oppositions could truly be re-

FIGURE 20. Elizabeth Robins in post-suffrage years (ca. 1926). Courtesy of Mabel Smith, Literary Executor, Elizabeth Robins Estate; The Elizabeth Robins Papers, Fales Library/Special Collections, New York University.

solved. In her New Woman mindset, Robins was not trying to divide but was seeking to find harmony at a higher level. Robins successfully conjoins art and politics, aesthetics and ideology, because she creatively invokes opposition and conflates negativity through networking and boundary-crossing. She fits into a specifically female tradition that runs the spectrum from Jane Austen to Virginia Woolf, illustrating just how effectively style can serve to move and instruct the most recalcitrant reader or audience member. Even the critics who didn't like Robins found themselves in the palm of her hand, their psychological refusal to submit to her arguments overcome by the artist's precise control of her medium. One of her contemporary supporters, Mrs. Patrick Campbell, called her "the first intellectual I had met on the stage," and Jane Marcus today extols her as a political genius. In the scope conjured up by these attributes, we can recognize an artist whose multiple skills compound one another, a polemicist who blends firebrand subject matter and aesthetic sensibility. When Robins coins and uses a key term like "sex antagonism," we know that she is putting negativity to a creative purpose. Like Audré Lorde, Robins realizes that "the master's tools will never dismantle the master's house"—and so she forges her own.[39]

Epilogue: The Female Quest Reconsidered

Having explored the female quest by applying my theory of creative negativity to four Victorian exemplars, I would like to conclude this study by considering some of the theory's implications for interrogating other authors and their texts. Casting my net over several examples from nineteenth-century popular culture should afford the reader an enjoyable but slightly different kind of accounting of how the female quest has been playing itself out. Although this last series of elaborations will remain relatively brief, it does reinforce how the working out of this theory (and any other new theory, for that matter) continues to test the boundaries of current language use. As new terms persist in cropping up, they determine their value by how well they help the reader to reconsider, revise, and extend the original theory. This retrofitting activity, after all, is always part of the process of theory formulation and validation. By implementing the theory of creative negativity in the context of other female quests, I intend to demonstrate its usefulness as a theory, not only because it sheds light on the new texts at hand but because its expansion further elucidates my overall argument about Cameron, Ritchie, Besant, and Robins. The texts that I have in mind are both central to our current cultural imagination and rich in opportunities to generate new insights into our past and future. After examining two male-authored texts, one from Victorian England and the other from turn-of-the century America, I will look back to Mary Shelley's *Frankenstein* as an exemplary case of an inverted female quest, one that turns creative negativity to parodic purpose in order to lay bare the process of identity formation and reconstruction.

Replaying the elements that I have been attributing to the female quest by studying its manifestations in popular culture allows us to recognize how popularity can confirm an intuitive endorsement that may not have been subject to continuous critical scrutiny. Two female-centered tales by male authors come readily to mind for their perennial appeal and the imagery they repeatedly assert—Lewis Carroll's *Alice's Adventures in Wonderland* (1865) and L. Frank Baum's *The Wonderful Wizard of Oz* (1900), both of which have since acquired the respectability that the label "classic" grants them. What both of these incarnations of the female quest highlight is the heroine's fight for sanity, a much more harrowing struggle than the typical male questor's linear search for an emblem reaffirming individual separateness. (This generalization is not entirely fair, of course, given spiritual quests by men who seek the selflessness of the transcendent self). Notably, the reward for these two girl-children goes well beyond mere social reinstatement to encompass a unique metaphysical awareness.

In both of these tales, the quest involves entering an aesthetic field that can be conveniently explained in terms of dreamworks and returning with a reified pearl of insight or perception, which in turn signals another step in the heroine's level or awareness of reality. For Alice, it's the pack of cards turning into falling leaves that confirms her combined experience of waking and dreaming as all of one piece.[1] Dorothy of the classic 1939 film version of Baum's tale literally moves into a world of color when she enters the kingdom of Oz, attaining a new aesthetic band that she can take back to inform her more mundane reality.[2] Whether the aesthetic field is a dream, an illusion, or a fantasy (such as going through the looking-glass in the second of the *Alice* books, which is a dream as well), the old aesthetics become redefined, newly minted by these heroines. In artistic terms the female quest operates to reinvent form, while in interpersonal terms its concomitant new perception of self or reality acts to erase boundaries between people, connecting rather than separating them.

MACROCOSM VERSUS MICROCOSM

However, neither resolution of these two female quests is reached without a disturbing prelude of madness or the threat of insanity being confronted and somehow incorporated into the heroine's overall self-realization, which is rendered all the more meaningful for its creative encounter with the forces of social negation. Apparently, the heroine must initially descend into a microcosm, a process I'll call *micromaterialization*. By using the term "micromaterialization," I am referring to the questor's descent into a world of madness from which she must try to escape with her prize. This descent is variously figured into the metaphors that inform Carol P. Christ's key feminist text, *Diving Deep and Surfacing: Women Writers on Spiritual Quest* (1980), and Adrienne Rich's poetry collection, *Diving into the Wreck* (1973). But for the child-woman, micromaterialization is usually non-volitional; it's something that happens to the heroine, seemingly brought about by intense, dissociative events, such as Alice tumbling down the rabbit hole or Dorothy pulled up into the air by the cyclone.[3] This passivity is itself indicative of the general female condition as more acted upon than acting, yet the very delay of externalized action in turn opens up the possibility for internalized exploration, however unsettling it may be. An extreme version of this allegory—extreme because it resists reentry into society and sanity—occurs in Charlotte Perkins Gilman's *The Yellow Wallpaper* (1899), whose heroine is forced by her physician-husband into the ostensibly therapeutic microcosm of the nursery room with its yellow wallpaper and goes irretrievably mad.

The mental picture that emerges from this process of micromaterialization is a *supra-image*, if you will, of the lesser or smaller universe that has frequently encased women. This is the image evoked by the very title of Henrik Ibsen's infamous play, *A Doll's House* (1889), demarcating as it does both the female as toy-object and the small-scale life-game she has thus far been willing to play. It is appropriate, perhaps even inevitable, that the female quest should take the form of entering this lesser universe in a symbolic mode and then battling to return triumphant into the "real" universe. And it is indeed a telling contrast that the standard male quest entails the much more direct path of going boldly forth into the real world from its onset. But once again the bravado of that male model tends to be self-limiting, for not even entering the dream world that is apparently set in opposition to reality may also mean that one's dream—that is, one's ideal or true goal—can never be fully realized or accomplished. Nora Helmer may spend most of Ibsen's play confined to the microcosm that is her domestic prison, but by play's end she exultantly slams the door on the box that has contained her—and most women of her period—for a lifetime.

In the Victorian period, we encounter a society very much intent on placing women into specific and well-defined boxes—possibly even more intent, in its growing insecurity, than British society had ever been. But Victorian women also found themselves being forced into definitional boxes that made less and less sense, even in the repressive terms of the dominant culture. The result of this state of affairs was a radical, albeit unintentional, decreation of the female self, wrought by Victorian society on women of the period. The situation was thus both perilous and rife with possibilities. A society which coerced one into incoherent self-definitions could quite easily drive one mad, a desperate consequence highlighted by a best-selling novel (and play) like Mrs. Henry Wood's *East Lynne* (1862). At the same time, however, a more positive recourse might occur in the kind of subversive rebellion undertaken by women with a fluid sense of self-definition, one that allowed them to grow internally and prosper externally while subtly critiquing the very culture that believed it was confining them. Such is the case for another best-selling novelist of the day, Mary Elizabeth Braddon, who penned the sensational *Lady Audley's Secret* (1862). Still another fascinating arena in which elements of this battle between the sexes played themselves out was that of the Victorian illustrated text. Here we frequently find depictions of women who are being forcibly compressed by the frames which surround them, but as the *fin de siècle* approaches, we also begin to discover more disturbing images of disruption—of metamorphosis and explosion—imagery that even finds its way into children's literature.[4]

Thus, the nineteenth-century female quest acts out the image of entering into a microcosm and discovering or bringing back something that will resolve the questor's externally (male) imposed plight. That "something" is an emblem of communication, a dissolution of the boundaries between individuals (even if, initially, someone like Nora's husband feels isolated and cut off by her insight). The struggle for lucidity in the female quest carries a concomitant necessity not just to achieve sanity but also to overcome, for oneself and others, the elements that might be inflicted on a woman's way of life that drive her insane. At their worst, men have attempted to keep women within their repressive, male-defined microcosms (we could say that some hegemonic societies have essentially tried to keep women from completing their quest), and it would seem that it is partly the role of the female questor to rescue such men from themselves, whether or not they know they need rescuing and, for that matter, redemption.

Completing the supraimage signaled by the female questor moving a symbolic object or insight from a lesser to a greater level or sphere of reality—of turning the potentially negative experience of micromaterialization to creative purpose—is the final stage of the process I will now call *metamaterialization*. The coinage "metamaterialization" was chosen in part to help signify the notion that the process works from a state of loss or absence. Thus, after the female questor plunges into, finds, or creates a dream, she then metamaterializes something from that dream, thereby initiating the movement from one ontological sphere to a more encompassing one. Poetry sometimes partakes of a parallel process, as we witness in Marianne Moore's poem about "imaginary gardens with real toads," for poetry's very ability to bring into being something real and viable through metaphor resonates with the same magical power of the female questor jumping from one level of reality to another. For the subjects of my book, metamaterialization is repeatedly engendered from an image of loss or absence, which is then overcome through intuitive and innovative application of the process I have been describing.[5] In the case of Cameron, metamaterialization is the resource for her allegorical imagery; in Ritchie, it becomes her rhetorical technique; in Besant, it develops into its own mode of religious evolution; and in Robins, it metamorphoses into a method of dramatic communication.

The operation of creative negativity has all along reflected the process expressed by the movement from *micromaterialization* to *metamaterialization* in the female quest. For example, combining *reality and illusion* recalls the female questor's ability to metamaterialize an illusory object or symbol into the real world to which she must finally return. A shift in *magnitude* may remind us of the activity of the female quest as well, for a sense of multifariousness or zooming out parallels metamaterialization, chiefly in terms of the enhanced perspective achieved by the creative negativist. I have even used the word "metamaterialization" several times earlier in this book without specifically defining it, since its meaning has seemed apparent in context. Accordingly, I describe how Wassily Kandinsky acknowledges the creative potential of interdisciplinary exchange for conjoining artists from different fields as well as for encouraging individual artists to experiment with artistic boundaries, in both instances to forge something previously unimagined. From the conjunction of spirituality and creativity, itself quite remarkable, he seems to be endorsing the emergence of something "non-material," or, in my terms, the activity of "meta-materialization" (hyphenated in this context and in other self-evident examples). Likewise, my meaning seems self-apparent when I depict Julia Margaret Cameron transfiguring—or "meta-materializing"—her autobiographical "jottings" into "the dignity of experience" as she pens "Annals of My Glass House," thereby creating her unique blend of the personal and transpersonal.

Nor is it difficult to envision how instances of micromaterialization explode into moments of metamaterialization for Annie Besant, for the two terms almost recapitulate her entire history of moving from microcosms into macrocosms, a process that now seems quite predictable from the rhetorical clues she provides in her two autobiographies. And for Robins, as both author and actress, the terminology makes a fitting commentary on her uncanny achievements. Not only did she create symbolic gestures like the one of her heroine Vida Levering turning a former lover's telegram announcing his candidacy into "political dynamite," but her acting style caused audience members to catapult from illusion into an uncomfortable new reality, an activity that itself closely resembles the process of conversion. For Ritchie, however, the mechanism of micromaterialization eliding into metamaterialization is even more fundamental: it informs her rhetorical strategy from the most minute word choices, through the subtle projection of imagery, to overall framing devices that celebrate the unremitting nature of the female quest.

In order to analyze Ritchie's distinctive brand of creative negativity, I have already had recourse to both the term and process of metamaterialization. Specifically, Ritchie's early period finds her experimenting with a sophisticated form of the supraimage of the microcosm, for *Old Kensington* (1873) actually culminates in an ironic reversal of metamaterialization. Quoting her description of the "fire leap[ing] brightly in its iron cage" at the end of the novel, I note how she accentuates the concluding irony of failed "meta-materialization" as "the sunlight . . . extinguished the flame" (56.531). Here Ritchie openly toys with a disturbing vision of a world where communication flounders and no quest seems possible, but acknowledging loss or absence, in this and other cases, simply constitutes part of her programmatic confrontation with and transformation of negativity. In almost elegiac fashion, she regularly evokes sister-practitioners of metamaterialization, particularly Julia Margaret Cameron. In these instances, Ritchie metamaterializes multiple definitions of friendship (*From an Island*), conjoins herself with Cameron to metamaterialize their shared creative activity ("Reminiscences" for *Alfred, Lord Tennyson, and His Friends*), and invokes microcosms only to metamaterialize us out again into the larger universe which frames them ("From Friend to Friend"). In the hands of a consummate practitioner like Anne Thackeray Ritchie, metamaterialization allows her to spin out the female quest as an individual and archetypal activity, as something that she both exalts and exemplifies, for her own and all time.

MALE VERSUS FEMALE

"To strive, to seek, to find, and not to yield!" These words comprise the final line of Victorian Poet Laureate Alfred Lord Tennyson's quintessential poem about the male quest entitled "Ulysses" (1833; 1842). For the male questor, in the tradition of the medieval romance or the long mythic and warring past, the goal is both desired and undesired. That is, the quest usually follows a clearly defined, linear route marked by a series of physical adventures toward a specific reward or treasure, like the famous Holy Grail sought by the Knights of the Round Table, yet the value largely inheres in the heroic journey itself, one that must either be repeated to stave off boredom or longed for through its loving evocation in multiple retellings. It is the striving and the seeking (highlighted by an unyielding stance) that are valued by this stereotypical male quest, not the finding itself. Necessary though it is as a spur to questing, the goal once achieved carries with it a static outcome that apparently must be overturned or exploded somehow. And if, as in the case of Ulysses, the goal appears to be home, then home represents that selfsame static nightmare that the questor eventually hopes to escape.

What's wrong with this scenario? Well, for one thing, it reflects an inner conflict that is apparently not recognized or acknowledged by the chief actor on the scene. In many respects, we could say that this male questor is unconsciously looking for ways to undermine or undo his very activity. It also smacks of a kind of insufferable narcissism; no one else seems to figure as a subjective consciousness here, especially not a heroine in distress who might need to be rescued to satisfy the stipulated goal of the mission. The unyielding stance of the hero bespeaks the kind of egotism that cries out, as if to an admiring crowd, "Look at me!" Of course, one could argue that in anthropological terms the entire scenario symbolizes a rite of passage, a significant step on the road to manhood and its attendant expectations of stoic self-defense. This is the pattern of the male quest in the Western tradition that has been variously documented by Lord Raglan, Otto Rank, Carl Jung, and Joseph Campbell, among others.[6] But what is this self that the male questor will be defending? Lacking self-awareness or insight into what drives him forward, this questor will evidently continue to seize opportunities to prolong or restart his quest, much as the Homeric Ulysses managed to protract his journey homeward, however often he protested to the contrary. This questor can finally be found dwelling on memories of a glorious past, for no present has meaning for him unless it can play a part in prompting the retelling of this backward-looking tale in which he is cast in the starring role.

For me, the preceding review of the male quest brings to the fore several questions: Does the author's gender figure into the concept of the female quest? Can males truly write or envision a female quest? And what are the limitations or advantages in such an undertaking? Carroll, Baum, and Ibsen all share an intuitive alignment with the female experience in the first place, if only because they are willing to imagine a tale with a female at its center. We know that Carroll, as the reclusive Oxford don Charles Lutwidge Dodgson, was already at some remove from the mainstream, and his peculiar case of feeling closely linked to young girls suggests his subjective attunement to the tale he recognizes will appeal to his female auditors and readers. As for Baum, he wrote adventure tales for both boys and girls, but his regular return to the heroines of the Oz books (Dorothy, Ozma, Trot, Betsy Bobbin) reflects a longing for the daughters he never had, ones whom it would seem he might have granted a genuine subject position. And Ibsen presents an intriguing case of a playwright whose iconoclastic parables have frequently involved a recentering from the margins of traditional societal alignments.

So, yes, it appears that males can certainly pen female quests, and perhaps even lend them additional weight through their male authority in a world that has traditionally been more friendly to the enterprise of males publishing books, staging plays, or making films. Their perspective can often be instructive, their satire biting, their leadership compelling. But something will always be missing, for each individual "project" is just that—a temporary taking-on of the subjective experience of the female, even if it is returned to with regularity and compassion. An apt analogy to this assertion can be found in racial discourse. The white civil rights worker, for example, no matter how rigorous and tiring a laborer in his cause, will always have recourse to the safety and security of his Caucasian skin. What Cameron, Ritchie, Besant, Robins, and other women share with respect to the female quest is an interplay between modes of expression and lived experience—the myriad yet patterned ways in which self-expression for women is embodied in the performative autobiographies of their lifelong acts of metamaterialization.

At this point, I must admit that a lingering fixation or obsession still haunts the depictions of Alice and Dorothy. There persists an immaturity, a youthfulness, an asexuality in these two female questors who have been authored by men. It may be that female sexuality remains a mystery to the average heterosexual male; it is either exploited from a blatantly sexualized perspective or evaded entirely. Dorothy's "asexuality" (namely, a femaleness generally unavailable to the male) via her cinematic incarnation as immortalized by Judy Garland has in fact been embraced by her openly gay adherents; apparently homosexuality is more comfortable acknowledging its sexuality in such frank endorsements.[7] But it is not mere coincidence that Carroll sets his tale underground, mirroring a move to the unconscious, or that Baum unleashes a cyclone's energy to propel his plot. Female sexual energy produces life (another way of claiming its drive toward micromaterialization), but before the female quest can be launched in a manner that will allow for self-exploration of the questor's inner universe, her sexuality must somehow be set aside. This plotline has an explanation that is sadly simple, I'm afraid, for without this disappearance, the marriage plot would undoubtedly take over and determine the contours of the female quest as we have often known it.[8]

Yet these two male authors are onto something, even if they cannot completely integrate it into their modus operandi, when they give us such asexual heroines. The female quest as I have been detailing it must of necessity begin by laying sexuality aside, but it is ultimately a refracted sexuality that fuels the metamaterialization that completes the journey. And herein lies a major distinction between the female quest as male- or female-authored. The male author cannot help treating the female heroine partially as an object (she is, after all, still the "other"), and so her asexuality can sometimes become uncomfortably close to infantilization. Carroll's infantilizing of Alice is both a verbal and a visual matter, for not only does he finally relegate her to a "little sister" status but his own portraits of her for the original *Alice's Adventures Under Ground* (1862–1863) depict growth uncomfortably constrained (and contained) by the dimensions of his tiny margins.[9] Clearly female adulthood is something unpleasant, even horrific, to be staved off as long as possible.

Baum comes closer to granting Dorothy a measure of development and maturity, although he does finally return her to a cocoon-like home environment on the Kansas farm. In this respect, it is intriguing to note Baum's later short story, "Little Dorothy and Toto," collected in his *Little Wizard Stories of Oz*

(1913). This tale concludes with the Wizard playing a trick on Dorothy and admonishing her, "I wanted to prove to you that it is really dangerous for a little girl to wander alone in a fairy country" (46). In both this and *The Wonderful Wizard of Oz*, Dorothy is much younger than her cinematic counterpart Judy Garland: Baum and his illustrators depict her as around five or six years of age. In contrast, Baum wrote a more adult boy's quest, *The Master Key: An Electrical Fairy Tale* (1901), dedicated to his son Robert and modeled after his son's "adventures" with electricity. The title page reads as follows: "Founded upon the mysteries of electricity and the optimism of its devotees. It was written for boys, but others may read it." Interestingly enough, Donald L. Greene and Douglas G. Greene, who introduce the book's 1974 reprint, observe that although Rob starts out as a "stock hero of the innumerable boy's adventure series," the story soon develops into a more complex novel of education (iv–v).

In contrast to the child-heroines of the popular quest stories I have been discussing, the women who comprise the subject matter of this book embody the concept of the female quest from the inside out in the intertwining of their lives and their self-expression. Their more fully realized and developed instances of metamaterialization demonstrate how differently (because the stakes are so much higher) adult women set aside issues of their own sexuality in order to achieve their inner and outer goals. The experiences of Besant and Robins recall the range and impact of such displacing of sexuality. For Besant, the rigorous self-honesty that finally led to the spirituality that she embraced as leader of the worldwide Theosophy movement first required that she distance herself from other human beings. The price she paid was great, particularly in the loss of her two children to her repressive clergyman-husband, but the rewards were even greater. Through Theosophy, in which she was eventually reunited with her children, she ascended from one to another level of increasingly transcendent circles. Robins made a similar choice but in all likelihood to a more delimited personal end. Her various responses to the suicide of her actor-husband led to a series of artistic decisions, both in the Ibsen roles she played and in the collaborations she undertook. Ultimately, the creativity she fashioned out of negativity emerged in a life and body of work that were in part shaped by a hidden restraint, namely the power of her self-contained and unspoken sexuality.

AN INVERTED FEMALE QUEST

Now that I have reconsidered elements of the female quest as performed through two popular nineteenth-century classics, in part to further illuminate the lives and work of my four female questors, I would like to demonstrate how creative negativity can be inverted in the service of parody. I have already shown how Cameron, Ritchie, Besant, and Robins variously redefined formal elements by pressing against old boundaries to create new forms. Yet, however seriously they took their work and set their goals, they retained a self-consciousness that allowed them to poke fun at themselves while they critiqued the Victorian society that tried to contain them. In this respect, they tested the fluidity of their multiple self-definitions, moving back and forth across playing fields of their own remaking. This sportive quality is inherent in the nature of creative negativity, for it requires the practitioner to be flexible about where she places her focus, to zoom in close to her subject and pull back to reframe it, to be ready always to overturn negation into creation. As a game, the operation of creative negativity ultimately sets aside the rules of time and space in order to free the player to develop a fresh game plan. Because my four exemplars often needed to exercise their options covertly, they developed strategies that can be called subversive, techniques that could at times even be considered parodic. Initially, this activity was perhaps most obvious in the case of Anne Thackeray Ritchie's retelling of her domestic fairytales, but she and her sister creative negativists found myriad ways to subtly seize their rhetorical and imagistic openings.

So, despite the fact that all four women experienced containment, they found ways out of and around their containers, sometimes even embellishing them by turning their own heartfelt efforts into playful self-parody. But what about the most immediate predecessors to these women, female creative artists who experienced similar constraints but who operated against less clear-cut opposition and without the sense of hidden cohesiveness I have been recounting? If we look at a sustained creative work from a pre-Victorian period, might we not find out that the Victorians in fact inherited some of the covert components I have been delineating? And might those elements have originally been buried yet deeper, emerging from an intermix of the unconscious and conscious, their parodic inversions covering up what might have seemed even more revolutionary for their times? Barred from active participation in the creative marketplace of their era, women writers of the eighteenth and early nineteenth centuries fashioned their own subversive strategies, their female quests anticipating some of the tools and activities of their Victorian successors.[10]

By now a well-worn staple of popular culture, Mary Wollstonecraft Godwin Shelley's *Frankenstein; Or, The Modern Prometheus* (1818; 1831) constitutes one of the most powerful myths of creativity ever invented. That it was written by a young woman in her late teens, the soon-to-be wife of a prolific and justly famous Romantic poet, has long imbued it with suspicions about the source of its own creative invention, but recent (largely feminist) scholarship has done a good job of providing a more equitable sounding board for discussing its inception and reputation.[11] For my purposes, this Gothic tale furnishes a prime opportunity to view creative negativity turned to parodic, even horrific, application. And horror is perhaps the most significant result of this inverted mode, for it raises the stakes in the aesthetic arena of Shelley's own making to reveal an art form that is genuinely disturbing, not just something that passes as mere diversion or pure entertainment. Ultimately, *Frankenstein*'s horrific inversions of creative negativity construct a parody that critiques male-governed society in productive ways, pointing the reader toward the values that the female quest espouses.

In this vein, I choose to read Victor Frankenstein's creation—the "creature," as he calls himself, not the "monster" of filmic legend—as the embodiment of negative creativity turned inward on itself in a parodic, horrific fashion. Through the specter of a male student of science attempting to create life, Shelley evokes a twisted parody of the technique envisioned: misguided machinery in the wrong hands produces doubly botched results. As each element of creative negativity is skewed by the god-preempting creation of human life, we witness the bounds of society broken down to their primal level. The creature emerges as a spliced-together monstrosity of different times, different lives, all uneasily focused into one terrible entity. And at novel's end, instead of fixation in space, we encounter the inverted—and potentially unending—wandering across the Arctic wasteland, where nothing is fixed and one's position is barely known. Within the parameters of this grotesque male effort at the supreme act of creation, Shelley places the consciousness of a woman, further encasing it within an almost parodic plethora of formal framing devices. To see the creature as an incarnation of female consciousness enables us to recognize the ways in which "woman" is constructed, contained, and imprisoned—as well as the risks those activities run should the object become a subject capable of breaking out of her prison and wrecking vengeance on those who have tried to control her to satisfy their own ends.

At the novel's (moral) center lies the creature's monologue. Six chapters in length, it tells "his" tale in a high-flown, emotional rhetoric which represents a basic working out of all the elements of creative negativity I have been elaborating. I am quoting in full the first paragraph of this account so that the reader can trace with me Shelley's mode of setting the stage for this unfolding process:

> It is with considerable difficulty that I remember the original era of my being; all the events of that period appear confused and indistinct. A strange multiplicity of sensations seized me, and I saw, felt, heard, and smelt at the same time; and it was, indeed, a long time before I learned to distinguish between the operations of my various senses. By degrees, I remember, a stronger light pressed upon my nerves, so that I was obliged to shut my eyes. Darkness then came over me and troubled me, but hardly had I felt this when, by opening my eyes, as I now suppose, the light poured in upon me again. I walked and, I believe, descended, but I presently found a great alteration in my

sensations. Before, dark and opaque bodies had surrounded me, impervious to my touch or sight; but I now found that I could wander on at liberty, with no obstacles which I could not either surmount or avoid. The light became more and more oppressive to me, and the heat wearying me as I walked, I sought a place where I could receive shade. This was the forest near Ingolstadt; and here I lay by the side of a brook resting from my fatigue, until I felt tormented by hunger and thirst. This roused me from my nearly dormant state, and I ate some berries which I found hanging on the trees or lying on the ground. I slaked my thirst at the brook, and then lying down, was overcome by sleep.[12]

First and foremost, we are presented with growth out of negativity, but rather than the philosophical or emotional exploration typical of the constructive creative negativity I have been detailing, this beginning out of nothingness is rendered as a very rooted physical occurrence, its isolated subjectivity forced to deal with a barrage of confusing emotions. These reflections, indeed the very act of remembering, will eventually turn to epistemological and moral meditations, but for now muddled physicality remains their primary subject matter. The multifariousness of these inchoate sensations further contributes to a sense of being lost in time; with no solid baseline in time, there can be no opportunity for time to be altered or played with to potentially creative ends. As a result, when the creature's synaesthetic perceptions combine reality and illusion, the conflation produces merely a temporary experience of freedom. Furthermore, when nothingness and disorientation do give way to the focus of light itself, it is painful; instead of enlightenment, this focus leads to more confusion, oppression, even torment, before near-dormancy drifts into sleep's unconsciousness.

Creative negativity usually occurs within a social context, in keeping with both the female creative negativist's sense of community and her awareness that her tools must link up to counteract the pressure of a larger social fiction. But Shelley gives us creative negativity within a vacuum. Entirely alone and without the ability to communicate, the creature needs to discover the nature of family and society itself through his own efforts. Significantly, true self-awareness (the equivalent of creative negativity's self-referentiality) comes only after a great delay, when the creature has (miraculously enough) taught himself language. Only then can he think: "The words induced me to turn towards myself" (13.114). Unfortunately, self-referentiality can result only in self-rejection in this scenario, as the creature concludes his reflections with the anguished rhetorical question of self-ascription, "Was I, then, a monster, a blot upon the earth, from which all men fled and whom all men disowned?" (115). Ironically, the full flowering of creative negativity occurs for the creature precisely when he becomes a social being, when he achieves a status from which he is immediately ejected.

At this point, the creature's attempted entrance into society reenacts in earnest all the elements of creative negativity, now with an agonizing degree of self-consciousness and self-referentiality as well as an hysterical (female) awareness of time pressure which both attenuates and constricts that effort. Having lovingly observed the De Lacey family from the safety of his hidden hovel, he entertains the possibility of introducing himself to them. The creature's indirect references to the family he has come to adore and wishes to unite with combine profound emotional truth with self-deception; reality and illusion thereby congeal and become twisted into a series of double meanings. And multifariousness surrounds the event: everything comes to depend on his interview with the blind patriarch of the family. But the climax, the moment of so-called truth, is simultaneously the anti-climax and the moment of untruth. So, once again, this version of creative negativity results in failure and frustration, for the attempt to turn illusion into reality is destroyed by the return of the sighted members of the family, who cannot see the reality—the human feeling—beneath the illusion of the creature's monstrous appearance. And now the creature feels his isolation all the more acutely because it entails loss of the society previously unknown to him.

The novel's many framing devices further point up the author's parodic proclivities and repeatedly return us to variations on the themes of isolation, obsession, and madness. Speaking for the first time as acknowledged author, Mary Shelley in her 1831 introduction invokes the inverse of the Romantic male myth of solitary creation; appreciating the creative environment produced by the collaborative/competitive enterprise of group storytelling at Lake Geneva in 1816, she recounts her own desire to "awaken thrilling horror" in both her listeners and eventual readers (ix). Next in the sequence of layers comes Percy Bysshe Shelley's unsigned preface, reprinted from the original 1818 edition; assuming the first-person prerogative of the then-anonymous author, this preface alternately ascribes the creative endeavor to "fancy," the unconscious reverberations of classic texts of poetry, and "casual conversation" (xiii). By allowing Percy's self-contradictions to coexist in juxtaposition with her own account, Mary thus silently comments on both the multiplicity of explanations of creativity (revealing herself comfortable with uncertainty, much in the manner invoked by Keats's negative capability) and the (male) hubris of trying to assign it a single provocation. Now that modern readers can credit authorship of this preface as well as an unpublished review of *Frankenstein* to Percy, we can recognize the degree to which he was both self-involved and obtuse about his young wife's project.[13] Aligning himself with Frankenstein as victim, Percy betrays an association we have long suspected. Certainly there are many parallels between Frankenstein's friend, Henry Clerval, and Percy, but it is also in Frankenstein's arrogance that we can read Mary's parodic critique of her husband's presumption and detachment as exemplary male Romantic poet.

Shelley's cautionary tale follows through with its own implications, detailing a series of catastrophes and unresolvable conflicts to reveal the dark side of the female quest. From Frankenstein's initially wrong choice of isolation from family and society proceeds his uncontrolled mania; his egotism unrestrained, he commits the audacious act of solitary creation, from which there is no deliverance. In a twisted, even obscene way, Frankenstein's inner pursuit metamaterializes as a monster. It takes the natural balance between male and female to produce a child. When that balance is somehow upset, as it is in Elizabeth Robins's play *Alan's Wife*, then the creative negativist portrays her alter-ego destroying the unbearable result. In contrast to the Robins heroine, who knows what she must do and acts accordingly, with full awareness of the repercussions, Frankenstein only half-heartedly tries to escape the implications of his heinous action. Repeatedly, he is drawn back into the self-destructive microcosm of his own making. Imprisoned by his hubris and lack of self-knowledge, he refuses to heed even his own warnings.

The female quest recognizes and confronts the danger of getting sucked back into the microcosm, for we witness an ominous trap of circularity when creative negativity goes awry and metamaterialization cannot occur. Given the challenging leap to the macrocosm in the first place, when ambivalence is heightened— as it is for Frankenstein—then that barrier becomes truly insurmountable. In contrast, Dorothy at the end of *The Wonderful Wizard of Oz* learns that she is considering the wrong method for returning home to Kansas by taking the false wizard's hot-air balloon. Instead, what she needs has been within her all along: she just has to come to that self-realization. Metamaterialization occurs, after all, as the creative outcome of dream or fantasy, but it can also fail to take place when the dream becomes a nightmare from which one cannot awake, cannot metamaterialize. Both Dorothy and Alice (of both *Alice's Adventures in Wonderland* and *Through the Looking-Glass*) experience the fearful tension between feeling lost forever within a fantasy world or being able to return—to metamaterialize. In Alice's case, the first breakthrough occurs when she can exclaim, "You're all nothing but a pack of cards!" With this epiphany—calling things for what they really are—she is able to awaken from her dream world and escape its efforts to contain her. And in the second instance, Alice takes charge even more actively, shaking the Red Queen until she turns into the black kitten on the familiar side of the looking-glass, thereby transporting herself back to the real world from which she had originally tried to escape.

Within Shelley's inverted female quest, in which creative negativity is turned into monster, Frankenstein's tragic flaw may well be his failure to make viable connections with other people. Even the two male figures he professes to love, his father and Henry, remain cut off from his trust and confidence. In contrast, creative negativity and the constructive female quest are redolent with connections, whether we look to Alice trying to find the anthropomorphic white rabbit or Dorothy linking up the various individuals she meets on the yellow brick road. Looking back to my Victorian exemplars, it is easy to see the numerous ways in which they reach out to connect the commonplace and the ineffable. Julia Margaret Cameron is remarkably adept at linking the material world and the divine, while Anne Thackeray Ritchie meets the rhetorical challenge of trying to connect with her readership via negative empathy, her unique brand of emotional magic. As for Annie Besant, worldwide spiritual unity becomes a real possibility from within the framework of Theosophy as she re-creates it. And Elizabeth Robins repeatedly demonstrates how the isolated individual can cut across division as she engages in countless boundary-crossings.

In the case of Frankenstein's creature, he is shown at perhaps his most sympathetic when he is gazing with longing at the life of the De Lacey family, as if it is both a microcosm of society and an emblem of the macrocosm into which he cannot metamaterialize. Though not of his own choosing, his isolation is also nightmarish; like Frankenstein, the creature finds sleep difficult, and he is haunted by his dreams. (Here the 1939 film version of *The Wonderful Wizard of Oz* stands in sharp contrast, for Judy Garland's Dorothy tries hard to remember what her dream experience apparently tries to occlude.) In many respects, the inverted female quest resembles a state of dissociation, wherein one cannot mate, procreate, or socialize. Unnamed and unwanted, the creature begs for nonexistence, but as he variously encounters his double in his creator, their combined deaths seem the only fitting termination. The rage, revenge, and hatred that have been building within creator and created, toward both self and other, reach a climax in the social near-sterility of the chase across the Arctic, where the only being to witness and record their tale is himself another isolate, a would-be Frankenstein, namely Robert Walton, the stranded ship captain.[14]

Reading *Frankenstein* as an inverted female quest suggests that the novel may be seen as an allegory of what man has done to woman in our society. Essentially placing her in a microcosmic, lesser universe, he has forced her to create herself—to metamaterialize herself—leaving her inherently dissociated, a self created from the fragments of the male. But this is also a symbolic tale of creation and vengeance, and in her covert fight for sanity, woman learns how to express and understand herself. In an horrific take on this tale, the female body remains central to the male, who is constantly putting it on view and judging it. Just as the creature finds himself in a monstrous body, in a nightmare version of woman's situation she finds her own body monstrous. One scenario that can result from this dilemma has woman turning on herself in self-destructive ways.

Another, more positive spin, can also be fostered, however, as women learn to trust one another, finding ways to effect their own healing. Perhaps the tension between these two responses helps to explain why Shelley's potent images continue to haunt us, as women today carry on the struggle for full existence in a world still subject to male reductionism.

How conscious of his or her technique must a writer be for us to say that he or she is employing a strategy? This is a thorny question, and not just because literary critics are leery of engaging in the intentional fallacy. For Mary Shelley, however, the issue must at least be acknowledged if I am to consider *Frankenstein* as an inverted female quest. Surely her many framing devices and even her subsequent revisions of the novel after Percy's death go a long way toward confirming an uncanny awareness of technique that borders on conscious choice. For further confirmation, her parodic tendencies can also be observed elsewhere in her canon. Her short story "Transformation" (1830), for example, shows her cheerfully reversing many of the incidents from Byron's diabolical doppelgänger drama *The Deformed Transformed* (1824), which Shelley knew intimately because she had transcribed it for him. As for my Victorian exemplars, they probably divide by time period: Cameron and Ritchie seem to claim their rebellious status less consciously than do Besant and Robins, yet the two earlier figures are nevertheless aware of their own inventiveness as they introduce creative innovations into their respective fields. As "gentle subversives," they managed to hone their intuitive choices into recognizable, even trademark, styles.

Already, I can recognize elements of creative negativity surfacing in the analyses of other literary critics. A serendipitous conjunction of subject and methodology occurs, for instance, in an article published by Julie Kane in *Twentieth Century Literature* (1995) which opens as follows: "If one were to catalogue the various types of 'mystical' experience appearing in the writings of Virginia Woolf, the list would be virtually indistinguishable from the topics of interest to the Theosophists and spiritualists of her day: telepathy, auras, astral travel, synaesthesia, reincarnation, the immortality of the soul, and the existence of a Universal Mind" (328). Besides citing specific comparisons among the writings of Besant, the New Physicists, and Woolf, Kane goes on to explore Woolf's paradoxical attraction to mysticism in terms reminiscent of my language of creative negativity: "The root 'mystical experience'—loss of self; merger with a greater unity; the apprehension of numinousness, timelessness, transcendence, and intensified meaning—is recognizable in many of [Woolf's] novels and in her personal writings" (332). Here we can identify echoes of creative negativity's emphasis on negation through loss, the evocation of timelessness, the intensity of the focal point (with its attendant boundary-crossing), the tension between reality and illusion, and a sense of magnitude. Applied to such key Woolf texts as

Mrs. Dalloway (1925), *To the Lighthouse* (1927), *Orlando* (1928), and *The Waves* (1931), these concepts can help us to gauge the Modernist sensibility as an extension of elements already present in Victorian texts, enabling us to stress continuity as well as difference between the two periods.[15]

The four women whose lives and work constitute the basis of this study achieved a considerable measure of personal and artistic freedom. That they had to persist against considerable odds is also true, but the rewards for their efforts stand today not only as model accomplishments but as exemplary strategy. In the course of uncovering their remarkable achievements and the interconnections among them, I became aware of other women's stories, untold or only partially recovered, that still need to be unlayered and explored. Besides some of the authors I mention in Chapter 1, their American counterparts merit at least an initial listing: Susan Fenimore Cooper, Margaret Fuller Ossoli, Harriet Wilson, Harriet Jacobs, Sophia Hawthorne, Louisa May Alcott, Fanny Fern (Sara Payson Willis Parton), Emily Dickinson, Mary Chesnut, Alice James, Lydia Maria Child, Sarah Orne Jewett, Elizabeth Stuart Phelps, Charlotte Perkins Gilman, Jane Addams, Edith Wharton, Willa Cather, and Gertrude Stein.[16] Still other figures who may be more well known—writers like Jane Austen, the Brontë sisters, even George Eliot and Virginia Woolf—deserve to be seen newly in light of their sister artists' reconsidered accomplishments. The cohesiveness that I am postulating in the operation of creative negativity for Cameron, Ritchie, Besant, and Robins may prove more elusive when applied to some of the other creative artists of their day, but it points toward a future where creative consciousness can be more readily communicated, shared, and built upon. For in fictional creations and life stories from the nineteenth century, we see the female quest beginning to take control of its communal destiny by writing its own script.

Reference Matter

Notes

Chapter 1. Creative Negativity and the Female Quest

1. Keats first advanced his concept of negative capability in a letter to his brothers George and Tom (21–27 December 1817). David Perkins cites W. J. Bate's paraphrase, which emphasizes negating the ego in order to develop the broad ability to perceive and embrace everything—in short, denying the intellect in an effort to avoid sweeping rejections (as applied to the Victorians specifically, to lay aside dogma and preconceptions). See Perkins, *English Romantic Writers*, 1209. Keats's expression briefly resurfaces in my chapters on Besant and Robins and with reference to Mary Shelley. For a recent forum that invokes negation as a critical aesthetic, see Daniel Fischlin, *Negation, Critical Theory, and Postmodern Textuality*. This collection contains an essay by Veronica Hollinger applicable to my reading of *Frankenstein* (developed in the Epilogue), "Putting on the Feminine: Gender and Negativity in *Frankenstein* and *The Handmaid's Tale*."

2. This last point informs many feminist studies, most notably Sandra M. Gilbert and Susan Gubar's *The Madwoman in the Attic: The Woman Writer and the Nineteenth-Century Literary Imagination*. I explore the issue of female anger with particular respect to Ritchie in a study entitled "Hate and Humor as Empathetic Whimsy in Anne Thackeray Ritchie."

3. I discuss *The Wonderful Wizard of Oz* (1900) as a Theosophical quest in Chapter 4, and it figures prominently in my elaboration of the female quest in the Epilogue. Apropos, the official journal of the Theosophical Society of America is the monthly publication entitled *The Quest*, founded in 1912. Sad to say, another aptly named journal, *Quest: A Feminist Quarterly*, had a short-lived history (1974–1982).

4. See A[nne] R[itchie], "Elizabeth Barrett Browning," and J[ulia] P[rinsep] S[tephen], "Julia Margaret Cameron," in the *Dictionary of National Biography: To 1900*, 3:78–82 and 752; S[eymour] V[esey] F[itz]G[erald], "Sir Richmond Thackeray Willoughby Ritchie," *DNB: 1912–1921*, 462–63; H. V. Lovett and Patrick Cadell, "Annie Besant," *DNB: 1931–1940*, 72–74; and Angela V. John, "Elizabeth Robins," *DNB: Missing Persons*, 560–61.

5. Two texts which invoke the concept of victimology only to actively overturn it are Martha Vicinus, *Suffer and Be Still: Women in the Victorian Age*, and Nina Auerbach, *Romantic Imprisonment: Women and Other Glorified Outcasts*, the former because its historical accounts document the cases of real working women, the latter because Auerbach so ably demonstrates the inherent strength out of which her female subjects operate.

6. See, for example, Margaret Macmillan, *Women of the Raj*, as well as the considerable body of travel literature by Victorian women that was republished or made available for the first time in the late twentieth century. Unfortunately, much of this literature has been allowed to go out of print again.

7. The Cameron Family Papers (Accession no. 850858) are available to scholars through the Special Collections at the J. Paul Getty Museum's Research Institute for the History of Art and the Humanities, which houses seventeen boxes of manuscript materials to support its extensive photographic collection of images by Julia Margaret Cameron. Besides her correspondence, the papers include an unpublished two-page fragment entitled "Reminiscences," written during her final years in Sri Lanka. Cf. Joanne Lukitsh, "'Simply Peasants': Artistry, Authorship, and Ideology in Julia Margaret Cameron's Photography in Sri Lanka."

8. A reliable source for this assertion about James's romantic interest in Robins is their mutual friend, Marie Belloc Lowndes (1868–1947), also a good friend of Anne Thackeray Ritchie, whose correspondence with Lowndes I discuss in Chapter 3. See Lowndes's remarks on the subject of the James–Robins friendship in Susan Lowndes, *Diaries and Letters of Marie Belloc Lowndes, 1911–1947*, 18.

9. Most of the names in this listing were first brought to the fore in twentieth-century feminist criticism by Patricia Meyer Spacks, *The Female Imagination*; Ellen Moers, *Literary Women: The Great Writers*; Elaine Showalter, *A Literature of Their Own: British Women Writers from Brontë to Lessing*; and Nina Auerbach, *Communities of Women: An Idea in Fiction*.

10. As I will be demonstrating in later chapters, George Bernard Shaw constitutes another fascinating link between Besant and Robins. He has been variously described as romantically interested in or desired by each of them, but the most obvious common element is their dislike at being provoked or teased by him. Besant was actually responsible for his early novels and drama reviews being published (through the editorship of her journal, *Our Corner*), while Robins's keeping him at bay helped him to gain access to the backstage theatrical maneuverings of the 1890s. He also reviewed Cameron's 1889 posthumous exhibition for *The Star* (London); see Chapter 2, n. 52.

11. See Wassily Kandinsky, *Rückblicke* (1913; reprint, Bern: Benteli, 1977), 24, as translated and discussed by Harriet Watts, "Arp, Kandinsky, and the Legacy of Jacob Bohme," 252. This language sounds very much like that of Arthur Koestler in *The Act of Creation: A Study of the Conscious and Unconscious in Art*. In *The Spiritual in Art: Abstract Painting, 1890–1985*, edited by Maurice Tuchman and Judith Freeman, Charles C. Eldredge observes that late-nineteenth-century aesthetics generally emphasized synaesthesia ("Nature Symbolized: American Painting from Ryder to Hartley," 124).

12. This is Watts's interpretation from Kandinsky's "Zwei Richtungen," *Kandinsky:*

Essays über Kunst und Künstler (1935; reprint, Teufen: Arthur Niggli and Willy Verkauf, 1955), 184, as translated and discussed in her essay cited above (240).

13. I am hardly alone in seeing the creature as female. For an extended interpretation of the creature as female, see especially Gilbert and Gubar's chapter "Horror's Twin: Mary Shelley's Monstrous Eve" in their *Madwoman in the Attic*, 213–47 and 671–74 (notes). This tradition is alive and well in the present day, as evidenced by Susan Stryker, "'My Words to Victor Frankenstein above the Village of Chamounix': Performing Transgender Rage."

Chapter 2. Julia Margaret Cameron

1. This mini-biography of Cameron only begins to scratch the surface, of course. The first book-length study of Cameron was Helmut Gernsheim's *Julia Margaret Cameron: Her Life and Work*, but it has been superseded by a combination of other, shorter accountings that are essentially exhibition catalogues which nonetheless contain innovative essay-articles or chapters. A high priority has been a sustained feminist perspective on her life, which Amanda Hopkinson provides in *Julia Margaret Cameron*, but a more extensive project is in progress by Victoria C. Olsen. In addition, a feature-length film is planned by Abby Freedman. (Unless otherwise indicated, all references to Gernsheim will be to the text cited above.)

2. Cameron made numerous prints of this image and created additional negatives using the same model on the same occasion in 1866, variously labeling them "Cassiopeia" and "The Mountain Nymph, Sweet Liberty" (taken from John Milton's "L'Allegro" of 1632). The model has finally been correctly identified as a Mrs. Keene, about whom no other information exists. The point I wish to make by providing these details is that references to individual images by me and other critics can often be confusing, since titles vary, different negatives have been used, and some titles were repeated with different models and poses over several years. When I reproduce images, I acknowledge their specific locations, and whenever possible (and appropriate) I narrow down the photographs I describe by title, model, and date.

3. In his preface to *Victorian Photographs of Famous Men and Fair Women by Julia Margaret Cameron*, Tristram Powell encapsulates this range accordingly: "Although she began as an amateur, Mrs. Cameron ended up a self-conscious artist" (10). I will be demonstrating that her amateur standing was extremely short-lived; moreover, her use of intuition, typically ascribed as a female trait, should not in itself signal a limitation.

4. Cameron has sometimes been grouped with the Pre-Raphaelites because their subject matter overlaps hers in certain respects, but their propensity to employ sharp detail contrasts radically with her blurred-focus technique. Mike Weaver provides a well-illustrated comparative study of Cameron and the Pre-Raphaelite school in his chapter "Legends and Idylls" in *Julia Margaret Cameron, 1815–1879*, 64–85.

5. Henry Peach Robinson, *Pictorial Effect in Photography, Being Hints on Composition and Chiaroscuro for Photographers*, 145. Robinson's critique of Cameron is nicely situated in relation to her defense by Peter Henry Emerson in Anita Ventura Mozley's catalogue copy for *Mrs. Cameron's Photographs from the Life*. See Emerson's account in W. Arthur

Boord, *Sun Artists: Original Series*, 33–42. Both Gernsheim and Joanne Lukitsh excerpt additional contemporary reviews that record the raging critical debate; see, respectively, *Julia Margaret Cameron: Her Life and Work* and *Julia Margaret Cameron: Her Work and Career*. Gerhard Joseph best articulates the interpretive strategies at issue here: "Her particular contribution to the dialectic of the hard-edged and the blurred that I have defined as oscillation between a post-Romantic aesthetic of particularity and an aesthetic of vagueness was to understand and demonstrate, first intuitively and then with increasing sophistication of purpose, that photography could become an art form precisely because of its unrivalled potentials for calibration of focus" (84); see his chapter, "The Sharp and the Blurred: Tennyson and Julia Margaret Cameron," in *Tennyson and the Text: The Weaver's Shuttle*, 75–87.

6. Critics have been aware of Cameron's various kinds of boundary-crossing for some time, but they have not always had the language to come to grips with it. For Jed Perl, that effort emerges in an awkward but awe-struck manner, as he tries to explain Cameron's "rapturous betwixt-and-betweenness"; see "The Trouble with Photography," 31.

7. Charles Darwin, *The Expression of the Emotions in Man and Animals*, 226. Reproducing one of Cameron's 1868 photographs of Darwin, Gernsheim records the scientist's response to it as follows: "I like this photograph very much more than any other which has been taken of me" (190).

8. Although I reproduce six of Cameron's images in this book (including the cover illustration), and describe a great many more, the reader who is not otherwise familiar with her photography would do well to examine one of the many fully illustrated books or catalogues of her work. Published in conjunction with the 1999 traveling exhibition organized by the Art Institute of Chicago, *Julia Margaret Cameron's Women* provides a splendid opportunity for the viewer to immerse himself or herself in Cameron's female portraits as well as to read the title essay by organizer Sylvia Wolf (22–85). Wolf also publishes a marked copy of "Mrs. Cameron's Photographs, Priced Catalogue" from an 1868 commercial showing that allows us to understand more about Cameron's self-awareness as a professional (208–18). For more about Cameron's substantial donations of her work to the South Kensington Museum, see Mark Haworth-Booth and Anne McCauley, *The Museum and the Photograph: Collecting Photography at the Victoria and Albert Museum 1853–1900*. Note, too, that various websites now produce their own Cameron "exhibitions."

9. This anecdote has been retold by numerous biographers and commentators; for one recounting, see Brian Hill, *Julia Margaret Cameron: A Victorian Family Portrait*, 109.

10. It should, of course, be observed that the Gernsheim Collection at the Harry Ransom Humanities Research Center at the University of Texas, Austin (hereafter abbreviated as HRHRC), contains a substantial number of images by Dodgson, which form the basis for Gernsheim's other breakthrough text, *Lewis Carroll, Photographer*. See also Lindsay Smith, "Further Thoughts on 'The Politics of Focus,'" 13–31, as well as the previous study which informs it, "The Politics of Focus: Feminism and Photography Theory." Smith raises a number of important questions regarding gender studies which I will be taking up later in this chapter.

11. "Annals of My Glass House" will be studied in extended detail at a later point, but

for now the reader is directed to n. 28 for information about its publishing history and my system of citation.

12. Gernsheim reprints the latter poem in his appendix C, 184, while Weaver reproduces both of them in *Cameron*, 158 and 154, respectively. Dated September 1875, "On a Portrait" was published in *Macmillan's Magazine* 33 (February 1876): 372, while "On receiving a copy of Arthur Clough's poems at Fresh Water Bay" was sent to his widow 20 July 1862 (Ms., Bodleian Library, Oxford). Two other manuscript poems, "Prayer written when I quickened with my first child" (8 July 1838) and "Farewell of the Body to the Soul" (n.d.), are held in the Special Collections of the J. Paul Getty Research Institute for the History of Art and the Humanities, Los Angeles, Calif. (Accession no. 850858—Series I: Cameron Family Papers, box 1, folder 10); they are both published in Weaver, *Whisper of the Muse: The Overstone Album and Other Photographs by Julia Margaret Cameron*, 62 and 68.

13. See Roy Flukinger, *The Formative Decades: Photography in Great Britain, 1839–1920*, 88. Regarding "Summer Days," Powell adds his own assessment of its nonconformity: "Freed from the over-artful influence of the Pre-Raphaelites, Mrs. Cameron's liveliness and sympathy towards her sitters are more apparent" (31).

14. For an extended analysis of soliloquies in relation to various other forms of discourse I call "autodiction," as well as how transcendence figures into the cosmic monologue, see Carol MacKay, *Soliloquy in Nineteenth-Century Fiction* (London: Macmillan; Totowa, N.J.: Barnes and Noble, 1987).

15. Quotations are from De Salluste, otherwise known as Seigneur du Bartas, *Divine Weekes and Workes, Sixth Day*; Shakespeare, *King Richard III*, 5.3.117; Whittier, *My Psalm*, stanza 2.

16. *Ruth*, published in 1853, appeared before Cameron's photographic career, while *Tess* and *Esther Waters* were published more than a decade after her death, in 1891 and 1894, respectively. Nonetheless, they are all representative of the Victorian mindset (and its tenacity) in Cameron's own time regarding the woman who was sexually active outside of marriage. For further reading, see, for example, George Watt, *The Fallen Woman in the 19th-Century English Novel*.

17. Elisabeth G. Gitter, "The Power of Women's Hair in the Victorian Imagination"; this quotation and the one that follows are both taken from p. 936.

18. Weaver's sustained argument on the Madonna–Magdalene conjunction occurs in *Whisper of the Muse*, 37–50 especially; my two citations are from 45 and 48, respectively. Of "The Angel at the Tomb" and "The Angel at the Sepulchre," Weaver further observes that they conjoin the dual aspects of Magdalene's experience—"as mourner and lover of Christ" (41). Gernsheim's labeling of the sitter for both these images as Cameron's adopted daughter Cyllene Wilson has been corrected by a consensus of photography historians, who now recognize the model as Mary Hillier.

19. Eleanor Locker's history is detailed in Winifred Gérin, *Anne Thackeray Ritchie: A Biography*, 214–16. Its significance in Ritchie's life story lies in the fact that the grieving widow nearly ran off with Richmond Ritchie, but after he elected to remain with his wife, Locker went on to marry Augustus Birrell. Lukitsh has studied the Cameron–Ritchie connection in depth in "The Thackeray Album: Looking at Julia Margaret Cameron's Gift to

Her Friend Annie Thackeray," while I acknowledge the ramifications of the friendship in "'Only Connect': The Multiple Roles of Anne Thackeray Ritchie."

20. In point of fact, Cameron's explosive treatment stands in contra-distinction to the typology expressed by one of her female sources of inspiration on this count, namely Anna Jameson (1794–1860). See Jameson's various studies of sacred and legendary art cited in my list of works consulted. Weaver, in his various publications, serves as the chief explanatory source of the Jameson–Cameron connection.

21. This reading corresponds with those developed by Jennifer Pearson Yamashiro in "Idylls in Conflict: Representations of Gender in Julia Margaret Cameron's Photographic Illustrations of Tennyson's *Idylls of the King*," and Lukitsh in "Julia Margaret Cameron's Photographic Illustrations to Alfred Tennyson's *Idylls of the King*."

22. See Auerbach, *Private Theatricals: The Lives of the Victorians*. Applying this concept of heightened theatricality to Cameron, Perl qualifies it by way of her eccentric inspiration: "The work has a 'backstage' excitement. Cameron wrests a crazily soulful experimental theatre from the dreariest scenarios of nineteenth-century painting" (31).

23. See Carol Armstrong, *Scenes in a Library: Reading the Photograph in the Book, 1843–1875*, 490 n. 31. Armstrong discusses at length the two pairings I have just been describing, as do many other feminist critics of Cameron's illustrations for *Idylls* who are uncovering their labyrinthine complexities; see, for one additional example, Debra N. Mancoff's essay in the Wolf catalogue (86–106). Armstrong draws our attention to the reversal of the title of Tennyson's poem "Merlin and Vivien" in Cameron's two images of "Vivien and Merlin," the new hierarchy further underscored by the photographer's doubling hand (391).

24. See Nicole Cooley, "Ideology and the Portrait: Recovering the 'Silent Image of Woman' in the Work of Julia Margaret Cameron," 374, as well as catalogue copy for "Summer Days" (55) by Therese Mulligan in the publication *For My Best Beloved Sister Mia: An Album of Photographs by Julia Margaret Cameron*, to which Eugenia Parry Janis, April Watson, and Lukitsh also contributed essays.

25. Many Victorian photographers have been lumped together as sentimental, but Elizabeth Lindquist-Cock does a good job of distinguishing among them. Finding Cameron's costume dramas "overly sentimental," Lindquist-Cock otherwise notes that Cameron "created a Rembrandtesque style" through which she displayed "great depths of feeling and empathy based on direct observation"; see "Sentiment, Compassion, Straight Record: The Mid-Victorians," 722.

26. Weaver writes: "In terms of her Christian beliefs Mrs. Cameron was a typological feminist. She accepted the uniquely female experience of life—the ability to give birth—but defended her sisters within the allegorical or typical framework of the Christian church from the slur of earth goddess. Because of, and in spite of, the female closeness to the rhythms of physical life, women 'thro' love' were, in her view, uniquely capable of understanding the emotions attendant upon nativity and cruxifixion, death and resurrection" (*Whisper of the Muse*, 30). I remain puzzled and disturbed by Weaver's own slur on the earth goddess, since he is himself generally feminist in his readings, almost New Age in fact, in his respect for Cameron as both centered and holistic (45).

27. See, for comparison, some of the photographs used as illustrations in Elaine Showalter's *The Female Malady*, as well as Cameron's various studies for "Ophelia." The theme of insanity remains a constant in the female quest, with the actual threat of the so-called rest cure rearing its ugly head for women writers Charlotte Perkins Gilman, Virginia Woolf, and Elizabeth Robins, among others. Incidentally, Emily Peacock was also Cameron's model for "The Angel in the House" (1871).

28. See "Mrs. Julia Margaret Cameron's 'Annals of My Glass House'." It has since been reprinted by various history-of-photography scholars, including Gernsheim, 180–83; Beaumont Newhall, *Photography: Essays and Images*, 135–38; Weaver, *Cameron*, 154–57; and Violet Hamilton, *Annals of My Glass House: Photographs by Julia Margaret Cameron*, 11–16, but because of its primary resource status, I am citing the 1927 printing. The original manuscript resides with the Royal Photographic Society in Bath. Cameron's namesake daughter, Julia Hay Norman, died in 1873, the only one of her children to predecease her.

29. Mary Ryan's tale is fairly well known and frequently retold, but for a succinct source for her life story and those of Cameron's many other female models, see Stephanie Lipscomb, "Sitters' Biographies," in the Wolf catalogue (219–27).

30. For a detailed study of Cameron's use of Hillier as a model, see Carol Mavor's chapter, "To Make Mary: Julia Margaret Cameron's Photographs of Altered Madonnas," in her book, *Pleasures Taken: Performances of Sexuality and Loss in Victorian Photographs*, 43–69 and 135–45. The subjects of class and race for the Cameron oeuvre are further explored by Lori Cavagnaro, "Julia Margaret Cameron: Focusing on the Orient," as well as by Lukitsh, "'Simply Pictures of Peasants'." For more on Cameron's efforts to continue her "pictorial" art in Kalutara, see Marianne North's autobiography, *Recollections of a Happy Life*, 1:313–16 and 322.

31. He has since been identified as Dr. Wilhelm Vogel, professor of photography and editor of the journal *Photographische Mitteilungen*. Hamilton notes that he was instrumental in organizing the Berlin International Photographic Exhibition, which granted Cameron a bronze and then a gold medal in 1865 and 1866 (14).

32. For further reading on this subject as it applies to a female tradition, see my article, "Hate and Humor as Empathetic Whimsy in Anne Thackeray Ritchie."

33. For additional discussion of the real versus the ideal in Cameron, especially as they relate to questions of commercialism and women's private sphere, see Victoria Olsen, "Idylls of Real Life."

34. "The Gardener's Daughter" (1875) is the title of another of Cameron's images, which she captured the year following the writing of "Annals" for the second volume of her miniature edition of *The Idylls of the King*; see Gernsheim Collection 964:0313:0022 (HRHRC).

35. For this 1847 edition of *Leonora*, another Magdalene-like story, Cameron also wrote a preface, reprinted as "Appendix B" in Gernsheim (184–85); the engravings for the 1847 edition were executed by John Thompson.

36. In addition to the various writings discussed in this chapter, Cameron reportedly completed at least half of a novel (Hopkinson, 15). H. H. H. Cameron labeled an image from 1867 (elsewhere identified as "The Passion Flower at the Gate," taken from Ten-

nyson's *Maude: A Monodrama* and cited in "Annals") accordingly: "Mary Pinnock as 'Maggie' (The Heroine of My Mother's Novel)"; see *Julia Margaret Cameron: An Album*, #23. Pinnock also posed several times as Ophelia.

37. Other contemporary translators of *Leonora* included Herschel, Dante Gabriel Rossetti, and the scientist William Whewell. Gernsheim reproduces part of *The Art-Union* review of Cameron's version, which describes it as "more faithful: but little of the spirit of the original is lost; the versification is at once smooth and vigorous" (February 1847; Gernsheim, 185). She is particularly to be commended for her shift (acknowledged in the preface) from the ballad meter of the quatrain to rhymed couplets when the rapid movement of the "spectral career" takes over the poem (stanza 39).

38. From one who knew her, Leslie Stephen, came the grumbling concession that Cameron had "the temperament, at least, of genius"; see Frederick William Maitland, *The Life and Letters of Sir Leslie Stephen*, 335. For a more recent (and celebratory) admission, we have only to look at the likes of a title such as the one proffered by Wilfred Blunt, "Julia Margaret Cameron: Early Genius of the Camera."

39. See Raymond Blathwayt, "How Celebrities Have Been Photographed," 639. The article deals primarily with the work of Cameron, here dubbed "the world-famed amateur photographer."

40. For more about the efforts to save "Dimbola," long a hotel (as is "Farringford"), as a National Treasure, see Ann Hills, "Idylls No More at Freshwater?," and Virginia Nicholson, "Dimbola: Julia Margaret Cameron at Freshwater."

41. Cameron shares with many other women autobiographers, notably Ritchie, an ambivalence about disclosing the private self or presuming to sum up a life; their fragmented self-portraits reflect both the complexities of their multiple relationships and their distaste for ego assertion. See, for example, Estelle C. Jelinek, *Women's Autobiography: Essays in Criticism*; Judith Kegan Gardiner, "On Female Identity and Writing by Women"; and Susan Stanford Friedman, "Women's Autobiographical Selves: Theory and Practice."

42. Cameron herself refers to her autobiographical fragment as "the truthful account of indefatigable work" (296), yet as Malcolm Daniel explains regarding her chosen field of endeavor, "the problem faced by any photographer choosing a mythical, literary, biblical, historical, or allegorical subject was to reconcile the assumed truthfulness of photography with the impossibility of the subject actually having been photographed"; see his "Darkroom vs. Greenroom: Victorian Art Photography and Popular Theatrical Entertainment," 16. Life-writing, especially by and about women, runs up against some very real problematics when photography enters the equation, but for Virginia Woolf, telling her-story in *A Room of One's Own* already means "one cannot hope to tell the truth," though "[f]iction here is likely to contain more truth than fact" (4).

43. Watson further supports her "revelation" by citing some of Cameron's earlier experimentation with Oscar Rejlander as recorded in the Mia Album. See Mulligan et al., 14–25; cf. Figure 5 for one of Rejlander's (ascribed) photographs of Cameron.

44. Rossetti, "Mr. Palgrave and Unprofessional Criticisms on Art," 333–34.

45. [Anne Thackeray Ritchie], "A Book of Photographs," first published anonymously

in *The Pall Mall Gazette* (10 April 1865): 10–11; reprinted in [Miss Thackeray], *Toilers and Spinsters and Other Essays* (1874). My citations are to the 1874 collection. Hardwicke Knight fails to recognize the timeliness of the "review" by assuming it was first written for the essay-collection some ten years after Cameron embarked on her photographic career; see "Anne Isabella Thackeray and Julia Margaret Cameron." By registering her images at Colnaghi's, Cameron was publicly and legally claiming copyright for her art.

46. Besides the letter just cited, the Gernsheim Collection contains other Cameron–Ritchie correspondence, including five letters to "Pinkie" Ritchie, one of Anne's cousins; excerpts from several of Cameron's letters to "Pinkie," another of her models, are reproduced in Gernsheim. Cameron and her artistic community can also be credited with serving as inspiration to Ritchie's novella, *From an Island* (initially published in *The Cornhill*), in which both an artist and a photographer bear some resemblance to Cameron herself. Ritchie's daughter, Hester Thackeray Ritchie Fuller, eventually drew upon several of her mother's studies to write her own *Three Freshwater Friends: Tennyson, Watts, and Mrs. Cameron*.

47. See his *Figures of Autobiography: The Language of Self-Writing*, 37.

48. Despite acknowledging Cameron's pioneer status and her "real artist's gift of piercing through the outward appearance to the soul of the individual," Gernsheim still takes the high road when comparisons with the Old Masters are raised: "Her illustrations to the Bible, Shakespeare, and Tennyson, though compared by her contemporaries with the paintings of the Old Masters, appear ludicrous to modern eyes. . . . [T]he realism of the medium inevitably reduces the sublime to the ridiculous"; see *A Concise History of Photography*, 58 and 75, respectively.

49. See especially Elizabeth French Boyd, *Bloomsbury Heritage: Their Mothers and Their Aunts*. Virginia Woolf's *Freshwater*, first written in 1923 and then revised for a private performance in 1935, has been edited for publication by Lucio Ruotolo, while *Night and Day*, Virginia's second novel, was published by her half-brother, Gerald Duckworth, in 1919. Val Williams has produced two pertinent studies, "Only Connecting: Julia M. Cameron and Bloomsbury" and "Carefully Constructing an Idyll: Vanessa Bell and Snapshot Photography, 1907–1946"; cf. Quentin Bell and Angelica Garnett, *Vanessa Bell's Family Album*. Clive Bell's introduction in autograph-manuscript, with accompanying letter (16 August 1947), resides in the Gernsheim Collection (HRHRC).

50. I am here alluding to the title of C. S. Lewis's novel, *Till We Have Faces*, which is described appropriately in its jacket notes as a "timeless" tale "of the struggle between sacred and profane love, of unselfish faith and selfish pride, of the spirit and of the flesh."

51. For further reading on the Cameron–Carroll comparison besides the citation to Smith in note 10, see Mavor, "Dream-Rushes: Lewis Carroll's Photographs of the Little Girl."

52. The quotation is from the 1889 issue of *The Star* (London), in which Shaw as art critic reviewed Cameron's first posthumous exhibition; reprinted in Gernsheim, 67. Gernsheim adds the observation that Shaw "stated the viewpoint generally accepted today as a correct estimation of Julia Cameron's work," a statement that can no longer be supported.

53. Dated 20 November 1876, this unpublished manuscript is housed at the Getty Research Institute, Research Library, 850858 (Series I, box 1, folder 10). Cameron and her husband moved back to Ceylon in October 1875, and they made a short visit to England in 1878, before she died 26 January 1879 at Dikoya Valley, Ceylon, predeceasing her husband by a year. Uttered in response to the sunset, her last word was "Beautiful."

54. The author of the headnote to *The Photographic Journal* reprinting of "Annals" is J. Dudley Johnston. Cameron's letter to Overstone is dated 5 November 1867; cited by Weaver in *Whisper of the Muse* (19), it is held by the University of London Library. Ward's article, "Tennyson at Freshwater," appeared in *The Dublin Review* for January 1912; it is cited by Colin Ford in *The Cameron Collection: An Album of Photographs by Julia Margaret Cameron Presented to Sir John Herschel* (10). Cameron's observations about Tennyson's remarks regarding Austen and Shakespeare (directed in private conversation to Ritchie and Leslie Stephen) were made in a letter to Sir Henry Taylor in 1860; they are quoted by Blathwayt in "How Celebrities Have Been Photographed" (640). Finally, Maurice's letter is cited by Marie A. Belloc in "The Art of Photography: Interview with Mr. H. Hay Herschel [*sic*] Cameron" (582).

55. The autograph-manuscript of Turner's sonnet is held by the Getty Research Institute, Research Library, 850858 (Series I, box 1, folder 13). Undated, it is addressed "To Mrs. Cameron / Ancient History illustrated / with 4 modern pictured faces." In closing, Turner writes, "My dear Mrs Cameron, Accept this tribute to your art. You kindly said you would take it in liquidation of my manifold debt to you." The poem was first published as a frontispiece to Cameron's 1874 limited edition of *The Idylls of the King*; most recently it was reproduced in John J. McKendry's *Four Victorian Photographers*, which was reissued as a 1968 calendar by the Metropolitan Museum of Art.

56. See *Women of Photography: An Historical Survey*, 16.

Chapter 3. Anne Thackeray Ritchie

1. Virginia Woolf, "Lady Ritchie" [Obituary Notice], reprinted in Winifred Gérin, *Anne Thackeray Ritchie: A Biography*. My citations are from Gérin's biography.

2. I have collected the centenary introductions in two volumes, where I introduce them in terms of Ritchie's own accomplishments as a woman of letters. See my introduction to *The Two Thackerays: Anne Thackeray Ritchie's Centenary Biographical Introductions to the Works of William Makepeace Thackeray*, as well as my essay, "Biography as Reflected Autobiography: The Self-Creation of Anne Thackeray Ritchie."

3. Smith-Elder, its successor John Murray, and Tauchnitz all published collective reissues. I am grateful to William B. Todd and Ann Bowden for verifying the numerous Tauchnitz impressions, which show two of Ritchie's fourteen titles still in print in 1939.

4. [Leonard Huxley], *The House of Smith, Elder*, 161.

5. Terry Eagleton, *Criticism and Ideology: A Study in Marxist Literary Theory*, 48.

6. Exceptions are always to be found in this complex accounting, however. For instance, both Thackeray and Thomas Hardy complained vocally and justly about subject-matter constraints imposed upon their fiction, and a number of women who wrote sen-

sation novels in the last half of the century began to gain economic control over their publishing outlets. See, for example, Elaine Showalter, *A Literature of Their Own: British Women Novelists from Brontë to Lessing*, 31, on the latter qualification. The baseline list of publishers in the period was nonetheless male: Richard Bentley, John Blackwood, Bradbury and Evans, Chapman and Hall, Henry Colburn, Alexander Macmillan, and George Smith.

7. N. N. Feltes, *Modes of Production of Victorian Novels*, 45. Eliot and the question of professionalism are discussed at some length by Feltes as well as by Susan M. Greenstein, "The Question of Vocation: From *Romola* to *Middlemarch*."

8. For an article on the substantial contribution that Ritchie and other women writers made to Victorian culture via the pages of *The Cornhill*, see Janice H. Harris, "Not Suffering and Not Still: Women Writers at *The Cornhill Magazine*, 1860–1900."

9. Much earlier, the young George Smith did try to work with Charlotte Brontë, who established an unusual mixture of independence from and dependence on her publisher's advice. After her father's death, Ritchie received very little guidance, though in her turn she was sought out as a mentor by other women writers like Rhoda Broughton and Cholmondeley. Cf. Percy Lubbock, *Mary Cholmondeley: A Sketch from Memory*, 47.

10. For Thackeray's quotation, see Huxley (160). His proud identification is cited by Gérin (119). Ritchie's correspondence is published in *Thackeray and His Daughter: The Letters and Journals of Anne Thackeray Ritchie, with Many Letters of William Makepeace Thackeray*, 124 and 201, respectively. The British edition is more appropriately (and neutrally) entitled *The Letters of Anne Thackeray Ritchie*. Pagination in the two volumes differs and each only slightly approximates the other. Unless otherwise indicated, page citations to Ritchie's letters will be to the American edition and will occur in parentheses in the text under *Letters*.

11. Anne Thackeray, "Little Scholars," reprinted in *Toilers and Spinsters and Other Essays*, 99.

12. Lady [A.I.T.] Ritchie, "From Friend to Friend: [Mrs. Tennyson and Mrs. Cameron]." The essay originally appeared in *The Cornhill Magazine* and was later reprinted in *From Friend to Friend*; my citations are to the original *Cornhill* article.

13. Jack Zipes, *Victorian Fairy Tales: The Revolt of the Fairies and the Elves*, xxvi; this volume contains a reprinting of Ritchie's "Cinderella" (103–26). Zipes is also the author of *Breaking the Magic Spell: Radical Theories of Folk and Fairy Tales*.

14. For a more complete breakdown of the "Cinderella" tale-type, see Stith Thompson, *Motif Index of Folk Literature*, as well as his earlier study, *The Folk Tale*.

15. Cf. Marta Weigle, *Spiders and Spinsters: Women and Mythology*. The quiet realism that Ritchie displays at the endpoint of "Cinderella" has a precedent in an earlier rendering of the tale-type. The young author wanted to end her first novel, *The Story of Elizabeth* (1862–1863), less "happily"; that is, she didn't want to marry off her heroine Elly to the hero. Reminiscent of the Reverend Patrick Brontë advising Charlotte about the ending of *Villette* (1853), Thackeray begged his daughter not to conclude on such a dismal note. As a compromise, she produced a muted conclusion that reports the marriage in retrospect, along with a description of the decay and destruction of the tale's primary setting.

16. Miss Thackeray, "Cinderella," 32. This volume also contains the following newly-told "Fairy Tales for Grown Folks": "The Sleeping Beauty in the Wood," "Beauty and the Beast," "Little Red Riding Hood," and "Jack the Giant Killer," while *Bluebeard's Keys and Other Stories* includes "Riquet à la Houppe," "Jack and the Beanstalk," and "The White Cat."

17. See George Cruikshank, "Cinderella and the Glass Slipper," and Louisa May Alcott, *A Modern Cinderella; or, The Little Old Shoe and Other Stories*, 5–69.

18. See Anne Sexton, "Cinderella." For other modern feminist renderings, see Angela Carter's own text, *The Bloody Chamber and Other Adult Tales*, as well as her edited volume, *Sleeping Beauty and Other Favourite Fairy Tales*, and Zipes's edited collection, *Don't Bet on the Prince: Contemporary Feminist Fairy Tales in North America and England*.

19. See Bruno Bettelheim, *The Uses of Enchantment: The Meaning and Importance of Fairy Tales*, and Erik H. Erikson, *Identity, Youth, and Crisis*. Nina Auerbach and U. C. Knoepflmacher also reprint two of Ritchie's fairytales—"The Sleeping Beauty in the Wood" (21–34) and "Beauty and the Beast" (35–74)—in their collection, *Forbidden Journeys*. Cf. Knoepflmacher's chapter, "Growing Up Ironic: Thackeray's *The Rose and the Ring*," in his volume *Ventures into Childhood*, 74–114. In this respect, Robin Sheets compares Ritchie's "Bluebeard's Keys" with Thackeray's use of the Bluebeard legend in her work in progress, *Curious Women, Murderous Men*.

20. Cf. Vineta Colby, *Yesterday's Women: Domestic Realism in the English Novel*, and Nancy Armstrong, *Desire and Domestic Fiction: A Social History of the Novel*.

21. Charlotte Brontë, *Jane Eyre: An Autobiography*, 117.

22. The original dates of publication were in *The Cornhill Magazine*: "Jane Austen," 24 (1871): 158–74; "Mrs. Barbauld," 44 (1881): 581–603; "Miss Edgeworth," 46 (1882): part 1, 404–26, and part 2, 526–45; and "Mrs. Opie," n.s. 1 (1883): 357–82. The Austen essay appeared contemporaneously in America in *Littell's Living Age* and was later revised for Ritchie's collection, *Toilers and Spinsters and Other Essays*, and then subsequently reprinted in *From an Island and Some Essays*. The essay began as an extended review of *Lady Susan* and *The Watsons*, recently published in conjunction with James Austen-Leigh's memoir of his aunt.

23. Quoted in Woolf, "George Eliot," 231.

24. William Makepeace Thackeray, *The History of Pendennis: His Fortunes and Misfortunes, His Friends and His Greatest Enemy*, 1.16.160–61, and *The Newcomes: Memoirs of a Most Respectable Family*, 1.29.332.

25. The history of the female essay has only recently come under serious scrutiny. In this regard, I am especially indebted to Tracy Seeley's article, "Victorian Women's Essays and Dinah Mulock's *Thoughts*: Creating an *Ethos* for Argument." Additional resources on this topic include Thaïs E. Morgan, *Victorian Sages and Cultural Discourse: Renegotiating Gender and Power*, and Ruth-Ellen Boetcher Joeres and Elizabeth Mittman, *The Politics of the Essay: Feminist Perspectives*. See also Manuela Mourão, "Delicate Balances: Gender and Power in Anne Thackeray Ritchie's Non-fiction."

26. Ritchie knew the value of letters as self-revelatory, for she used letters quite freely to explore her own verbal resources. Her letters (and selected journals) have now been

made public in three formats: her daughter Hester's 1924 edition, *Thackeray and His Daughter*; Hester Thackeray Fuller's later attempt in 1951, with Violet Hammersley, to weave together some of the more personal correspondence in memoir-like form, *Thackeray's Daughter: Some Recollections of Anne Thackeray Ritchie*; and most recently the 1994 volume that includes some of Gordon Ray's private collection, edited and introduced by Lillian F. Shankman, Abigail Burnham Bloom, and John Maynard, *Anne Thackeray Ritchie: Journals and Letters*. Many more letters on deposit at the University of London Library and the Eton College Library (donated by Ritchie's granddaughter, Belinda Norman-Butler) remain unpublished, as are the letters in the John Murray Archives (London); Ray's collection now resides at the Pierpont Morgan Library (New York). I will return to Ritchie's letter-writing style in more detail later in this chapter.

27. Diary entry dated 5 March 1919, a week after Ritchie's death; see *The Diary of Virginia Woolf*, 1:247–48. For further discussion of this playful incarnation, see my article "The Thackeray Connection: Virginia Woolf's Aunt Anny."

28. In addition to its original publication in *The Cornhill Magazine*, "Heroines and Their Grandmothers" is reprinted in Ritchie's *Toilers and Spinsters*, in Dale Spender and Janet Todd's *British Women Writers: An Anthology from the Fourteenth Century to the Present*, and in Andrea Broomfield and Sally Mitchell's *Prose by Victorian Women Writers: An Anthology*. "A Discourse on Modern Sibyls" is collected in Ritchie's *From the Porch*.

29. Leslie Stephen recognized the inheritance of genius from Thackeray to Ritchie, playfully intimating that it might have skipped over to his family lineage through his first wife Minny Thackeray to his own daughter Virginia (by Julia Duckworth) while sadly escaping him. For Stephen's views on Ritchie, see *Sir Leslie Stephen's Mausoleum Book*, 14; these are reflected as well in Seymour Vesey FitzGerald's entry (under her husband Richmond's name) in the *Dictionary of National Biography* (1927), 462–63. For more on Richmond, see P[hilip] L[eigh]-S[mith], *Record of an Ascent: A Memoir of Sir Richmond Thackeray Ritchie*. We know from a letter by Anne to the young novelist Rhoda Broughton what Richmond thought of one of Robins's key Ibsen roles—"Richmond has just come home, in utter scorn of *Hedda Gabler*" (9 May [1891]; *Letters*, 232)—but Anne herself remains teasingly, possibly conspiratorially, silent about her own views. She became Lady Ritchie in 1907 when her husband was knighted for his services to the India Office.

30. Ritchie, *Madame de Sévigné*, 116–17.

31. Leslie Stephen was less than happy about this marriage, largely because it meant he was no longer the central male figure in Ritchie's life; fortunately, he was soon to marry the widowed Julia Duckworth, thus sparing Ritchie the role of being his caretaker. George Eliot, on the other hand, gained courage from Ritchie's example when she in turn chose a marriage partner some twenty years her junior.

32. Woolf cites this last image in her review-essay celebrating Ritchie's life, "The Enchanted Organ," written on the occasion of Hester's publication of her mother's letters in 1924.

33. Gérin reproduces part of the Ritchie–James correspondence held by the Houghton Library, Harvard University, in appendix B of her biography (284–92); my citations

are to her text, 288 and 290 respectively. Cf. James, "The Art of fiction," *Longman's Magazine* (September 1884); rpt. *Theory of Fiction: Henry James*, ed. and intro. James E. Miller, Jr. (Lincoln: University of Nebraska Press, 1972), 35. James's essay is actually a rebuttal to a lecture of the same name delivered by Walter Besant, Annie Besant's brother-in-law, at the Royal Institute in London earlier that same year.

34. "Anne Thackeray Ritchie," review of *Thackeray's Daughter*, compiled by Hester Thackeray Fuller and Violet Hammersley, *Times Literary Supplement*, 1 February 1952.

35. To date, Gérin's is the only full-length biographical study of Ritchie, but Henrietta Garnett intends to remedy that omission.

36. *Old Kensington* was first published in *The Cornhill Magazine* 25–27 (1872–1873). I cite the Esther Schwartz-McKinzie reprint, which also includes *The Story of Elizabeth*. The subheading, "For we think back through our mothers if we are women," is taken from Woolf's *A Room of One's Own* (79).

37. *From an Island* was first published in *The Cornhill Magazine* 18–19 (1868–1869), and it has been variously reprinted in book form. I cite the American edition of *The Village on the Cliff, with Other Stories and Sketches*. Gérin and Shankman mistakenly assume the novella was published in 1877, when it was reissued by Tauchnitz, thereby reading it in relation to the question of an older woman being courted by a younger man.

38. *Alfred, Lord Tennyson, and His Friends* (London: T. Fisher Unwin, 1893) was limited to 400 copies and is primarily available in rare book libraries. Harriet Devine Jump has reprinted an abridged version of Ritchie's "Reminiscences" in *Women's Writing of the Victorian Period 1837–1901: An Anthology*.

39. From a previously unpublished letter (ca. 1890) quoted by Howard Overing Sturgis in "Anne Isabella Thackeray (Lady Ritchie)," 465. Stevenson waxes eloquent on the subject of Ritchie's writing: "I never see why you make your breaks, all your craft is magic and mystery in my matter-of-fact eyes; but the result is indeed exquisite and in your small volume I have made a troop of friends. I beg of you to give me more: a second volume: Joanna Bailie [*sic*], Mary Wollstonecraft, Mrs. Fry, Mrs. Inchbald and (please) Mrs. Radcliffe. My wife (in a state of delight about equal to mine) joins me in my pleading." The remainder of this letter appears in Desmond MacCarthy's foreword to Hester Thackeray Fuller, *Thackeray's Daughter* (9–10).

40. For example, Ritchie's writing about Barrett Browning represents a cyclical return. She began writing about her for the entry in the *Dictionary of National Biography* (commissioned by her brother-in-law Leslie Stephen), then developed it for an article in *Harper's New Monthly Magazine* in 1892, and finally recast it for *Records of Tennyson, Ruskin, and [Elizabeth and Robert] Browning* later that year. In this last incarnation, Ritchie speaks of sometimes consulting with "a recording friend and neighbor, to whom I sometimes go for the magic of a suggestive touch when together we conjure up things out of the past"; see *Records*, 143.

41. [Virginia Stephen], Review of *Blackstick Papers*. In her introductory essay on Haydn, Ritchie pays tribute to the Fairy Blackstick, first created by her father for his tale *The Rose and the Ring* (1854), as well as citing his creation (in the original manuscript) of the wicked Fairy Hopstick, whose manner of demise prefigures that of the Wicked Witch

of the West in L. Frank Baum's *The Wonderful Wizard of Oz* (1900); see Ritchie, *Blackstick Papers*, 1–3.

42. [Anne Isabella Thackeray], "In Friendship," *The Cornhill Magazine* 27 (June 1873): 666–70; reprinted in *Toilers and Spinsters*, 288–97. The quotation constitutes the final paragraph of the final essay in the collected volume.

Chapter 4. Annie Wood Besant

1. Again Besant argued her own defense. For a full narrative of the trial waged by Besant and Charles Bradlaugh for the right to birth-control information, see S. Chandrasekhar, *"A Dirty, Filthy Book": The Writings of Charles Knowlton and Annie Besant on Reproductive Physiology and Birth Control and an Account of the Bradlaugh-Besant Trial*.

2. Garuri Viswanathan provides a well-reasoned study of how Besant's life pattern could never fully dismiss certain elitist tendencies associated with Empire. While finding that Western historiography has generally failed to see continuity in Besant's various conversions, she uncovers not paradox but irony in Besant's stance regarding India and Commonwealth status: "If the sentiments of anticolonialism and imperialism become virtually indistinguishable, their blurring can be partly attributed to the racial doctrine that animates both, a doctrine that by the time of the Home Rule League offered striking ways of articulating the complex attitudes toward national and imperial consolidation" (*Outside the Fold*, 207); see also her chapter, "Conversion, Theosophy, and Race Theory," in ibid., 177–208 and 288–91 (notes).

3. I am grateful to Leah Madge Young Renold, whose on-site study of the history of Benares Hindu University fills a gap in the scholarship about Besant's role in educational reform and her firm commitment to the education of women. Renold also discusses at length two of Besant's long-time contributions to the BHU curriculum, *Sanatana Dharma: An Elementary Text-book of Hindu Religion and Ethics* and *Sanatana Dharma: An Advanced Text-book of Hindu Religion and Ethics*, both first published in 1903. See Renold, "Hindu Identity at Banaras Hindu University 1915–1947."

4. Starting in 1879, Besant and Bradlaugh's two daughters had begun to follow the scientific curriculum at London University, and by 1881 Besant had taken all the courses required for the degrees of Bachelor of Science and of Medicine. However, one of the professors who served on the examining committee absolutely refused to ratify her as a recipient of the actual B.Sc. degree.

5. For useful introductions to Theosophy, see especially Bruce F. Campbell, *Ancient Wisdom Revived: A History of the Theosophical Movement*, and Robert Ellwood, *Theosophy: A Modern Expression of the Wisdom of the Ages*.

6. For further reading on this subject, see Mary G. Mason, "The Other Voice: Auto-biographies of Women Writers"; Felicity Nussbaum, *The Autobiographical Subject: Gender and Ideology in Eighteenth-Century England*; Virginia Lieson Brereton, *From Sin to Salvation: Stories of Women's Conversions, 1800 to the Present*; and Peter A. Dorsey, "Women's Autobiography and the Hermeneutics of Conversion."

7. See *Annie Besant: A Biography*. For an example of Taylor's attitude toward her sub-

ject, note her remarks about Besant's slow recovery from her second pregnancy: "When such a highly strung and forceful personality was curbed, and deeply at odds with its apparent destiny, explosions were bound to occur. Frank had no experience of how to cope with hysteria; no wonder he shook her from time to time, as Annie complained" (35). The opening of the biography's final paragraph qualifies Taylor's overall judgment of Besant's success, however: "The exception is her *Autobiography*, which compels attention, astonishment, and sympathy in equal measure" (332).

8. For Indian biographies, see, for example, Sri Prakasa, *Annie Besant as Woman and as Leader*, and C. P. Ramaswami Aiyar, *Annie Besant*. Unfortunately, neither Anne Taylor nor Peter Washington in his *Madame Blavatsky's Baboon: Theosophy and the Emergence of the Western Guru* updates the recent recanting of the Society of Psychical Research regarding its previous charges against Blavatsky as an impostor. For a corrective, see Sylvia Cranston, *HPB: The Extraordinary Life and Influence of Helena Blavatsky, Founder of the Modern Theosophical Movement*. For three new feminist readings, see Rosemary Dinnage, *Annie Besant*; Olivia Bennett, *Annie Besant*; and Catherine Wessinger, *Annie Besant and Progressive Messianism, 1847–1933*. Clearly geared toward younger readers, Rebecca Bartholomew's *Lost Heroines: Little-Known Women Who Changed History* helps to fill a very real gap; see her chapter on Besant, indexed under the discipline of "Liberator of the Factory Workers/Labor Reformer" (17–23).

9. See John D. Barbour, *Versions of Deconversion: Autobiography and the Loss of Faith*, 2. He goes on to observe that "deconversion" is especially apt for his study "because it suggests the paradoxical ways in which narratives of lost faith mirror conversion stories. . . . One of my central interests is in how autobiographers try to break away not only from discredited religious beliefs but from the forms of narrative associated with those beliefs" (4). Cf. the list of six "psychic situations favourable for the occurrence of religious conversion" enumerated by Sante De Sanctis in *Religious Conversions* (258–61)—all of which obtain for Besant according to Geoffrey West [Geoffrey Harry Wells]; see West's chapter "Interlude on Conversion" in *The Life of Annie Besant* (143–52).

10. For a beginning—though hardly retroactive—corrective, see Thaïs E. Morgan, *Victorian Sages and Cultural Discourse: Renegotiating Gender and Power*. Linda Peterson specifically contextualizes the problem for women's self-writing about deconversion, explaining that "they did not compose retrospective accounts of spiritual or psychological progress" not only because of the prohibitions against self-expression but because of those against their application of the biblical typology available to their male counterparts; see "Gender and Autobiographical Form: The Case of the Spiritual Autobiography," 212.

11. Annie Besant, *Autobiographical Sketches* (London: Freethought Publishing Company, 1885), 3. The sketches originally appeared in *Our Corner* 3–5 (1884–1895); all references to this text will be to the Freethought edition, abbreviated in parenthetical page citations as "S."

12. Annie Besant, *An Autobiography*, 6; all subsequent references are to the 1894 edition and will be noted in parentheses in the body of the text by the abbreviation "A." One important addition to this autobiographical account is an index. The advertisement for the 1893 first edition by T. Fisher Unwin reads as follows: "Sincerest among icono-

clasts is Mrs. Besant. Atheism and Theosophy are poles asunder, but she has fearlessly made the journey in pursuit of Truth. Her life has been brimful of excitement, and she tells her story with lucidity and *verve*, dwelling, as she proceeds, on the interesting people she has known, from Bradlaugh to Blavatsky." After assuming official leadership of Theosophy in Europe and India in 1891, Besant published almost exclusively with Theosophical publishing houses for the remainder of her life. *An Autobiography* has remained in constant reprint under the auspices of the Theosophical Society, while *Sketches* was never reissued in Besant's lifetime, largely, I suspect, because Besant felt it had been essentially superseded; I have found only one recorded reprint of *Sketches*, listed by Gordon Press Publishers, New York, in 1972. The various editions of *An Autobiography* are discussed in relation to their illustrations later in this chapter.

13. This language of longing to be saved and regret that she hasn't yet had a conversion experience reflects some of the sentiments expressed by the American poet Emily Dickinson (1830–1886). In private correspondence, written at home and at school, Dickinson initially speaks about her sorrow at not being able to convert, but after a while she reacts negatively to the social pressure that she do so, eventually rejecting entirely this kind of public commitment. See *The Letters of Emily Dickinson*, vol. 1. For an intriguing study of deconversion as counter-conversion, see Julie Graf, "Reconfiguring Conversion: The Construction of Identity in the Counter-Conversion Narratives of Emily Dickinson, Elizabeth Cady Stanton, and Jane Addams."

14. Keats, quoted by David Perkins, *English Romantic Writers*, 1209. The discomfiture that Keats invokes reminds us that most of Besant's contemporaries would readily settle for belief while she almost seems to prefer a religion of doubt.

15. Needless to say, Besant's public revelations of Stanley's generous spirit proved compromising to him in the eyes of the religious community. Himself another boundary-crosser, Stanley demonstrates an ability to celebrate a "symbol of unity, not of strife" (S81). "I think," he explains to Annie, "that I am of more service to true religion by remaining in the Church and striving to widen its boundaries from within, than if I left it and worked from without" (S82). This enlightened outlook sets him in remarkable contrast to the narrow dogmatism of Dr. Pusey, who shudders at Besant's slightest intimation of doubt (A109).

16. See especially the foreword to *Esoteric Christianity*, which emphasizes the need to look behind all forms for the essence that originally inspired them: "The object of this book is to suggest certain lines of thought as to the deep truths underlying Christianity, truths generally overlooked, and only too often denied" (vii).

17. Sri Prakasa, "Mrs. Besant and the India of Tomorrow," 43.

18. Arthur Digby Besant also includes in his appendix to *The Besant Pedigree* a reply from W. E. Gladstone (prime minister from 1868–1874, 1880–1886, and 1892–1894), to whom he has written remonstrating against some of Gladstone's remarks in a review of *An Autobiography*. Gladstone replies (4 October 1894), "It scarcely admits of argument from my side—for who would argue with a profoundly affectionate son to prove to him (and I cannot prove, for I have only such conjectural knowledge as the book supplies) that his mother was not exempt from the general law of human kind, and consequently had

imperfections?" (271–72). Cf. Gladstone's review, "True and False Conceptions of the Atonement," *Nineteenth-Century* 36, no. 211 (September 1894): 317–31. Digby was chairman of Besant and Company, which published his family history and later became the Theosophical Bookshop, located in the shadow of the British Museum through the 1980s.

19. The parallel passage in *An Autobiography* reads as follows: "He saved me from the superficiality that my 'fatal facility' of speech might so easily have induced; and when I began to taste the intoxication of easily won applause, his criticism of weak points, his challenge of weak arguments, his trained judgement, were of priceless service to me, and what of value there is in my work is very largely due to his influence, which at once stimulated and restrained" (A138). Besant then proceeds to commend Bradlaugh for his courtesy to women and his indifference to class (A138–39).

20. Note how the language of the budding rebel emerges much more strongly from the pages of *An Autobiography*: "My religious past became the worst enemy of the suffering present. . . . All the hitherto dormant and unsuspected strength of my nature rose up in rebellion; I did not yet dream of denial, but I would no longer kneel" (A90–91). This time omitting the dramatic description of her "dark night of the soul," she sums up vehemently and unequivocally, "For now I no longer doubted, I had rejected, and the time for silence was past" (A114).

21. Although most of the details of the custody trial are consolidated and practically buried in chapter 9 of *An Autobiography*, Besant does prefigure the emotional wrenching of losing her daughter through a description of her that might very well in turn serve as a self-portrait: "She was the sweetness and joy of my life, my curly-headed darling, with her red-gold hair and glorious eyes, and passionate, wilful loving nature" (A129).

22. See Besant's translation of *The Bhagavad-Gītā: or, The Lord's Story* (1895). Although Sir Edwin Arnold's translation, *The Song Celestial* (1885), was apparently Mohandas Gandhi's first encounter with this sacred Hindu text, Besant's edition also played a part in his return to the religion of his ancestors. Westerners are probably more familiar with the phrase as it appears in T. S. Eliot's notes to *The Waste Land* (1922). Invoking "Shantih" three times to end his poem, Eliot explains that "the Peace which passeth understanding" is our best equivalent to this word, traditionally repeated to conclude each of the Upanishads.

23. In a similar vein, Besant speaks of "The Masters," "Brotherhood," and "The White Brotherhood." See, for example, her self-citation from *Our Corner* (February 1888), when she recalls the work she and Stead were engaged in: "Lately there has been dawning on the minds of men far apart in questions of theology, the idea of founding a new Brotherhood, in which the service of Man should take place erstwhile given to service of God—a brotherhood in which work should be worship and love should be baptism, in which none should be regarded as alien who was willing to work for human good" (A329). Following closely upon this recollection, she acknowledges, "How unconsciously I was marching towards the Theosophy which was to become the glory of my life, groping blindly in the darkness for that very brotherhood, definitely formulated on these very lines by those Elder Brothers of our race, at whose feet I was so soon to throw myself" (A330). And when she is fully prepared to make the break to Theosophy,

she asks the key rhetorical question, "The Socialist position sufficed on the economic side, but where to gain the inspiration, the motive, which should lead to the realisation of the Brotherhood of Man?" (A338). For a discussion about adopting non-sexist language within Theosophy, see Robert Ellwood and Catherine Wessinger, "The Feminism of 'Universal Brotherhood': Women in the Theosophical Movement."

24. For Besant's role in highlighting the pernicious practice of evictions by landlords in Ireland, see the column that she instituted in *Our Corner* (October 1886): "I propose to publish during the autumn and winter a monthly list of the evictions occurring in Ireland. Outrages may come, and I am anxious that any whom I can influence may clearly understand the connexion between evictions and outrages, and may see how landlord oppression leads to peasant [*sic*] revenge" (245). The accounts become increasingly detailed, functioning like a listing of statistics-plus-commentary in an editorial mode. With the advent of 1887 (vol. 9), the column is retitled "The War in Ireland," now treated much more in the manner of a *cause célèbre*, reflecting a full-fledged argument and its espousal.

25. Besant goes on to comment further on her mother's hair turning white overnight and her out-of-body episode of "witnessing" her husband's funeral: "With my present knowledge the matter is simple enough, for I now know that the consciousness can leave the body, take part in events going on at a distance, and returning, impress on the physical brain what it has experienced" (A26). She concludes this chapter by adding, "But there was a more serious side to this dreamful fancy when it joined hands with religion" (A28).

26. This account is omitted in *An Autobiography*. In its place occurs a mini-essay on how the imagination of childhood parallels that of the mystic: "The dreamy tendency in the child, that on its worldly side is fancy, imagination, on its religious side is the gem of mysticism, and I believe it to be far more common than many people think" (A40).

27. The phrase "To see, to know, to understand" invoked by both texts also recalls Tennyson's poem "Ulysses," discussed later, in the Epilogue. The odyssey metaphor in relation to Besant is picked up by Janet Oppenheim in her article, "The Odyssey of Annie Besant."

28. Earlier in the text Besant speaks of the tie between organized religion and ethics in the following terms: "What Religion has to face in the controversies of to-day is not the unbelief in the sty, but the unbelief of the educated conscience and of the soaring intellect; and unless it can arm itself with a loftier ethic and a grander philosophy than its opponent, it will lose its hold over the purest and the strongest of the younger generation" (A100). In her own case, she explains, "To a woman of my temperament, filled with passionate desire for the bettering of the world, the elevation of humanity, a lofty system of ethics was of even more importance than a logical, intellectual conception of the universe; and the total loss of all faith in a righteous God only made me more strenuously assertive of the binding nature of duty and the overwhelming importance of conduct" (A153; taken from her 1874 pamphlet, *The True Basis of Morality*).

29. Studies like Wessinger's *Annie Besant and Progressive Messianism, 1847–1933* already point the way; the title of her dissertation, "Millenarianism in the Thought of Annie Besant," more overtly asserts Besant's progressive model in contrast to catastrophic millennialism. Of Wessinger's articles, two seem especially apropos: "Democracy vs. Hierar-

chy: The Evolution of Authority in the Theosophical Society," and "Annie Besant and Issues in Contemporary Feminist Spirituality." See also Joy Dixon, "Sexology and the Occult: Sexuality and Subjectivity in Theosophy's New Age," as well as Diana Burfield, "Theosophy and Feminism: Some Explorations in Nineteenth Century Biography."

30. We can witness some of the last days of Besant and Bradlaugh's public playing-out of their growing division in the pages of *Our Corner*. Besant publishes her exchange of views on Socialism with Bradlaugh on a monthly basis in 1887, starting in April and ending in June (volume 9). He begins with "Socialism: Its Fallacies and Dangers"; she responds with "Its Truths and Its Hopes." He then tries a "Rejoinder," to which she provides in the same issue "A Final Reply"—thereby getting the last word!

31. For bibliographies of Besant's writings, see the various biographies in my list of Works Consulted, most notably under Aiyar, Bennet, Besterman, Cousins, Dinnage, Kumar, Nethercot, Prakasa, Taylor, and West. Moreover, interested readers can always review issues of the monthly journal, *The Quest*, published by the American branch of the Theosophical Society in America (Wheaton, Ill.). There have even been Internet exchanges providing information to readers who have not had ready access to her history or writings. One such posting at <http://www.indiana.edu/libref/victoria> (21 April 1997) from Teresa Malafaia at the University of Lisbon reported that she had recently supervised an M.A. thesis on the Besant autobiographies. Excerpts from *An Autobiography* appear in at least one anthology, namely Janet Horowitz Murray's *Strong-Minded Women and Other Lost Voices from Nineteenth-Century England*; they are reproduced under the following headings: "Decision to Marry" (1866), "Her Daughter's Illness" (1871), "Her First Lecture" (1873), and "The 'White Slavery' of London Match Workers" (1888).

32. Serialized in *Our Corner* over a twenty-three-month period in 1885 and 1886, *The Irrational Knot* was not published in book form until 1905, when Shaw referred to it as "The Second Novel of His Nonage" (London: Archibald Constable). Intriguingly, its preface goes on to read, "It may be regarded as an early attempt on the part of the Life Force to write a Doll's House in English by the instrumentality of a very immature writer aged twenty-four." Cf. Besant's 1879 pamphlet on the subject, *Marriage: Its Past, Present and Future*. Shaw's note to the reader of *Love Among the Artists*, serialized in fourteen monthly installments in 1887–1888 and published in book form in 1900 by Herbert S. Stone of Chicago, offers a back-handed acknowledgment of Besant: "If you find yourself displeased with my story, remember that it is not I, but the generous and appreciative editor of this magazine, who puts it forward as worth reading" (*Our Corner* 10: 265). For more on their stormy relationship, albeit slanted in Shaw's favor, see Michael Holroyd, *Bernard Shaw: The Search for Love (1856–1898)*, vol. 1; for a more even-handed account, see Sally Peters, *Bernard Shaw: The Ascent of the Superman*.

33. See *Arms and the Man: A Pleasant Play*. Shaw's shorthand notes sum up the play accordingly: "The comedy begins in the conflict between [Raina's] romantic ideas of heroic soldiering and the reality before her in the person of this extremely matter-of-fact Swiss *homme de metier*." In his undated instructions to the producer of a film version of the play, he writes, "Raina must be pretty enough to be readily forgiven her affectations and little lies; and she must have some comic talent." This last comment is espe-

cially intriguing given his views on Besant's lack of humor. See extensive files on the play in the Hanley Collection, HRHRC. Cf. Donald P. Costello, *The Serpent's Eye: Shaw and the Cinema*, appendix D: "The Entire Screen Play for a Projected Film Version of *Arms and the Man*" (Notre Dame, Ind.: University of Notre Dame Press, 1965), 189–96. Shaw's confirmation of "Mrs. Besant" as the model for Raina comes in the postscript of a letter [21 April 1898] sent to fellow drama critic William Archer; see *Bernard Shaw: Collected Letters, 1898–1910*, 2:341. It is interesting to note that Shaw wrote the part of Raina for the actress Florence Farr, with whom he had one of his many theatrical dalliances; Farr subsequently became involved with W. B. Yeats, who continued to be influenced by Theosophy long after his official break with it in 1889. Incidentally, Shaw has also acknowledged that the character of Mrs. Clandon, "a leader of the sex emancipation movement" in *You Never Can Tell* (1898), another "pleasant play," is modeled after Besant.

34. The letters are dated 30 December 1907 and 6 February 1908, and both are at the HRHRC; the second letter is reprinted in *Bernard Shaw: Collected Letters, 1898–1910* 2:755–57. This later letter ends with the exasperated exclamation "Demon—demon—demon!"

35. See Shaw, "Annie Besant and the 'Secret Doctrine'"; the HRHRC has the galley proofs for this article. Cf. the exchange in *The Freethinker* between H. Cutner (21 December 1947) and Shaw (11 January 1948) regarding the Besant–Shaw connection. The year 1947 also saw a reprint of Shaw's article, "Mrs. Besant as a Fabian Socialist" (originally published in *The Theosophist*), which he had first reissued as "Mrs. Besant's Passage through Fabian Socialism," in *Dr. Annie Besant: Fifty Years in Public Work*; see Cousins, *The Annie Besant Centenary Book*. Stanley Weintraub weaves the two articles together to form the "complete" story in his edition, *Shaw: An Autobiography*, 1:138–43, where he also repeats Shaw's outrageous claims (from his 1887 diary) that Besant's hair turned gray and she contemplated suicide when they parted company (303 n. 11).

36. For Stead's letter to Blavatsky, see the Adyar Archives, The Theosophical Society, Madras, India. Besant's report about how she wrote the review of *The Secret Doctrine* has been reprinted in the *Theosophical Journal* 15, no. 6 (1974): 3–5. In the interim, Blavatsky's reply to Besant was published in *The Theosophist* 53, pt. 1 (January 1932): 377 (reprinted in Cranston 363).

37. The HRHRC copy of this Limited Editions Club publication of *Great Expectations* bears some fascinating autograph exchanges among Shaw and his editor and publisher—all of which betray a playful indifference to fact over fiction.

38. See John Algeo, "*The Wizard of Oz*: The Perilous Journey"; he cites the Besant–Blavatsky quotation on p. 295. Algeo's previous article, "A Notable Theosophist: L. Frank Baum," discusses Baum's involvement with Theosophy, particularly through his mother-in-law, Matilda Joslyn Gage. Cf. Gage, *Woman, Church and State: The Original Exposé of Male Collaboration Against the Female Sex*, as well as Michael Patrick Hearn's acknowledgment of Baum's Theosophical interests in *The Annotated Wizard of Oz*, 72–73 especially. Also pertinent are Paul Nathanson, *Over the Rainbow: The Wizard of Oz as Secular Myth*, and Linda Hansen, "Experiencing the World as Home: Reflections on Dorothy's Quest in *The Wizard of Oz*." Of further interest is Frederick Buechner's crediting

the *Oz* books as influencing his own spiritual quest; see William Zinsser, *Spiritual Quests: The Art and Craft of Religious Writing*, 178–79.

39. Ruth Brandon's recent study, *The New Woman and the Old Men: Love, Sex and the Woman Question*, provides an example of yet another body of research that needs to be taken into account. In addition, there are other contemporary works to be considered or reconsidered, either for their influence, reflection of the cultural ambience, or attempt to write character from Besant's example. See, especially, Mrs. [Edith Lees] Havelock Ellis's *Attainment*, whose heroine Rachel is clearly modeled on Besant and her journey. Rachel moves from philanthropy to Theosophy, wherein the sun and the moon blend the light of their mysteries to create a union "beyond motion and beyond speech" (316). See also the children's book, *The Story of an Amulet*, written by Besant's good friend E. Nesbit. In this text, the Queen of Babylon travels forward in time to Edwardian England, only to wreck havoc at the British Museum when she tries to reclaim her possessions on display. As she sweeps down the museum steps, a passing journalist inquires, "Theosophy, I suppose. Is she Mrs. Besant?" Given a "reckless" affirmation, the journalist rushes off to Fleet Street to publish his article, "Impertinent Miracle at the British Museum" (128).

40. See Barbara Strickland, Review of the Texas Book Festival panel "Plucked from Obscurity: Writing Biographies of Not-so-Famous People," 42. Desley Deacon is the author of the biography *Elsie Crews Parson: Inventing a Modern Life* (Chicago: University of Chicago Press, 1997). One amazing statistic about Besant that I cannot resist citing as confirmation of her indefatigable energy in pursuing her quest is that during a single year, June 1892 to June 1893, just after she had assumed the mantle from Blavatsky, she gave a total of some 223 lectures; see Nethercot, *The First Five Lives of Annie Besant*, 389.

Chapter 5. Elizabeth Robins

1. Long out of print, *Alan's Wife* (co-authored with Florence Bell and originally published anonymously in 1893) is now available in Linda Fitzsimmons and Viv Gardner, *New Women Plays*, 1–25. Although the "New Woman" label is perhaps questionable for the play, it is appropriate as authorial ascription.

2. Besides being Robins's long-time companion and sometime collaborator, Octavia Wilberforce was also Virginia Woolf's consulting physician. Wilberforce's autobiography, "The Eighth Child," has recently been edited and published by Pat Jalland as *Octavia Wilberforce: The Autobiography of a Pioneer Woman Doctor*.

3. Sue Ellen Case, *Feminism and Theatre*, 129. For more extended discussion about how feminism informs autobiographical theory, see Bella Brodzki and Celeste Schenck, *Life/Lines: Theorizing Women's Autobiography*; Sidonie Smith, *A Poetics of Women's Autobiography: Marginality and the Fictions of Self-Representation*; and Leigh Gilmore, *Autobiographics: A Feminist Theory of Women's Self-Representation*; as well as the works cited in Chapter 2, note 41. Considering the fragmentary nature of women's self-writing, it is especially ironic that a substantial portion of Robins's autobiographical manuscript material was lost during one of her transatlantic crossings, toward the end of World War II.

4. The quotation comes from Robins, *Both Sides of the Curtain*, 330. The title of this

autobiographical account stems from a suggestion made by Virginia Woolf around the time she and her husband Leonard published Robins's "communal" memoir, *Ibsen and the Actress* (1928), through their joint enterprise of the Hogarth Press.

5. Ann L. Ardis provides a representative source for historical background on the New Woman in *New Women, New Novels: Feminism and Early Modernism*. For discussions specifically pertinent to Elizabeth Robins and the theatre, respectively, see Catherine Wiley, "The Matter with Manners: The New Woman and the Problem Play," and Vivien Gardner and Susan Rutherford, *The New Woman and Her Sisters: Feminism and Theatre, 1850–1914*.

6. See especially Elaine Showalter's third chapter, "New Women," and accompanying notes, in *Sexual Anarchy: Gender and Culture at the Fin de Siècle*. Notably, the 1995 Association for Theatre in Higher Education Conference was entitled "Gateways to the Next Millennium."

7. For just one concrete example, the appellation of "genius" is resolutely invoked in *The Standard*'s review of Robins's novel *Magnetic North* (1904): "The reader who is not indolent is rewarded by gaining a fresh aspect of the earth and man, and by knowing a work of genius. This is a large word, but nothing short of genius would bring such unfamiliar matter home to inexperienced imagination" (qtd. from inside front cover of William Heinemann's 1919 Popular Edition of the novel).

8. See the scrapbooks of theatrical reviews kept by Robins on deposit at the Fales Library/Special Collections (Series IIA, book 7), Elmer Holmes Bobst Library, New York University; subsequent references to unpublished material in the Elizabeth Robins Papers will appear in parentheses in the text, with the numbering representing series, box, and folder. The finding aid for primary source material in the collection has been made available online at < http://www.nyu.edu/library/bobst/research/fales/coll_mss/robins >. Running to some one hundred linear feet of materials, the Elizabeth Robins Collection was acquired from Leonard Woolf after the death of Octavia Wilberforce in 1963. The opening of the Robins Papers to the public was celebrated on 28 April 1986 by a dramatic program in which the actress Katherine Houghton "performed" Robins before the Friends of the Library.

9. See the introduction to Joanne E. Gates, *Elizabeth Robins, 1862–1952: Actress, Novelist, Feminist*, 1–4; unless otherwise indicated, references to Gates will be to this text. This was the first published full-length biography of Robins, immediately followed by Angela John, *Elizabeth Robins: Staging a Life, 1862–1952*. Until their publication, scholars had to rely on unpublished dissertations by Jane Marcus (Northwestern, 1973), Mary Cima (Cornell, 1978), and Gates herself ("'Sometimes Suppressed and Sometimes Embroidered': The Life and Writing of Elizabeth Robins, 1862–1952") for extensive background information on Robins. Cf. Sue Thomas, *Elizabeth Robins (1862–1952): A Bibliography*.

10. The story has been introduced and published by Gates in *American Voice*. Cf. Gates's lecture on the art and craft of biographical research, "Elizabeth Robins: A Life in Letters." The text takes an epistolary form, a series of imaginary letters in which Gates as biographer addresses Robins as subject in order to demonstrate her ongoing engagement with the writing of this life story.

11.   See Robins to Virginia Woolf, 11 December 1936 (Monks House Papers, University of Sussex Library). Robins was present when Woolf received the 1928 Femina-Vie Heureuse Prize for *To the Lighthouse* at the Institut Français and spoke in striking terms of her mother Julia as "the most beautiful Madonna & at the same time the most complete woman of the world" (4 May 1928; Woolf, *Diary* 3:183). Like Ritchie before her, Robins (despite her own chronic fatigue) expressed an almost vigilant concern about Woolf's health over a period of many years. During Woolf's last months in 1940–1941, Wilberforce regularly supplied Woolf with milk and cream from the Jersey cows on Robins's farmland.

12.   The typescript of this autobiographical novel, in its various states of revision, is on deposit at the Fales Library (7A.63–66); the dedication to volume 1, "A Study in Egoism," invokes Robins's concept of the "composite portrait" (7A.63.1). "In many ways," Gates observes, "'Theodora' invites comparison with the struggles with the self depicted in Dreiser's *Sister Carrie* and Willa Cather's *The Song of the Lark*, two other American novels about Midwestern young women who work their way toward self-fulfillment and recognition on the New York stage" (191–92).

13.   Intriguingly, Robins was working on an historical drama set in Rachel's time when she turned her attention to something more contemporary, namely her suffrage vehicle *Votes for Women!* (1907).

14.   I am primarily drawing here from "chapters" entitled "Stages on the Road" and "The End," both on file at the Fales (7A.4.1–4); since these typescripts are still somewhat fragmentary and involve pagination that overlaps and repeats itself, I have chosen to avoid confusion by not citing page numbers in my own text.

15.   The date of Besant's appearance was 30 August 1891. She later reprinted her remarks in *1875 to 1891: A Fragment of Autobiography*, published by the Theosophical Society; this pamphlet temporarily filled the gap between *Autobiographical Sketches* (1885) and the disclosures of *An Autobiography* (1893). See my discussion of her speech and its publishing history in Chapter 4.

16.   Robins, *Way Stations*, 321–30, now available online (see note 26).

17.   The Robins–Shaw correspondence that follows is on deposit at the HRHRC; the dates of these exchanges are, respectively, 12, 17, 28, and 29 November 1936. Early in the new year, Robins writes to "Geoffrey West," pseudonym of Geoffrey Harry Wells and another biographer of Besant (1927 and 1929), "My book is all but finished, but not of course yet copied fair, or fit for publisher's inspection" (31 January 1937; HRHRC).

18.   Shaw's letter about the so-called interview with Robins is at NYU and reprinted in *Bernard Shaw: Collected Letters, 1874–1897*, 1:379–81. Gates explicates some of this same Shaw–Robins animosity in "The Theatrical Politics of Elizabeth Robins and Bernard Shaw." It was only after Gates delivered this paper to "The Shaw and Theatre Conference," Virginia Tech University, 4–7 November 1992, that she by chance discovered the Wilberforce envelope with Robins's scribblings intact at the Fales Library (6A.3.23); see her discussion of Robins's response in her "Lecture" (12–16).

19.   William Archer, Introduction to *Alan's Wife: A Dramatic Study in Three Scenes*, xlvii. Both Robins and coauthor Florence Bell were embarrassed by the excessive analy-

sis and documentation that surrounded the published play. In fact, Archer's introduction was much longer than the play itself, suggesting his own overwrought involvement with the issues raised by the production.

20. T. S. Eliot, "Hamlet and His Problems," 100. Formulated in an effort to address the obscurities Eliot found in *Hamlet*, the "objective correlative" has since become what F. O. Matthiessen calls "a *locus classicus* of criticism"; see *The Achievement of T. S. Eliot: An Essay on the Nature of Poetry*, 58.

21. With respect to synaesthetic boundary-crossing, we can also look to the Russian painter Wassily Kandinsky (1866–1944) on the spiritual and emotional meaning of different colors; ultimately, his artwork can be seen as a synaesthetic embodiment, in opposition to the work of most abstract artists. On the subject of new literary forms being sought by women at the turn of the century, Showalter cites Laura Marholm Hanson accordingly: "Seeking to tell a new story, the New Woman writer 'needs an artistic mode of expression; she flings aside the old forms and searches for new'"; see Hanson, *Modern Women*, trans. Hermione Ramsden (London, 1896), 78–79, as quoted in Showalter, *Daughters of Decadence: Women Writers of the Fin de Siècle*, ix.

22. See Elin Diamond, "Mimesis, Mimicry, and the 'True-Real,'" 378, as well as "Realism and Hysteria: Toward a Feminist Mimesis." Cf. Gates's biography throughout, as well as Tillie Olsen, *Silences*. *Woman's Secret* has been reprinted in Robins's collection of her suffrage writings, *Way Stations* (1–17); this text was originally intended as the introduction to *The Convert* (my citations are to the proof pages on file at the Fales Library, 12A.3.19). For further analysis of the role of silence in fiction and on the stage, see Peter Brooks, *The Melodramatic Imagination: Balzac, Henry James, Melodrama, and the Mode of Excess*.

23. See Shaw to Charles Charrington, 28 January 1890, in *Bernard Shaw: Collected Letters, 1874–1897*, 1:239. Ibsen engendered yet another curious Besant–Robins linkage. The history of *A Doll's House*, that emblematic text for Besant and the first Ibsen vehicle for Robins, traces an intriguing trajectory. Apparently Walter Besant, Annie's judgmental brother-in-law, wrote a sequel to *A Doll's House* which Shaw considered "of enormous importance as a representative middle class evangelical verdict on the play"—and so he wrote his own sequel to the sequel! Shaw goes on to report how Archer joined ranks with Mrs. Aveling [Eleanor Marx], "agreeing with her [criticisms] to the point of begging me for the sake of my reputation not to publish it." It would seem he took their advice to heart.

24. See Jane Marcus's Introduction to *The Convert*, and Jan McDonald, "'The Second Act Was Glorious': The Staging of the Trafalgar Square Scene from *Votes for Women!* at the Court Theatre." For more on the implications of comedy for suffrage drama, see Susan Carlson, "The Suffragettes and Shakespeare: Marriage, Comedy, and Politics in the Edwardian Theatre" (paper delivered at the "Women in Theatre" conference, Hofstra University, 7 October 1994). My citations to *Votes for Women!* refer to the first published edition as reprinted in the anthology selected and introduced by Dale Spender and Carole Hayman, *"How the Vote Was Won" and Other Suffragette Plays*. The text of the play is also available in W. B. Worthen, ed., *Modern Drama: Plays/Criticism/Theory* (Fort

Worth: Harcourt Brace College Publishers, 1995), 174–202, which republishes as well Robins's 1907 essay, "The Feministe Movement in England" (203–4), taken from *Way Stations*, and also available at Indiana University's Victorian Women Writers Project: An Electronic Collection <http://www.indiana.edu/letrs/vwwp/robins/votes.html>. More information about the staging of the play is available by studying director Harley Granville-Barker's promptbook (Fales 8B.1.12), which has been reproduced by Gates in a recent anthology edited by Katherine E. Kelly, *Modern Drama by Women, 1880s–1930s: An International Anthology*, 108–46.

25. Gates would concur on this count; see especially her discussions of these two texts in her biography (159–66). For more on Robins and the links between suffrage and drama, see Leslie Hill's fifth chapter, "Suffragettes," in her dissertation, "Representations of Women in British Drama: 1890–1914." Cf. Robins's "The Meaning of It," her self-described "impression of the great Hyde Park Suffrage Demonstration," which appeared in the *Daily Mail* (in June 1908); this article, as well as many of her suffrage speeches, has been collected in *Way Stations* (74–76).

26. Most critics have yet to appreciate that *The Convert* is much more than a novelization of *Votes for Women!* The two major exceptions to this generalization are Marcus, in her critical introduction cited in note 24, and Gates, in her article tracing the development from Robins's 1905 novel to this 1907 work of autobiographical fiction, "Elizabeth Robins: From *A Dark Lantern* to *The Convert*—A Study of Her Fictional Style and Feminist Viewpoint." Of Robins's some fifteen novels, *The Convert* is the only one in recent print, although Gates has done a splendid job of putting the texts of both *The Mills of the Gods* (1908) and *My Little Sister* (1913) on her website, "The Elizabeth Robins Web Home Page" at <http://www.jsu.edu/depart/english/robins/index.htm>. The website also reproduces a detailed chronology, several short stories, the article "On Seeing Madame Bernhardt's Hamlet" (1900), and the full text of *Way Stations*, as well as linking to the On-Line Guide to the Papers of Elizabeth Robins at the Fales Library at NYU.

27. The conjunction of aesthetics and ideology is a vexed one for feminism. Marcus tackles it head-on regarding Robins and Woolf specifically, as well as for feminist scholars more generally; see "Art and Anger" and "Still Practice: A/Wrested Alphabet: Towards a Feminist Aesthetic." Marcus concludes the former article by asserting, "Anger is *not* anathema in art; it is a primary source of creative energy. Rage and savage indignation sear the hearts of female poets and female critics. Why not spit it out, as Woolf said, blow the blessed horn as Robins said?" (94). Cf. Mary Poovey, *The Proper Lady and the Woman Writer: Ideology as Style in the Works of Mary Wollstonecraft, Mary Shelley, and Jane Austen*, and Karen Laughlin, "Introduction: Why Feminist Aesthetics?"

28. On the subject of women's lives inspiring the performance of those lives, see Anita Plath Helle, "Representing Women Writers Onstage: A Retrospective to the Present." For an example of one of the pageant plays of the suffrage era, see Cicely Hamilton's *A Pageant of Great Women* (first performed 12 November 1909) in Viv Gardner, *Sketches from the Actresses' Franchise League*, 41–50. Robins wrote a preview of the historical women who would figure in the Women's Coronation Pageant, "Come and See," for the *Westminster Gazette*, 16 June 1911 (reprinted in *Way Stations* [246–52]).

29. Marcus conjoins these two women autobiographers, along with composer Ethel Smyth, anthropologist Jean Ellen Harrison, and mathematician Sophie Kovalevsky, in her study of "a deliberate resignation from the public world and patriarchal history," in which these women "re/signed their private lives into domestic discourse" ("Invincible Mediocrity," 114); the latter two Marcus joins with Robins as choosing autobiographical forms "structured as drama, and characters act their parts on the stage of the text" (127). Moreover, in a reference that connects back to my evocation of the superpersonal with respect to Robins, Marcus observes of Bashkirtseff that in 1911 her journal "was still popular enough to inspire an anonymous parody: *Super Soul: The Memoirs of Marie Mushenough*" (136)!

30. The review of *The Magnetic North* is cited on the inside cover of the 1919 Popular Edition published by William Heinemann, while the assessment of *Come and Find Me* was made by Gates in her dissertation, "'Sometimes Suppressed and Sometimes Embroidered': The Life and Writing of Elizabeth Robins, 1862–1952" (292). Virginia Woolf reviewed *A Dark Lantern* for the *Guardian* (24 May 1905), finding that "Miss Robins has the gift of charging her air with electricity, and her readers wait for the expected explosion in a state of high tension"; see Woolf, Review of *A Dark Lantern*, 42. These last two projects journeyed a checkered road — encouraged by both Bell and Granville-Barker, Robins came close to producing "Bowarra" for Tree's theatre, but it has never seen the stage, while *Raymond and I*, written during her brother's six-week absence in 1932 due to amnesia, reached only posthumous publication because Raymond refused to see it in print during his own lifetime.

31. Robins's *My Little Sister* bears comparison with Besant's "White Slavery in London" in *The Link* (1888), which exposed the deplorable working conditions for women in the Byrant and May match factory, as well as with Stead's more notorious — and all-too-personal — handling of the issue of young girls being kidnapped into prostitution and even sold abroad, which he had made public in his inflammatory eyewitness accounts in *The Pall Mall Gazette*, "The Maiden Tribute of Modern Babylon" (July 1885). Robins's fictional contribution underwent several incarnations: its genesis dates to a play co-scripted with John Masefield; after Robins had taken back the project and published the novel, it was adapted for the stage by Cicely Hamilton (although Archer apparently objected to the ending as too close to the novel, so Robins rewrote it herself, now making Bettina's fate more explicit); and it finally arrived on the American silent screen in 1919 (directed by Kenean Buel for William Fox Corporation).

32. All page citations are to Robins's edition of *Theatre and Friendship: Some Henry James Letters with a Commentary*.

33. See Susan Carlson's extended discussion of these two plays and the leading-lady roles earmarked for Robins in *Women of Grace: James's Plays and the Comedy of Manners*, 79–86. Alice James notes in her diary that her brother said Robins was "the most intelligent creature, next to [Benoît Constant] Coquelin[,] with whom he ever talked about her art"; see *The Diary of Alice James*, 211. Henry James's most well-known play, *Guy Domville*, met a dismal critical reception on its opening in London in 1895; see the prefatory matter in the edition of *Guy Domville: A Play in Three Acts* edited and introduced by

Leon Edel, who reproduced commentary by Bernard Shaw, H. G. Wells, and Arnold Bennett.

34. Bell to Robins, 1 November 1909 (Fales 5B.8.5). Bell wrote a "mini-biography" of Robins, "Personalities and Powers: Elizabeth Robins," for the inaugural issue of the suffrage weekly *Time and Tide* in 1920 (7–8), which is reprinted in her *Landmarks: A Reprint of Some Essays and Other Pieces Published Between the Years 1894 and 1922.*

35. The Pankhurst and Granville-Barker correspondence to which I am referring resides at the HRHRC. For the Case citation, see *Performing Feminisms: Feminist Critical Theory and Theatre*, 6.

36. Besides the letters cited from *Theatre and Friendship*, I have been consulting James's extensive rough notes on the evolution of *Votes for Women!* on file at the Fales (T.S., 13 November 1906, 49 pp.; 7A.71.5).

37. See Robins's chapter "Even Dead" in *Ancilla's Share: An Indictment of Sex Antagonism*, 130–32. For an informed discussion of this critique, see J. Ellen Gainor, *Shaw's Daughters: Dramatic and Narrative Constructions of Gender*, 108–10. Might Mr. Shaw have needed to rethink some of his credentials for later entitling one of his books *The Intelligent Woman's Guide to Socialism* (1928)?

38. Unpublished notes, 12 April 1907, citing also novelist James Barrie's confused (i.e., typically male) accord: "A novel should be long. It should take time to read. We ought to be able to lose ourselves in it as one does in a wood. That is to get the effect of detachment from our own concerns, etc., etc." (HRHRC).

39. See Hélène Cixous, "The Laugh of the Medusa"; Mrs. Patrick Campbell, *My Life and Some Letters*; Jane Marcus, Introduction to *The Convert*, vii; and Audré Lorde, "The Master's Tools Will Never Dismantle the Master's House."

Epilogue

1. For *Through the Looking-Glass and What Alice Found There* (1872), Alice actively initiates the transition by shaking the Red Queen of her dream state until she transforms into the black kitten of her waking reality. In general, Alice is much more single-minded in pursuit of her quest in this second tale, in this case moving across the chessboard landscape in order to become a queen. Perhaps it is the game-like competition that makes this adventure more akin to the usual male quest. For a modern-day effort to bring together Alice, Dorothy, and C. S. Lewis's Susan (from *The Lion, the Witch, and the Wardrobe* and subsequent tales)—all seeking to rediscover their respective dreamlands—see *Hungry for Fairyland*, written by Dan Gordon for the 1996 Winnipeg Fringe Festival.

2. The novel supports this decision on the part of the filmmakers, for Baum describes Kansas (and its inhabitants) as fundamentally gray while Oz is replete with different color codings (*The Annotated Wizard of Oz*, 92–93). Baum treats his fairyland Oz as a real place, however; perhaps this line of thinking makes it less necessary for Dorothy to bring back an actual object, since she can apparently return to this magic kingdom, as she does in many subsequent volumes.

3. Intriguingly, R. D. Laing offers a view of dissociation as part of the normal order

of (modern) human experience in *The Politics of Experience*: "The condition of alienation, of being asleep, of being unconscious, of being out of one's mind, is the condition of the normal man" (28).

4. See, for example, Percy H. Muir, *Victorian Illustrated Books*, and Forrest Reid, *Illustrators of the Eighteen-Sixties: An Illustrated Survey of the Work of 58 British Artists*.

5. This sense of loss is portrayed throughout another underacknowledged tradition, that of the female elegy. Jane Marcus has articulated this subgenre vis-à-vis Virginia Woolf; see, especially, her essay "Storming the Toolshed."

6. As I have been arguing, there are by comparison far fewer resources about the female quest in literature, but two examples provide good starting points: Carol Pearson and Katherine Pope, *The Female Hero in American and British Literature*, and Rachel M. Brownstein, *Becoming a Heroine: Reading about Women in Novels*.

7. The gay quest has yet to be fully articulated, but some examples of lesbian self-writing begin to contribute to the overarching scope of the female quest. See, for instance, Lisa Alther's comedic "fiction" *Kinflicks* and Catharine R. Stimpson's semi-autobiographical *Classnotes: A Novel*. See also Robert H. Hopcke, "Dorothy and Her Friends: Symbols of Gay Male Individuation." Tracing how Dorothy "finds herself" by mediating between outer and inner worlds, this Jungian reading supports my notion of metamaterialization; her "model" thus serves as inspiration to the gay male quest to reconcile reality and appearance, that is, masculinity and femininity. As an indicator of how much the *Oz* tale has become integrated into a symbolic rallying point for the gay community, see Nicola Field's *Over the Rainbow: Money, Class and Homophobia*, which never finds it necessary to actually mention Baum's text or Fleming's film.

8. The history of the screenplay for the 1939 production of *The Wizard of Oz* (directed by Victor Fleming) records the near-disaster of imposing the typical Hollywood romance plot on this key female quest. Apparently Noel Langley, the first to draft the script that would undergo numerous revisions with the advent of two other screenwriters, originally wanted to link Dorothy romantically with the farmhand Hickory, who in turn would become the Scarecrow; see Langley, Florence Ryerson, and Edgar Allan Woolf, *The Wizard of Oz: The Screenplay*, 11. For a revisionary study of women as readers and writers of the romance plot, see Janice Radway, *Reading the Romance: Women, Patriarchy, and Popular Literature*.

9. See Lewis Carroll [Charles Dodgson], *Alice's Adventures Under Ground*. For an extended discussion of these illustrations as compared to the ones by John Tenniel for the 1865 publication, consult Nina Auerbach, "Falling Alice, Fallen Women, and Victorian Dream Children." It can be argued that Dodgson wrote the first *Alice* book in an effort to "freeze" or "encapsulate" Alice Liddell—the subject and recipient of his tale—in her youthful prime when their friendship flourished.

10. This is not the place to expound upon the many eighteenth-century women writers whose methodologies might be explored in this context, but suffice it to say that this work has already been undertaken by a number of feminist scholars. For now, let me suggest three resources to consult as a follow-up to my comments: Catherine Gallagher, *Nobody's Story: The Vanishing Acts of Women Writers in the Marketplace, 1670–1820*; Mary

Schofield and Cecelia Macheski, *Fettr'd or Free: British Women Novelists, 1670–1815*; and Dale Spender, *Women of Ideas (And What Men Have Done to Them)*. Of course, some of this work has precedence in Ritchie's "Heroines and Their Grandmothers" (1865) and *A Book of Sibyls: Mrs Barbauld, Miss Edgeworth, Mrs Opie, and Miss Austen* (1883).

11. Typical of the tendency to judge Mary Shelley as significant only in relation to her husband's talents is Richard Garnett's entry on her in the *Dictionary of National Biography*, in which he dismisses her in the following terms: "Mary undoubtedly received more than she gave. Nothing but an absolute magnetising of her brain by Shelley's can account for her having risen so far above her usual self as in 'Frankenstein.'" See *DNB: To 1900*, 18:29, as well as Garnett's typescript draft at the HRHRC. Feminist critiques now offer an extensive countervoice.

12. Shelley, *Frankenstein: Or, The Modern Prometheus*, ed. Harold Bloom, ch. 11, p. 98. I am in accord with Stephen C. Behrendt's decision to select the most readily available paperback version of the revised 1831 text; see Behrendt, *Approaches to Teaching Shelley's Frankenstein*.

13. For ready access to this review, see William Veeder, *Mary Shelley and Frankenstein: The Fate of Androgyny*, 225–27, whose text in general argues for Percy's influence on Mary's novel-writing in general and *Frankenstein* in particular. For an argument that by implication takes an opposing view, see James P. Davis, "*Frankenstein* and the Subversion of the Masculine Voice."

14. Shelley depicts Frankenstein as manipulating the negative emotions of hatred and rage to help him focus the revenge he hopes to enact upon his creation as he brings his tale to its albeit inverted end (see especially ch. 23, p. 189). In distinct contrast, Ritchie's canon repeatedly demonstrates her transforming hate into humor, which in turn informs the kind of functional critiques that convert others to her point of view.

15. See Julie Kane, "Varieties of Mystical Experience in the Writings of Virginia Woolf." Of course, I have been connecting Woolf with Cameron, Ritchie, and Robins throughout this study, but seeing Woolf in conjunction with Besant, the most independent figure in my accounting, is especially illuminating. Woolf was actually in the audience when Besant spoke to the "1917 Club," founded in part by Woolf's husband Leonard; her description was hardly flattering: "She—a massive, & sulky featured old lady, with a capacious head, however, thickly covered with curly white hair,—began by comparing London, lit up & festive, with Lahore. And then she pitched into us for our maltreatment of India, she, apparently, being 'them' & not 'us.' But I don't think she made her case very solid, though superficially it was all believable, & the 1917 Club applauded & agreed" (19 July 1917; *Diary* 1:293). The links between the two women become more apparent, though, in comparing their autobiographical texts; see Woolf's incomplete *Moments of Being: Unpublished Autobiographical Writings* (1976), edited and published some thirty-five years after her death.

16. At a later stage of scholarly application of the theory of creative negativity to Victorian authors and their texts, it would be interesting to study some of the male novelists and their female creations. To start with, I immediately think of Thackeray's Becky Sharp (*Vanity Fair*) and Ethel Newcome (*The Newcomes*); Dickens's Esther Summerson (*Bleak*

House), Amy Dorrit (*Little Dorrit*), and Estella/Miss Havisham (*Great Expectations*); Wilkie Collins's Marian Halcombe (*The Woman in White*) and Lydia Gwilt (*Armadale*); Anthony Trollope's Alice Vavasor (*Can You Forgive Her?*) and Lizzie Eustace (*The Eustace Diamonds*); George Meredith's Clara Middleton (*The Egoist*) and the eponymous Diana of the Crossways; Henry James's Isabel Archer (*The Portrait of a Lady*); George Moore's Esther Waters; and Thomas Hardy's Tess of the D'Urbervilles and Sue Bridehead (*Jude the Obscure*). To these I would add the heroines in the poetry of Robert Browning, William Morris, and Tennyson (given his ties with Cameron and his application of the male quest formula, especially those in *The Idylls of the King*), as well as the female leads from the dramas of Ibsen, Shaw, and Wilde. Such studies might well point up the protofeminism in many of these male authors.

Works Consulted

Abel, Elizabeth, Marianne Hirsch, and Elizabeth Langland, eds. *The Voyage In: Fictions of Female Development*. Hanover, N.H.: University Press of New England, 1983.

Abrams, M. H. *The Mirror and the Lamp: Romantic Theory and the Critical Tradition*. 1953. Reprint, New York: W. W. Norton, 1958.

Aiyar, C. P. Ramaswami. *Annie Besant*. Delhi: Ministry of Information and Broadcasting, 1963.

Alcott, Louisa May. *A Modern Cinderella, or, The Little Old Shoe and Other Stories*. New York: Hurst, [1904].

Aldrich, Marcia, and Richard Isomaki. "The Woman Writer as Frankenstein." In *Approaches to Teaching Shelley's Frankenstein*, edited by Stephen C. Behrendt. New York: Modern Language Association, 1990. 121–26.

Algeo, John. "A Notable Theosophist: L. Frank Baum." *The American Theosophist* 74 (August–September 1986): 270–73.

———. "*The Wizard of Oz*: The Perilous Journey." *The American Theosophist* 74 (October 1986): 291–97.

Alther, Lisa. *Kinflicks*. New York: Knopf, 1976.

Altick, Richard D. *The English Common Reader: A Social History of the Mass Reading Public, 1800–1900*. Chicago: University of Chicago Press, 1957.

———. "The Sociology of Authorship." *Bulletin of the New York Public Library* 66 (1962): 389–404.

Apostolos-Cappadona, Diane, and Lucinda Ebersole, eds. *Women, Creativity, and the Arts: Critical and Autobiographical Perspectives*. New York: Continuum, 1995.

Archer, C[harles]. *William Archer: Life, Work and Friendships*. New Haven, Conn.: Yale University Press, 1931.

Archer, William. Introduction to *Alan's Wife: A Dramatic Study in Three Scenes*, by [Elizabeth Robins and Frances Bell], edited by J. T. Grein. London: Henry, 1893. ix–lii.

Ardis, Ann L. *New Women, New Novels: Feminism and Early Modernism*. New Brunswick, N.J.: Rutgers University Press, 1990.

Armstrong, Carol. "Cupid's Pencil of Light: Julia Margaret Cameron and the Maternalization of Photography." *October*, no. 76 (1996): 114–41.

———. *Scenes in a Library: Reading the Photograph in the Book, 1843–1875*. Boston: MIT Press, 1998.

Armstrong, Nancy. *Desire and Domestic Fiction: A Political History of the Novel*. New York: Oxford University Press, 1987.

———. "Emily's Ghost: The Cultural Politics of Victorian Fiction, Folklore, and Photography." *Novel* 25, no. 3 (1992): 245–67.

———. "Imperialist Nostalgia and *Wuthering Heights*." In *Wuthering Heights*, edited by Linda Peterson. Boston: St. Martin's Press, 1992. 428–49.

———. "The Occidental Alice." *Differences* 2, no. 2 (1990): 3–40.

Arnstein, Walter L. *The Bradlaugh Case: A Study in Late Victorian Opinion and Politics*. Oxford: Clarendon Press, 1965.

Aston, Elaine. *An Introduction to Feminism and Theatre*. London: Routledge, 1995.

Auerbach, Nina. *Communities of Women: An Idea in Fiction*. Cambridge: Harvard University Press, 1978.

———. *Ellen Terry: Player in Her Time*. New York: W. W. Norton, 1987.

———. "Falling Alice, Fallen Women, and Victorian Dream Children." *English Language Notes* 20, no. 3 (1982): 46–64. Reprinted in *Romantic Imprisonment: Women and Other Glorified Outcasts* (New York: Columbia University Press, 1985), 149–68.

———. *Private Theatricals: The Lives of the Victorians*. Cambridge: Harvard University Press, 1990.

———. *Woman and the Demon: The Life of a Victorian Myth*. Cambridge: Harvard University Press, 1982.

Auerbach, Nina, and U. C. Knoepflmacher, eds. *Forbidden Journeys: Fairy Tales and Fantasies by Victorian Women Writers*. Chicago: University of Chicago Press, 1992.

Bailey, Alice A. *The Unfinished Autobiography*. New York: Lucis, 1951.

Baldick, Chris. *In Frankenstein's Shadow: Myth, Monstrosity, and Nineteenth-Century Writing*. Oxford: Clarendon, 1987.

Bann, Stephen, ed. *Frankenstein, Creation and Monstrosity*. London: Reaktion, 1994.

Barbauld, Anna Laeticia. *The Works of Anna Laeticia Barbauld, with a Memoir by Lucy Aikin*. 2 vols. London: Longman, Hurst, Rees, Orme, Brown and Green, 1825.

Barbour, John D. *Versions of Deconversion: Autobiography and the Loss of Faith*. Charlottesville: University Press of Virginia, 1994.

Barthes, Roland. *Camera Lucida: Reflections on Photography*. Translated by Richard Howard. New York: Hill and Wang, 1981.

Bartholomew, Rebecca. *Lost Heroines: Little-Known Women Who Changed History*. West Valley, Utah: Uintah Springs Press, 1996.

Bartram, Michael. *The Pre-Raphaelite Camera: Aspects of Victorian Photography*. New York: Graphic Society; Boston: Little, Brown, 1985.

Basch, Françoise. *Relative Creatures: Victorian Women in Society and the Novel*. New York: Schocken Books, 1974.

Baum, Frank Joslyn, and Russell P. MacFall. *To Please a Child: A Biography of L. Frank Baum, Royal Historian of Oz*. Chicago: Reilly and Lee, 1961.

Baum, L. Frank. *The Annotated Wizard of Oz. [The Wonderful Wizard of Oz.]* Illustrated by W. W. Denslow. 1900. Reprint, edited and with an introduction by Michael Patrick Hearn, New York: Clarkson N. Potter, 1973.

———. *Little Wizard Stories of Oz*. Illustrated by John R. Neill. 1914. Reprint, with an introduction by Michael Patrick Hearn, New York: Schocken Books, 1985.

———. *The Master Key: An Electrical Fairy Tale*. Illustrated by F. Y. Cory. 1901. Reprint, with an introduction by Donald L. Greene and Douglas G. Greene, Westport, Conn.: Hyperion Press, 1974.

———. *The Wizard of Oz*. 1900. Reprint, with illustrations by Lisbeth Zwerger, New York: North-South Books, 1996.

Baxter, I. *A Brief Guide to Biographical Sources*. London: British Library, 1990.

Behrendt, Stephen C., ed. *Approaches to Teaching Shelley's Frankenstein*. New York: Modern Language Association, 1990.

Belenky, Mary Field, Blythe McVicker Clinchy, Nancy Rule Goldberger, and Jill Marruck Tarule. *Women's Ways of Knowing: The Development of Self, Voice, and Mind*. New York: Basic Books, 1986.

Bell, Florence. *Landmarks: A Reprint of Some Essays and Other Pieces Published Between the Years 1894 and 1922*. London: Ernest Benn, 1929.

Bell, Susan Groag, and Marilyn Yalom, eds. *Revealing Lives: Autobiography, Biography, and Gender*. Albany: State University of New York Press, 1990.

Bell, Quentin, and Angelica Garnett, eds. *Vanessa Bell's Family Album*. London: Jill Norman and Hobhouse, 1981.

Belloc, Marie A. "The Art of Photography: Interview with Mr. H. Hay Herschel [*sic*] Cameron." *The Woman at Home* 8 (April 1897): 581–90.

Bennett, Betty T. "Feminism and Editing Mary Wollstonecraft Shelley: The Editor and?/or? the Text." In *Palimpsest: Editorial Theory in the Humanities*, edited by George Bornstein and Ralph G. Williams. Ann Arbor: University of Michigan Press, 1993. 67–96.

Bennett, Olivia. *Annie Besant*. London: Hamish Hamilton, 1988.

Benstock, Shari, ed. *Feminist Issues in Literary Scholarship*. Bloomington: Indiana University Press, 1987.

Bernstein, Susan David. *Confessional Subjects: Revelations of Gender and Power in Victorian Literature and Culture*. Chapel Hill: University of North Carolina Press, 1997.

Besant, Annie. *1875 to 1891: A Fragment of Autobiography*. London: Theosophical Publishing Society, 1891.

———. *The Ancient Wisdom: An Outline of Theosophical Teachings*. 1897. Reprint, Adyar: Theosophical Publishing House, 1939.

——. *Autobiographical Sketches*. London: Freethought Publishing Company, 1885. Originally published in *Our Corner* 3–5 (1884–1885).

——. *An Autobiography*. 1893. 2nd impression, London: Theosophical Publishing Society, 1894. 2nd ed., Benares: Theosophical Publishing Society, 1908. 3rd ed., Adyar: Theosophical Publishing House, 1939.

——. *The Education of Indian Girls*. Benares: Theosophical Publishing Society, 1904.

——. *Esoteric Christianity*. 1901. Reprint, Adyar: Theosophical Publishing House, 1987.

——. *Death—and After?* London: Theosophical Publishing Society, 1894.

——. *Duties of the Theosophist*. Adyar: Theosophical Publishing House, 1917.

——. *Essays on Socialism*. London: Freethought Publishing Company, 1887.

——. *The Future of Indian Politics: A Contribution to the Understanding of Present-Day Problems*. Adyar: Theosophical Publishing House, 1922.

——. *How India Wrought for Freedom: The Story of the National Congress Told from Official Records*. Adyar and London: Theosophical Publishing House, n.d.

——. *The Immediate Future and Other Lectures*. London: Theosophical Publishing Society, 1911.

——. *In the Outer Court*. London: Theosophical Publishing House, 1918.

——. *India: Bond or Free?* New York: G. P. Putnam's Sons, 1926.

——. *An Introduction to Yoga*. 1908. Reprint, Adyar: Theosophical Publishing House, 1927.

——. "The Legalisation of Female Slavery in England." *National Reformer* (London), 4 June 1876.

——. *Man and His Bodies*. 1896. Reprint, Adyar: Theosophical Publishing House, 1967.

——. *Marriage: Its Past, Present and Future* (1879 brochure). Reprint, People's Pocket Series No. 83, edited by E. Haldeman-Julius, Girard, Kans.: Appeal to Reason, [1921].

——. *The Path of Discipleship*. London: Theosophical Publishing Society, 1899.

——. *The Political Status of Women*. London: Watts, 1885.

——. *Popular Lectures on Theosophy*. Los Angeles: Theosophical Publishing House, 1919.

——. *Psychology: Science of the Soul*. Los Angeles: Theosophical Publishing House, 1919.

——. *Theosophical Christianity*. London: St. Alban Press, 1922.

——. *Theosophy and Imperialism*. Adyar: Theosophical Publishing Society, 1902.

——. *The True Basis of Morality*. London: Watts, 1874.

——. *Wake Up, India*. London and Adyar: Theosophical Publishing House, 1913.

——, ed. *The Secular Song and Hymn Book*. Issued by Authority of the National Secular Society. 2nd ed. London: C. Watts, [1875].

——, trans. *The Bhagavad-Gītā, or, The Lord's Song*. 15th ed. 1895. Reprint, Madras: G. A. Nateson, [1945].

Besant, Annie, and C. W. Leadbeater. *Thought Forms*. Benares: Theosophical Publishing Society, 1905.

Besant, Arthur Digby. *The Besant Pedigree*. London: Besant & Company, 1930.

Besant, Walter. *The Autobiography of Sir Walter Besant.* Preface by S. Squire Sprigge. New York: Dodd, Mead, 1902.

Besterman, Theodore. *Mrs. Annie Besant: A Modern Prophet.* London: Kegan Paul, Trench, Trübner, 1934.

Bettelheim, Bruno. *The Uses of Enchantment: The Meaning and Importance of Fairy Tales.* New York: Alfred A. Knopf, 1977.

Bevir, Mark. "Annie Besant's Quest for Truth: Christianity, Secularism and New Age Thought." *The Journal of Ecclesiastical History* 50, no. 1 (1999): 62–93.

Bingle, Richard J. "An Introduction to the India Office Library and Records (Oriental and India Office Collections), British Library, London." *Sagar: South Asia Graduate Research Journal* 3, no. 2 (1996): 12–33.

Black, Sir Frederick. *An Outline Sketch of the Parliamentary History of the Isle of Wight.* Newport, Isle of Wight: County Press, 1929.

Blathwayt, Raymond. "How Celebrities Have Been Photographed." Illustrated by Julia Margaret Cameron and Henry Herschel Cameron. *The Windsor Magazine* 2 (December 1895): 639–48.

Blavatsky, H[elena] P[etrovna]. *The Key to Theosophy, Being a Clear Exposition, in the Form of Question and Answer, of the Ethics, Science, and Philosophy for the Study.* 1889. Reprint, Pasadena: Theosophical University Press, 1946.

———. *Isis Unveiled: A Master-Key to the Mysteries of Ancient and Modern Science and Theology.* 2 vols. 1877. Reprint, Point Loma, Calif.: Theosophical Publishing Company, 1910.

———. *The Secret Doctrine: The Synthesis of Science, Religion, and Philosophy.* 2 vols. 1888. Reprint, Los Angeles: Theosophical Company, 1925.

Bloom, Harold. *The Anxiety of Influence: A Theory of Poetry.* New York: Oxford University Press, 1973.

Blunt, Wilfred. "Julia Margaret Cameron: Early Genius of the Camera." In *The British Eccentric*, edited by Harriet Bridgeman and Elizabeth Drury. New York: Clarkson N. Potter, 1975. 127–36.

Bolen, Jean Shinoda. *Crossing to Avalon: A Woman's Midlife Pilgrimage.* New York: HarperCollins, 1994.

Bonner, Hypatia Bradlaugh, and John M. Robertson. *Charles Bradlaugh: A Record of His Life and Work.* 2 vols. London: T. Fisher Unwin, 1898.

Boord, W. Arthur, ed. *Sun Artists: Original Series.* London: Kegan Paul, Trench, Trübner, 1891.

Boyd, Elizabeth French. *Bloomsbury Heritage: Their Mothers and Their Aunts.* New York: Taplinger, 1976.

Braddon, Mary Elizabeth. *Lady Audley's Secret.* 1862. Reprint, edited and with an introduction by David Skilton, Oxford: Oxford University Press, 1986.

Brandon, Ruth. *The New Women and the Old Men: Love, Sex and the Woman Question.* New York: W. W. Norton, 1990.

Brereton, Virginia Lieson. *From Sin to Salvation: Stories of Women's Conversions, 1800 to the Present.* Bloomington: Indiana University Press, 1991.

Bright, Esther. *Old Memories and Letters of Annie Besant*. London: Theosophical
    Publishing House, 1936.

Brightwell, Cecilia Lucy. *Memorials of the Life of Amelia Opie*. 2nd ed. Norwich, U.K.:
    Fletcher and Alexander, 1854.

Brodzki, Bella, and Celeste Schenck, eds. *Life/Lines: Theorizing Women's Autobiography*.
    Ithaca, N.Y.: Cornell University Press, 1988.

Brontë, Charlotte. *Jane Eyre: An Autobiography*. 1847. Reprint, edited and with an
    introduction by Q. D. Leavis, Harmondsworth, U.K.: Penguin, 1966.

Brooks, Peter. *The Melodramatic Imagination: Balzac, Henry James, Melodrama, and the
    Mode of Excess*. New Haven, Conn.: Yale University Press, 1976.

Brotman, Jordan. "A Late Wanderer in Oz." *Chicago Review*, December 1969. Reprinted
    in Sheila Egoff, G. T. Stubbs, and L. F. Ashley, eds., *Only Connect: Readings
    on Children's Literature*, 2nd ed. (New York: Oxford University Press, 1980),
    156–69.

Brown, Marshall. "A Philosophical View of the Gothic Novel." *Studies in Romanticism*
    26, no. 2 (1987): 275–301.

Browning, Elizabeth Barrett. *Aurora Leigh: A Poem*. 1855. Reprint, with an introduction
    by Gardner B. Taplin, Chicago: Cassandra Books, 1979.

Brownstein, Rachel M. *Becoming a Heroine: Reading about Women in Novels*. New York:
    Viking Press, 1982.

———. *Tragic Muse: Rachel of the Comédie-Française*. New York: A. A. Knopf, 1993.

Bruson, Jean-Marie, ed. *Hommage de Julia Cameron à Victor Hugo*. Paris: Maison de
    Victor Hugo, 1980.

Bump, Jerome. "Mary Shelley's Subversion of Male Myths of Creativity in *Franken-
    stein*." In *The Ethics of Popular Culture: From Frankenstein to Cyberculture*,
    edited by Ingo R. Stoehr. Kilgore, Tx.: Second Dimension Press, 1995. 18–42.

Bunch, Charlotte. Introduction to *Building Feminist Theory: Essays from Quest, A
    Feminist Quarterly*, foreword by Gloria Steinem. New York: Longman, 1981.

Burfield, Diana. "Theosophy and Feminism: Some Explorations in Nineteenth
    Century Biography." In *Women's Religious Experience*, edited by Pat Holden.
    Beckenham, U.K.: Croom Helm, 1983. 27–56.

Bürger, Gottfried August. *Leonora*. Translated by Julia Margaret Cameron. Illustrations
    by D. Maclise, R.A. Engraved by John Thompson. London: Longman,
    Brown, Green and Longmans, 1847.

Butler, Judith. "Conclusion: From Parody to Politics." In *Gender Trouble: Feminism and
    the Subversion of Identity*. London: Routledge, 1990. 142–490.

Butler, Marilyn. *Maria Edgeworth: A Literary Biography*. Oxford: Clarendon Press, 1972.

Byatt, A. S. *Angels and Insects: Two Novellas*. New York: Random House, 1992.

Caine, Barbara. *Victorian Feminists*. Oxford: Oxford University Press, 1992.

Cameron, Julia Margaret. *Illustrations to Tennyson's "Idylls of the King" and Other Poems*.
    2 vols. London: Henry S. King, 1875.

Campbell, Bruce F. *Ancient Wisdom Revived: A History of the Theosophical Movement*.
    Berkeley: University of California Press, 1980.

Campbell, Joseph. *The Hero with a Thousand Faces.* Cleveland and New York: Meridian Books, 1956.

Campbell, Mrs. Patrick. *My Life and Some Letters.* London: Hutchinson, n.d.

Carlson, Susan. *Women and Comedy: Rewriting the British Theatrical Tradition.* Ann Arbor, Mich.: UMI Research Press, 1991.

——. *Women of Grace: James's Plays and the Comedy of Manners.* Studies in Modern Literature No. 48. Ann Arbor, Mich.: UMI Research Press, 1985.

Carlyle, Thomas. *Sartor Resartus: The Life and Opinions of Herr Teufelsdrökh.* 1836. Reprint, edited by Charles Frederick Harrold, New York: Odyssey Press, 1937.

Carroll, Lewis [Charles Dodgson]. *Alice's Adventures in Wonderland* and *Through the Looking-Glass and What Alice Found There.* Illustrations by John Tenniel. 1865 and 1872. Reprint, edited and with an introduction by Roger Lancelyn Green, Oxford: Oxford University Press, 1971.

——. *Alice's Adventures Under Ground.* [Facsimile of the 1862–1863 original manuscript.] 1886. Reprint, Ann Arbor, Mich.: University Microfilms, 1964.

Carter, Angela. *The Bloody Chamber and Other Adult Tales.* New York: Harper, 1981.

——, ed. *Sleeping Beauty and Other Favourite Fairy Tales.* Illustrations by Michael Foreman. London: Victor Gollancz, 1982.

Case, Sue-Ellen. *Feminism and Theatre.* London: Macmillan, 1988.

——, ed. *Performing Feminisms: Feminist Critical Theory and Theatre.* Baltimore, Md.: Johns Hopkins University Press, 1990.

Case, Sue-Ellen, and Janelle Reinelt, eds. *The Performance of Power: Theatrical Discourse and Politics.* Iowa City: University of Iowa Press, 1991.

Cavagnaro, Lori. "Julia Margaret Cameron: Focusing on the Orient." *The Library Chronicle of the University of Texas* 26, no. 4 (1996): 117–43. Reprinted in *Gendered Territory: Photographs of Women by Julia Margaret Cameron*, edited and with an introduction by Dave Oliphant (Austin: Harry Ransom Humanities Research Center, 1996).

Chandrasekhar, S. *"A Dirty, Filthy Book": The Writings of Charles Knowlton and Annie Besant on Reproductive Physiology and Birth Control and an Account of the Bradlaugh-Besant Trial.* Berkeley: University of California Press, 1981.

Chodorow, Nancy. *The Reproduction of Mothering: Psychoanalysis and the Sociology of Gender.* Berkeley: University of California Press, 1978.

Christ, Carol P. *Diving Deep and Surfacing: Women Writers on Spiritual Quest.* Boston: Beacon Press, 1980.

Christ, Carol T., and John O. Jordan, eds. *Victorian Literature and the Victorian Visual Imagination.* Berkeley: University of California Press, 1995.

Cima, Gay Gibson. "Discovering Signs: The Emergence of the Critical Actor in Ibsen." *Theatre Journal* 35, no. 1 (1983): 5–22.

——. "Elizabeth Robins: The Genius of an Independent Manageress." *Theatre Survey* 21, no. 2 (1980): 145–63.

——. *Performing Women: Female Characters, Male Playwrights, and the Modern Stage.* Ithaca, N.Y.: Cornell University Press, 1993.

Cixous, Hélène. "The Laugh of the Medusa." Translated by Keith Cohen and Paula Cohen. *Signs: Journal of Women in Culture and Society* 1, no. 4 (1976): 875–94.

Colby, Robert A. "'What Fools Authors Be!': The Authors' Syndicate, 1890–1920." *The Library Chronicle*, n.s. 35 (1986): 61–87.

Colby, Vineta. *Yesterday's Woman: Domestic Realism in the English Novel*. Princeton: Princeton University Press, 1974.

Colby, Vineta, and Robert A. Colby. *The Equivocal Virtue: Mrs. Oliphant and the Victorian Literary Market Place*. Hamden, Conn.: Archon, 1966.

Colvin, Christina, ed. *Maria Edgeworth: Letters from England, 1813–1844*. Oxford: Clarendon Press, 1971.

Conger, Sydny M. "Aporia and Radical Empathy: *Frankenstein*." In *Approaches to Teaching Shelley's Frankenstein*, edited by Stephen C. Behrendt. New York: Modern Language Association, 1990. 60–66.

Conway, Moncure Daniel. *Autobiography: Memories and Experiences*. 2 vols. Boston: Houghton Mifflin, 1904.

——. *My Pilgrimage to the Wise Men of the East*. Boston: Houghton Mifflin, 1906.

Cook, Blanche Wiessen. "Female Support Networks and Political Activism: Lillian Wald, Crystal Eastman, Emma Goldman." *Chrysalis*, no. 3 (1977): 43–61.

Cooley, Nicole. "Ideology and the Portrait: Recovering the 'Silent Image of Woman' in the Work of Julia Margaret Cameron." *Women's Studies: An Interdisciplinary Journal* 24, no. 4 (1995): 369–84.

Corbett, Mary Jean. "Feminine Authorship and Spiritual Authority in Victorian Women's Autobiographies." *Women's Studies* 18, no. 1 (1990): 13–30.

Cosslett, Tess. *Science and Religion in the Nineteenth Century*. Cambridge: Cambridge University Press, 1983.

——. *Woman to Woman: Female Friendship in Victorian Fiction*. Brighton, U.K.: Harvester, 1988.

Cousins, James, ed. *The Annie Besant Centenary Book*. Madras: Theosophical Publishing House, 1947.

Cox, Julian. "Julia Margaret Cameron: The Creative Process." Los Angeles: J. Paul Getty Museum, 1996.

——. *Julia Margaret Cameron: Photographs from the J. Paul Getty Museum*. "In Focus" Series. Los Angeles: J. Paul Getty Museum, 1996.

Cranston, Sylvia. *HPB: The Extraordinary Life and Influence of Helena Blavatsky, Founder of the Modern Theosophical Movement*. New York: G. P. Putnam's Sons, 1993.

Cross, Nigel. *The Common Writer: Life in Nineteenth-Century Grub Street*. Cambridge: Cambridge University Press, 1985.

Cruikshank, George. "Cinderella and the Glass Slipper" (1854). In *Victorian Fairy Tales: The Revolt of the Fairies and the Elves*, edited by Jack Zipes. New York: Methuen, 1987. 39–57.

Cuthbertson, Yvonne. "Julia Margaret Cameron: Classic Portraits from the Victorian Age." *Darkroom Photography* 12, no. 4 (1990): 24–29.

Daniel, Malcolm. "Darkroom vs. Greenroom: Victorian Art Photography and Popular Entertainment." *Image* 33, no. 1/2 (1990): 13–19.

Darwin, Charles. *The Expression of the Emotions in Man and Animals.* London: J. Murray, 1872.

David, Deirdre. *Intellectual Women and Victorian Patriarchy.* London: Macmillan, 1987.

Davis, James P. "*Frankenstein* and the Subversion of the Masculine Voice." *Women's Studies* 21, no. 3 (1992): 307–22.

Davis, Tracy C. "Acting in Ibsen." *Theatre Notebook* 39, no. 3 (1985): 113–23.

———. *Actresses as Working Women: Their Social Identity in Victorian Culture.* London: Routledge, 1992.

de Laclos, Choderlos. *Les Liaisons Dangereuses.* 1782. Reprint, translated and with an introduction by P. W. K. Stone, Harmondsworth, U.K.: Penguin, 1961.

De Sanctis, Sante. *Religious Conversion: A Bio-Psychological Study.* London: Keagan Paul, 1927.

de Sévigné, Madame. *Selected Letters.* Translated and with an introduction by Leonard Tancock. Harmondsworth, U.K.: Penguin, 1982.

Denny, Barbara, comp. *Kensington in Old Photographs.* London: CPL Publishing, 1974.

Diamond, Elin. "Mimesis, Mimicry, and the 'True-Real.'" *Modern Drama* 32, no. 1 (1989): 58–72. Reprinted in *Acting Out: Feminist Performances,* edited by Lynda Hart and Peggy Phelan (Ann Arbor: University of Michigan Press, 1993), 363–82.

———. "Realism and Hysteria: Toward a Feminist Mimesis." *Discourse* 13, no. 1 (1990–1991): 59–92.

Dickinson, Emily. *The Letters of Emily Dickinson.* Vol. 1. Edited by Thomas H. Johnson and Theodora Ward. Cambridge: Harvard University Press, 1958.

Dinnage, Rosemary. *Annie Besant.* Middlesex, U.K.: Penguin, 1986.

Dixon, Joy. "Sexology and the Occult: Sexuality and Subjectivity in Theosophy's New Age." *Journal of the History of Sexuality* 7, no. 3 (1997): 409–33.

Dodier, Virginia. *Clementina, Lady Hawarden: Studies from Life, 1857–1864.* Introduction by Marina Warner. Afterword by Mark Haworth-Booth. New York: Aperture, 1999.

Dolan, Jill. *The Feminist Spectator as Critic.* Ann Arbor: University of Michigan Press, 1991.

Dorsey, Peter A. "Women's Autobiography and the Hermeneutics of Conversion." *a/b: Auto/Biography Studies* 8, no. 1 (1993): 72–90.

Dunlap, Barbara J. "Anne Thackeray Ritchie." In *Victorian Novelists after 1885,* edited by Ira B. Nadel and William E. Freedman. Vol. 18 of *Dictionary of Literary Biography.* Detroit: Gale Research, 1983. 251–57.

Dusinberre, Juliet. *Alice to the Lighthouse: Children's Books and Radical Experiments in Art.* New York: St. Martin's Press, 1987.

Eagleton, Terry. *Criticism and Ideology: A Study in Marxist Literary Theory.* New York: Schocken, 1978.

[Eastlake, Lady Elizabeth]. "Photography." *Quarterly Review* 101 (April 1857): 442–68.

Edel, Leon. *Henry James: The Treacherous Years, 1895–1901*. Philadelphia: Lippincott, 1969.

Egan, Michael. *Ibsen: The Critical Heritage*. London: Routledge and Kegan Paul, 1972.

Eldredge, Charles C. "Nature Symbolized: American Painting from Ryder to Hartley." In *The Spiritual in Art: Abstract Painting, 1890–1985*, edited by Maurice Tuchman and Judith Freeman. New York: Abbeville Press, 1986. 113–29.

Eliot, George. "Silly Novels by Lady Novelists." *Westminster Foreign Quarterly Review* 66 (October 1856): 442–61.

Eliot, T. S. "Hamlet and His Problems." In *The Sacred Wood: Essays on Poetry and Criticism*. 1920. Reprint, London: Methuen, 1969. 95–103.

Ellis, Mrs. [Edith Lees] Havelock. *Attainment*. London: Alston Rivers, 1909.

Ellis, Kate Ferguson. "Subversive Surfaces: The Limits of Domestic Affection in Mary Shelley's Later Fiction." In *The Other Mary Shelley: Beyond Frankenstein*, edited by Audrey A. Fisch, Anne K. Mellor, and Esther H. Schor. Oxford: Oxford University Press, 1993. 220–34.

Ellwood, Robert. *Alternative Altars*. Chicago: Chicago University Press, 1979.

——. *Theosophy: A Modern Expression of the Wisdom of the Ages*. Wheaton, Ill.: Quest, 1986.

Ellwood, Robert, and Catherine Wessinger. "The Feminism of 'Universal Brotherhood': Women in the Theosophical Movement." In *Women's Leadership in Marginal Religions: Explorations Outside the Mainstream*, edited by Catherine Wessinger. Urbana and Chicago: University of Illinois Press, 1993. 68–87.

Erikson, Erik H. *Identity and the Life Cycle. Psychological Issues*. Vol. 1. New York: International Universities Presses, 1959.

——. *Identity, Youth, and Crisis*. New York: W. W. Norton, 1968.

Ewbank, Inga-Stina. "The Last Plays." In *The Cambridge Companion to Ibsen*, edited by James McFarlane. Cambridge: Cambridge University Press, 1994. 126–54.

"The Exhibition of the Photographic Society." *The Art-Journal*, n.s. 9 (December 1870): 376.

Farfan, Penny. "From Hedda Gabler to Votes for Women: Elizabeth Robins's Early Feminist Critique of Ibsen." *Theatre Journal* 48, no. 1 (1996): 59–79.

Feldman, Paula R., and Theresa M. Kelley, eds. *Romantic Women Writers: Voices and Countervoices*. Hanover, N.H.: University Press of New England, 1995.

Felski, Rita. *Beyond Feminist Aesthetics*. Cambridge, Mass.: Harvard University Press, 1989.

Feltes, N. N. *Modes of Production of Victorian Novels*. Chicago: University of Chicago Press, 1986.

Fernando, Lloyd. *"New Women" in the Late Victorian Novel*. University Park: Pennsylvania State University Press, 1977.

Ferris, Lesley. "The Female Self and Performance: The Case of *The First Actress*." In *Theatre and Feminist Aesthetics*, edited by Karen Laughlin and Catherine Schuler. London: Associated University Presses, 1995. 242–57.

Field, Nicola. *Over the Rainbow: Money, Class and Homophobia*. London and East Haven, Conn.: Pluto Press, 1995.

Filmer, Kath, ed. *The Victorian Fantasists: Essays on Culture, Society and Belief in the Mythopoeic Fiction of the Victorian Age*. Foreword by David Jasper. London: Macmillan, 1991.

F[itz]G[erald], S[eymour] V[esey]. "Sir Richmond Thackeray Willoughby Ritchie." In *The Dictionary of National Biography: 1912–1921*, edited by H. W. C. Davis and J. R. H. Weaver. Oxford: Oxford University Press, 1927. 462–63.

Fitzsimmons, Linda, and Viv Gardner, eds. *New Women Plays*. London: Methuen, 1991.

Fleishman, Avrom. *Figures of Autobiography: The Language of Self-Writing*. Berkeley: University of California Press, 1983.

Flinders, Carol Lee. *Enduring Grace: Living Portraits of Seven Women Mystics*. San Francisco: HarperCollins, 1993.

Flukinger, Roy. *The Formative Decades: Photography in Great Britain, 1839–1920*. Austin: University of Texas Press, 1985.

Flynn, Elizabeth A., and Patrocinio P. Schweickart, eds. *Gender and Reading: Essays on Readers, Texts, and Contexts*. Baltimore, Md.: Johns Hopkins University Press, 1986.

Ford, Colin. *The Cameron Collection: An Album of Photographs by Julia Margaret Cameron Presented to Sir John Herschel*. Wokingham, U.K.: Van Nostrand Reinhold, 1975.

Foucault, Michel. *The History of Sexuality*. Vol. 1. Translated by Robert Hurley. New York: Pantheon Books, 1978.

Fox, Matthew, ed. *Hildegard of Bingen's Book of Divine Works with Letters and Songs*. Santa Fe, N.M.: Bear and Company, 1987.

Fraser, Kennedy. *Ornament and Silence: Essays on Women's Lives*. New York: Alfred A. Knopf, 1996.

Fricke, John, Jay Scarfone, and William Stillman. *The Wizard of Oz: The Official 50th Anniversary Pictorial History*. Introduction by Jack Haley, Jr. New York: Warner Books, 1989.

Friedman, Susan Stanford. "Women's Autobiographical Selves: Theory and Practice." In *The Private Self: Theory and Practice of Women's Autobiographical Writings*, edited by Sheri Benstock. Chapel Hill: University of North Carolina Press, 1988. 34–62.

Fry, Roger. Introduction to *Victorian Photographs of Famous Men and Fair Women by Julia Margaret Cameron* [1926]. Edited by Tristam Powell and with a second introduction by Virginia Woolf. London: Hogarth Press, 1973.

Fuller, Hester Thackeray Ritchie. *Three Freshwater Friends: Tennyson, Watts, and Mrs. Cameron*. Newport, Isle of Wight: County Press, 1933.

Fuller, Hester Thackeray, with Violet Hammersley. *Thackeray's Daughter: Some Recollections of Anne Thackeray Ritchie*. Introduction by Desmond MacCarthy. Dublin: Euphorion, 1951.

Gage, Matilda Joslyn. *Woman, Church and State: The Original Exposé of Male*

Collaboration Against the Female Sex. 1893. Reprint, with an introduction by Sally Roesch Wagner and a foreword by Mary Daly, Watertown, Mass.: Persephone Press, 1980.

Gainor, J. Ellen. *Shaw's Daughters: Dramatic and Narrative Constructions of Gender*. Ann Arbor: University of Michigan Press, 1991.

Gallagher, Catherine. *Nobody's Story: The Vanishing Acts of Women Writers in the Marketplace, 1670–1820*. Berkeley and Los Angeles: University of California Press, 1994.

Gallagher, Catherine, and Thomas Laqueur, eds. *The Making of the Modern Body: Sexuality and Society in the Nineteenth Century*. Berkeley: University of California Press, 1987.

Gardiner, Judith Kegan. "On Female Identity and Writing by Women." *Critical Inquiry* 8, no. 2 (1981): 347–61.

Gardner, Martin. "A Child's Garden of Bewilderment." *Saturday Review*, 17 July 1965. Reprinted in Sheila Egoff, G. T. Stubbs, and L. F. Ashley, eds., *Only Connect: Readings on Children's Literature*, 2nd ed. (New York: Oxford University Press, 1980), 150–55.

Gardner, Vivien, and Susan Rutherford, eds. *The New Woman and Her Sisters: Feminism and Theatre, 1850–1914*. Ann Arbor: University of Michigan Press, 1992.

Gardner, Viv, ed. *Sketches from the Actresses' Franchise League*. Nottingham, U.K.: Nottingham Drama Texts, 1985.

Garnett, Richard. "Mary Wollstonecraft Shelley." In vol. 18 of *The Dictionary of National Biography: To 1900*, edited by Leslie Stephen and Sidney Lee. Oxford: Oxford University Press, 1917. 29–31.

Gaskell, Mrs. [Elizabeth]. *Cranford*. 1853. Reprint, with an introduction by Anne Thackeray Ritchie, London: Macmillan, 1891.

——. *The Life of Charlotte Brontë*. 1857. Reprint, with an introduction by Alan Shelston, Harmondsworth, U.K.: Penguin, 1975.

Gately, Patricia D., D. Cole Woodcox, and N. Dennis Leavens, eds. *Perspectives on Self and Community in George Eliot: Dorothea's Window*. Lewiston, N.Y.: Mellen Press, 1997.

Gates, Joanne E. *Elizabeth Robins, 1862–1952: Actress, Novelist, Feminist*. Tuscaloosa: University of Alabama Press, 1994.

——. "Elizabeth Robins: A Life in Letters." Faculty Scholar Lecture, Jacksonville State University, 23 February 1995.

——. "Elizabeth Robins: From *A Dark Lantern* to *The Convert*—A Study of Her Fictional Style and Feminist Viewpoint." *Massachusetts Studies in English* 6, no. 3/4 (1978): 25–40.

——. The Elizabeth Robins Web Home Page: Texts and Contexts. <http://www.jsu.edu/depart/english/robins/index.htm>.

——. Introduction to "The Herstory of a Button," by Elizabeth Robins. *American Voice*, no. 19 (1990): 35–38.

———. "'Sometimes Suppressed and Sometimes Embroidered': The Life and Writing of Elizabeth Robins, 1862–1952." Ph.D. diss., University of Massachusetts at Amherst, 1987.

———. "Stitches in a Critical Time: The Diaries of Elizabeth Robins, American Feminist in England." *a/b: auto/biography* 4, no. 2 (1988): 130–39.

———. "The Theatrical Politics of Elizabeth Robins and Bernard Shaw." *Shaw: The Annual of Bernard Shaw Studies* 14 (1994): 43–53. Reprinted in *1992: Shaw and the Last Hundred Years,* edited by Bernard F. Dukone (University Park: Pennsylvania State University Press, 1994).

Gaylor, Annie Laurie, ed. *Women without Superstition, "No Gods—No Masters": The Collected Writings of Women Freethinkers of the Nineteenth and Twentieth Centuries.* Madison, Wisc.: Freedom from Religion Foundation, 1997.

Gérin, Winifred. *Anne Thackeray Ritchie: A Biography.* Oxford: Oxford University Press, 1981.

Gernsheim, Helmut. *A Concise History of Photography.* 3rd rev. ed. New York: Dover, 1986.

———. *Julia Margaret Cameron: Her Life and Work.* 1948. Reprint, New York: Aperture, 1975.

———. *Lewis Carroll, Photographer.* New York: Dover, 1969.

Gernsheim, Helmut, and Alison Gernsheim. *Queen Victoria: A Biography in Word and Picture.* London: Longmans, 1959.

Gibbs-Smith, Charles Harvard. "Mrs. Julia Margaret Cameron, Victorian Photographer." In *One Hundred Years of Photography: Essays in Honor of Beaumont Newhall,* edited by Van Deren Coke. Albuquerque: University of New Mexico Press, 1975. 69–76.

Gilbert, Sandra, and Susan Gubar. *The Madwoman in the Attic: The Woman Writer and the Nineteenth-Century Imagination.* New Haven, Conn.: Yale University Press, 1979.

Gilchrist, Cherry. *Theosophy: The Wisdom of the Ages.* London: Labyrinth, 1996.

Gillespie, Diane Filby. *The Sisters' Arts: The Writing and Painting of Virginia Woolf and Vanessa Bell.* Syracuse, N.Y.: Syracuse University Press, 1988.

Gillespie, Diane Filby, and Elizabeth Steele, eds. *Julia Duckworth Stephen: Stories for Children, Essays for Adults.* Syracuse, N.Y.: Syracuse University Press, 1987.

Gilligan, Carol. *In a Different Voice: Psychological Theory and Women's Development.* Cambridge: Harvard University Press, 1982.

Gilman, Charlotte Perkins. *The Yellow Wallpaper.* 1899. Reprint, with an afterword by Elaine R. Hodges, New York: Feminist Press, 1973.

Gilmore, Leigh. *Autobiographics: A Feminist Theory of Self-Representation.* Ithaca, N.Y.: Cornell University Press, 1994.

Gissing, George. *New Grub Street.* 1891. Reprint, with an introduction by Bernard Bergonzi, Harmondsworth, U.K.: Penguin, 1968.

Gitter, Elisabeth G. "The Power of Women's Hair in the Victorian Imagination." *Publications of the Modern Language Association* 99, no. 5 (1984): 936–54.

Glance, Jonathan C. "'Beyond the Usual Bounds of Reverie?': Another Look at the Dreams in *Frankenstein*." *Journal of the Fantastic in the Arts* 7, no. 4 (1996): 30–47.

[Goodrich, S. G.]. "Mrs. Barbauld." In *Lives of Celebrated Women*. Boston: Wm. J. Reynolds, 1852.

Gordon, Dan. *Hungry for Fairyland*. Winnipeg Fringe Festival, 1996. <http://www.pangea.ca/dan/fairyland.html>.

Graf, Julie. "Reconfiguring Conversion: The Construction of Identity in the Counter-Conversion Narratives of Emily Dickinson, Elizabeth Cady Stanton, and Jane Addams." Master's thesis, University of Texas (Austin), 1994.

Greene, Gayle, and Coppélia Kahn, eds. *Making a Difference: Feminist Literary Criticism*. London: Methuen, 1985.

Greenstein, Susan M. "The Question of Vocation: From *Romola* to *Middlemarch*." *Nineteenth-Century Fiction* 35, no. 4 (1981): 487–505.

Griest, Guinevere L. *Mudie's Circulating Library and the Victorian Novel*. Bloomington: Indiana University Press, 1970.

Gubar, Susan. "'The Blank Page' and the Issues of Female Creativity." *Critical Inquiry* 8, no. 2 (1981): 243–63. Reprinted in *New Feminist Criticism: Essays on Women, Literature, and Theory*, edited by Elaine Showalter (New York: Pantheon Books, 1985), 292–313.

Hamilton, Charles. *The Illustrated Letter*. New York: Universe Books, 1987.

Hamilton, Susan, ed. *"Criminals, Idiots, Women, and Minors": Victorian Writing by Women on Women*. Peterborough, Ont.: Broadview Press, 1995.

Hamilton, Violet. *Annals of My Glass House: Photographs by Julia Margaret Cameron*. Claremont, Calif.: Perpetua Press, 1996.

Handy, Elizabeth. "Ways of Seeing." Ph.D. diss., London Polytechnic, 1990.

Hansen, Linda. "Experiencing the World as Home: Reflections on Dorothy's Quest in *The Wizard of Oz*." *Soundings* 67, no. 1 (1984): 91–102.

Harker, Margaret. *Julia Margaret Cameron*. "The Great Photographers" Series. London: Collins, 1983.

Harris, Janice H. "Not Suffering and Not Still: Women Writers at the *Cornhill Magazine*, 1860–1900." *Modern Language Quarterly* 47, no. 4 (1986): 382–92.

Harvey, John. *Victorian Novelists and Their Illustrators*. New York: New York University Press, 1971.

Haworth-Booth, Mark. *An Independent Art: Photographs from the Victoria and Albert Museum, 1839–1996*. Princeton: Princeton University Press, 1997.

Haworth-Booth, Mark, and Anne McCauley. *The Museum and the Photograph: Collecting Photography at the Victoria and Albert Museum, 1853–1900*. Williamstown, Mass.: Sterling and Francine Clark Art Institute, 1998.

Heilbrun, Carolyn G. *Writing a Woman's Life*. New York: W. W. Norton, 1988.

Helle, Anita Plath. "Representing Women Writers Onstage: A Retrospective to the Present." In *Making a Spectacle: Feminist Essays on Contemporary Women's*

Theatre, edited and with an introduction by Lynda Hart. Ann Arbor: University of Michigan Press, 1989. 195–208.

Hellwege, Pamela. "The Photographic Work of Laurie Simmons." *School Arts* 93, no. 9 (1994): 23–26.

Heyert, Elizabeth. *The Glass-House Years: Victorian Portrait Photography, 1839–1870*. Montclair: Allanheld & Schram; London: George Prior, 1979.

Hill, Brian. *Julia Margaret Cameron: A Victorian Family Portrait*. London: Peter Owen, 1973.

Hill, Leslie. "Representations of Women in British Drama: 1890–1914." Ph.D. diss., University of Glasgow, 1996.

Hill, Paul, and Thomas Cooper. *Dialogue with Photography*. New York: Farrar, Straus, Giroux, 1979.

Hillier, Bevis. *Victorian Studio Photographs: Biographical Portraits of Eminent Victorians*. Boston: David R. Godine, 1975.

Hill-Miller, Katherine C. "'The Skies and Trees of the Past': Anne Thackeray Ritchie and William Makepeace Thackeray." In *Daughters and Fathers*, edited by Lynda E. Boose and Betty S. Flowers. Baltimore, Md.: Johns Hopkins University Press, 1989. 361–83.

Hills, Ann. "Idylls No More at Freshwater?" *History Today* 42 (July 1992): 3–4.

Hinton, Brian. *Immortal Faces: Julia Margaret Cameron on the Isle of Wight*. Newport: Isle of Wight County Press, 1992.

Hobbs, Colleen. "Reading the Symptoms: An Exploration of Repression and Hysteria in Mary Shelley's *Frankenstein*." *Studies in the Novel* 25, no. 2 (1993): 152–69.

Hodges, Devon. "*Frankenstein* and the Feminine Subversion of the Novel." *Tulsa Studies in Women's Literature* 2, no. 2 (1983): 155–64.

Holledge, Julie. *Innocent Flowers: Women in the Edwardian Theatre*. London: Virago Press, 1981.

Hollinger, Veronica. "Putting on the Feminine: Gender and Negativity in *Frankenstein* and *The Handmaid's Tale*." In *Negation, Critical Theory, and Postmodern Textuality*, edited by Daniel Fischlin. Dordrecht, Netherlands: Kluwer Academinic Publishers, 1994. 203–24.

Hollis, Patricia. *Ladies Elect: Women in English Local Government, 1865–1914*. Oxford: Clarendon Press, 1987.

Holroyd, Michael. *Bernard Shaw: The Search for Love (1856–1898)*; *The Pursuit of Power (1898–1918)*; *The Lure of Fantasy (1918–1950)*; *The Last Laugh (1950–1991)*; and *The Last Laugh: An Epilogue (1950–1991)*. 5 vols. New York: Random House, 1988–1992.

Homans, Margaret. *Bearing the Word: Language and Female Experience in Nineteenth-Century Women's Writing*. Chicago: University of Chicago Press, 1986.

Homans, Margaret, and Adrienne Munich, eds. *Remaking Queen Victoria*. Cambridge: Cambridge University Press, 1997.

Hon, G. Thomas. "The Melange that Was Julia Margaret Cameron." *The Photographic Journal* 128 (July 1988): 302–3.

Hopcke, Robert H. "Dorothy and Her Friends: Symbols of Gay Male Individuation." *Quadrant* 22, no. 2 (1989): 65–76.

Hopkins, Lisa. *A Hall of Mirrors: Mary Shelley's Frankenstein*. Sheffield, U.K.: City Polytechnic School of Cultural Studies, 1991.

Hopkinson, Amanda. *Julia Margaret Cameron*. "Virago Pioneers" Series. London: Virago, 1986.

Horney, Karen. *Feminine Psychology*. Edited and with an introduction by Harold Kelman. New York: W. W. Norton, 1973.

Howard, Jeremy, ed. *Whisper of the Muse: The World of Julia Margaret Cameron*. London: Colnaghi, 1990.

Huizinga, Johan. *Homo Ludens: A Study of the Play-element in Culture*. 1950. Reprint, Boston: Beacon Press, 1955.

[Huxley, Leonard]. *The House of Smith, Elder*. London: [privately printed], 1923.

Hynes, Samuel. *The Edwardian Turn of Mind*. Princeton: Princeton University Press, 1968.

Ibsen, Henrik. *A Doll's House*. 1889. Reprint, translated by Egil Tornqvist, Cambridge: Cambridge University Press, 1995.

———. *When We Dead Awaken*. Copenhagen: Gyldendal, 1899. Reprinted in James Walter McFarland, ed. and trans., *The Oxford Ibsen*, vol. 8 (Oxford: Oxford University Press, 1977), 235–97.

In Honour of Dr. Annie Besant: Lectures by Eminent Persons, 1952–88. Kamachha: Indian Section of the Theosophical Society, 1990.

Jacobus, Mary. "Is There a Woman in This Text?" *New Literary History* 14, no. 1 (1982): 117–41.

Jalland, Pat, ed. *Octavia Wilberforce: The Autobiography of a Pioneer Woman Doctor*. London: Cassell, 1989.

James, Alice. *The Diary of Alice James*. Edited by Leon Edel. New York: Dodd, Mead, 1964.

James, Henry. "The Art of Fiction." *Longman's Magazine*, September 1884. Reprinted in *Theory of Fiction: Henry James*, edited by James E. Miller, Jr. (Lincoln: University of Nebraska Press, 1972), 27–44.

———. *Guy Domville: A Play in Three Acts*. With Comments by Bernard Shaw, H. G. Wells, and Arnold Bennett. Edited by and with an introduction by Leon Edel. London: Rupert Hart-Davis, 1961.

Jameson, Mrs. [Anna Brownell Murphy]. *Legends of the Madonna as Represented in the Fine Arts*. Boston: Houghton Mifflin, 1852.

———. *Sacred and Legendary Art*. 2 vols. 1848. Reprint, New York: AMS Press, 1970.

———. *Shakespeare's Characters of the Intellect and Affections*. 1846. Reprint, New York: Leavitt and Allen, 1911.

———. "Woman's Mission and Woman's Position." In *Memoirs and Essays Illustrative of Art, Literature and Social Morals*. New York: Wily & Putnam, 1846.

Jamieson, Michael. "An American Actress at Balmoral." *Theatre Research International* 2, no. 2 (1977): 717–31.

Jay, Elisabeth. *Faith and Doubt in Victorian England*. London: Macmillan, 1986.

Jinarajadasa, C[urppumullage]. *A Short Biography of Annie Besant*. 1932. Reprint, Adyar: Theosophical Publishing House, 1996.

Jelinek, Estelle C., ed. *Women's Autobiography: Essays in Criticism*. Bloomington: Indiana University Press, 1980.

Joeres, Ruth-Ellen Boetcher, and Elizabeth Mittman, eds. *The Politics of the Essay: Feminist Perspectives*. Bloomington: Indiana University Press, 1993.

John, Angela V. "Elizabeth Robins." In *The Dictionary of National Biography: Missing Persons*, edited by C. S. Nicholls. Oxford: Oxford University Press, 1993. 560–61.

——. *Elizabeth Robins: Staging a Life, 1862–1952*. London: Routledge, 1995.

The J[ohn] Paul Getty Museum Handbook of the Photographs Collection. Malibu, Calif.: The Museum, 1995.

Johnson, Barbara. "My Monster/My Self." *Diacritics* 12, no. 2 (1982): 2–10.

Johnson, William S. *Nineteenth-Century Photography: An Annotated Bibliography, 1839–1879*. Boston: G. K. Hall, 1990.

Jones, Barbara. *The Isle of Wight*. Harmondsworth, U.K.: Penguin, 1950.

Jordan, Judith V., Alexandra G. Kaplan, Jean Baker Miller, Irene P. Stiver, and Janet L. Surrey. *Women's Growth in Connection: Writings from the Stone Center*. New York and London: Guilford Press, 1991.

Joseph, Gerhard. *Tennyson and the Text: The Weaver's Shuttle*. Cambridge: Cambridge University Press, 1992.

Julia Margaret Cameron: An Album. Washington, D.C.: Lunn Gallery/Graphics International, 1975.

Jung, Carl. *Man and His Symbols*. New York: Dell, 1968.

Kandinsky, Wassily. *Concerning the Spiritual in Art*. 1914. Reprint, translated and with an introduction by H. T. H. Sadler, New York: Dover, 1977.

Kane, Julie. "Varieties of Mystical Experience in the Writings of Virginia Woolf." *Twentieth Century Literature* 41, no. 4 (1995): 328–49.

Karpinski, Gloria. *Where Two Worlds Touch: Spiritual Rites of Passage*. London: Rider, 1990.

Kelly, Katherine E., ed. *Modern Drama by Women, 1880s–1930s: An International Anthology*. London: Routledge, 1996.

Kestner, Joseph. "Narcissism as Symptom and Structure: The Case of Mary Shelley's *Frankenstein*." In *The Nature of Identity*, edited by Winston Weathers. Tulsa: University of Tulsa Press, 1981. 15–25.

Kincaid, James R. "Alice's Invasion of Wonderland." *Publications of the Modern Language Association* 88, no. 1 (1973): 92–99.

——. *Child-Loving: The Erotic Child and Victorian Culture*. New York: Routledge, 1992.

King, Ursula. *Women and Spirituality: Voices of Protest and Promise*. 2nd ed. London: Macmillan, 1993.

Klein, Julie Thompson. *Crossing Boundaries: Knowledge, Disciplinarities, and Interdisciplinarities*. Charlottesville: University Press of Virginia, 1996.

Knight, Hardwicke. "Anne Isabella Thackeray and Julia Margaret Cameron." *History of Photography* 7, no. 3 (1983): 247–48.

Knoepflmacher, U. C. "Thoughts on the Aggression of Daughters." In *The Endurance of Frankenstein: Essays on Mary Shelley's Novel*, edited by George Levine and U. C. Knoepflmacher. Berkeley: University of California Press, 1979. 88–91.

———. *Ventures into Childhood: Victorians, Fairy Tales, and Femininity*. Chicago: University of Chicago Press, 1998.

Koestler, Arthur. *The Act of Creation: A Study of the Conscious and Unconscious in Art*. 1964. Reprint, New York: Dell, 1967.

Krishnamurti, J[iddu]. *Education and the Significance of Life*. 1953. Reprint, San Francisco: Harper & Row, 1981.

———. *Krishnamurti on Education*. 1974. Reprint, New York: Harper & Row, 1977.

———. *On Mind and Thought*. San Francisco: Harper, 1993.

Kristeva, Julia. "Women's Time." *Signs* 7, no. 1 (1981): 13–35.

Kuhn, Thomas S. *The Structure of Scientific Revolutions*. 2nd ed. Chicago: University of Chicago Press, 1970.

Kumar, Raj. *Annie Besant's Rise to Power in Indian Politics, 1914–1917*. Delhi: Concept Publishing House, 1981.

Laing, R. D. *The Divided Self: An Existential Study of Sanity and Madness*. Baltimore: Penguin Books, 1971.

———. *The Politics of Experience*. New York: Ballantine Books, 1967.

Landow, George P., ed. *Approaches to Victorian Autobiography*. Athens: Ohio University Press, 1979.

Langley, Noel, Florence Ryerson, and Edgar Allan Woolf. *The Wizard of Oz: The Screenplay*. 1939. Reprint, edited and with an introduction by Michael Patrick Hearn, New York: Delta Books, 1989.

Laughlin, Karen. "Introduction: Why Feminist Aesthetics?" In *Theatre and Feminist Aesthetics*, edited by Karen Laughlin and Catherine Schuler. London: Associated University Presses, 1995. 9–21.

Leadbeater, C. W. *Clairvoyance*. 1899. Reprint, Adyar: Theosophical Publishing House, 1983.

———. *Freemasonry and Its Ancient Mystic Rites*. 1986. Reprint, New York: Gramercy Books, 1998.

Lee, Hermione. *Virginia Woolf*. London: Chatto and Windus, 1996.

LeFevre, Karen Burke. *Invention as a Social Act*. Carbondale: Southern Illinois University Press, 1987.

L[eigh]-S[mith], P[hilip]. *Record of an Ascent: A Memoir of Sir Richmond Ritchie*. London: Dillon's University Bookshop, 1961.

Lennox, Charlotte. *The Female Quixote; or, The Adventures of Arabella*. 1752. Reprint, with an introduction by Sandra Shulman, London: Pandora, 1986.

Lessing, Doris. *Martha Quest*. New York: New American Library, 1952.

Levine, George. *The Realistic Imagination: English Fiction from Frankenstein to Lady Chatterley*. Chicago: University of Chicago Press, 1981.

Levine, Philippa. *Feminist Lives in Victorian Britain: Private Roles and Public Commitment*. London: Basil Blackwell, 1990.

——. *Victorian Feminism (1850–1900)*. London: Hutchinson, 1987.

Lewis, C. S. *Till We Have Faces*. New York: Harcourt, Brace, 1956.

Lindquist-Cock, Elizabeth. "Sentiment, Compassion, Straight Record: The Mid-Victorians." *Massachusetts Review* 19, no. 4 (1978): 717–28.

Lionnet, Françoise. *Autobiographical Voices: Race, Gender, Self-Portraiture*. Ithaca, N.Y.: Cornell University Press, 1989.

London, Bette. "Mary Shelley, *Frankenstein*, and the Spectacle of Masculinity." *Publications of the Modern Language Association* 108, no. 2 (1993): 253–67.

Longford, Elizabeth. "Annie Besant." In *Eminent Victorian Women*. New York: Alfred A. Knopf, 1981. 129–50.

Lorde, Audré. "The Master's Tools Will Never Dismantle the Master's House." Comments delivered at "The Personal and Political Panel," Second Sex Conference, New York, 29 November 1979. Reprinted in *Sister Outsider: Essays and Speeches* (Freedom, Calif.: Crossing Press, 1988), 110–13.

Lovett, H. V., and Patrick Cadell. "Annie Besant." In *The Dictionary of National Biography: 1931–1940*, edited by L. G. Wickham Legg. Oxford: Oxford University Press, 1949. 72–74.

Lowndes, Susan, ed. *Diaries and Letters of Marie Belloc Lowndes, 1911–1947*. London: Chatto & Windus, 1971.

Lubbock, Percy. *Mary Cholmondeley: A Sketch from Memory*. London: Jonathan Cape, 1928.

Lukitsh, Joanne. "Julia Margaret Cameron and the 'Ennoblement' of Photographic Portraiture." In *Victorian Scandals: Representations of Gender and Class*, edited by Kristine Ottesen Garrigan. Athens: Ohio University Press, 1992. 207–32.

——. *Julia Margaret Cameron: Her Work and Career*. Rochester, N.Y.: International Museum of Photography at George Eastman House, 1986.

——. "Julia Margaret Cameron's Photographic Illustrations to Alfred Tennyson's *Idylls of the King*." *Arthurian Literature* 7 (1987): 145–57. Reprinted in *Arthurian Women: A Casebook*, edited and with an introduction by Thelma S. Fenster (New York: Garland Publishing, 1996), 247–62.

——. "'Simply Pictures of Peasants': Artistry, Authorship, and Ideology in Julia Margaret Cameron's Photography in Sri Lanka, 1875–1879." *Yale Journal of Criticism* 9, no. 2 (1996): 283–308.

——. "The Thackeray Album: Looking at Julia Margaret Cameron's Gift to Her Friend Annie Thackeray." *The Library Chronicle* 26, no. 4 (1996): 33–61. Reprinted in *Gendered Territory: Photographs of Women by Julia Margaret Cameron*, edited and with an introduction by Dave Oliphant (Austin: Harry Ransom Humanities Research Center, 1996).

Lyles, W. H. *Mary Shelley: An Annotated Bibliography*. New York: Garland, 1975.

Lytton, Edward Bulwer. *Zanoni*. 1845. Reprint, Boston: Dana Estes, 1890.

MacCarthy, Mary Warre Cornish. *A Nineteenth-Century Childhood*. London: M. Secker, 1929.

Macgregor, Margaret Eliot. "Amelia Alderson Opie: Worldling and Friend." *Smith College Studies in Modern Languages* 14, no. 1/2 (1932/1933): iii–xv, 3–146.

MacKay, Carol Hanbery. "Biography as Reflected Autobiography: The Self-Creation of Anne Thackeray Ritchie." In *Revealing Lives: Autobiography, Biography, and Gender*, edited by Marilyn Yalom and Susan Groag Bell. Foreword by Lillian S. Robinson. Albany: State University of New York Press, 1990. 65–80 and 217–20 (notes).

———. "'Both Sides of the Curtain': Elizabeth Robins, Synaesthesia, and the Subjective Correlative." *TPQ: Text and Performance Quarterly* 17, no. 4 (1997): 299–316.

———. "Hate and Humor as Empathetic Whimsy in Anne Thackeray Ritchie." *Women's Studies* 15/16 (1987/88): 117–33. Reprinted in *Last Laughs: Perspectives on Women and Comedy*, edited by Regina Barreca, Studies in Gender and Culture Series (New York: Gordon and Breach, 1988).

———. "'Only Connect': The Multiple Roles of Anne Thackeray Ritchie." *The Library Chronicle*, n.s. 30 (1985): 83–112.

———. "'Soaring between home and heaven—': Julia Margaret Cameron's Visual Meditations on the Self." *The Library Chronicle* 26, no. 4 (1996): 63–87. Reprinted in *Gendered Territory: Photographs of Women by Julia Margaret Cameron*, edited and with an introduction by Dave Oliphant (Austin: Harry Ransom Humanities Research Center, 1996).

———. "The Thackeray Connection: Virginia Woolf's Aunt Anny." In *Virginia Woolf and Bloomsbury: A Centennial Celebration*, edited by Jane Marcus. Bloomington: Indiana University Press; London: Macmillan, 1987. 66–95.

———. Introduction to *The Two Thackerays: Anne Thackeray Ritchie's Biographical Introductions to the Centenary Edition of the Works of William Makepeace Thackeray*. Edited by Carol Hanbery MacKay. Bibliography apparatus by Peter Shillingsburg and Julia Maxey. 2 vols. New York: AMS Press, 1988. 1:xi–lxxxvii.

Macmillan, Margaret. *Women of the Raj*. 1988. Reprint, London: Thames and Hudson, 1996.

Madden, William A. "Framing the Alices." *Publications of the Modern Language Association* 101, no. 3 (1986): 362–73.

Maitland, Frederick William. *The Life and Letters of Sir Leslie Stephen*. London: Duckworth, 1906.

Malcolm, Janet. "The Genius of the Glass House." *New York Review of Books* 46, no. 2 (4 February 1999): 10–14.

Manvell, Roger. *The Trial of Annie Besant and Charles Bradlaugh*. New York: Horizon Press, 1976.

Marcus, Jane. "Art and Anger: [Elizabeth Robins and Virginia Woolf]." *Feminist Studies* 4, no. 1 (1978): 69–97. Reprinted in *Art and Anger: Reading Like a Woman* (Columbus: Ohio State University Press, 1988), 122–54.

———. Introduction to *The Convert*, by Elizabeth Robins. New York: Feminist Press, 1980.

———. "Invincible Mediocrity: The Private Selves of Public Women." In *The Private Self: Theory and Practice of Women's Autobiographical Writings*, edited by Sheri Benstock. Chapel Hill: University of North Carolina Press, 1988. 114–46.

———. "Liberty, Sorority, Misogyny." In *Virginia Woolf and the Languages of Patriarchy*. Bloomington: Indiana University Press, 1987. 75–95 and 198–201 (notes).

———. "Nostalgia Is Not Enough: Why Elizabeth Hardwick Misreads Ibsen, Plath, and Woolf." In *Art and Anger: Reading Like a Woman*. Columbus: Ohio State University Press, 1988. 49–70.

———. "Still Practice, A/Wrested Alphabet: Towards a Feminist Aesthetic." In *Feminist Issues in Literary Scholarship*, edited by Shari Benstock. Bloomington: Indiana University Press, 1987. 79–97. Reprinted in *Art and Anger: Reading Like a Woman* (Columbus: Ohio State University Press, 1988), 215–49.

———. "Storming the Toolshed." In *Art and Anger: Reading Like a Woman*. Columbus: Ohio State University Press, 1988. 182–200.

———. "Transatlantic Sisterhood: Labor and Suffrage Links in the Letters of Elizabeth Robins and Emmeline Pankhurst." *Signs* 3, no. 3 (1978): 744–55.

———, ed. *Suffrage and the Pankhursts*. London: Routledge & Kegan Paul, 1987.

Marsh, Jan. "An Abbess and a Cannon." Review of *Annie Besant: A Biography*, by Anne Taylor, and *Beatrice Webb: Woman of Conflict*, by Carol Seymour-Jones. *New Statesman and Society* 5, no. 200 (1992): 38–39.

Mason, Mary G. "The Other Voice: Autobiographies of Women Writers." In *Life/Lines: Theorizing Women's Autobiography*, edited by Bella Brodzki and Celeste Schenck. Ithaca, N.Y.: Cornell University Press, 1988. 19–44.

Matlaw, Myron. "Robins Hits the Road: Trouping with O'Neill in the 1880s." *Theatre Survey* 29, no. 2 (1988): 175–92.

Matthiessen, F. O. *The Achievement of T. S. Eliot: An Essay on the Nature of Poetry*. 3rd ed. London: Oxford University Press, 1958.

Mavor, Carol. "Dream-Rushes: Lewis Carroll's Photographs of the Little Girl." In *The Girl's Own: Cultural Histories of the Anglo-American Girl, 1830–1915*, edited by Claudia Nelson and Lynne Vallone. Athens: University of Georgia Press, 1994. 156–93.

———. *Pleasures Taken: Performances of Sexuality and Loss in Victorian Photographs*. Durham, N.C.: Duke University Press, 1995.

McCarthy, William, and Elizabeth Kraft, eds. *The Poems of Anna Leticia Barbauld*. Athens: University of Georgia Press, 1994.

McDonald, Jan. "'The Second Act Was Glorious'—The Staging of the Trafalgar Scene from *Votes for Women!* at the Court Theatre." *Theatre History Studies* 15 (1995): 139–60.

McKendry, John J. *Four Victorian Photographers*. New York: Metropolitan Museum of Art, 1967.

Mellor, Anne K. *English Romantic Irony*. Cambridge, Mass.: Harvard University Press, 1980.

———. *Mary Shelley: Her Life, Her Fiction, Her Monsters*. New York: Methuen, 1988.

———. "Possessing Nature: The Female in *Frankenstein*." In *Romanticism and Feminism*, edited and with an introduction by Anne K. Mellor. Bloomington: Indiana University Press, 1988. 220–32.

———. *Romanticism and Gender*. London: Routledge, 1993.

Melon, Marc. "Beyond Reality: Art Photography." In *A History of Photography: Social and Cultural Perspectives*, edited by Jean-Claude Lemagny and André Rouillé. Cambridge: Cambridge University Press, 1987. 82–101.

Melton, J. Gordon, ed. *The Origins of Theosophy: Annie Besant—The Atheist Years*. New York: Garland Publishing, 1990.

Mermin, Dorothy. "Gender and Genre in *Aurora Leigh*." *Victorian Newsletter*, no. 69 (1986): 7–11.

Meyers, Jeffrey. *Married to Genius*. London: Magazine Editions, 1977.

Michie, Elsie B. "Production Replaces Creation: Market Forces and *Frankenstein* as Critique of Romanticism." *Nineteenth-Century Contexts* 12, no. 1 (1988): 27–33.

Millard, Charles W. "Julia Margaret Cameron and Tennyson's *Idylls of the King*." *Harvard Library Bulletin* 21, no. 2 (1973): 187–201.

Miller, Nancy K., ed. *The Poetics of Gender*. New York: Columbia University Press, 1986.

Miners, Scott, ed. *A Spiritual Approach to Male/Female Relations*. Wheaton, Ill.: Theosophical Publishing House, 1984.

Miyoshi, Masao. *The Divided Self: A Perspective on the Literature of the Victorians*. New York: New York University Press, 1969.

Moers, Ellen. *Literary Women: The Great Writers*. Garden City, N.J.: Anchor Books, 1977.

Moir, M. *A General Guide to the India Office Records*. London: British Library, 1988.

Moore, Catherine E. "'Ladies . . . Taking the Pen in Hand': Mrs. Barbauld's Criticism of Eighteenth-Century Women Novelists." In *Fettr'd or Free: British Women Novelists, 1670–1815*, edited by Mary Schofield and Cecelia Macheski. Athens: Ohio University Press, 1986. 383–97.

Moore, Marianne. *The Complete Poems of Marianne Moore*. New York: Macmillan and Viking, 1967.

Morgan, Charles. *The House of Macmillan (1843–1943)*. London: Macmillan, 1943.

Morgan, Thaïs E., ed. *Victorian Sages and Cultural Discourse: Renegotiating Gender and Power*. New Brunswick, N.J.: Rutgers University Press, 1990.

Mourão, Manuela. "Delicate Balances: Gender and Power in Anne Thackeray Ritchie's Nonfiction." *Women's Writing* 4, no. 1 (1997): 73–89.

Mozley, Anita Ventura. *Mrs. Cameron's Photographs from the Life*. Stanford, Calif.: Stanford University Department of Art, 1974.

"Mrs. Cameron's Photographs." *Intellectual Observer* 11 (February 1867): 30–33.

"Mrs. Julia Margaret Cameron's 'Annals of My Glass House.'" *The Photographic Journal* 67, no. 7 (1927): 296–301.

Muir, Percy H. *Victorian Illustrated Books*. London: Batsford, 1971.

Mulligan, Therese, Eugenia Parry Janis, April Watson, and Joanne Lukitsh. *For My Best Beloved Sister Mia, An Album of Photographs by Julia Margaret Cameron*. Albuquerque: University of New Mexico Art Museum, 1995.

Munich, Adrienne. *Queen Victoria's Secrets*. New York: Columbia University Press, 1996.

Murray, Janet Horowitz, ed. *Strong-Minded Women and Other Lost Voices from Nineteenth-Century England*. New York: Pantheon Books, 1982.

Nadel, Ira Bruce. *Biography: Fiction, Fact, and Form*. New York: St. Martin's, 1984.

[Nair, T. M.]. *Evolution of Mrs. Besant: Being the Life and Public Activities of Mrs. Annie Besant, Secularist, Socialist, Theosophist and Politician, with Sidelights on the Inner Workings of the Theosophical Society and Methods by Which Mr. Leadbeater Arrived at the Threshold of Divinity*. Madras: Justice Printing Works, 1918.

Nalbantian, Suzanne. *Aesthetic Autobiography: From Life to Art in Marcel Proust, James Joyce, Virginia Woolf and Anaïs Nin*. London: Macmillan, 1994.

Nathanson, Paul. *Over the Rainbow: The Wizard of Oz as a Secular Myth*. Albany: State University of New York Press, 1991.

Nesbit, E[dith]. *The Story of the Amulet*. Illustrations by H. R. Millar. 1906. Reprint, London: Ernest Benn, 1957.

Nethercot, Arthur H. *The First Five Lives of Annie Besant*. Chicago: University of Chicago Press, 1960.

———. *The Last Four Lives of Annie Besant*. Chicago: University of Chicago Press, 1963.

Newey, Vincent, and Philip Shaw, eds. *Mortal Pages, Literary Lives: Studies in Nineteenth-Century Autobiography*. Aldershot, U.K.: Scolar Press; Brookfield, Vt.: Ashgate Publishing, 1996.

Newhall, Beaumont. *The History of Photography from 1839 to the Present Day*. Rev. ed. New York: Museum of Modern Art, 1964.

———. *Photography: Essays and Images*. New York: Museum of Modern Art, 1980.

Newman, Beth. "Narratives of Seduction and the Seduction of Narrative: The Frame Structure of *Frankenstein*." *English Literary History* 53, no. 1 (1986): 141–61.

Newton, Judith, and Deborah Rosenfelt, eds. *Feminist Criticism and Social Change*. London: Methuen, 1985.

Nicholson, Virginia. "Dimbola: Julia Margaret Cameron at Freshwater (1990)." *Charleston Magazine*, no. 11 (1995): 23–30.

Nord, Deborah Epstein. "Political Mystic." Review of *Annie Besant: A Biography*, by Anne Taylor. *Women's Review of Books* 10, no. 9 (1993): 25–26.

North, Marianne. *Recollections of a Happy Life*. Vol. 1. Edited by Mrs. John Addington Symonds. London: Macmillan, 1894.

Nussbaum, Felicity. *The Autobiographical Subject: Gender and Ideology in Eighteenth-Century England*. Baltimore, Md.: Johns Hopkins University Press, 1989.

Oates, Joyce Carol. "*Frankenstein*'s Fallen Angel." *Critical Inquiry* 10, no. 3 (1984): 543–54.

Olsen, Victoria C. "Idylls of Real Life." *Victorian Poetry* 33, no. 3/4 (1995): 371–89.

———. "Representing Culture: Women and Cultural Politics in Mid-Victorian England." Ph.D. diss., Stanford University, 1994.

Olsen, Tillie. *Silences*. New York: Delacorte Press, 1978.

Oost, Regina B. "Marketing *Frankenstein*: The Shelleys' Enigmatic Preface." *English Language Notes* 35, no. 1 (1987): 26–35.

Opie, Amelia. *Adeline Mowbray, or, The Mother and the Daughter*. 3 vols. 1805. Reprint, edited and with an introduction by Gina Luria, New York: Garland Publishing, 1974.

———. *The Works of Mrs. Amelia Opie*. 3 vols. 1843. Reprint, New York: AMS Press, 1974.

Oppenheim, Janet. "The Odyssey of Annie Besant." *History Today* 39 (September 1989): 12–18.

Our Corner. Edited by Annie Besant. Vols. 5–12. London: Freethought Publishing Company, 1885–1888.

Ovenden, Graham, ed. *Pre-Raphaelite Photography*. 1972. Reprint, London: Academy Editions; New York: St. Martin's Press, 1984.

———, ed. *A Victorian Album: Julia Margaret Cameron and Her Circle*. Introduction by Lord David Cecil. New York: Da Capo Press, 1975.

Owen, Alex[andra]. *The Darkened Room: Women, Power and Spiritualism in Late Victorian England*. Philadelphia: University of Pennsylvania Press, 1990.

[Patmore, Coventry]. "Mrs. Cameron's Photographs." *Macmillan's Magazine* 13 (January 1866): 230–31.

Pearson, Carol, and Katherine Pope. *The Female Hero in American and British Literature*. New York: R. R. Bowker, 1981.

Perkins, David, ed. *English Romantic Writers*. New York: Harcourt, Brace and World, 1967.

Perl, Jed. "The Trouble with Photography." *The New Republic* 219, no. 16 (19 October 1998): 31–36.

Perry, Ruth. *Women, Letters, and the Novel*. New York: AMS Press, 1980.

Personal Narratives Group, eds. *Interpreting Women's Lives: Feminist Theory and Personal Narrative*. Bloomington: Indiana University Press, 1989.

Peters, Margot. *Shaw and the Actresses*. New York: Doubleday, 1980.

Peters, Sally. *Bernard Shaw: The Ascent of the Superman*. New Haven, Conn.: Yale University Press, 1996.

Peterson, Linda. "Gender and Autobiographical Form: The Case of the Spiritual Autobiography." In *Studies in Autobiography*, edited by James Olney. New York: Oxford University Press, 1988. 211–22.

———. *Victorian Autobiography: The Tradition of Self-Interpretation*. New Haven, Conn.: Yale University Press, 1986.

Phelan, Peggy. *Unmarked: The Politics of Performance*. London: Routledge, 1993.

"Photography: A Woman's Eye." Review of Julia Margaret Cameron's "Portraits of Women" at the Museum of Modern Art. *The Economist* 351, no. 8114 (10 April 1999): 85.

Poovey, Mary. *The Proper Lady and the Woman Writer: Ideology as Style in the Works of Mary Wollstonecraft, Mary Shelley, and Jane Austen.* Chicago: University of Chicago Press, 1984.

Postlewait, Thomas. "Autobiography and Theatre History." In *Interpreting the Theatrical Past: Essays in the Historiography of Performance*, edited by Thomas Postlewait and Bruce A. McConachie. Iowa City: University of Iowa Press, 1989. 248–72.

———. *Prophet of the New Drama: William Archer and the Ibsen Campaign.* Westport, Conn.: Greenwood Press, 1986.

———, ed. *William Archer on Ibsen: The Major Essays, 1889–1919.* Westport, Conn.: Greenwood Press, 1984.

Powell, Kerry. "Oscar Wilde, Elizabeth Robins, and the Theatre of the Future." *Modern Drama* 37, no. 1 (1994): 220–37.

Powell, Tristram, ed. *Victorian Photographs of Famous Men and Fair Women by Julia Margaret Cameron.* Introductions by Virginia Woolf and Roger Fry. 1926. Reprint, London: Hogarth Press, 1973.

Prakasa, Sri. *Annie Besant as Woman and as Leader.* 1940. Reprint, Bombay: Bharatiya Vidya Bhavan, 1962.

———. "Mrs. Besant and the India of Tomorrow." In *In Honour of Dr. Annie Besant: Lectures by Eminent Persons, 1952–88*, foreword by Radha Burnier, President of the Theosophical Society. Kamachha: Indian Section of the Theosophical Society, 1990. 25–43.

Prose, Francine. "Scent of a Woman's Ink: Are Women Writers Really Inferior?" *Harper's Magazine* (June 1998): 61–70.

Quenell, Peter. *Victorian Panorama: A Survey of Life and Fashion from Contemporary Photographs.* New York: Charles Scribner's Sons; London: B. T. Batsford, 1937.

The Quest: Journal of the Theosophical Society in America. Wheaton, Ill.: Theosophical Publishing House, 1912– .

Rabkin, Eric S. *The Fantastic in Literature.* Princeton: Princeton University Press, 1976.

Rackin, Donald. "Alice's Journey to the End of Night." *Publications of the Modern Language Association* 81, no. 5 (1966): 313–26.

———. "Love and Death in Carroll's Alices." *English Language Notes* 20, no. 2 (1982): 26–45.

Radway, Janice. *Reading the Romance: Women, Patriarchy, and Popular Literature.* Chapel Hill: University of North Carolina Press, 1984.

Raglan, Lord. *The Hero: A Study in Tradition, Myth and Drama.* New York: Oxford University Press, 1937.

Rambler [pseud.]. "The Most Remarkable Stage Crowd Ever Seen: How Trafalgar

Square Is Reproduced at the Court." *The Evening News* (London), 10 April 1907.

Ransom, Hazel Harrod. *Elizabeth Barrett Browning: Poet-Reformer*. Edited and with an introduction by Miguel González-Gerth. Austin: University of Texas Special Publications Project, 1997.

Reed, John R. *Victorian Conventions*. Athens: Ohio University Press, 1975.

Reid, Forrest. *Illustrators of the Eighteen-Sixties: An Illustrated Survey of the Work of 58 British Artists*. 1928. Reprint, New York: Dover, 1975.

Renold, Leah Madge Young. "Hindu Identity at Banaras Hindu University." Ph.D. diss., University of Texas at Austin, 1999.

Reynolds, Kimberley, and Nicola Humble. *Victorian Heroines: Representations of Femininity in Nineteenth-Century Literature and Art*. New York: New York University Press, 1993.

Rich, Adrienne. *Diving into the Wreck*. New York: W. W. Norton, 1973.

——. "*When We Dead Awaken*: Writing as Re-vision." *College English* 34, no. 1 (1972). Reprinted in *On Lies, Secrets, and Silence: Selected Prose* (New York: Norton, 1979), 33–50.

Ritchie, Anne Thackeray. *Anne Thackeray Ritchie: Journals and Letters*. Edited by Abigail Burnham Bloom and John Maynard. Commentary and notes by Lillian F. Shankman. Columbus: Ohio State University Press, 1994.

——. *Blackstick Papers*. London: Smith, Elder, 1908.

——. *Bluebeard's Keys and Other Stories*. 1874. Reprint, London: Smith, Elder, 1902.

——. "A Book of Photographs." *Pall Mall Gazette* (10 April 1865): 10–11. Reprinted in *Toilers and Spinsters and Other Essays* (London: Smith, Elder, 1874), 224–29.

——. *A Book of Sibyls: Mrs Barbauld, Miss Edgeworth, Mrs Opie, and Miss Austen*. London: Smith, Elder, 1883.

——. "Barrett Browning, Elizabeth." In vol. 3 of *The Dictionary of National Biography: To 1900*, edited by Leslie Stephen and Sidney Lee. Oxford: Oxford University Press, 1917. 78–82.

——. *Chapters from Some Memoirs*. London: Macmillan, 1894. Published in the United States as *Chapters from Some Unwritten Memoirs* (New York: Harper's, 1894).

——. "A Discourse on Modern Sibyls." In *From the Porch*. London: Smith, Elder, 1913. Reprint, Freeport, N.Y.: Books for Libraries, 1971. 3–30.

——. "Cinderella." In *Five Old Friends and a Young Prince*. 1868. Reprint, London: Smith, Elder, 1905.

——. *From an Island*. *The Cornhill Magazine* 18–19 (1868–1869): 610–25, 739–60, and 62–78. Reprinted in *The Village on the Cliff, with Other Stories and Sketches* (Boston: Fields, Osgood, 1869), 155–201.

—— "From Friend to Friend: [Mrs. Tennyson and Mrs. Cameron]." *The Cornhill Magazine*, n.s. 41, no. 241 (1916): 21–43. Reprinted in *From Friend to Friend*, edited by Emily Ritchie (1919; reprint, New York: E. P. Dutton, 1920), 1–39.

——. "Heroines and Their Grandmothers." *The Cornhill Magazine* 11 (May 1865): 630–40. Reprinted in *Toilers and Spinsters and Other Essays* (London: Smith,

Elder, 1874), 72–98; *British Women Writers: An Anthology from the Fourteenth Century to the Present*, edited by Dale Spender and Janet Todd (New York: Peter Bedrick Books, 1989), 630–42; and *Prose by Victorian Women Writers: An Anthology*, edited by Andrea Broomfield and Sally Mitchell (New York: Garland, 1996), 487–504.

———. Introductions to the following works by Maria Edgeworth: *Castle Rackrent* and *The Absentee* (London: Macmillan, 1895), *Ormond* (London: Macmillan, 1895), *Popular Tales* (London: Macmillan, 1895), and *Helen* (London: Macmillan, 1896).

———. "Little Scholars." *The Cornhill Magazine* 1 (May 1860): 549–59. Reprinted in *Toilers and Spinsters and Other Essays* (London: Smith, Elder, 1874), 99–122.

———. *Madame de Sévigné*. Edited by Mrs. Oliphant. Foreign Classics for English Readers. Edinburgh and London: William Blackwood, 1881. Reprint, New York: AMS Press, 1973.

———. *Miss Angel*. [Life of Angelica Kauffman.] London: Smith, Elder, 1875.

———. *Miss Williamson's Divagations*. London: Smith, Elder, 1881.

———. *Records of Tennyson, Ruskin, and [Robert and Elizabeth] Browning*. London: Macmillan, 1892. Reprint, New York: Harper and Brothers, 1893.

———. "Reminiscences." Text written to accompany *Alfred, Lord Tennyson and His Friends*, a Series of 25 Portraits and Frontispiece in Photogravure from the Negatives of Mrs. Julia Margaret Cameron and H. H. Cameron, with an Introduction by H. H. Hay Cameron. London: T. Fisher Unwin, 1893. [Edition limited to 400 copies]. "Reminiscences" reprinted and abridged in Harriet Devine Jump, ed., *Women's Writing of the Victorian Period, 1837–1901: An Anthology* (New York: St. Martin's Press, 1999), 281–83.

———. *The Story of Elizabeth* [1863] and *Old Kensington* [1873]. Reprinted and with an introduction by Esther Schwartz-McKinzie. Bristol: Thoemmes Press, 1995.

———. *Thackeray and His Daughter: The Letters and Journals of Anne Thackeray Ritchie, with Many Letters of William Makepeace Thackeray*. Edited by Hester Thackeray Ritchie. New York: Harper and Brothers, 1924. Published in Great Britain as *The Letters of Anne Thackeray Ritchie* (London: John Murray, 1924).

Ritchie, Anne Thackeray, and Richardson Evans. *Lord Amherst and the British Advance Eastwards to Burma*. Edited by William Wilson Hunter. Rulers of India Series. Oxford: Clarendon Press, 1909.

Roberts, Pam. "Julia Margaret Cameron: A Triumph over Criticism." In *The Portrait in Photography*, edited by Graham Clarke. London: Reaktion Books, 1992. 47–70.

[Robins, Elizabeth]. *Ancilla's Share: An Indictment of Sex Antagonism*. London: Hutchinson, 1924. Reprinted in "Pioneers of the Woman's Movement" Series, Westport, Conn.: Hyperion Press, 1976.

Robins, Elizabeth. *The Alaska-Klondike Diary of Elizabeth Robins, 1900*. Edited and with an introduction by Victoria Joan Moessner and Joanne E. Gates. Fairbanks: University of Alaska Press, 1999.

———. "Annie Besant." [Typescript draft of unpublished memoir.] The Elizabeth
Robins Papers, Fales Library, Elmer Holmes Bobst Library, New York
University.

———. *Both Sides of the Curtain*. London: William Heinemann, 1940.

———. *Come and Find Me*. New York: Century, 1908.

———. *The Convert*. 1907. Reprint, with an introduction by Jane Marcus, New York:
Feminist Press, 1980.

———. "The Herstory of a Button." Introduction by Joanne E. Gates. *American Voice*,
no. 19 (1990): 35–38.

———. *Ibsen and the Actress*. London: Hogarth Press, 1928.

———. Introduction to the Bath Classics edition of "Uncle Tom's Cabin." Reprinted in
Author 20, no. 1 (1909): 23–25.

———. *The Magnetic North*. New York: Frederick A. Stokes, 1904.

———. *My Little Sister*. New York: Dodd, Mead, 1913. Published in London and
Toronto as *Where Are You Going to . . . ?* (1913).

———. "On Seeing Madame Bernhardt's Hamlet." *North American Review* 171, no. 529
(1900): 908–19.

———. *Raymond and I*. Foreword by Leonard Woolf. New York: Macmillan, 1956.

———. *Theatre and Friendship: Some Henry James Letters with a Commentary*. London:
Jonathan Cape, 1932.

———. *Under the Southern Cross*. Illustrations by John Rae. New York: Frederick A.
Stokes, 1907.

———. *Votes for Women!* 1907. Reprinted in *"How the Vote Was Won" and Other
Suffragette Plays*, edited and with an introduction by Dale Spender and Carole
Hayman (London: Methuen Theatrefile, 1985), 35–87. [Also available at
< http:/www.indiana.edu/letrs/vwwwp/robins/votes.html >.]

———. *Way Stations*. London: Hodder & Stoughton, 1913.

———. *Woman's Secret*. Letchworth, U.K.: Garden City Press, [1907].

[Robins, Elizabeth, and Florence Bell]. *Alan's Wife: A Dramatic Study in Three Scenes*.
Edited by J. T. Grein. Introduction by William Archer. London: Henry, 1893.

Robinson, Charles E. "The Devil as Doppelgänger in *The Deformed Transformed*: The
Sources and Meaning of Byron's Unfinished Drama." *Bulletin of the New York
Public Library* 74 (1970): 177–202.

Robinson, Henry Peach. *Pictorial Effect in Photography, Being Hints on Composition and
Chiaroscuro for Photographers*. Edited by Robert A. Sobieszek. 1869. Reprint,
Pawlet, Vt.: Helios, 1971.

Rogers, Katharine M. "Anna Barbauld's Criticism of Fiction—Johnsonian Mode,
Female Vision." *Studies in 18th-Century Culture* 21 (1997): 27–41.

Rose, Phyllis. *Parallel Lives: Five Victorian Marriages*. New York: Vintage Books, 1983.

Rosen, Jeff. "Cameron's Photographic Double Takes." In *Orientalism Transposed: The
Impact of the Colonies on British Culture*. London: Ashgate, 1998. 158–80.

Rosenblum, Naomi. *A History of Women Photographers*. New York: Abbeville Press,
1994.

Rosmarin, Adena. *The Power of Genre*. Minneapolis: University of Minnesota Press, 1985.

Rossetti, William Michael. "Mr. Palgrave and Unprofessional Criticisms on Art." *Fine Arts Quarterly Review* (1866). Reprinted in *Fine Art, Chiefly Contemporary: Notices Re-printed, with Revisions* (London: Macmillan, 1867), 324–34.

Roszak, Theodore. *The Memoirs of Elizabeth Frankenstein*. New York: Random House, 1995.

Rowe, Karen E. "Feminism and Fairy Tales." In *The Voyage In: Fictions of Female Development*, edited by Elizabeth Abel, Marianne Hirsch, and Elizabeth Langland. Hanover, N.H.: University Press of New England, 1983. 69–89 and 327–30 (notes).

Royle, Edward. *Radicals, Secularists, and Republicans: Popular Freethought in Britain, 1866–1915*. Manchester, U.K.: Manchester University Press, 1980.

Rubenstein, Marc A. "'My Accursed Origin': The Search for the Mother in *Frankenstein*." *Studies in Romanticism* 15, no. 2 (1976): 165–94.

Russ, Joanna. *How to Suppress Women's Writing*. Austin: University of Texas Press, 1983.

Ruthven, K. K. *Feminist Literary Studies: An Introduction*. Cambridge: Cambridge University Press, 1984.

Sanders, Valerie. *The Private Lives of Victorian Women: Autobiography in Nineteenth-Century England*. London: Harvester Wheatsheaf, 1989.

Scheinker, Andrea. "Appropriation of Play in a Victorian Album: Idylls of the King and Other Poems Illustrated by Julia Margaret Cameron." *Athanor* 15 (1997): 33–37.

Schofield, Mary, and Cecelia Macheski, eds. *Fettr'd or Free: British Women Novelists, 1670–1815*. Athens: Ohio University Press, 1986.

Seeley, Tracy. "Victorian Women's Essays and Dinah Mulock's *Thoughts*: Creating an Ethos for Argument." *Prose Studies: History, Theory, Criticism* 19, no. 1 (1996): 93–109.

Sellers, Susan, ed. *Feminist Criticism: Theory and Practice*. Toronto: University of Toronto Press, 1991.

Sexton, Anne. "Cinderella." In *Transformations*. Boston: Houghton Mifflin, 1972.

Shaw, G[eorge] Bernard. "Annie Besant and the 'Secret Doctrine.'" *The Freethinker* 67 (14 December 1947): 450.

———. *Arms and the Man: A Pleasant Play*. 1898. Reprint, New York: Penguin, 1975.

———. *Bernard Shaw: Collected Letters, 1874–1950*. 4 vols. Edited by Dan H. Laurence. London: Max Reinhardt; New York: Viking, 1965–1988.

———. *The Diaries, 1874–1897*. Edited by Stanley Weintraub. 2 vols. University Park: Pennsylvania State University Press, 1986.

———. *Fabian Essays*. Jubilee Edition. London: G. Allen & Unwin, 1947.

———. "In Memory of Mrs. Annie Besant." [Message to Remembrance Meeting by Women's Indian Association, London.] *Times* (London), 20 October 1933, sec. 10, p. 5.

———. "Mrs. Besant as a Fabian Socialist." *The Theosophist* 39 (October 1917): 9–19.

Reprinted as "Mrs. Besant's Passage through Fabian Socialism" in *Dr. Annie Besant: Fifty Years in Public Work* (London: [privately printed], 1924), 3–14, and in James Cousins, ed., *The Annie Besant Centenary Book* (Madras: Theosophical Publishing House, 1947), 17–24.

——. *The Quintessence of Ibsenism*. London: W. Scott, 1891.

——. *Theatrics: Selected Correspondence*. Edited by Dan H. Laurence. Toronto: University of Toronto Press, 1995.

——. *You Never Can Tell: A Pleasant Play*. 1898. Reprint, with an introduction by S. N. Behrman, Lincoln: University of Nebraska Press, 1961.

Shelley, Mary Wollstonecraft. *The Annotated Frankenstein*. Edited by Leonard Wolf. New York: Potter, 1977.

——. *Collected Tales and Stories*. Edited by Charles E. Robinson. Baltimore, Md.: Johns Hopkins University Press, 1976.

——. *Frankenstein*. With an introduction by the author. 1831. Reprint, edited and with a second introduction by Johanna M. Smith, Boston: St. Martin's Press, 1992.

——. *Frankenstein*. 1818. Reprint, edited by James Rieger, Chicago: University of Chicago Press, 1984.

——. *Frankenstein: or, The Modern Prometheus*. 1831. Reprint, edited and with an afterword by Harold Bloom, New York: Signet-New American Library, 1965.

——. *Frankenstein; or, The Modern Prometheus*. 1818. Reprint, edited by D. L. Macdonald and Kathleen Scherf. Peterborough, Ont.: Broadview Press, 1994.

——. *The Journals of Mary Shelley, 1814–1844*. Edited by Paula Feldman and Diana Scott-Kilvert. 2 vols. Oxford: Clarendon, 1987.

——. *The Letters of Mary Wollstonecraft Shelley*. Edited by Betty T. Bennett. 3 vols. Baltimore, Md.: Johns Hopkins University Press, 1980–1988.

Sherwin, Paul. "*Frankenstein*: Creation as Catastrophe." *Publications of the Modern Language Association* 96, no. 5 (1981): 883–903.

Shires, Linda, ed. *Rewriting the Victorians: Theory, History, and the Politics of Gender*. New York: Routledge, 1992.

Showalter, Elaine, ed. *Daughters of Decadence: Women Writers of the Fin de Siècle*. London: Virago, 1993.

——. "Dinah Mulock Craik and the Tactics of Sentiment: A Case Study in Victorian Female Authorship." *Feminist Studies* 2, no. 1 (1975): 5–23.

——. *The Female Malady: Women, Madness, and English Culture, 1830–1980*. New York: Pantheon Books, 1985.

——. *A Literature of Their Own: British Women Novelists from Brontë to Lessing*. Princeton: Princeton University Press, 1977.

——. *Sexual Anarchy: Gender and Culture at the Fin de Siècle*. New York: Viking, 1990.

Silver, Carole G. *Strange and Secret People: Fairies and Victorian Consciousness*. Oxford: Oxford University Press, 1998.

Singley, Carol, and Susan Sweeney, eds. *Anxious Power: Reading, Writing, and Ambivalence in Narrative by Women*. Albany: State University of New York Press, 1993.

Sitwell, Edith. *English Eccentrics*. New York: Vanguard, 1957.

Smidt, Kristian. "T. S. Eliot, William Archer, and Henrik Ibsen." In *The Importance of Recognition: Six Chapters on T. S. Eliot*. Tromso, Norway: A. S. Peder Norbye, 1973. 62–80.

Smith, Helen Zenna. *Not So Quiet . . . Stepdaughters of War*. 1930. Reprint, with an afterword by Jane Marcus, New York: The Feminist Press, 1989.

Smith, Johanna M. "'Hideous Progenies': Texts of *Frankenstein*." In *Texts and Textuality: Textual Instability, Theory, and Interpretation*, edited and with an introduction by Philip Cohen. New York: Garland, 1997. 121–40.

Smith, Lindsay. "Further Thoughts on 'The Politics of Focus.'" *The Library Chronicle* 26, no. 4 (1996): 13–31. Reprinted in *Gendered Territory: Photographs of Women by Julia Margaret Cameron*, edited and with an introduction by Dave Oliphant (Austin: Harry Ransom Humanities Research Center, 1996).

———. "The Politics of Focus: Feminism and Photography Theory." In *New Feminist Discourses*, edited by Isobel Armstrong. London: Routledge, 1992. 238–62.

Smith, Sidonie. *A Poetics of Women's Autobiography: Marginality and the Fictions of Self-Representation*. Bloomington: Indiana University Press, 1987.

Solomon, Deborah. "Sorority Sisters: In All-Girl Exhibitions, Do You Admire the Art or Bond with the Women in It?" *New York Times Magazine*, 22 November 1995, 36.

Spacks, Patricia Meyer. *The Female Imagination*. New York: Avon Books, 1975.

Spalding, Frances. *Vanessa Bell*. New Haven and New York: Ticknor and Fields, 1983.

Spark, Muriel. *Mary Shelley: A Biography*. Rev. ed. New York: Dutton, 1987.

Spender, Dale. *Mothers of the Novel*. London: Pandora, 1986.

———. *Women of Ideas (And What Men Have Done to Them)*. London: Ark, 1983.

Spivak, Gayatri Chakravorty. "Three Women's Texts and a Critique of Imperialism." *Critical Inquiry* 12, no. 1 (1985): 243–61.

Squier, Susan M. "The Modern City and the Construction of Female Desire: Wells's *In the Days of the Comet* and Robins's *The Convert*." *Tulsa Studies in Women's Literature* 8, no. 1 (1989): 63–75.

Stephen, Dorothea Jane. *Studies in Early Indian Thought*. Cambridge: Cambridge University Press, 1918.

S[tephen], J[ulia] P[rinsep]. "Julia Margaret Cameron." In vol. 3 of *The Dictionary of National Biography: To 1900*, edited by Leslie Stephen and Sidney Lee. Oxford: Oxford University Press, 1917. 752.

Stephen, Leslie. *Sir Leslie Stephen's Mausoleum Book*. Introduction by Alan Bell. Oxford: Clarendon Press, 1977.

Stephens, Autumn. *Wild Women: Crusaders, Curmudgeons and Completely Corsetless Ladies in the Otherwise Virtuous Victorian Era*. Berkeley, Calif.: Conari Press, 1992.

Stern, Carol Simpson, and Bruce Henderson. *Performance: Texts and Contexts*. New York: Longman, 1993.

Stimpson, Catharine R. *Classnotes: A Novel*. New York: Times Books, 1979.

Stowell, Sheila. *A Stage of Their Own: Feminist Playwrights of the Suffrage Era.* Manchester, U.K.: Manchester University Press, 1992.

Strasser, Alexander. *Immortal Portraits.* London: Focal Press, 1941.

Strickland, Barbara. Review of the Texas Book Festival panel entitled "Plucked from Obscurity: Writing Biographies of Not-so-Famous People." *The Austin Chronicle,* 6 November 1997, 42.

Stryker, Susan. "'My Words to Victor Frankenstein above the Village of Chamounix': Performing Transgender Rage." *Glq: A Journal of Lesbian & Gay Studies* 1, no. 3 (1994): 237–54. Reprinted in *States of Rage: Emotional Eruption, Violence, and Social Change,* edited and with an introduction by Renee R. Curry and Terry L. Allison (New York: New York University Press, 1996), 195–215.

Sturgis, Howard Overing. "Anne Isabella Thackeray (Lady Ritchie)." *The Cornhill Magazine,* n.s. 47 (November 1919): 449–67.

Suleri, Sara. *The Rhetoric of English India.* Chicago: University of Chicago Press, 1992.

Sutherland, John. "Failed Lawyers and Precocious Women." *The Dickens World* 3 (1987): 1–4.

———. *Victorian Novelists and Publishers.* Chicago: University of Chicago Press, 1976.

Swindells, Julia. *The Victorian Writing and Working Woman: The Other Side of Silence.* Minneapolis: University of Minnesota Press, 1985.

Tammany, Jane Ellert. *Henrik Ibsen's Theatre Aesthetic and Dramatic Art.* New York: Philosophical Library, 1980.

Tanzy, Conrad Eugene. "Publishing the Victorian Novel: A Study of the Economic Relationships of Novelists and Publishers in England, 1830–1880." Ph.D. diss., Ohio State University, 1961.

Taylor, Anne. *Annie Besant: A Biography.* Oxford: Oxford University Press, 1992.

Templeton, Joan. *Ibsen's Women.* Cambridge: Cambridge University Press, 1997.

Tennyson, Alfred, Lord. *The Poems of Tennyson.* Edited by Christopher Ricks. London: Longmans, 1969.

Thackeray, William Makepeace. *The History of Pendennis: His Fortunes and Misfortunes, His Friends and His Greatest Enemy.* Illustrations by Thackeray. 2 vols. 1848–1850. Reprint, London: Smith, Elder, 1878–1879.

———. *The Letters and Papers of William Makepeace Thackeray.* Edited by Gordon N. Ray. 4 vols. Cambridge, Mass.: Harvard University Press, 1945.

———. *The Newcomes: Memoirs of a Most Respectable Family.* Illustrations by Richard Doyle. 2 vols. 1853–1855. Reprint, London: Smith, Elder, 1878–1879.

Thomas, G. "That Oriental Streak in Julia Margaret Cameron's Ancestry." *History of Photography* 12, no. 2 (1998): 175–78.

Thomas, Sue. *Elizabeth Robins (1862–1952): A Bibliography.* Victorian Fiction Research Guide 22. Queensland, Australia: University of Queensland, Department of English, 1994.

———. "Sexual Matter and 'Votes for Women.'" *Papers on Language and Literature* 33, no. 1 (1997): 47–70.

Thompson, Stilth. *Motif Index of Folk Literature*. 6 vols. Bloomington: University of Indiana Press, 1955.

——. *The Folk Tale*. New York: Dryden Press, 1946.

Tickner, Lisa. *The Spectacle of Women: Imagery of the Suffrage Campaign, 1907–1914*. Chicago: University of Chicago Press, 1988.

Thorndike, Sybil. "Elizabeth Robins as I Knew Her." *The Listener* (London), 17 July 1952, 108–9.

Timbs, John. *English Eccentrics and Eccentricities*. Rev. ed. London: Chatto & Windus, 1898.

Tomalin, Claire. *The Invisible Woman: The Story of Nelly Ternan and Charles Dickens*. London: Viking, 1990.

Todd, Janet, ed. *A Dictionary of British and American Women Writers, 1660–1800*. Totowa, N.J.: Roman & Littlefield, 1987.

Trela, D. J., ed. *Margaret Oliphant: Critical Essays on a Gentle Subversive*. Selinsgrove, Pa.: Susquehanna University Press; London: Associated University Presses, 1995.

Tropp, Martin. *Mary Shelley's Monster: The Story of Frankenstein*. Boston: Houghton Mifflin, 1976.

Truss, Lynn. *Tennyson's Gift*. London: Hamish Hamilton, 1996.

Tuchman, Gaye, and Nina Fortin. "Edging Women Out: Some Suggestions about the Structure of Opportunities and the Victorian Novel." *Signs* 6, no. 2 (1980): 308–25.

Vann, J. Don, and Rosemary T. VanArsdel, eds. *Victorian Periodicals: A Guide to Research*. New York: Modern Language Association, 1978.

Varlow, Sally. *A Reader's Guide to Writers' Britain*. London: Prion Books, 1997.

Veeder, William. *Mary Shelley and Frankenstein: The Fate of Androgyny*. Chicago: University of Chicago Press, 1986.

Vicinus, Martha. *Independent Women: Work and Community for Single Women, 1850–1920*. Chicago: University of Chicago Press, 1985.

——, ed. *Suffer and Be Still: Women in the Victorian Age*. Bloomington: Indiana University Press, 1973.

Victoria's World: A Photographic Portrait Drawn from the Gernsheim Collection. Austin: The University of Texas Art Museum, 1968.

Viswanathan, Gauri. *Masks of Conquest: Literary Study and British Rule in India*. New York: Columbia University Press, 1989.

——. *Outside the Fold: Conversion, Modernity, and Belief*. Princeton: Princeton University Press, 1998.

Wagenknecht, Edward. "The Yellow Brick Road." In *As Far as Yesterday: Memories and Reflections*. Norman: University of Oklahoma Press, 1968. 63–79.

Wagner-Martin, Linda. *Telling Women's Lives: The New Biography*. New Brunswick, N.J.: Rutgers University Press, 1994.

Warner, Marina. *From the Beast to the Blonde: On Fairy Tales and Their Tellers*. New York: Farrar, Straus and Giroux, 1994.

Washington, Peter. *Madame Blavatsky's Baboon: Theosophy and the Emergence of the Western Guru.* London: Secker & Warburg, 1993.

Watt, George. *The Fallen Woman in the 19th-Century English Novel.* Totowa, N.J.: Barnes and Noble, 1984.

Watts, Harriet. "Arp, Kandinsky, and the Legacy of Jakob Bohme." In *The Spiritual in Art: Abstract Painting, 1890–1985,* edited by Maurice Tuchman and Judith Freeman. New York: Abbeville Press, 1986. 239–55.

Weaver, Mike. *Julia Margaret Cameron, 1815–1879.* Boston: Little, Brown, 1984.

———. "Julia Margaret Cameron: The Stamp of Divinity." In *British Photography in the Nineteenth Century,* edited by Mike Weaver. Cambridge: Cambridge University Press, 1989. 151–61.

———. *Whisper of the Muse: The Overstone Album and Other Photographs by Julia Margaret Cameron.* Malibu, Calif.: The J. Paul Getty Museum, 1986.

Weigle, Marta. *Spiders and Spinsters: Women and Mythology.* Albuquerque: University of New Mexico Press, 1982.

Weintraub, Stanley, ed. *Shaw: An Autobiography.* 2 vols. New York: Weybright and Talley, 1969–1970.

Wells, H[erbert] G[eorge]. *Experiment in Autobiography: Discoveries and Conclusions of a Very Ordinary Brain (Since 1866).* New York: Macmillan, 1934.

Welsh, Alexander. *The City of Dickens.* Oxford: Clarendon Press, 1971.

Wessinger, Catherine. "Annie Besant and Issues in Contemporary Feminist Spirituality," parts 1 and 2. *The Quest* 10, no. 1 (1997): 26–33; no. 2 (1997): 42–49 and 51.

———. *Annie Besant and Progressive Messianism, 1847–1933.* Lewiston, N.Y.: Edwin Mellen Press, 1988.

———. "Democracy vs. Hierarchy: The Evolution of Authority in the Theosophical Society." In *When Prophets Die: The Postcharismatic Fate of New Religious Movements,* edited by Timothy Miller with an introduction by J. Gordon Melton. Albany: State University of New York Press, 1991. 93–106 and 218–22 (notes).

———. "Service to India: Annie Besant's Work in India for Human Rights," parts 1 and 2. *Theosophical History* 3 (January 1990): 19–32 and (April 1990): 51–60.

———, ed. *Religious Institutions and Women's Leadership: New Roles Inside the Mainstream.* Columbia: University of South Carolina Press, 1996.

West, Alick. *George Bernard Shaw: "A Good Man Fallen Among Fabians."* New York: International Publishers, 1950.

West, Geoffrey [Geoffrey Harry Wells]. *The Life of Annie Besant.* London: Gerald Howe Limited, 1929.

Wiley, Catherine. "The Matter with Manners: The New Woman and the Problem Play." *Themes in Drama: Women in Theatre* 11 (1989): 109–27.

———. "Staging Infanticide: The Refusal of Representation in Elizabeth Robins's *Alan's Wife.*" *Theatre Journal* 42, no. 4 (1990): 432–46.

Williams, Gertrude Marvin. *The Passionate Pilgrim*. New York: Coward-McCann, 1931.

Williams, Val. "Carefully Creating an Idyll: Vanessa Bell and Snapshot Photography, 1907–1946." In *Women Photographers: The Other Observers, 1900 to the Present*. London: Virago, 1986.

———. "Only Connecting: Julia M. Cameron and Bloomsbury." *Photographic Collector* 4, no. 1 (1983): 40–49.

Wilson, A. N. *Eminent Victorians*. London: BBC Books, 1989.

Wilson, Colin. *Rudolf Steiner: The Man and His Vision*. Wellingborough, N.H.: Aquarian Press, 1985.

Wolf, Sylvia. *Focus: Five Women Photographers*. Morton Grove, Ill.: Albert Whitman, 1994.

———. *Julia Margaret Cameron's Women*. Contributions by Stephanie Lipscomb, Deborah N. Mancoff, and Phyllis Rose. Chicago: The Art Institute; New Haven, Conn.: Yale University Press, 1998.

Wolfson, Susan J. "Feminist Inquiry and *Frankenstein*." In *Approaches to Teaching Shelley's Frankenstein*, edited by Stephen C. Behrendt. New York: Modern Language Association, 1990. 50–59.

Women of Photography: An Historical Survey. Exhibition Catalogue of exhibit organized by the San Francisco Museum of Art, 18 April–15 June 1975.

Wood, Mrs. Henry. *East Lynne*. 1862. Reprint, with an introduction by Sally Mitchell, New Brunswick, N.J.: Rutgers University Press, 1984.

Woof, Robert. *Tennyson, 1809–1892: A Centenary Celebration*. Grasmere: Wordsworth Trust, 1992.

Woolf, Virginia. *The Common Reader*. 1925, 1932. Reprint, New York: Harcourt, Brace, 1948.

———. *The Diary of Virginia Woolf*. Edited by Anne Oliver Bell with Andrew McNeillie. 5 vols. New York: Harcourt Brace Jovanovich, 1977–1984.

———. "The Enchanted Organ." Review of *Thackeray and His Daughter*, edited by Hester Thackeray Ritchie. In vol. 4 of *The Collected Essays*, edited by Leonard Woolf. New York: Harcourt, Brace and World, 1967. 74–75.

———. *Freshwater: A Comedy*. Edited by Lucio P. Ruotolo. New York: Harcourt, Brace, Jovanovich, 1976.

———. "George Eliot." In *The Common Reader*. 1925. Reprint, New York: Harcourt, Brace, 1953. 166–176.

———. Introduction to *Victorian Photographs of Famous Men and Fair Women by Julia Margaret Cameron* [1926]. Edited by Tristam Powell and with a second introduction by Roger Fry. London: Hogarth Press, 1973.

———. "Lady Ritchie." [Obituary Notice.] *Times Literary Supplement*, 6 March 1919. Reprinted in Winifred Gérin, *Anne Thackeray Ritchie: A Biography* (Oxford: Oxford University Press, 1981), 278–83.

———. *The Letters of Virginia Woolf*. Edited by Nigel Nicolson and Joanne Trautmann. 6 vols. New York: Harcourt Brace Jovanovich, 1975–1980.

———. *Moments of Being: Unpublished Autobiographical Writings*. Edited and with an introduction by Jeanne Schulkind. New York: Harcourt Brace Jovanovich, 1976.

———. *Mrs. Dalloway*. 1925. Reprint, New York: Harcourt, Brace and World, 1953.

———. *Night and Day*. 1919. Reprint, London: Hogarth Press, 1960.

———. *Orlando*. 1928. Reprint, New York: Harcourt Brace Jovanovich, 1956.

——— Review of *Blackstick Papers*, by Anne Thackeray Ritchie. *Times Literary Supplement*, 19 November 1908. Reprinted in *The Essays of Virginia Woolf*, vol. 1, *1904–1912*, edited by Andrew McNeillie (New York: Harcourt Brace Jovanovich, 1986), 228–29.

———. Review of *A Dark Lantern*, by Elizabeth Robins. *Guardian* (London), 24 May 1905. Reprinted in *The Essays of Virginia Woolf*, vol. 1, *1904–1912*, edited by Andrew McNeillie (New York: Harcourt Brace Jovanovich, 1986), 42–43.

———. *A Room of One's Own*. 1929. Reprint, New York: Harcourt, Brace and World, 1957.

———. *To the Lighthouse*. 1927. Reprint, New York: Harcourt, Brace and World, 1953.

———. *The Waves*. New York: Harcourt, Brace, 1931.

Worthen, W. B., ed. *Modern Drama: Plays/Criticism/Theory*. Fort Worth: Harcourt Brace College Publishers, 1995.

Wyatt-Brown, Anne M., and Janice Rossen, eds. *Aging and Gender in Literature: Studies in Creativity*. Charlottesville: University Press of Virginia, 1993.

Yamashiro, Jennifer Pearson. "Idylls in Conflict: Victorian Representations of Gender in Julia Margaret Cameron's 'Idylls of the King.'" *The Library Chronicle* 26, no. 4 (1996): 117–43. Reprinted in *Gendered Territory: Photographs of Women by Julia Margaret Cameron*, edited and with an introduction by Dave Oliphant (Austin: Harry Ransom Humanities Research Center, 1996).

Yeats, W[illiam] B[utler]. *The Trembling of the Veil*. London: T. W. Laurie, 1922.

———. *A Vision: An Explanation of Life Founded upon the Writings of Giraldus and upon Certain Doctrines Attributed to Kusta ben Luka*. London: T. W. Laurie, 1925.

Young, Arlene. "The Monster Within: The Alien Self in *Jane Eyre* and *Frankenstein*." *Studies in the Novel* 23, no. 3 (1991): 325–38.

Zinsser, William, ed. *Spiritual Quests: The Art and Craft of Religious Writing*. Boston: Houghton Mifflin, 1988.

Zipes, Jack. *Breaking the Magic Spell: Radical Theories of Folk and Fairy Tales*. Austin: University of Texas Press, 1979.

———, ed. *Don't Bet on the Prince: Contemporary Feminist Fairy Tales in North America and England*. New York: Routledge, 1989.

———. *Victorian Fairy Tales: The Revolt of the Fairies and the Elves*. New York: Methuen, 1987.

Zuckerman, Joanne. "Anne Thackeray Ritchie as a Model for Mrs. Hilbery in Virginia Woolf's *Night and Day*." *Virginia Woolf Quarterly* 1, no. 3 (1973): 32–46.

Index

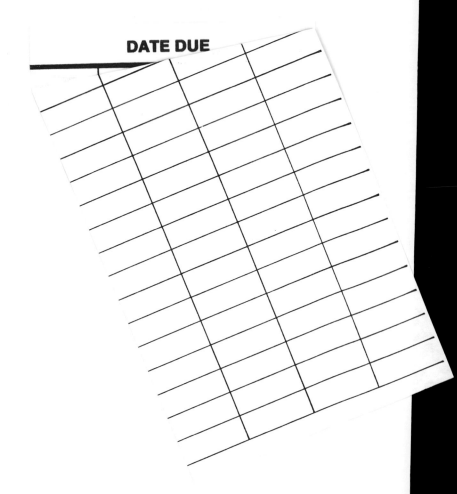

DATE DUE